PLIÉ

Plié Ball!

Baseball Meets Dance
on Stage and Screen

Jeffrey M. Katz

Foreword by Edward Villella

McFarland & Company, Inc., Publishers
Jefferson, North Carolina

ISBN (print) 978-0-7864-6406-7
ISBN (ebook) 978-1-4766-2535-5

LIBRARY OF CONGRESS CATALOGUING DATA ARE AVAILABLE

British Library cataloguing data are available

On the cover: Gwen Verdon in the Broadway production of *Damn Yankees*
1955-1957 (Photofest); *inset from left to right*: Frank Sinatra, Gene Kelly,
Jules Munshin in *Take Me Out to the Ball Game*, 1949 (MGM/Photofest)

Printed in the United States of America

*McFarland & Company, Inc., Publishers
Box 611, Jefferson, North Carolina 28640
www.mcfarlandpub.com*

Table of Contents

Acknowledgments and Dedication

It has taken quite a long time for this project to be completed. What this means is that, with each passing month and year, I become indebted to more and more people for the moral and practical (and, in the case of my small but loyal Kickstarter crew, financial) support that is and has been provided to me. There is no doubt that I will fail to name some of the wonderful individuals who have helped me in some fashion along the way. However, I will strive, in this section, to acknowledge as many "angels" as possible.

First and foremost, I must mention those members of my family who have given me not only incredible support and encouragement, but also many useful and, in some cases, brilliant suggestions and ideas. Helice Koffler has provided me with so much insight and so many fabulous ideas and she helped develop my knowledge of and love for dance. I can never thank her enough for what she has given and continues to give to me, which includes her love, her trust, and her belief. She is an absolutely astounding person and I cannot imagine life without her.

Steve Katz launched me on this voyage when he alerted me to the 2009 Cooperstown Symposium on Baseball and American Culture and attended the symposium with me (as did Helice) after my paper was selected to be presented. He also helped instill in me, at the earliest age, a love of baseball, and he, his wife, Isabelle, and his daughters, Melissa and Linda, always have been filled with enthusiasm and excitement about this project, and I am truly grateful. And Bobbi and Bob Turner, along with their daughter, Kathy, have been there every step of the way and are, quite simply, three of the greatest, most generous people on the planet.

I also must thank Helice's parents, Jerry and Eleanor Koffler, for their kindness, for constantly offering assistance, and for raising my cultural awareness acutely. Additionally, a great debt is owed to the late Lillian Goldstein for helping to guide me to and keep me on the right track. I also wish to express gratitude to friends and teachers who, at various points over decades of my life, pushed me to keep writing and researching. These friends include Cleo Brooks, Tim Firth, Josephine Paltin, Drew Wanderman, and Kenny Young; these teachers include Judy Breshin, Joseph Cotter, Kenneth Feldman, Tamara Green, Adele Haft, Joe Hassett, Alice Jourdain, Elaine Lang, Evelyn Popper, Judith Saltman, William Sinnigen, and Jane and Robert White. Finally, I must acknowledge my late parents, Monroe and Muriel Katz. I wish we had more time together and I wish I could have known you better.

I now mention some of the many people who contributed directly to the making of this book. Since this component is so large, I will attempt to make the nature of the contribution as clear as possible. Again, if anyone has been left out, please accept my sincere apology and please know that I am eternally thankful for whatever degree of help you provided. Thank you to:

- Charles Perrier, Tanisha Jones, Susan Kraft, George Boziwick, Daisy Pommer, and the frontline staff at the New York Public Library for the Performing Arts;
- Christopher Pennington of the Jerome Robbins Foundation;
- Bob Sloane and the frontline staff at the Harold Washington Library branch of the Chicago Public Library;
- The staff at the Newbery Library of Chicago;
- Jeni Dahmus and Max Grafe of the Juilliard School Archives (Peter Jay Sharp Special Collections) in New York City;
- Chad Gneiting of the Juilliard School's Lila Acheson Wallace Library;
- Ashley Swinnerton of the Museum of Modern Art's Department of Film;
- The staff at the Paley Center for Media in New York City;
- Maryann Chach, Mark Swartz, and the entire Shubert Archive staff;
- The three individuals connected to the National Baseball Hall of Fame and the 2009 Cooperstown Symposium on Baseball and American Culture who played such an important role in the birth of this study: Jim Gates, William Simons, and Tim Wiles;
- Those attendees at the 2009 Cooperstown Symposium on Baseball and American Culture (including sportswriters) whose positive comments about my presentation were so inspirational;
- My Kickstarter supporters: Ellen Bar, Ana Rosa Blue, Linda Katz, Steve and Isabelle Katz, Eleanor and Jerry Koffler, Helice Koffler, Katie O'Leary, Josephine Paltin, Rod Richards, Bobbi and Bob Turner, Zoe Waldron, and Drew Wanderman;
- The seventeen magnificent and talented artists and professionals who allowed me so generously to interview them for this book and who never ceased to lend support: Chris Black, Renee Bucciarelli, Dean Caswell, Steve Cohen, Gail Conrad, Lisa de Ribere, Christopher Fleming, Louis Kavouras, Ana Maria Tekina-eirú Maynard, Lynn Parkerson, Moses Pendelton, Peter Pucci, Joan Quatrano, Nick Ross, Gail Heilbron Steinitz, Maria Tcherkassky, and Edward Villella.
- Those fabulous photographers who permitted me to use their photos for little or, in most cases, no compensation: David Becker, Nicholas Coppula, Johan Elbers, Christina Harkness, John Kane, Susan Kettering, Marc Levine, Kegan Marling, Rosalie O'Connor, Michael O'Neill, Terrence Orr, Robert Shomler, Alexandre Silva, Rich Sofranko, Zera Thompson, and Will Waghorn;
- Ron Mandelbaum and the great team at Photofest;
- Those individuals who are associated with dance companies, choreographers, dancers, baseball teams, etc., who gave their time and energy to solve problems, make contacts, and retrieve information for me and my book: Lisa Auel, Ellen Bar, Samantha Barczak, Beth Blickers, Amanda Braverman, Shana Daum, Kristine Elliott, David Farmerie, Demetrius Grant, Billy Harner, Gina Hasson, Donna Lenchuk, Carla DeBeasi Ruiz, Staci Slaughter, Bob Vickrey, Linda Villella, and Aimee Waeltz;
- Dance companies and baseball teams that lent support in some capacity: Ballet Fleming, Brooklyn Ballet, Brooklyn Cyclones, Chris Black Dance, City Stage New West, Co-Motion Dance, MOMIX, Nicholas Andre Dance Company,

Peter Pucci Plus, Pittsburgh Ballet Theatre, Potrzebie Dance Project, Puerto Rican Folkloric Dance and Cultural Center (Austin, TX), San Francisco Giants, Seattle Mariners;

- Author Stephen Manes, for encouragement and entertaining lunches;
- All of the writers and researchers who came before me and whose work I read, referenced, and enjoyed (with special recognition to Ann Barzel, A. Bartlett Giamatti, James Mote, Edward J. Rielly, and Harold Seymour);
- All of the people who shared articles and websites and photos with me and those who suggested television shows, movies, theatrical works, pieces of choreography, and names of players and dancers;
- All of the incredible, phenomenal, beautiful dancers, choreographers, and ballplayers who have inspired me over the years. This group includes the great Edward Villella, a wonderful and generous man and an immortal figure in the world of dance.

Finally, my dedication. This is tricky. I certainly wish to dedicate this book to Helice and I wish to dedicate it, too, to my brother and sister and late father and mother. I also wish to dedicate it to the dancers, choreographers, and players whom I love so dearly and who have given me and so many countless others so much joy and such satisfaction. But I did make a promise to Helice, who suggested that it would be fun to reference the 1945 film *Leave Her to Heaven* and borrow the dedication used for the "latest" novel produced by the film's main character, Richard Harland (played in the movie by Cornel Wilde). And so, in the words of Mr. Harland (as recorded in the original book by Ben Ames Williams and the later screenplay by Jo Swerling), I dedicate this book "to the girl with the hoe."

Foreword by Edward Villella

I grew up with a need to move. I never walked, I always ran. I never reached for something over my head—I jumped. I couldn't stay still and I constantly fidgeted. I was always happy in action at the local sandlot and the local schoolyard. I played stickball in the streets, along with bicycle tag and running bases between two sewer covers. This last activity is what eventually got me into ballet. I was knocked unconscious when I got hit in the back of the head by a baseball. After that, I was dragged to my sister's ballet classes. I sat there bored and restless, watching the little girls trying to be graceful, until, at the end of class, they started to run and jump across the floor. That was more like it. It was like running and jumping for the ball. Hey, I thought, maybe this isn't so bad. Standing at the back of the room imitating these silly girls earned me a punishment of standing at the ballet barre the next day. The similarities between baseball and ballet became abundantly apparent while I was beginning my new love of a more sophisticated physicality and throughout the years, as I developed into a dancer, I never lost my love for baseball.

This book helps to shine a beautiful light on the similarities, the connections between these two great disciplines, these two incredible art forms. The observations ring true and the descriptions and stories are fascinating. It is a huge subject and a book like this is long overdue. As I said to Jeff in our initial conversation way back in 2011, I was a far better baseball player for having taken ballet as a kid. From a very early age, I understood the connections between dance and baseball. This wonderful examination of the very close relationship between dance and baseball will help others understand and will serve, very simply, to entertain and enlighten readers whose knowledge of baseball and/or dance is great or small or even nonexistent. Enjoy.

Edward Villella, award-winning dancer and choreographer, preformed as a principal dancer for the New York City Ballet. A lifelong athlete, Mr. Villella has a special appreciation for baseball.

Preface

I love baseball and I love dance. In truth, that is how the story of this book begins. My introduction to and passion for baseball came first, thanks primarily to the fact that I was born into what could be termed a "baseball family." My father had been a part-time Major League Baseball scout for more than twenty years prior to my birth and my brother, who idolized Mickey Mantle, played for high school and sandlot teams while I was still in diapers. As a result, before even entering kindergarten, I already had been taken to numerous games at Yankee Stadium (in addition to a couple at Shea) and schooled in the art of scorekeeping by my baseball-crazy brother. Little League was a given, of course, and I even had the astounding good fortune to be selected as Flying A Gasoline Honorary New York Yankees Bat Boy when I was nine years old, an honor that earned me the right to attend a double-header against the Oakland Athletics for free, meet members of the New York Yankees in the home dugout during batting practice, walk on the field at Yankee Stadium, and have photographs taken with my favorite Yankees at the time (Bobby Murcer and Bill Robinson). And, to top it all off, I got to be on television, standing next to pitcher Jack Aker and announcer Jerry Coleman as the drawing for the next Honorary Bat Boy took place. Add to this the fact that I received a free Mel Stottlemyre–model baseball glove and was the subject of a story, along with my father, that appeared in the *Bronx Press Review* and what you wind up with is an even deeper love for the game. Heck, I even exchanged letters with Brooks Robinson, whom I met by chance outside of Yankee Stadium (while I was holding a massive hero sandwich, purchased by my brother after a Yankees–Orioles night game), and was called "my little pal" by Rod Carew, a Hall of Fame player whom my father "discovered" and signed while he, my father, was working as a temporary, "fill in" scout for the Minnesota Twins in the early 1960s.

The love for dance developed more gradually, revealing itself over time, as I recognized slowly the signs of my passion. As a child, I enjoyed dancing to songs on the radio and on records, just like my brother and sister, and seemed to possess, also like my older siblings, a kind of natural rhythm (which, in my case, led very quickly to an interest in and aptitude for drumming). There is a wonderful black-and-white photograph of me (wearing a white shirt with a bow tie and dark-colored short pants) doing the Twist with my cousin at some bar mitzvah when I was probably about four or five years old and I recall vividly that I always was ready to jump up and get down when the music came on at gatherings and events or just at home. Additionally, I remember enjoying the dancers that I saw on television—people like Sammy Davis, Jr., and Peter Gennaro and ensembles such as the Lockers and the June Taylor Dancers, as well as the many unnamed performers who appeared in the "chorus" on variety shows, dancing with or behind the "headline" entertainers. Most of all, though, I admired the slick, sultry, and supersonic movements of singers and musical groups (the Temptations, Sly Stone, James Brown, the Jackson Five, etc.) and the kids who demonstrated a universe of

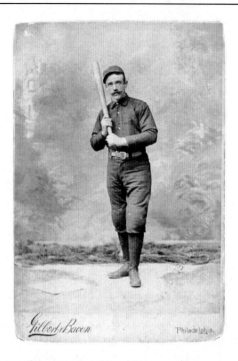

Deacon McGuire of the Philadelphia Quakers, c. 1888 (New York Public Library, A.G. Spalding Baseball Collection; photograph by Gilbert & Bacon).

Left: William "Kid" Gleason of the Philadelphia Quakers, c. 1888 (New York Public Library, A. G. Spalding Baseball Collection; photograph by Gilbert & Bacon).
   Right: Jim Fogarty of the Philadelphia Quakers, c. 1888 (New York Public Library, A. G. Spalding Baseball Collection; photograph by Gilbert & Bacon).

Women dancing and two Washington Senators/Nationals baseball players clowning on a baseball field, 1924 (Library of Congress Prints and Photographs Division).

new steps on shows like *Soul Train, Shindig!, Hullabaloo,* and *American Bandstand.* It was fun and I was a speedy learner and admirable copycat, with some ability to improvise. Still, though, any kind of "formal" dance training or dance education was about as far outside of the zone of familiarity in my family and neighborhood as it is possible to conceive.

Nevertheless, I did realize, despite my inability to articulate these thoughts, that what I liked especially about baseball, even more than the other sports I played in my childhood (football, basketball, and a wee bit of hockey and soccer), was its grace and sophistication of movement, its pace, its rhythm, its visual beauty, and the opportunities it provided to be involved and to shine in many different ways (you could field and throw and run and hit for power and/or average and/or accuracy and so much more!). Also, it was clear that baseball was a sport of *tradition,* with a rich history, played at hallowed, mythic venues, such as Fenway Park, Yankee Stadium, and Wrigley Field, all of which are were referred to as "cathedrals" by worshipful fans. When I reached my teen years and began to fully grasp the strong attraction that I felt for the arts, I also began to recognize that baseball—unlike football or hockey or even basketball—possessed a genuine connection to this new world that was beginning to open up. There was, I understood on some level, a relationship between baseball and music, baseball and theater, baseball and *dance.* It was New York City in the 1970s and '80s and I started attending as many shows as I could fit into my schedule and budget. In many cases, friends—primarily female friends—made suggestions and I was avidly reading publications such as the *Village Voice,* the *Soho News, Creem* magazine, the *New York Rocker,* and the *New York Times.* I went to see Off Broadway and Off Off Broadway productions, attended and sometimes participated in poetry readings, visited art galleries and museums, listened and moved to bands and solo musical artists in tiny, often filthy clubs, as well as makeshift performance spaces and big arenas, played in small and slightly larger musical groups for little or no pay, and witnessed frequently thrilling and occasionally consciousness-altering dance exhibitions by the likes of the Alwin Nikolais ensemble, Murray Louis, the Alvin Ailey American Dance Theater, the Joffrey Ballet, Twyla Tharp, the Paul Taylor Dance Company, and the New York City Ballet. All along the way, though, I continued to follow baseball closely, go to games (mostly at Yankee Stadium), play for fun (whenever I had the chance to do so), and even collect baseball cards. The link between baseball and the arts may not have been something that I could articulate and explain in a convincing manner, but it certainly was possible for me to detect the presence of the very same forces of enchantment at work.

As I got older, this "relationship" or "kinship" awareness did seem to become more transparent, particularly in relation to dance. I grew to love both baseball and dance with a high degree of intensity. For the bulk of my pre-college youth, when not musing on a future as a great writer or rock star, I dreamed of becoming a professional baseball player—a dream, ultimately, that was dashed by organized baseball performance anxiety in high school. Once I reached college, I took a few modern dance classes, caught the instructor's eye, got inspired, and dreamed again, this time of enhancing my skills as a dancer and one day joining the Nikolais company or some other admired dance group that featured brilliant and personally affecting choreography. Sadly, though, this dream got quashed, too (and rather quickly)—this time, due to a fear of "the unknown" and a concern that pursuing dance, in any case was a little "out of my league." Playing baseball and dancing *felt good*—and in somewhat similar ways. There was that same sense of satisfaction, that same sense of artistry, both of which also extended to music. And the many comparisons that one heard constantly—the "ballet of baseball" and "music of baseball"—seemed to strike a note that was absolutely true. I realized that the players I admired most—graceful, elegant, hardworking, and intelligent practitioners like Ernie Banks, Paul Blair, Rod Carew, Ron Guidry, Reggie Jackson, Sandy Koufax, Thurman Munson, Tony Oliva, Willie Randolph, Merv Rettenmund, Steve Rogers, Joe Rudi, Celerino Sanchez, Roy White, and the three Robinsons—Bill, Brooks, and Frank—were those who did seem, in many ways, like dancers on the field. The resolution in the picture was growing sharper and sharper.

Then, in late 2008 or early 2009, my brother, a dues-paying member of the National Baseball Hall of Fame Library and Museum, alerted me to a call for papers for an upcoming conference, about which, previously, I had known nothing (I am a little ashamed to say). The conference was the 21st Cooperstown Symposium on Baseball and American Culture (how had those first twenty slipped by me?), to be held at the National Baseball Hall of Fame, from late May to early June 2009. I considered the scope of the conference—an examination of baseball's impact on the culture of the United States—and, in very short order, realized that a golden opportunity had presented itself. It would be possible to devote real time and attention to the subject of baseball and dance in the U.S.: how these two disciplines connect and intersect, what kinds of commonalities may be found, and where their points of variance lie. I did a bit of preliminary research and discovered a surprising number of dance pieces that had been created using baseball as an inspiration and observed that most of these pieces were not widely known. It also became evident that baseball had played a role, and sometimes a significant one, in the actual lives of a great many dancers. I knew that a handful of films, musicals, and television shows with a baseball and dance component were relatively well known to the general American population (for example, *Damn Yankees*, *Take Me Out to the Ball Game*, and one episode of *I Love Lucy*); however, because most Americans do not attend shows that feature dance alone (also known as *concert dance*), it was quite apparent that not only are examples of baseball- inspired choreography a mystery to the majority of the American people, but also that a widespread belief exists in American society that sports (which is considered a more "masculine" pursuit) and dance (which, even in the 21st century, is viewed by an overwhelming number of men, as noted above, as a "feminine" activity and not truly athletic) are two separate, unrelated entities and that dance is an "esoteric" art form and not meant for the appreciation of the "average," "everyday" citizen.

How could I pass up a chance to look into and address all of these issues?

And so, my proposal was submitted and, happily, accepted. I spent a few, painstaking months creating my paper, which targeted concert dance, and, finally, delivered my presentation, with some nice, eye-catching visuals, on June 3, 2009, in Cooperstown. Much to my delight, the paper was received well and some suggestions were made by attendees that I should consider producing an expanded, book-length study. A couple of representatives from the National Baseball Hall of Fame, shortly thereafter, contacted me and reiterated this suggestion, encouraging me to explore the topic even more broadly—to go beyond concert dance. After my paper was accepted for publication in the Symposium anthology by William H. Simons, the book's editor, I made a decision to work on a book and, well, thanks to McFarland and Company, here we are—a few years and many hundreds, actually thousands, of hours of research, writing, rewriting, and more rewriting later. The title of the book is almost identical to the title of my original paper and much of the text from the original paper has made its way into this book, as well. However, what we have here is an investigation of the relationship between baseball and dance that covers much more than concert dance. And it is hoped that this study, which is a hefty component of an even larger study, will illuminate the breadth and the depth of this intimate, incredibly powerful, and it may be argued, truly *primal* relationship. At the very least, it is hoped that the book will be fun to read and perhaps even occasionally eye-opening, educational, and inspirational.

The Structure of the Book

In a sense, *Plié Ball!* consists of two alternating, but interrelated segments. There are, on the one hand, five distinct chapters, covering the subjects of theater (in its varied forms), concert dance (a subset of theater, but presented in this book as a distinct performance art), and "the screen" (comprising film, television, and video). Simultaneously, winding their way in serpentine fashion between these five chapters are four sets of excerpted interview transcripts. Then, following the last chapter, is what may be viewed as the book's "culminating" section, bearing the title, "Final Thoughts," which features two full-length interview transcripts. All of the transcripts, excerpted and otherwise, are included in order to delve even deeper into the profound, intimate relationship between baseball and dance. Interviews were conducted with fifteen brilliant professionals, representing the worlds of dance, baseball, and medicine, between 2009 and 2013. Each interviewee was selected because of his or her experience with *both* disciplines and each has a *lot* to say about the relationship. These contributions were critical for this book and are vital to the achievement of a better understanding of this topic as a whole. Interviews were conducted on the telephone, face to face, and via e-mail. In some cases, the interview subjects and I engaged in multiple communications, while in other cases, only a single, "formal" interview took place.

As for photographs, images, and illustrations, there are, literally, *hundreds* that I would have loved to use. Most, unfortunately, were a bit too difficult or costly to obtain. Still, the ones that are included are very important and I am incredibly grateful to have the opportunity to share them in this book. It is good to keep in mind, though, that a staggering number of additional visuals exist—and this is not even taking into account the equally staggering number of moving images. Many of these moving images are rare and are accessible only through a visit to an archival repository (such as the New York Public Library for the Performing Arts, Chicago's Newberry Library, the Paley Center for Media, which has branches in both New York City and Los Angeles, and, of course, the National Baseball Hall of Fame in Cooperstown, New York); however, a substantial portion may be accessed through the Internet, free of charge. The same, of course, holds true in the case of still images, as well as publications, paper documents, clippings, and ephemera.

There also is an appendix, which provides further information about a related topic (dance and baseball in literature for youth).

It is also important for me, once again, to acknowledge the very special and genuinely beautiful foreword contributed so generously and with such kindness and care by the astounding Edward Villella. Mr. Villella, I must confess, is a hero of mine and the fact that he not only agreed to be interviewed for this book, but also that he consented to compose a foreword is almost beyond comprehension. I have no doubt that this will be a source of pleasure and enlightenment for all readers.

Introduction—
The Ballet of Baseball
*Pirouettes on the Pitcher's Mound
and Jetés in the Outfield*

To characterize the year 1986 as "memorable" for fans of both the New York Mets and the Boston Red Sox would be an understatement of the most monumental kind. After phenomenal seasons, the two teams faced off in a World Series that is considered by most baseball experts to be among the very best in the modern era. For the Boston Red Sox, of course, the results were tinged with anguish and controversy, but the fact that the team itself had a brilliant year cannot be disputed. As far as the Mets were concerned, it was a year of pure magic, capped by a championship that seemed to display divine intervention.

Shortly after the Series victory, as the magnificence of the Mets was reviewed and analyzed by sports writers and baseball historians, a small article appeared in the *New York Post*, penned by the legendary New York baseball journalist Maury Allen.[1] The purpose of this article was to examine more closely a very unusual baseball reality. In 1986, with the exception of a minor thumb ailment suffered by catcher Gary Carter, the New York Mets were virtually injury-free. What could possibly be credited with keeping the hard-playing, rough-and-tumble, and, in many cases, wild-living Mets players so healthy for 175 games? For some insight, Allen consulted the Mets' team physician, Dr. James Parkes. Parkes, without hesitation, responded that at least part of the explanation could be traced to the "ballet legwork" and "linear stretching exercises" the Mets received from Steve Cedros, a dancer and ballet teacher hired by the team.

It was ballet that helped the Mets become the top team in baseball.

Coincidentally, one of the millions of disappointed and stunned Red Sox fans watching the World Series in 1986 was a man named Moses Pendleton. When the terrible moment of Mookie Wilson's ground ball scooting through the legs of Bill Buckner occurred in Game Six, Moses, who witnessed the shocking event on television, slammed down his foot so violently that a four-inch piece of wood from his parquet floor was dislodged and wound up piercing his skin, causing him, as he puts it, to "literally bleed for his team."[2] Pendleton at the time was working with his new dance troupe, Momix, after a long period of choreography and performance with the Pilobolus Dance Theater. In just a few years, with Momix, Mr. Pendleton would pay tribute to his beloved sport by creating a piece called, very simply, "Baseball."

Why begin with this two-part story? Quite simply, these two related anecdotes serve to illustrate the very strong, but often overlooked, connection that exists, in the United States, between baseball and dance. For most Americans, this connection is recognized on sporadic occasions. The baseball-themed musical comedy, *Damn Yankees*, for example, has been revived repeatedly on stages around the world since it premiered on Broadway in 1955, and its 1958 film version continues to be shown with some regularity on television and in movie theaters; fans of the classic television series I Love Lucy can still watch rerun after rerun of episode 1 from season 6, in which Lucy, Ricky, and special guest Bob Hope perform a rousing song-and-dance rendition of "Nobody Loves the Ump"; and innumerable ball park denizens have not only witnessed the gyrations of dancing groundskeepers, cheerleading squads, and baseball clowns like Max Patkin and Al Schacht, but also have "busted a move" of their own (sometimes for the benefit of the scoreboard camera) as stadium loudspeakers blast out songs with big, infectious beats, such as "Who Let the Dogs Out?" "Cotton-Eyed Joe," and, of course, "The Macarena."

However, the extent of this baseball-dance connection is not understood as widely or comprehensively by most Americans. Yet, the surprising reality is that baseball has been a powerful source of inspiration for both choreographers and dancers for decades. Moreover, the similarities that exist between these two disciplines, upon closer examination, prove to be startling. Baseball players and dancers have much in common and it is the goal of this book to shed a bright light on these points of convergence. In particular, this book seeks to scrutinize the theater, the concert stage, and the big and little screens of motion pictures, television, and video in order to reveal the many ways in which this close relationship has been—and continues to be—expressed through *performance*. As it turns out, the history is both fascinating and entertaining, and the examples are bountiful—much more bountiful, in fact, than had been anticipated when this project was initiated in 2008. Along these lines, it is important to note that more detailed studies of certain aspects of the relationship between baseball and dance had to be placed on hold temporarily due to the time and space required for the present stage and screen study. A lengthy look at the incredible and multifaceted phenomenon of ball park dancing (a genuinely huge subject) and the extraordinary parallels that may be found in the areas of training, preparation, injuries, fan psychology, and cultural traditions (also subjects of surprising enormity) needed to be postponed. Still, these subjects will be touched upon at various points and in various ways throughout the book, meaning that the spotlight will reach even these less exhaustively covered areas at least in an introductory manner, setting the stage for what I intend to be a follow-up study (to be completed in the very near future).

In order to pave the way for the broad examination of baseball and dance on stage and screen, a few more "elemental" subjects, including some of those mentioned at the end of the previous paragraph, need to be addressed. The initial question with which we are faced, after all, is the following: What are the *essential qualities and characteristics* that are shared by baseball and dance? Attempting to answer this fundamental question will provide us with a critical added layer of foundation upon which we may be able to create a more complete picture of the dynamic relationship that has existed and continues to exist, particularly in America, between these two distinct and beautiful forms of human expression.

Similarities and Connections

To be sure, baseball and dance have much in common. In spite of dismissive sentiments that may be voiced by those who falsely and foolishly equate baseball (and, in general, all sports) with masculinity, while viewing dance as a non-athletic, intrinsically "feminine" pursuit, links between the two disciplines have been observed by writers and those who participate in either dance or baseball (or both) for almost as long as baseball has been played in the United States.[3] Baseball's grace of movement, the line and form of the players, the extraordinary emphasis on timing—all of these elements are stunningly dance-like. In the synopsis provided by filmmakers Ken Burns and Lynn Novick for their award-winning 1994 Public Broadcasting System television documentary *Baseball*, the term "ballet of baseball" is used to describe the physical and aesthetic beauty of the game,[4] and dancers such as Gene Kelly and Edward Villella have spoken with eloquence on these similarities. Kelly, for example, remarked in his 1958 CBS television special, "Dancing—A Man's Game," that when Mickey Mantle (who actually appears on the program) catches and throws a baseball, what we are witnessing is *dance*. To quote Kelly, "It is … a beautiful, rhythmic thing to watch."[5] And, in a 1979 segment of the CBS television news magazine *Monday Morning*, Villella ponders the outstanding fielding prowess of the New York Yankees' third baseman Graig Nettles in the 1978 World Series and exclaims, "I think he was as graceful and as lovely as the best of classical dancers."[6]

The similarities, however, do not end with movement. When taking into account such areas as training and preparation, focus and concentration, the pursuit of excellence, and the simultaneous love and fear among dancers and players of those who attend the performance (or game), the connections appear to be even stronger and more far-reaching.[7] Baseball players, such as George Brett and Derek Jeter, may talk about "being in the zone" (when the game "slows down," becomes "simple," and every pitcher's pitch, in Brett's famous words, seems as big as a "beach ball")[8]; yet, dancers, too, describe frequently the much-sought-after feeling of *ease*, when the body and mind seem to be aligned perfectly. To once again quote Edward Villella, "When you're having a great performance, you're aware of the fact that it's *so easy*, it's so smooth, and, when you're finished, you say … 'Wow, that was something—that was extra special.'"[9]

Additionally, the world of the professional baseball player and that of the professional dancer are marked not simply by intense training and physical development, leading to excitement, exhilaration, and moments of seeming perfection, but also by pain, fear, and, not infrequently, tragedy. In a 1987 interview conducted for the cable television program *Eye on Dance*, this less pleasant link in the dance-baseball chain is revealed most vividly.[10] As dancer-choreographer Kirk Peterson, dance company director Ian (Ernie) Horvath, sports physician Joel Solomon, and New York Mets pitcher Ron Darling discuss the ways in which sports and dance intersect, the complicated subject of injuries is raised. What becomes crystal clear in just a few moments is how strikingly similar the mindset of an injured baseball player and that of an injured dancer happens to be. Peterson, Horvath, Solomon, and Darling are in almost unwavering agreement that players and dancers often will continue to perform with pain, for three primary reasons: (1) reluctance to disappoint fellow players and/or fans; (2) fear of being perceived as weak or vulnerable; and (3) fear of being replaced or overshadowed by an eager reserve player or lower-level dancer (what Ron Darling refers to, in familiar baseball lingo, as the "Wally Pipp Syndrome").

In spite of their super-human, larger-than-life images and despite the perpetual quest for the sublime, the dancer and the baseball player are confronted constantly with mortality, uncooperative bodies, and the byproducts of competition at its extreme. And, yet, to quote

A. Bartlett Giamatti, "The rage to get it right, to make things fit as they never have before, to show a sight or make a sound that is completely coherent, as fully a law unto itself, as close to completely what glistens within, as possible"[11] never ceases to motivate the dancer and the baseball player, even as he or she hobbles on to the field or grimaces with pain during a *grand jeté*.

Finally, it may be said that a consideration and review of the ways in which baseball and dance in America germinated, developed, and evolved—beginning in the mid-19th century—necessarily lead to revelations of historical parallels that are quite remarkable. Such revelations will be addressed in the body of the book, particularly in the opening sections of chapter 1 and chapter 3.

Baseball's Influence on American Dancers

In the coming chapters, there also will be plenty of discussion of the many choreographers, theatrical producers, dance directors, and musical stagers who have found the "Great American Pastime," for one reason or another, to be a source of inspiration. However, in addition to these baseball-minded dance and show creators, there are far more numerous cases that exist of dancers, most of whom do not create dances, who have been influenced dramatically in some very real way by baseball's beauty and fluidity of movement or, in certain instances, by the sheer composition and construct of the game, as well as the overriding sense of fairness and civility and the potential for explosive change that seems to hover over every pitch and each at-bat.

Like Edward Villella (whose own high school and college years were punctuated not only by dance classes and performances, but also by baseball games and awards), Marianna Tcherkassky, a former principal dancer with the American Ballet Theatre, was a great admirer of New York Yankees' third baseman Graig Nettles. Speaking of the fielding miracles performed by Nettles in the aforementioned 1978 World Series, Tcherkassky exclaimed, "Talk about dance moves.... [Nettles] seemed to have an entire repertoire."[12]

Similarly, Tom Rawe, a former member of the Twyla Tharp company, has explained with a sense of awe how an afternoon's viewing of a televised baseball game (with the sound turned off) provided him with an opportunity to refine his own approach to dance: "I was watching a pitcher with his motion.... If I knew my dance movements as well as he knew his pitcher's motion, wouldn't that be phenomenal? He not only knows the motion, but the sequences, the timing, everything working together.... I started thinking, 'Oh, I want to incorporate that into my dance.'"[13]

Many dancers, of course, have pursued baseball careers, only to find that their own skills were not strong enough to carry them to the highest levels of the game. Oakland Ballet's Ron Thiele, for example, pitched in semi-professional baseball leagues; Jim Morrow, founder of the Instruments of Movement Dance Company, and Broadway "triple threat" performer Shuler Hensley all entered college on baseball scholarships; Jeff Richards, who was a featured dancer in the blockbuster film version of the classic Broadway musical *Seven Brides for Seven Brothers* played in the Minor Leagues (for the Portland Beavers and Salem Senators); and Nick Ross, who performed in the companies of such esteemed choreographers as Peter Pucci and Jennifer Muller before establishing his own dance troupe, played baseball well enough in high school to earn a tryout with a major league team. All of these dancers, ultimately, understood that professional baseball, in all likelihood, was not a realistic option. Yet, what each *also* came to understand fairly quickly was that a lifetime of baseball training could transfer quite nicely to a dance environment and his own athletic abilities, combined with the grace and precision learned specifically on the baseball diamond, might prove to be a dynamic starting point from which to launch a dance career (provided that a love of and passion for dance itself also was present).

Again and again, it is possible to discover irrefutable evidence that proves the existence of a wonderful, powerful, deep-rooted, and truly historic connection between baseball and dance in the United States. Indeed, it may be said with confidence that at this point in history, this connection is not only stronger than ever before, but also that it seems to be in the process of actually *growing* in strength. In just this earliest part of the 21st century, specifically from 2001 to 2013, it is possible to identify more than thirty examples of baseball and dance merging on the stage and screen. At the same time, during this same period, a bevy of baseball players and managers—including Craig Counsell of the Milwaukee Brewers, Tony LaRussa of the St. Louis Cardinals, Don Mattingly of the Los Angeles Dodgers, and retired All-Star, Hall of Fame catcher Mike Piazza—have been invited by professional dance companies to appear as guest performers in such productions as *The Nutcracker* and *Slaughter on Tenth Avenue*. Taken together, this seems to be a small but significant indication that the line between both art forms is becoming less and less pronounced in the minds of professional athletes, as well as those of the American (and global) public. More and more, the words spoken in 1979 by Edward Villella regarding the close connection between dance and baseball ring tremendously true. Villella, who was described in 1967 as a "star of the new generation of male dancers that is exciting the world of ballet with breathtaking speed, power, and manly art,"[14] said of dancers and baseball players, "What we do is make the unnatural natural to ourselves and we make the difficult look easy."[15] Skilled on the ball field and virtuosic on the concert dance stage, who would understand the similarities better than Villella?

1

On Stage I

Music Halls, Vaudeville, Broadway
and More—19th Century through
Early 20th Century

In 1908 … [Mike] Donlin set a new standard for that strange American hyphenate,
the athlete-actor. An adept base stealer on the ball field, he proved he could shake
a mean leg on the stage, too.[1]

The passage above appears in Noel Hynd's 1996 book, *Marquard and Seeley*, a fascinating
examination of the personal and professional relationship that developed between star baseball pitcher Rube Marquard and stage luminary Blossom Seeley during the first quarter of
the 20th century. Marquard, who was known as "King of the Diamond," and Seeley, who was
billed as "Queen of Ragtime," performed together in such rousing stage shows as *Breaking
the Record; or Nineteen Straight* and *The Suffragette Pitcher*, both of which featured plenty of
dancing as well as singing. In the passage above, Hynd refers to Mike Donlin, another star
baseball player who also gained fame as a vaudeville entertainer—an outfielder who not only
could track down a fly ball and beat out a bunt at the Polo Grounds, but also could dance
skillfully enough to bring down the house and cause a "small pandemonium of uproar" in a
Times Square music hall.[2]

In Hynd's book, as well as in such extraordinary accounts of American vaudeville as
John DiMeglio's *Vaudeville U.S.A.*, Joe Laurie, Jr.'s *Vaudeville: From Honky-Tonks to the Palace*,
and Anthony Slide's *The Encyclopedia of Vaudeville*, it becomes extremely clear that early 20th-
century America was a period when theatrical depictions of baseball through dance and the
active participation of baseball personnel in stage shows that incorporate dance were both
common and wildly in demand. According to Hynd, "[B]aseball and show business were
beginning to intertwine very neatly" in this era.[3] The connections were remarkably close and
Hynd observes that, in many ways, baseball and the spectacle known as vaudeville were cut
from the same cloth and became popular for similar reasons. To quote Hynd, "Baseball and
vaudeville mirrored each other in this era, both playing the big, booming, rowdy, bustling
American cities as well as the smallest, quietest, most God-fearing towns that could clear a
diamond in the village or erect a stage in a storefront."[4] Acknowledging this kinship, Joe
Laurie, Jr., points out that one of the most popular and glorious theaters in New York City
during this period before and during World War I, Hammerstein's, was frequented so heavily
by members of the baseball world (both on and off the stage) that it became known as "the
baseball player's home plate."[5]

Of course, the era when vaudeville was "king" was but one segment of U.S. entertainment history that provided members of the public with opportunities to experience the connections between dance and baseball in the context of live, non-ballpark theater. And it was not even the *earliest* period in American entertainment history where baseball and dance merged on the theatrical stage. In this chapter, we will look more closely at these aforementioned "theatrical depictions of baseball through dance" and explore in greater detail the "active participation of baseball personnel in stage shows that incorporate dance." We also will spend more time in the vaudeville era and meet more hoofing hurlers and sashaying shortstops. In fact, the history of theater productions which feature baseball-related dance numbers and/or dancing baseball players can be traced from baseball's beginnings all the way to the modern day.

The remainder of this chapter is divided into two sections, arranged chronologically: 19th century and early 20th century. The forthcoming chapter will focus on three subsequent periods: mid-20th century, 1960s-1980s, and 1990s to the present. The information provided in each of the five sections is not intended to be exhaustive; however, a hefty sampling of significant and representative people, productions, endeavors, movements, and events will be highlighted. Additionally, as background and context are offered, some important parallels to and overlaps with other portions of this book will become readily apparent. Peter Pucci, for example, who created baseball choreography for the 2010 musical *Johnny Baseball*, also choreographed a baseball-themed work for the concert dance stage; *Damn Yankees* was a cinema and Broadway hit; and the popularity of baseball players performing in vaudeville is described vividly in the 1918 children's novel, *Baseball Joe Around the World*. The nature of the subject, baseball and dance, is attuned quite perfectly to parallels and overlaps. Speaking of the world-famous baseball owner and eccentric, Bill Veeck, biographer Ed Linn remarks that Veeck, the man who hired baseball clowns, encouraged fan participation at ball games, and introduced the exploding scoreboard, always "viewed the baseball park as the theater in which he operated."[6]

19th Century

The period of human development that is associated most frequently with change and identity formation, growth and experimentation is adolescence. As Patrick Jones, who has devoted thousands of pages of text to the teenage years, has said, teenagers can be characterized as "works in progress."[7] If we take a bit of a leap and apply this definition to the history of the United States, a claim can be made that the mid-to-late 19th century, in turn, was the country's "adolescent" stage—a period when the United States, having gained and defended its independence only recently, was able finally to create an identity for itself, to grow, and to begin to decide what to do with its newfound freedom and autonomy. Lots of questions were still unanswered and many pieces of the national puzzle were still missing, but, after the turmoil of infancy and childhood, the country, at last, could focus on its cultural development.

It is not at all surprising, therefore, that the mid-to-late 19th century was precisely the time when distinctly American forms of sport and performing arts began to emerge and flourish. Of these sports and art forms, it has been pointed out by many cultural historians that baseball and theater (in all its manifestations) were the primary disciplines to materialize and to be embraced by the burgeoning population. Indeed, as George B. Kirsch remarks, in his study of baseball's origin, "[T]here were important similarities between the cultures of baseball and the theater during this era."[8] Kirsch describes how baseball and theater appealed to all segments of society and how members of the upper and lower classes found both joy and meaning, entertainment and enlightenment in the observance of a baseball game and a theatrical event. To quote Kirsch, "Like the world of theater, baseball had associations with both respectable society and the less reputable life of Victorian popular amusements. People flocked to games for many of the same reasons they attended plays produced for the masses; their tastes were both high-brow and low-brow."[9]

In a very real sense, baseball and theater were linked.

Simultaneously, as baseball's popularity spread, as the rules of baseball coalesced, and as the movement towards organized leagues advanced, a body of what can be termed "baseball music" was being introduced. Edward J. Rielly, in his sweeping and meticulously researched reference work, *Baseball: An Encyclopedia of Popular Culture*, declares that "music has been part of baseball since the sport's earliest days" and explains that "when people like something, they compose songs about it."[10] Rielly then cites the song that is believed to be the "first piece of baseball music" ever published, a lively ditty called "The Base Ball Polka."[11] This song, which dates from 1858 (approximately eleven years before the generally accepted inaugural year of professional baseball, 1869), turns out to be noteworthy for a second reason. If we consider the very title of the song, it becomes immediately clear that what we have is not only the first recorded example of baseball music, but also the first recorded example of a baseball *dance*. A polka, after all, is, first and foremost, a dance and, while it is difficult to know whether or not couples and groups of friends were actively bouncing around ballroom and parlor floors to "The Base Ball Polka" in 1858, there is no doubt that such a song was written with dancers and dancing in mind.

Soon afterwards, in the 1860s, other baseball-themed dance songs made their debuts. "Live Oak Polka," a song composed in honor of the Live Oak Base Ball Club of Rochester, New York, was released in 1860, as was "Home Run Quick Step," a "dedication to the members of the Mercantile Base Ball Club of Philadelphia, Pennsylvania." These were followed by such crowd-pleasers as "Union Base Ball Club March," "Home Run Polka," and "Home Run Galop," all penned prior to the landmark year of 1869.[12] In these formative years, as baseball's structure solidified and as its popularity ascended, its close connection to dance was quite evident and, it is possible to say, well understood by the general public.

Owing to the nature of these songs and considering that a large number of widely known tunes, particularly those with themes that reflected timely topics and popular pursuits, were performed frequently in dance and music halls and at social gatherings, there is every reason to believe, in this period before the phonograph and the radio, that American audiences listened to musicians playing and singers singing songs like "The Temple Cup, Two-Step March," "The Base Ball Fever," and "Slide, Kelly, Slide" within the sometimes cozy, sometimes vast confines of 19th-century American theaters and that corresponding dances either were performed or observed by the assembled spectators.

Famed 20th-century American dancer and choreographer Agnes deMille has commented that, from the mid-to-late 1800s, "America's own kind of dancing was developing ... in barrooms, tents, and low-grade theaters."[13] Ballet, in the 19th century, also was developing rapidly, but innovations were occurring primarily in Europe and Russia. The United States produced some notable ballet stars, such as Mary Ann Lee, Augusta Maywood, and George Washington Smith, and ballet shows became more and more popular in the U.S. as the century progressed; however, until the latter part of the 19th century, ballet was still tied, almost suffocatingly, to European and Russian forms and forebears.[14] The dancing styles to which deMille was referring were those that were on display in minstrel shows and popular theaters, dances that were inspired, in many cases, by America's black population, by its folk and indigenous traditions, and by the waves of immigrants resettling throughout the country, but chiefly in America's rapidly expanding urban centers. America's search for identity was reflected in its quest for art forms and styles, vocabularies and themes that were distinctly American. This quest, which, in truth, constituted a genuine *cultural movement*, is referred to, quite simply, as "Americana" and operating at the very center of this movement was *dance*.

In the 19th century, when the Americana movement was in its germination stage (as we shall examine more closely in pages to come, it reached its full flowering in the 1920s, '30s, '40s, and '50s), the theatrical forum which displayed and provided access to the widest range of "homegrown" entertainment, as well as entertainers and art forms from abroad (which, subsequently, often served to inspire American hybrids, variations, and offshoots), was vaudeville. In vaudeville, all were invited to exhibit their wares and, like another distinctly American enterprise, the *automat*, all tastes were catered to and all manner of dishes were offered and even celebrated. To quote dance historian Walter Terry: "With the establishment of vaudeville … variety—including variety in dance—became the rage."[15] Vaudeville was popular theater, entertainment for the masses, and, as such, the producers and promoters were on the lookout constantly for acts, concepts, costumes, and set designs that would attract customers, who, in most cases, could attend as many shows in one day as they desired for the price of a single ticket (which, in general, was kept quite low).

It was not long before these aforementioned producers and promoters began to set their sights on the nation's sports arenas, actively recruiting star performers who were admired and adored by the general public. After all, considering how important athletics was becoming in the United States in the mid-to-late 19th century, how could audiences resist the opportunity to see a beloved athlete make a live appearance on the stage and perhaps even sing or dance with an equally beloved music or dance hall entertainer? The potential for big crowds and, therefore, sizable box-office receipts, was enormous. At the same time, professional athletes were always on the prowl for off-season employment that could sustain them until the start of the next playing season.[16] Vaudeville, surely, was a perfect fit for sporting greats and, in terms of sports in America, by the late 1800s, as the *Sporting News* pointed out in an 1891 issue, "[N]o game [had] taken so strong a hold on Americans as base ball."[17] Consequently, in the latter part of the 19th century, the back-and-forth shuttle between the baseball field and the vaudeville stage began to operate in earnest. And, as the 1949 MGM film *Take Me Out to the Ball Game* illustrates—in a somewhat exaggerated fashion—a jaunty baseball-themed or baseball-inspired vaudeville song-and-dance routine was, quite often, a highlight of this circular journey.

John Montgomery Ward and Helen Dauvray

While the connection between vaudeville and baseball became especially pronounced and involved the highest number of participants during the first quarter of the 20th century, this late 19th century period featured an intriguing array of personalities and occurrences. Prominent among the players, former players, and baseball-loving actors who helped to establish and broaden this connection were Cap Anson, Mike "King" Kelly, De Wolf Hopper, and Digby Bell, all of whom shall be discussed briefly below. As Noel Hynd reminds us, though, one very early "major link" was contributed by another figure who never set foot on either a vaudeville, Broadway, or burlesque stage: the remarkable ballplayer-turned-lawyer John Montgomery Ward.[18] Described in an 1887 *New York Times* article as a "thorough gentleman and a splendid fellow,"[19] Ward began his professional baseball career in 1877 as a brilliant pitcher with the Providence Grays of the National League. In the early 1880s, although continuing to pitch effectively, Ward developed arm problems and attempted other positions. In 1883, he traded in his Grays uniform for a uniform of the New York Gothams (forerunner of the Giants) and, one year later, he swapped positions permanently and transformed himself into a stellar shortstop. While still playing, he also earned a law degree from Columbia University in 1886, helped to organize the National Brotherhood of Base Ball Players in 1885, and was an instrumental force in the founding of the short-lived Players League in 1890. However, the experience that may have provided the multitalented Ward with his widest acclaim was his marriage, in 1887, to one of the most popular stage actresses of the era, Helen Dauvray.

Dauvray, who harbored a great "love for the national game" and could be spotted in the stands of the Polo Grounds on a fairly regular basis during the baseball season,[20] was known for her acting, rather than singing and dancing, abilities. However, Dauvray loved music and musical entertainment and, in 1886, she composed a rollicking and popular dance song, entitled "One of Our Girls Polka." Thus, the Ward-Dauvray union in 1887 served to forge a small but not insignificant "link" in the baseball-dance chain. Furthermore, it not only focused an additional light on the parallel lives of the ballpark and the vaudeville house in America, but also managed to reinforce the notion that baseball and vaudeville (as well as other forms of popular entertainment) contained elements that were simultaneously low- and high-brow and could appeal to members of all classes. In the 1887 *New York Times* article, Dauvray makes a point of reassuring her fans (and, by extension, all denizens of "high society") that Ward "is a most charming and cultured man," who "speaks five or six languages fluently, and is otherwise well informed and well bred." At the same time, Dauvray did her part to celebrate and promote the game that she loved by establishing and financing, in the very same year as her marriage to Ward, an early version of the World Series, termed, appropriately, "The Helen Dauvray Cup." The cup was intended to reward the "champion baseball team of the world" and included "a gold medal cast for each member of the winning team." The first recipient of the Dauvray Cup (and corresponding "badges"), the Detroit Wolverines, succeeded in defeating the St. Louis Browns, ten games to five, in the championship showdown. Dauvray's illustrious cup continued to be presented until 1893, after which it was "retired" and replaced, one year later, by the Temple Cup, which had no affiliation with Helen Dauvray.

Anson, Kelly, Hopper and Bell

During the 1880s and 1890s, the belief that true similarities may be found in the requisite movements of baseball and dance was advanced significantly by four figures who crossed paths on a regular basis, both inside the ballpark and on the stages of dance and music halls. Conveniently, two of the four, Cap Anson and Mike "King" Kelly, were members of baseball royalty, while the remaining two, Digby Bell and De Wolf Hopper, were hugely successful and widely known actor-comedians. What brought them together with relatively great frequency during the closing decades of the 19th century was the strong, even passionate interest each pair shared in the other respective profession. While Anson and Kelly were theater lovers with a yen to perform, Bell and Hopper were baseball fanatics who socialized enthusiastically with ballplayers (including Anson and Kelly) and sprinkled baseball ideas, movements, and language into their theatrical skits and musical numbers as much as possible.

For Bell and Hopper, 1885 was a pivotal year in terms of baseball-themed theatrics. As Howard W. Rosenberg recounts in his expansive study of Cap Anson, an 1885 musical starring Bell and Hopper, *The Black Hussar*, premiered at Wallack's Theatre in New York City and included "a song with a baseball stanza" that was performed with what can only be described as true baseball choreography.[21] The subsequent review in the *New York Times*, cited by Rosenberg, makes this very clear: "Mr. Hopper enacts ... the pitcher, Mr. Bell, with a bird cage on his head and boxing gloves on his hands, plays catcher, while Mme. [Mathilde] Cottrelly handles a diminutive bat as striker and endeavors to make a 'home run.'"[22] Three years later, in 1888, Hopper, Bell, and Bell's wife, Laura Joyce, revived this scene at a benefit show for the pennant-winning New York Giants and, once again, the *New York Times* provided a description: "Bell, wearing a bird cage for a mask, a washboard for a [chest] protector, and boxing gloves, stood behind a china plate, while Laura Joyce Bell gracefully wielded a bat and waited eagerly for Hopper, standing in a low-neck dry goods box to pitch."[23] As in 1885, the *Times* raved and called the number "irresistibly comic."[24]

Bell and Hopper, in February 1889, drew once more from the baseball diamond in the staging of Franz von Suppe's *Boccaccio*, which was presented, once again, at Wallack's Theatre in New York City. This time, Rosenberg cites a review that appeared in the *Brooklyn Eagle*, which provides a vivid account of the skit performed in the show's third encore by Bell, Hopper, and "fellow McCaull Opera Company actor," Jefferson De Angelis.[25] As the *Eagle* reporter notes, all three actors, respectively playing the roles of catcher (Bell), pitcher (De Angelis), and batter (Hopper), carry out exaggerated movements associated with their particular positions; the scene ends with Bell being knocked down by a sliding Hopper, who then does a somersault. A comic argument ensues and Hopper, Bell, and De Angelis then turn directly to the audience and ask for help in deciding whether or not Hopper was safe or out. This appeal manages to rile the three principals even further, leading to an angry exit, in which, according to the *Eagle*, Hopper and Bell "go off kicking like [real-life players] Anson and [Buck] Ewing," adding, "It is a rich gag and takes immediately."[26] Once again, audience members were being treated to a piece of baseball-inspired choreography.

It is also important to be reminded that Hopper organized an actors' baseball team in 1886 and even helped to create the Actor's Amateur Athletic Association of America (AAAAA) in 1889—ideas and efforts which were forerunners of such still-existing entities as the Broadway Show League in New York City. Additionally, Hopper's dramatic rendition of Ernest Thayer's baseball poem "Casey at the Bat," presented initially in 1888 (when the poem was still unknown to most Americans), was a source of tremendous popularity for "several decades," according to Hynd,[27] and grew to be almost as legendary as the poem itself from the late 1800s through the early 20th century. Indeed, in 1906, the ongoing popularity of Hopper's recital led to its being released as a phonograph record and, by 1922, Hopper's performance was still considered marketable enough for it to be captured on film, complete with sound, courtesy of Lee DeForest's new and exciting Phonofilm process.

Bell, in turn, recorded his own version of Thayer's tale of the "Mudville Nine," entitled "The Man Who Fanned Casey," which was released in 1909.[28] Moreover, his relationship with the "national game" stretched at least as far back as 1867, when he played right field for the New York

Knickerbockers, the amateur team founded in 1845 by baseball pioneer Alexander Cartwright. Bell also was a longtime member of Hopper's rotating team of actor-athletes and was so "thoroughly saturated" with baseball, as he confessed to the *Baltimore Sun* in 1894, that, during one performance of Gilbert and Sullivan's *The Mikado*, he went so far as to pepper his own dialogue and actions with self-created baseball references.[29]

For Cap Anson and Mike "King" Kelly, of course, baseball was not just a passion and a pastime, it was also a livelihood—a livelihood at which, to put it mildly, they excelled. Anson's lengthy career spanned twenty-seven years, from 1871–1897, while Kelly, who "burned the candle at both ends,"[30] played only sixteen years, from 1878–1893, and died in his first year of retirement, 1894, at the age of thirty-six. Anson and Kelly were superstars of the era and their statistics alone are remarkable. Anson, for example, collected a total of 3,435 hits, as well as 2,075 career runs batted in, and a lifetime batting average of .334, while Kelly compiled 1,813 overall hits and a final batting average of .308, including two seasons in which he boasted averages of .354 (1884) and an astounding .388 (1886). If one takes into consideration that Kelly's last three

Mike "King" Kelly, wearing a Boston Bean-eaters uniform, 1887 (Library of Congress Prints and Photographs Division; photograph by George H. Hastings).

years of professional play were marked by distraction, disruption, ill health, and limited on-field action, his cumulative statistics are even more impressive. However, with Anson and, even more so, with Kelly, a great deal more than cold, hard statistics accounted for their mass appeal. In a word, Anson and Kelly were *showmen*.

From 1880–1886, Anson and Kelly played together on one of the most powerful major league clubs of the period, the Chicago White Stockings, a team that, from 1883–1887, also featured on its roster the future dancing preacher, Billy Sunday (who will be discussed at greater length later in this book). During this seven-year stretch of ball field solidarity, Anson's well-established reputation as a spectacular ballplayer (and, on the terrible flipside, a frighteningly unapologetic racist) grew exponentially, while the "flamboyant, fast-living" Kelly[31] became perhaps the most popular player in the game—to quote Steve Henson, the "first larger-than-life pro baseball player,"[32] who, in the words of Lieb, had "much the same hold on fans of the '80s" as Babe Ruth would in the coming century.[33] As irrefutable celebrities of baseball, Anson and Kelly also were attractive to theater promoters, who were always on the prowl for both crowd-pleasing acts and popular stars who could either perform in or publicize shows and venues. Once again, this was particularly true in the case of Kelly, who, as Henson reveals, liked "to address the crowd between pitches, banter with the umpire and bait the opposition, blurring the lines between baseball and performance art" (characteristics that may have been adopted by Kelly from African American baseball players and teams, as we shall see shortly).[34] Like many players of the time, Anson and Kelly accepted many invitations to attend vaudeville and musical theater performances and "rubbed elbows" with actors, singers, dancers, and comedians backstage, in nightclubs, and even at the ball park. It was, in truth, only a matter of time before the urge to perform would become too great and both Anson and Kelly would make their way from the area below and behind the footlights to center stage.

Unsurprisingly, this occurred first with Kelly. The ballplayer nicknamed "King," who was "the kind of athlete tailor-made for baseball legend,"[35] departed Chicago for Boston in 1887 and celebrated the home opener of his new club, the Boston Beaneaters, by attending a gala the very same night at the Boston Theatre.[36] Immediately, Kelly, a player regarded so highly that the regal sum of $10,000 was paid to the White Stockings by the Beaneaters for his release, became an even more glittering star. "Within two years," writes Henson, "Kelly was the subject of America's first pop music hit" ("Slide, Kelly, Slide," composed in 1889 by unrelated comedian J. W. Kelly, and performed by dance hall star Maggie Cline) and "[w]ithin four years, he was moonlighting as a Vaudeville act, reciting 'Casey at the Bat,' often substituting Kelly for Casey."[37] Between his appearance at the Boston Theatre in 1887 and his death from pneumonia in 1894, Kelly, whose name, since his debut in 1878, had been "synonymous" with baseball, was also linked closely with vaudeville, burlesque, and musical theater.

Though "Casey at the Bat" was Kelly's primary performance piece on the vaudeville stage, he also began appearing in sketches. This was due, in large part, to his affiliation with Charles Hoyt, one of the most creative and well-known theatrical figures of the late 19th century.[38] Hoyt, who, as we shall explore in greater detail below, also helped to introduce Cap Anson to the world of vaudeville, was a producer, writer, and composer with a love for baseball. In 1888, Hoyt began what would be a seven-year theatrical relationship with Mike "King" Kelly, persuading him to take on a small part in a stage piece called "A Rag Baby," which was performed in Boston. Kelly, at this point, was hooked. "A Rag Baby" was followed by appearances in such shows as *A Tin Soldier* (1889, in New York) and *Temperance Town* (1892, in Boston), both of which were created by Hoyt. Then, after a one-performance role as a baseball-playing minstrel in a Boston-based show called *Winning Cards* (in January 1893), Kelly, in March of the same year, performed "Casey" and three songs, including "Mamma Wouldn't Buy Me a Bow-Wow," in the show, *Vaudeville Club*, a revue put together by Kelly's stage partner, Billy Jerome (which took place at the Madison Street Opera House in Chicago). When the 1893 baseball season opened, Kelly became a member of the New York Giants; however, he appeared in only twenty games before being released to his old club, the Boston Beaneaters, who refused to accept him. Kelly opted to leave Major League Baseball entirely and decided, instead, to open a saloon in New York and devote himself to performing.

In late 1893, Kelly signed on with Mark Murphy's touring vaudeville company and began to appear in a popular show called *O'Dowd's Neighbors*. Kelly was billed as a "Special Added Attraction" (and referred to as "The Former $10,000 Beauty"[39]) and had the daunting task of delivering three song-and-dance parodies ("Two Little Girls Won't Do," "The Patch I Left Behind," and "The Monte Carlo"), as well as another recital of "Casey at the Bat."[40] The show and Kelly were applauded by critics and the general public alike, and rumors, generated primarily by Kelly himself, started flying of Kelly's co-starring in a baseball-themed comedy, *The Irish Adonis*, in late 1894.[41] In the meantime, though, Kelly hooked onto a semi-professional baseball team based in Allentown, Pennsylvania, which was part of the Pennsylvania State League and owned by a friend named Albert Johnson.[42] After the Allentown team folded in August of 1894, Kelly and a number of Allentown teammates proceeded to join another team owned by Johnson in Yonkers, New York.[43] For both teams, Kelly played, in many ways, like the "King" of old, batting .305 for Allentown and .375 for Yonkers. Once the season was over, though, Kelly was ready to concentrate again on his stage career. After reuniting with Murphy and "his funny associates"[44] for a few more performances of *O'Dowd's Neighbors*, Kelly was off to Boston, where, according to Rob Hudson, he would join the London Gaiety Girls Theatrical Company "to perform small comedy parts."[45] Sadly, though, en route to his latest show business opportunity, Kelly contracted pneumonia and passed away on November 8. Certainly, a life too short; yet, in this relatively small space of time, Kelly did much to connect baseball, music, theater, and dance in America.

Cap Anson, as mentioned above, was introduced to the stage by Charles Hoyt, the same man responsible for helping to launch the vaudeville and music hall career of Mike "King" Kelly. Coincidentally, Anson received his first taste of performing outside of the ball field in 1888, the year that Kelly began his own professional relationship with Hoyt (1888 also marked the inauguration of what is believed to be the first baseball opera, *Angela, or the Umpire's Revenge*, with libretto by Paul Eaton and music by John Philip Sousa, which premiered on June 29 at the Grand Opera House in Philadelphia). In the case of Anson, this virgin effort occurred at the Theatre Comique in New York City, where Anson was given a small part in one of Hoyt's madcap shows. The show itself has been identified by Rosenberg as *A Bunch of Keys* and by Smith, Smith, and Herschfield as *A Parlor Match*.[46] Either way, there is universal agreement that Anson's role consisted of a single line of dialogue, likely delivered rather stiffly. It also is clear that both shows, in a style typical of Hoyt and of the era in general, offered spectators an opportunity to experience a smorgasbord of theatrics. The *New York Times*, for example, noted, in 1884, that *A Bunch of Keys* contained "horse play, acrobatic feats, clog dances, the throwing of various missiles by the performers, the blowing of flour by one actor in the face of another, and such like pleasantry."[47] Likewise, an 1889 review of *A Parlor Match* in *The Spokesman-Review* of Spokane, Washington, observes that a new, local rendition displayed "[a] dozen vaudeville features," including "the cake walk," one of the hottest dances of the age, while a review in the *Daily Alta California* from May 15, 1888, exclaims of the traveling production, "The singing is good, the dancing is good, the jokes are good."[48] Anson, in his 1888 debut, may not have been "shaking a mean leg" on stage, but his proximity to dance was exceedingly close.

Interestingly, Hoyt's theatrical "courtship" with Anson actually commenced five years earlier, in 1883, when Hoyt, then a sports editor with the *Boston Post*, wrote a kind of comic ode, a parody of the contemporary hit song, "Baby Mine," to Anson and his fearsome White Stockings.[49] Local baseball favorites, the Boston Beaneaters, had just swept a four-game series with the White Stockings, catapulting the Boston team into first place, and Hoyt found himself unable to resist a smidgen of respectful gloating, resulting in the composition and publication of the lyric, "To the Gallant Captain of the C.B.B.C. (Chicago Base Ball Club)." From that point forward, Hoyt and Anson became correspondents and friends and Hoyt set himself to the task of wooing Anson onto the stage.

Eventually, of course, Anson did surrender to Hoyt's persistent theatrical overtures; however, their full-fledged vaudeville "marriage" was in no way immediate following the brief 1888 collaboration. To the contrary, in spite of Hoyt's ongoing attempts at seduction and Anson's unvarnished desires to step back into the theatrical limelight, a proper vehicle and time did not emerge for another seven years. As Rosenberg points out, the few ideas and titles that were proposed by Hoyt (such as "My Boyhood Days; or How We Played Ball in 1763" and "Only a Kick; or An Umpire That Died the Death") never seemed to advance much further than the dinner table.[50] When 1895 arrived, though, the partnership between Anson and Hoyt resumed with full force in the form of *A Runaway Colt*, a baseball-centered entertainment created specifically for Anson by Hoyt.

The title of the play, devised by Hoyt, referred directly to Anson's White Stockings, who, in the 1890s, were given the nickname "Anson's Colts."[51] Anson, a great celebrity on the ball field, but still very much a novice actor, played himself, "The Captain of the Chicagos." In his biography of Anson, David L. Fleitz describes the opening act, in which, according to the original script, "Capt. Anson captures the Runaway Colt":

> The play concerned a handsome young man named Manley Manners, a minister's son and college baseball player who receives an invitation to pitch for Chicago, but runs into opposition from his parents, who view baseball as a low-class sport and an unfit calling for the son of a reverend. The local bishop, however, is a baseball fan, and invites a "Mr. Adrian" [Anson] to dinner to meet the Manners family, who do not know that their guest is actually Cap Anson, manager of the Colts.[52]

As both Rosenberg and Fleitz illustrate with humor and panache, the three acts that follow are jam-packed with plot twists, melodrama, and whimsy. A perusal of the show's official playbill, though, reveals a bit more. To be sure, *A Runaway Colt* provided theatergoers with an opportunity to hear clever dialogue and watch a star baseball player perform live in a completely different medium; however, the show also treated audience members to a bevy of songs, an exhibition of gymnastics, some actual on-stage ball-playing, and, in Act II, a series of dances, "rendered by Little Flossie."[53] A baseball show, infused with baseball-inspired dance blended with genuine baseball movements, enacted, in many cases, by authentic Major League Baseball players (in addition to Anson, other members of the White Stockings and some representatives from the Baltimore Orioles were recruited for the show). Even the terminology used for the playbill was seasoned with baseball: the list of cast members was presented as "The Batting Order" and no intermission was scheduled between the two segments (or "tableaux") of Act IV so that audience members could "please imagine that eight innings have been played."

In the end, *A Runaway Colt*, which played for three weeks in December 1895 (at the American Theatre in New York City), was not a great success, and Cap Anson's reviews were somewhat less than favorable. Anson, though, relished the experience. Although he advised reporters, as well as baseball and show business colleagues, that he was more comfortable on the ball field than the Broadway stage, Anson continued to perform. In fact, it was only two years after *A Runaway Colt* that Anson retired from baseball and devoted much of his remaining life to vaudeville. In the next section of this chapter, we will return briefly to Anson and examine some of his work in that medium. Nevertheless, it is difficult, at this time, to resist quoting a passage about these future excursions that is supplied by Peter Golenbock in his entertaining history of the Chicago Cubs, *Wrigleyville*. Aside from providing us with another fine illustration of Anson's own position on the "baseball and dance chain," it, quite simply, makes for a truly enjoyable read:

> Anson was part of a slapstick vaudeville routine that required him to wear green whiskers, receive squirts of soapy water in the face, have buckets emptied upon him from above, and participate in snatching his fellow actors through a trapdoor. Between these antics, he and the other actors did a short hoedown and sang a song entitled "We're Ten Chubelin [Shoveling] Tipperary Turks."[54]

Black Baseball

Finally, it is impossible to discuss the connections between baseball and dance in the context of 19th-century theater without making reference to a separate, but parallel, professional baseball world—the world that was comprised of teams and leagues populated by non-white players who were unwelcome in (and, unofficially, banned by) the major leagues. It is important, at this point, to be reminded of the contributions made by these non-white players, teams, and leagues and to emphasize the fact that the dancing and theatrics performed on the field (or to and from the field) by players in the Negro Leagues and on teams that existed prior to their formation were often repeated in nightclubs, in vaudeville houses, and at social gatherings. It is, moreover, equally important to bear in mind that the connections between non-white ballplayers and performing artists were exceptionally strong and, in many instances, what occurred on the vaudeville or nightclub stage had a *direct influence* on what took place not only on the baseball field, but also on those streets and roads across America that led to the ballparks where African American teams were scheduled to play their games. Edward J. Rielly comments, "In the African American community, baseball and jazz went hand in glove"[55]; Michael E. Lomax, speaking about the Cuban Giants of the Negro Leagues, remarks, "The social interaction with theatrical performers had absolutely influenced their [the Giants'] vaudevillian flair on the diamond"[56]; Jules Tygiel observes, "Entertainers often could be found at the ballparks, rooting for their favorite clubs and clowning around with their favorite players"[57]; and Donn Rogosin states in no uncertain terms, "The ballplayers became an ingredient, a major one, of the black entertainment world."[58] The interconnectedness between black baseball and black theater, of which dance was an integral component, was unmistakably real and quite powerful.

This interconnectedness, as we shall see in the next two sections, would become most evident in the first half of the 20th century, commonly considered the heyday of the Negro Leagues. Yet, even at this early point in the history of black baseball, examples of baseball-inspired dance in non-ballpark venues can be identified. Lomax, in his extraordinary *Black Baseball Entrepreneurs, 1860–1901*, points out that, during the "winter months" of the late 19th century, players affiliated with the Cuban Giants, the team that, according to James Weldon Johnson, "originated and introduced baseball comedy," were known to perform in the "hotel industry."[59] The Giants, who were managed for a time by stage actor S.K. Govern, also spent many non-playing hours in vaudeville houses and music halls, where the players studied the routines of black comedians and dancers—"lessons" that "undoubtedly provided insights for the Cubans to create their own comic style."[60] There is every reason to believe that, during the late 19th century, the presence of such popular players in a vaudeville house and the close relationships that existed between such players and many star vaudeville performers would have resulted, from time to time, in the appearance of a baseball-playing guest on the stage of that very same vaudeville house, alongside one or more of those very same star performers. To once again quote Lomax, "Many of the personalities who frequented Black Bohemia were drawn from the baseball field."[61] Accordingly, if the attendance at a baseball game by a dancer or comedian from "Black Bohemia" could lead very easily to an invitation to entertain the ballpark spectators, would it not be relatively safe to assume that the attendance at a vaudeville performance by a member of a team like the Cuban Giants also might lead to an invitation to jump on the stage and participate in a comedy skit or song-and-dance number?

As the 19th century came to a close, the cultural landscape of America was in the midst of massive change, "mirroring," in many ways, the tremendous social, political, technological, and geographic changes that were taking place in the country. The "Americana" movement was picking up great steam; cities were growing at breakneck pace; tens of thousands of new immigrants were quickly enlarging and diversifying the population; new forms of dance were being created by bold innovators like Isadora Duncan and Loie Fuller; a broadening interest in fitness, health, and sanitation was developing; and the popularity of both baseball and theater was increasing dramatically. In a piece co-written in 1910 by Major League Baseball player Johnny Evers and famed journalist Hugh S. Fullerton, the following statement is made: "As an amusement enterprise ... baseball today is scarcely second to the theater."[62] The early 20th century in America was a period when the theater would prove to be an almost ideal venue for the demonstration of the intimate connections between baseball and dance.

Early 20th Century

In their landmark book, *Baseball: The Early Years*, Harold Seymour and Dorothy Seymour Mills write, "By the turn of the [20th] century, baseball had thrust itself sharply onto the American scene."[63] In fact, this may be a slight understatement. As numerous historians point out, and as we learn from reading the literature and journalism of the period (such as the 1891 *Sporting News* article, quoted above), baseball, in the early 1900s, was, to quote Noel Hynd, the "most popular sport in America."[64] Simultaneously, according to Hynd, "[L]ive on-stage theatrical performances" were equally popular in the United States and, of the many types of theater available to American citizens, vaudeville held the widest and strongest appeal. John DiMeglio, in *Vaudeville U.S.A.*, points out that, although vaudeville's so-called "golden age"— the first quarter of the 20th century—was relatively brief, it can be said, nevertheless, that during this "short but extremely significant time," vaudeville was "the most popular of all fields of entertainment."[65] Other forms of theater, from burlesque to Broadway, reflected the influence of vaudeville in the early 20th century and performers from every walk of life and every corner of the country, continent, and planet were attracted to the glamor, the diversity, and the potential for reaching mass audiences (as well as the potential for earning much-needed cash) that vaudeville presented. People with dancing skills, certainly, were in demand and, as Walter Terry reveals, opportunities existed for "[b]allet dancers, tap dancers, eccentric dancers, lovely chorus girls, skirt dancers and the like."[66] Additionally, in this era before television and "talking" films, heroes from the sporting world were sought constantly and, in the words of Edward J. Rielly, throughout "the early decades of the 20th century," a multitude of baseball players "found financially rewarding off-season jobs in vaudeville."[67] The "actor-athlete" ("singer-athlete," "dancer-athlete") precedent that had been established in the late 19th century was continued in a much more pronounced fashion, to put it very mildly, in the early 20th century.

In this galaxy of spectacle and variety, the fact that baseball players were particularly attractive to theater and vaudeville producers made perfect sense. As such early 20th century social theorists as H. Addington Bruce (author of the influential 1913 article "Baseball and the National Life") expressed in an almost scientific manner, baseball players were viewed in this period as athletes who were not only physically fit and "manly," but also graceful, agile, fair-minded, and team-oriented.[68] They were, in many respects, ideal candidates for both solo performances and "team" numbers, which included physical comedy acts and song-and-dance routines: they were strong enough to assume the roles of solid male partners, graceful enough to learn complex movements and execute them in an aesthetically pleasing manner, fair-minded enough to laugh at themselves, and appropriately team-oriented to share a scene with co-stars and chorus members. Thanks in large part to the efforts of sportswriters and baseball marketers, baseball players were being molded into genuine role models and, as Steven A. Riess discusses so effectively in his book *Touching Base: Professional Baseball and American Culture in the Progressive Era*, baseball itself was portrayed as "an edifying institution which taught traditional 19th-century qualities, such as courage, honesty, individualism, patience, and temperance, as well as certain contemporary values, like teamwork" (as well as "quick thinking" and "self-sacrifice").[69] Furthermore, baseball was believed to possess "the power to improve the character of its players and spectators" and "[y]oung men were supposedly taught to become better people by watching and playing baseball and by emulating the conduct of the professionals."[70]

In much the same way, Walter Terry observes that dance, in the early 20th century, was seen as a discipline which had the ability to help "strengthen the body, correct (in most cases) faults, develop co-ordination, enhance accuracy of movement and ... provide a more thorough physical education to the student than calisthenics normally can."[71] Terry goes on to explain that dance also was considered an exemplary antidote to emotional distress and social woes: "Emotionally ... dance aids students in adjusting themselves to group activity, to leadership, to discipline, and it helps them in matters of personal poise, in articulation, in the expression of ideas."[72]

Dance and baseball, in essence, were "good" for Americans for the very same reasons. That being said, it would seem, at this point, that a few general realities can be stated in terms of entertainment and culture in early 20th century America: (1) the American people were passionate about theater, and especially vaudeville; (2) the American people were wild about variety; (3) the American people were enthusiastic about dance numbers and choreography in their entertainment; and (4) the American people had a near-fanatical love of baseball. It would not be amiss to conclude that the merging of dance and baseball in live theater in the early 20th century was entirely unavoidable.

It is no wonder, therefore, that the early 20th century presents us with a cornucopia of examples to examine—too many, in all honesty, to describe in extensive detail in this book. Highlights, though, are very much in order, and the remainder of this section will attempt to present and illustrate briefly some of the most intriguing and representative occurrences of the intersection of baseball and dance within the realm of the early 20th-century theater.

The section will be divided into three parts, the first of which will focus on performers from the world of major league and semi-professional baseball (non-Negro League players who danced theatrically or appeared in shows that incorporated dance). The second part will look at shows, vaudeville and non-vaudeville, that included baseball-related dance routines, while the third part will return to black baseball and explore continuing connections in the Negro Leagues between theatrical dance and dance on the baseball field. Information within each of the three parts will be arranged chronologically.

Performances Involving Major League Baseball Players

Although Noel Hynd states accurately that the aforementioned New York Giants' outfielder Mike Donlin "almost single-handedly revivified the stage as a place for ballplayers to make money in the off-season" when he appeared in the baseball-themed musical production *Stealing Home* in 1908.[73] it may be even more accurate to cite the legendary stage and screen comedian Joe E. Brown as the 20th century's first dancing baseball player. Much more will be said very shortly about Donlin and his work with and without veteran singer-comedienne Mabel Hite; however, it is worthwhile to begin with Brown, who played semi-professional baseball in Toledo, Ohio, while performing dance-like acrobatics (including flying somersaults) as a member of the circus and vaudeville act, the Marvelous Ashtons, from 1903–1906.[74]

In the 21st century, Brown is likely best remembered for his role as Osgood Fielding III in the 1959 comedy film classic *Some Like It Hot* (in which he uttered the legendary closing line, "Nobody's perfect," to the object of his affection, the female-attired Jack Lemmon). Yet, as immortal and beloved as this role happens to be, it is actually a role that Brown played at the tail-end of a lengthy and highly successful career in show business—a career that Brown selected over baseball in the early 1900s. Wes D. Gehring, who produced a lovely, richly detailed biography of Joe E. Brown in 2006, reveals how much baseball meant to Brown and how talented a player he was—talented enough, in fact, to have been scouted by the New York Yankees while playing with "various baseball clubs" during the first two decades of the 20th century. Gehring writes that "one of young Brown's perennial part-time jobs" was playing semi-professional baseball.[75] Of course, when Brown was not playing ball, he was learning his craft as an actor, acrobat, singer, and dancer. After he left the Marvelous Ashtons in 1906, he joined another acrobatic ensemble, the Bell-Prevost Trio, and continued to seek work as an individual entertainer, often landing parts that called for what were termed "specialty" or "eccentric" dances. Gehring describes one such dance that Brown devised and which he would utilize repeatedly over the years:

> Brown kept a trampoline hidden in the theater's orchestra pit and he would regularly, but ever so casually, walk and/or dance off stage only to bounce back with a sporty, nonchalant air.[76]

In 1919, when Brown managed to secure a small part in the touring company of the Broadway show *Listen Lester*, he was showcased in another "eccentric dance" number and, once more, was able to make use of the "hidden trampoline" illusion (Gehring reminds us that variations of this exact routine have been preserved on screen—in *Top Speed*, from 1930, and *Bright Lights*, from 1935).[77] Brown also kept vaudeville audiences entertained with comic skits and acts that took advantage of his skills as a dancer, acrobat, and baseball player. Moreover, as Gehring points out, "As a touring vaudevillian, Brown frequently found himself in the company of on-the-road baseball players."[78] Relationships such as these reinforced Brown's reputation as a dancer-comedian-ballplayer and, even as late as the 1940s, when Brown volunteered to perform for U.S. troops overseas, "[P]opular demand required that part of his stand-up [comedy] schtick be diamond-directed."[79] For Joe E. Brown, acrobatics, dance, and baseball were three branches that sprung from the trunk of a common family tree, and Brown's special gifts as a showman enabled audiences to experience this genealogical reality in a seamless, joyful way.

Before launching into our discussion of professional baseball players who danced on stage in the first four decades of the 20th century, it also is important to say a few words about one the period's most respected, cherished, and prolific composers, John Philip Sousa. In the 19th century, Sousa not only played baseball religiously and dreamed of making baseball a career,[80] but also contributed the music, as noted earlier, to what is believed to be the first baseball opera, *Angela, or the Umpire's Revenge* (1888). In the early 20th century, Sousa's devotion to baseball soared to even higher levels. He and the musicians of his "incredible" band organized their own baseball team and, during the band's many concert tours throughout the United States and the world, baseball games during "off hours" were a staple.[81] In a sense, Sousa acted as a genuine "Ambassador of Americana," bringing American-bred music, sport, and optimism to all corners of the earth. In 1925, a kind of "apex" was reached when the stalwart commissioner of Major League Baseball, Judge Kenesaw Mountain Landis, requested that the man referred to commonly as the "March King" compose a special piece of music that celebrated the most popular sport in the United States.[82] Sousa accepted the request gladly and soon produced a triumphant, glorious, heartfelt march, intended, of course, to be performed in theaters, in parades, and at ballparks. He provided baseball with yet another anthem, thereby enhancing the sport's mystique and helping to solidify its lofty place in the American consciousness.

Thanks to vivid accounts contributed by a myriad of vaudeville historians, such as Joe Laurie, Jr., Anthony Slide, and Noel Hynd, as well as a plentiful quantity of contemporary, and often colorful, newspaper articles, reviews, and advertisements, we have access to a substantial amount of information regarding the presence of professional baseball players in live theatrical performances in early 20th-century America. Such performances were major news items, worthy of ample space in period press and serious coverage in works of history. It is possible, therefore, to identify a sizable portion of the professional baseball players who sought added fame and fortune in the footlights of the American stage. Certainly, as we have seen, Mike "King" Kelly and Cap Anson were 19th-century pioneers. Once the 20th century dawned, though, the proverbial "floodgates" were thrown wide open and a near torrent of stage-struck baseballers inundated the dance halls, burlesque joints, vaudeville houses, and "legit" theaters of the United States and beyond—encouraged energetically by the nation's theater producers and promoters.

Particularly useful data may be found in two newspaper articles from the period. On October 22, 1911, the *New York Times* published a story entitled, "Stage Attracts Baseball Stars," while, clear across the continent, the *San Francisco Call-Bulletin* released a story on November 8, 1911, with the headline, "Noted Ball Players Who Will Be Stars of the Stage."[83] The players named came from a variety of teams and represented a full range of positions on the baseball field—from pitchers to infielders, outfielders to catchers to managers. Additionally, the styles of performance that these players were scheduled to exhibit and the venues in which they would be carrying out such performances also ran the gamut in each case. The articles, taken together, make it very clear that the presence of a baseball player in any kind of theatrical production, be it a musical revue, a farcical skit, a dramatic reading, or a comic play, was a very big deal, indeed. Novelist Lester Chadwick, in 1918, expresses this sentiment effectively in *Baseball Joe Around the World*, when he has the narrator describe how much the fictional character, "Baseball Joe" Matson, looks forward to the sight of his ball field hero, Nick Altman, on the vaudeville stage: "There were three or four sketches and vaudeville turns before Altman, who, of course, was the chief attraction as far as Joe and his folks were concerned, came on stage."[84]

Two of the players identified by these two articles, Mike Donlin and Herman "Germany" Schaefer, are also cited by most historical sources as being the first full-fledged baseball professionals to moonlight as performing artists. Donlin, a New York Giants' outfielder, and Schaefer, then a second baseman for the Detroit Tigers, broke "into the business" in 1907 and 1908, respectively, with song-and-dance acts, but in very different arenas—both in terms of geography and status—and with very different results.[85] Donlin and Schaefer each possessed a distinct and well-publicized fondness for the nightlife and enjoyed socializing with theatrical personalities. Donlin, having the good fortune to be based in New York City, had somewhat of an advantage in terms of access to "big-time show business people."[86] As a result, his socializing led him, in short order, to Mabel Hite, whom Hynd describes as "a successful stage woman who had an excellent career as a singer-comedienne before meeting Donlin."[87] Donlin and Hite hit it off instantly and it was not long before the two of them "formed an act both on and off stage, the latter of which resulted in marriage."[88]

Known as "Turkey Mike" because of his distinctive stride,[89] Donlin had a natural sense of rhythm that was well suited to music, dance, and dramatic timing. In 1907, one year after he met Mabel Hite, Donlin opted to take a year off from his career with the Giants and hit the vaudeville circuit with his wife and stage partner. Incredibly, this would turn out to be one of three "theater sabbatical" years in his professional baseball life (the others being 1909 and 1910). Donlin and Hite's stage show consisted of singing and dancing, and their popularity led to an offer of a featured, original theatrical production, in 1908, called *Stealing Home*, which premiered at the close of the 1908 baseball season at Hammerstein's Theatre in New York.[90] In the baseball-themed show, Donlin was required to do a lot of dancing and, in spite of a smattering of negative reviews, most papers and nearly all spectators were exceedingly upbeat. Laurie, who actually attended the show, referred to it as "really a great act,"[91] and Hynd shares a number of positive media responses, including the following passage from *Variety*:

> If you haven't already attended the Big 42nd Street Ovation, by all means beg off from the office and do so without delay. Mike Donlin as a polite comedian is the most delightful vaudeville surprise you ever enjoyed, and if you miss him you do yourself an injustice.[92]

The success of *Stealing Home* and the personal satisfaction that Donlin attained from performing in the show resulted in his second and third years of non-baseball playing, during which time he devoted himself to singing, dancing, and acting. He would resume his career in baseball in 1911, but his work in show business never ceased. Although Hite, tragically, passed away in 1912, Donlin sang and danced in vaudeville with veteran entertainer Tom Lewis and fellow big-league ballplayer Marty McHale, and, once his days as an outfielder came to a close, he answered the call of Hollywood and became a screen actor, ultimately

Mike Donlin and Mabel Hite, c. 1910 (Library of Congress Prints and Photographs Division).

appearing in more than fifty films.[93] (This segment of Donlin's entertainment life, which included his starring role in the 1915 baseball-driven *Right Off the Bat*, will be discussed in chapter 5.)

Germany Schaefer's stage debut, in 1908, occurred in a boozy Chicago burlesque hall, where, according to a few sources, he teamed up with Detroit Tigers' shortstop, Charley O'Leary, to perform an Irish song-and-dance number that was greeted fairly derisively, despite the fact that Schaefer, whom the *New York Times* dubbed "the greatest base-

Germany Schaefer, Washington Senators, 1913 (Library of Congress Prints and Photographs Division).

ball comedian of the age," and O'Leary were resplendent in matching leprechaun outfits.[94] Schaefer, however, was undaunted. Honing his skills as a physical comedian inside the ballpark, he became a more and more effective stage performer, and it was not long before his act with O'Leary drew critical praise and attracted hordes of fans to vaudeville theaters. Furthermore, it was not long before Schaefer, like Donlin, became paired with a veteran female theater star. In Schaefer's case, the veteran star was Grace Belmont and, once the two formed a team, the demand for their services was enormous. As reported in the *New York Times*, before Schaefer and Belmont had set even a single foot on stage as a vaudeville team, they already had been "offered ten weeks booking" and the prediction was that they "should have no trouble getting more."[95] It was, by this time, 1911, and Schaefer was now one of the most accomplished song-and-dance performers to have been recruited from the world of professional baseball.

Schaefer continued to work with O'Leary and he continued to entertain audiences inside the ballpark and in theaters and vaudeville houses throughout America. He also teamed up with other stage personalities and with other baseball players, including former teammate, Nick Altrock. Interestingly, the influence and legacy of Schaefer (and Schaefer's partnership with O'Leary) survives in the Hollywood films *They Learned About Women* (1930) and *Take Me Out to the Ball Game* (1949).[96] In these two films, particularly the latter, the viewer is treated to scenes of on-field clowning and vaudeville song-and-dance numbers that are peppered amply with baseball-inspired choreography. According to almost all accounts of Schaefer and O'Leary, these depictions are very close to the mark.

It would seem natural, at this point, to shine a spotlight on Nick Altrock; however, in truth, the height of Altrock's fame as a vaudeville comedian and eccentric dancer (specializing in exaggerated baseball movements) would not come until after he joined with the second

"Clown Prince of Baseball" (Schaefer having been the first), Al Schacht, to form a baseball comedy mega-team in 1919. Instead, from a chronological standpoint, it seems best to describe a few of the many other ballplayers (and baseball personnel) who "took a chance with dance" in the period between 1910 and 1918. Of these, the unmistakable standout, the figure who managed to inspire the most glittering accolades as both a player and a performer, who was so popular that a dance song (which he himself introduced in one of his own hit shows) was composed in his honor, and whose personal life was the subject of the most intense public scandal of all the well-known actor-athletes, had to have been Richard LeMarquis, known more commonly as Rube Marquard.

Marquard, in 1908, received an $11,000 bonus to sign with the New York Giants as a hard-throwing pitcher and, initially, his career sputtered.[97] However, in 1911, he led the Giants to the National League championship with a remarkable 24–7 record, including a season total of 237 strikeouts. Although the Giants eventually lost the World Series to the American League champion Philadelphia Athletics, Marquard continued to pitch brilliantly and became the "toast" of New York (along with teammate Christy Mathewson, who finished 1911 with twenty-six wins). This sudden rise to stardom and popularity attracted the attention of theater producer Willie Hammerstein, who extended an invitation to Marquard in November 1911 to appear in a show at his eponymous theater in New York City. Marquard agreed and was paired with vaudeville entertainer Annie Kent in an act that was billed, according to Hynd, as "Rube Marquard and Annie Kent."[98]

Rube Marquard (center) early in his career, with Mike Donlin (right) and Libe Washburn, wearing New York Giants uniforms, early 1900s (Library of Congress Prints and Photographs Division).

The routine lasted fourteen minutes and featured a mixture of stage patter, singing, and more than a little dancing. Hynd provides us with a snippet of the review that appeared in *Variety*:

> The first to reach here used up all the cream. A number of people walked out of Hammerstein's Monday night before Marquard made his appearance at 10:28. Pretty late, of course, but still the Giants $11,000 pitcher is to be taken seriously. Annie Kent did what was practically a single singing and dancing specialty. For a finish, they do a few steps together—or rather Rube took one step to each three of Miss Kent's.[99]

Certainly not the most illustrious of starts, but not the most embarrassing, either. And what the show meant for Marquard was a bigger name for himself, a true taste of the stage, a corresponding confidence boost, and an opportunity for romance (he and Kent were believed to have had an affair). Marquard definitely was on his way as an actor-athlete.

The New York Giants, in 1912,

won another pennant and lost another World Series (this time to the Boston Red Sox). Once again, Marquard and Mathewson displayed incredible prowess on the mound; however, in this baseball season, Marquard's performance edged out that of Mathewson in terms of magnificence. It was not simply the fact that Marquard won more regular season games than Mathewson (twenty-six to twenty-three), nor was it the fact that Marquard was able to win (and complete) both of his World Series starts, while Mathewson, though outstanding, finished the Series with no wins and two losses. Even more so, Marquard was able to achieve the title, "King of the Diamond," in 1912 as a result of his record-setting nineteen consecutive wins, which began with his very first decision of the year and which was heralded in the film *Rube Marquard Wins* (co-starring Alice Joyce), released in the latter part of the baseball season, on August 24, 1912. It is easy to understand, therefore, that more than a few theatrical promoters would be targeting Marquard, seeking to capitalize on his immense popularity, once the baseball season was over.

Marquard's prime pursuer turned out to be Joe Kane, the manager and husband of Blossom Seeley, one of the most popular stage performers in America.[100] As Hynd reports, Kane arranged for a meeting with Marquard and Seeley on October 8, 1912, just two days after the Giants had been defeated by the Red Sox in the World Series, and a deal was made. Marquard and Seeley would be teamed in a vaudeville sketch that would premiere, once again, at Hammerstein's in New York City. Kane hired two of the most talented writers in show business, Thomas Gray and W. Ray Walker, to handle the dialogue and songs, and at least a few dance numbers featuring the two stars would be included. To top off everything, the sketch would be focused squarely on baseball. Even the title paid homage to Marquard's astounding 1912 feat: "Breaking the Record; or Nineteen Straight."[101]

Laurie—and particularly Hynd—offer wonderful details of the twenty-four-minute sketch, which turned out to be a great success and established Marquard and Seeley as a genuine song-and-dance-and-comedy duet.[102] Hynd informs readers that "New York went crazy over the prospects of seeing Marquard and Seeley live on stage together," and then shares an exciting "play-by-play" chronicle of the action, including almost step-by-step descriptions of the dance routines. One such dance was the finale, "The Gasotzky," a "quick-tempoed rag," which, according to Hynd, was "apparently invented" by Marquard and Seeley. The effect of this number was reported the day after the premiere in such publications as *Billboard* and the *New York Telegraph* and Hynd generously shares these enthusiastic reviews. *Billboard* exclaimed, "Rube brought down the house!" while the *New York Telegraph* raved, "The spectacle of the lengthy Rube dancing around the stage with the diminutive Miss Seeley is a wondrous sight and supplied a whirlwind finish!"[103]

Rube Marquard, wearing Brooklyn Robins uniform, 1916 (Library of Congress Prints and Photographs Division).

"Breaking the Record" also boasted a tune called "Baseball," which featured a singing solo by Marquard that ended with a dancing duet involving Seeley, as well as a jaunty (and familiar) song-and-dance number performed alone by Seeley, entitled, "Those Ragtime Melodies." However, the most memorable and, ultimately, famous segment of the show occurred when Marquard and Seeley performed the number that would henceforth be linked perpetually with the hoofing Giant hero, "The Marquard Glide." A true celebration of Marquard's accomplishments as a pitcher, the song also celebrated the beauty, grace, elegance, power, and sheer joy of baseball. It even can be said that the song expresses how closely baseball is linked to dance. Consider the second stanza[104]:

> He's going down to second,
> Watch him slide!
> He's king of the pitcher's box
> Stood up through all the knocks,
> Had it on those Red Sox,
> You can bet all your rocks on
> Reuben! Reuben!
> He's some pitcher,
> So we'll all do that Marquard Glide,
> All do that Marquard Glide,
> All do that Marquard Glide!

Keeping in mind that, at the start of the song, a curtain bearing the exterior image of the Polo Grounds was displayed, only to be replaced by a backdrop that portrayed the stadium's interior, in front of which stood the iconic figure of Marquard in his Giants uniform, it is hard to imagine that audience members did not recognize the artistry of movement—the essential dance-like quality—that is so much a part of baseball.

The teaming of Marquard and Seeley also served to ignite a passionate romance, leading to a well-publicized scandal that included secret trysts, private detectives hired by Kane, and, of course, a tabloid circus.[105] With the threesome of Marquard, Seeley, and Kane still feuding and in the midst of scandal, the newly minted song-and-dance team took their act on the road. The combination of pre-scandal fame, enticing reviews, and curiosity brought on by the romantic escapade translated into big audiences and high demand. Marquard and Seeley were a sensation. Yet, unlike Mike Donlin, Rube Marquard was not prepared to sacrifice his baseball career for vaudeville at this point. In 1913, after Seeley was granted a divorce by Joe Kane, she and Marquard were married and, as Kane was issuing threats to sue Marquard for damages, rumors began to circulate that Marquard, indeed, was preparing to retire from baseball. However, on March 12, 1913, with spring training close at hand, the *New York Times* reported that Marquard was beginning to disavow such rumors and, though he was wary of "what sort of a welcome" he might receive from his Giants teammates, he made it clear that he had every intention of returning to the team. Sure enough, when the 1913 baseball season began, Marquard was back on the pitcher's mound at the Polo Grounds and back to performing exquisitely. Of course, at the end of the season, after another battle for team pitching leadership with Christy Mathewson (as well as the underrated Jeff Tesreau), another National League championship title, another World Series loss (once more to the powerhouse Philadelphia Athletics), Marquard and Seeley were ready for another turn at vaudeville.

In the autumn of 1913, a new, shorter sketch—created, once again, by the winning partnership of Thomas Gray and W. Ray Walker and saturated with baseball—was commissioned by Marquard and Seeley, and "opening week" of the scheduled vaudeville tour was booked for November at the majestic Palace Theater in New York City, a venue at which Blossom Seeley herself had never before appeared as a performer.[106] The nine-minute turn was given the timely title, "The Suffragette Pitcher," and it did not fail to please. A catchy new number, "My Baseball Man," prompted loud and vigorous cheers, and the sight of Marquard in drag, pitching for Seeley's "all-women team," provoked much delight. Critics of the time certainly acknowledged the new act's appeal, although there were certain reservations. Hynd notes that one *Variety* reviewer, for example, had this to say: "Mr. Marquard seems to get as much fun out of his singing and dancing as does the audience…. But while Rube is onstage, you can't help but remark that his given name is well chosen."[107]

The tour proceeded as planned and turned out to be a success. In the years that followed, Marquard and Seeley continued to perform as a vaudeville team whenever the opportunity presented itself, but Seeley found herself busier and busier as a solo act, while Marquard's devotion to baseball remained constant. Eventually, the two separated (varying sources claim either 1916 or 1918), and, in 1920, an official divorce was decreed.[108] Joe Laurie, Jr., reveals that Marquard did some additional vaudeville work (singing, dancing, and patter) in 1917 with Billy Dooley "of the famous Dooley family"[109]; however, once the marriage between Marquard and Seeley ended, so, too, did Marquard's stage career. Rob Neyer and Eddie Epstein, in *Baseball Dynasties*, describe the Marquard-Seeley relationship as "an early, lesser version of the Joe DiMaggio-Marilyn Monroe story," and, to a certain extent, this may be true.[110] Still, as graceful and "dancer-like" as Joe DiMaggio was on the ball field, he never did attempt a soft-shoe or a "rag dance" on the stage of a glittering Times Square theater.

Coincidentally, more than a few of the many other baseball players and personnel who attracted the attention of theater producers and promoters between 1910 and 1918 were team-mates and World Series opponents of Rube Marquard. One such player was Marquard's pitching partner on the Giants, the phenomenal Christy Mathewson. Mathewson, who is generally considered to be one of the greatest pitchers in the history of Major League Baseball, was a prime target for the stage. Tall and elegant, with a tremendous sense of timing and a reputation for being honorable and soft-spoken, Mathewson was, to quote Steven A. Riess, "especially idolized" by fans, in addition to being respected and admired by other players.[111] He is even believed to have been the model for the hero of Lester Chadwick's Baseball Joe book series, Joe Matson.[112] Possessing such an abundance of qualities, it would have been impossible for Mathewson to avoid the watchful eyes of vaudeville scouts. Offers were made and, in spite of initial reluctance, Mathewson, in 1910, agreed to participate in a specially designed vaudeville sketch. Written by sportswriter Bozeman Bugler, it was called "Curves" and it would also feature Mathewson's "battery mate" on the Giants, catcher Chief Meyers, as well as stage actress May Tully. For a wee bit of singing, a little dancing, and the tossing around of some comic lines, Mathewson would be paid the tidy sum of $1,000 per week.[113]

As reported in the *New York Times*, the act wound up running from the end of the 1910 baseball season until the start of spring training in 1911. A great financial haul for Christy Mathewson, to say the least. Mathewson, though, was not interested in a second act. "He has no further desire to be an actor," announced the *New York Times*.[114] On the other hand, Meyers had been stung sufficiently by the "acting bee" and arranged for a return to the vaudeville circuit in the winter of 1911.[115] The rewards of the theater were turning out to be too thrilling and, of course, lucrative to pass up for so many baseball professionals—and managers were no exception. Indeed, in 1912, the fiery but venerable skipper of the New York Giants, John J. McGraw, was persuaded to venture into vaudeville and, although it is unlikely that McGraw himself did much dancing, it has been documented by Hynd and other historians that many of the performers with whom McGraw shared the stage were either dancers or eccentric "movement artists."[116] Of these, perhaps the most widely cited is "Odiva, the Goldfish Lady," who, while dressed in a "thin, diaphanous gold gown," would demonstrate a series of eye-opening underwater tricks and contortions.[117] It is also worth noting that McGraw had many acquaintances in the theater world, including two (the actors Walter Knight and John C. Slavin) who wound up bearing the brunt of McGraw's intoxicated rage at the popular New York City society club, The Lambs—incidents that resulted in suspensions and fines for McGraw from the Giants.[118]

Members of the World Series champion Philadelphia Athletics and Boston Red Sox, the vanquishers of the Giants from 1911–13, also were well represented in singing and dancing acts on the vaudeville circuit. During the 1911 baseball season, theatrical promoter John R. Robinson was able to sign three top Athletics pitchers—Chief Bender, Jack Coombs, and Cy Morgan—to an off-season vaudeville contract.[119] At the time, the Athletics were mired in second place, as the front-running Detroit Tigers seemed destined for the American League championship. Miraculously, though, the Athletics surged ahead of the Tigers and went on to defeat the Giants in the World Series. Suddenly, the pitching trio was a hot commodity—proving Robinson to be either very lucky or shrewdly clairvoyant.

As Laurie, the *New York Times*, and the *San Francisco Call-Bulletin* all point out, Robinson arranged for Bender, Coombs, and Morgan—each of whom, save Morgan, was a theater novice—to be accompanied on stage by the sister act Kathryn and Violet Pearl.[120] The routine was christened "Learning the Game" and, once again, the performance would feature music, comedy, and dancing. At the same time, four members of the Boston Red Sox (first baseman Hugh Bradley, third baseman Larry Gardner, pitcher Marty McHale, and pitcher Buck O'Brien) were hard at work preparing a song-and-dance act that was "booked over the better class of New England theaters" for the winter of 1911.[121]

Other prominent figures from the world of professional baseball who took their turns singing and dancing on theater stages between 1910 and 1918 included the following[122]:

- King Cole: Short-lived pitcher with the Chicago Cubs, Pittsburgh Pirates, and New York Yankees, who had a single spectacular year in 1910, after which he was made universally famous by legendary baseball writer Ring Lardner. Cole teamed with Jules Von Tilzer, brother of Albert Von Tilzer (who composed "Take Me Out to the Ball Game" with Jack Norworth in 1908), in a successful vaudeville act that toured during the winter months of 1910 and 1911. Cole died tragically of tuberculosis at the age of twenty-nine in 1916.
- Charlie "Red" Dooin: Catcher-manager of the Philadelphia Phillies, who was a member of Dumont's Minstrels in Philadelphia and the Steel Pier Minstrels in Atlantic City. Dooin also performed in the sketch "After the Game" with another member of Dumont's Minstrels, Jim McCool, in 1911.
- Hugh Jennings: Manager of the Detroit Tigers, who, for many years, participated in a popular vaudeville act with the veteran comedian Ben Smith.
- Joe Tinker: Chicago Cubs shortstop who was one-third of the fabled "Tinker-to-Evers-to-Chance" double-play combination. Tinker had a long-running

vaudeville relationship and, as Harold Seymour and Dorothy Seymour Mills relate in *Baseball: The Golden Age*, he got such positive reviews from show business critics that, in 1913, he "decided to quit baseball … and stay on the stage."[123] Quickly, though, Tinker "changed his mind" and joined the Cincinnati Reds as a player-manager. Included in Tinker's vaudeville résumé is a sketch called "A Great Catch," which he performed with the "petite" and versatile stage entertainer Sadie Sherman in 1910.

Two additional baseball players who kicked up their heels for vaudeville audiences between 1910 and 1918 were Nick Altrock and Cap Anson, both of whom were mentioned earlier in this chapter. Altrock, a lanky pitcher with rubbery limbs and a theatrically malleable face, had a moderately successful playing career, most of which was spent with the Chicago White Sox and Washington Senators. Yet Altrock was a fan favorite and somewhat of a "household name" as a result of his skills as a "funnyman," both on and off the field.[124] From early on, Altrock enjoyed entertaining fans at the ballpark from the "sidelines" with "broad physical comedy." A commemorative article by John Kelly in a 2011 issue of the *Washington Post* provides a few examples, such as "pretending to golf, imitating the [opposing] pitcher's windup, wrestling with himself, [and] reenacting Jack Dempsey's prizefights."[125] Umpire mocking, juggling, and rowing boats during rain delays also were part of Altrock's repertoire.

In 1909, Altrock came to the Washington Senators from the White Sox and, in that very same year, another player was acquired by the Senators from the Detroit Tigers. His name was Germany Schaefer, the so-called "Clown Prince of Baseball." This convergence would prove to be comedy heaven for fans in Washington, as well as other American League cities. Almost immediately, Altrock and Schaefer were doing ballpark comedy routines together and bringing their pantomimes, imitations, and madcap musical numbers to vaudeville stages

Al Schacht and Nick Altrock, October 4, 1924 (Library of Congress Prints and Photographs Division).

throughout the "American League circuit." Some baseball historians, such as Paul Votano, even claim that Altrock was the inspiration for the character, Nat Goldberg, in the previously mentioned 1949 film, *Take Me Out to the Ball Game*.[126] Whether or not this is true is difficult to say (Goldberg, for example, is portrayed as a first baseman, while Altrock, in spite of playing five games at first base in his fairly substantial career, was almost exclusively a pitcher). However, there is no denying the fact that Altrock and Schaefer were two members of a baseball comedy team that pleased crowds both inside and outside the ballpark.

Interestingly, though, the Altrock-Schaefer partnership was relatively brief, it was not until 1919 that Nick Altrock became a true comedy star. For, in 1919, the Senators acquired another pitcher with dwindling baseball skills but unlimited appeal as a baseball comedian, the *second* "Clown Prince of Baseball," Al Schacht.[127] Clark Griffith, owner of the Senators, had fan entertainment fully in that mind when he brought in Schacht and, unsurprisingly, the Altrock-Schacht partnership became an even quicker and bigger success than that of Altrock and Schaefer. In fact, it was a smash hit. The team of Altrock and Schacht would entertain everywhere, not only at Senators games, but also at All-Star games, World Series contests, inside National League parks, and, of course, in vaudeville houses throughout the United States (and beyond). Their act included an

Nick Altrock, Washington Senators, 1912 (Library of Congress Prints and Photographs Division).

abundance of pantomimes and physical comedy routines that can be classified very easily and accurately as *dance*. Repeated squabbles and a new job for Schacht in 1934 as a coach for the Boston Red Sox ended their partnership in the early 1930s, but the team of Altrock and Schacht did much to instill in the minds of the American public the notion that baseball and dance are close relatives.

Cap Anson's theatrical exploits, as noted previously, commenced in the late 1800s. Yet, according to a variety of period newspapers, Anson's full-fledged embrace of vaudeville, which created numerous opportunities for him to show off his limited but effective dancing skills, did not occur until the early 1910s, when he took to the stage as a solo performer.[128] Anson's maiden vaudeville voyage incorporated a monologue prepared by George M. Cohan, the recital of at least one poem ("The Courtship of a Son of Swat") by Grantland Rice, and a "buck and wing" dance ("for the boys," as Anson phrased it) to the old favorite "Turkey in the Straw." Good reviews piled up ("Cap Anson a Hit," read one headline), Anson earned some much needed money, and a new vaudeville career was launched. Anson, on occasion, even had opportunities to work with fellow ballplayer-entertainers on the vaudeville circuit, such as Charlie "Red" Dooin and Rube Marquard, to say nothing of Anson's former teammate, Billy Sunday, upon whose preaching platform Anson periodically would climb.

In later years, Anson also would have the chance to work with his "two beautiful daughters," Adele and Dorothy. In 1917, for example, Anson and his daughters performed a sketch, "First Aid for Father," created specifically for Cap, Adele, and Dorothy by the extraordinary team of George M. Cohan and Ring Lardner.[129] "First Aid for Father" contained sizable portions of baseball and dance, including a joyful finale featuring Anson and his daughters, dressed uniformly in "sports clothes," pitching and batting papier-mâché baseballs into the audience. A review in the *Chicago Tribune,* cited by David L. Fleitz, paints the act in upbeat tones: "The sketch is ideal for the captain's purposes … combining as it does wit, humor, melody, dancing, and a soupçon of the sentiment which is said to cling around the memory of historic personages."[130]

Anson's affair with vaudeville lasted until 1921, just one year before his death at the age of sixty-nine. Fittingly, his farewell act gave him another chance to work with his daughters and to present material that had been created by the most superb artists of the day (in this case, Ring Lardner and Herman Timberg).[131] Despite Anson's controversial personal life and his countless foibles in business and elsewhere, the poetry and appropriateness of a once-great baseball player saying his goodbyes through music and movement could be appreciated by all.

The discussion of dancing ballplayers in the early 20th century would be incomplete without a reverential nod and wink to the man upon whom Grantland Rice would bestow the title "Sultan of Swat" for eternity, Babe Ruth. Ruth's presence in vaudeville and in film is well documented, as is his close relationship to the theater (his second wife, Claire, for example, was a chorus girl who appeared in a variety of stage shows). Throughout the 1920s and into the 1930s, Ruth took part in a number of sketches and routines, delivering monologues, doing a smidgen of comedy, attempting a song or two (accompanied by top-flight partners and pianists), and treating the fans to a few dance steps.[132] What is not-so-common knowledge is that Ruth himself truly enjoyed dancing, a fact that is revealed by his daughter, Julia Ruth Stevens, in a memoir published in 2001, *Major League Dad.* In this sweet and highly personal reminiscence, Stevens refers to her father as a "beautiful dancer, who loved the fox-trot and delighted in teaching it to me."[133] Furthermore, Ruth "had a superb sense of timing on the dance floor" and Stevens suggests that this sense of dance-floor timing was reflected in his performance as a ballplayer: "[M]aybe the same timing … made him such a great pitcher and hitter."[134] In the 1996 children's picture book, *The Babe Ruth Ballet School* (written and illustrated by Tim Shortt), a fictionalized, ballet-dancing Babe Ruth claims that "dance … helps my balance and my movement."[135] It is interesting to consider that this scenario may not be as far-fetched as one might initially believe.

Baseball players continued to perform in vaudeville until it became clear that vaudeville's popularity was in steep decline. Such outstanding players as Mickey Cochrane, Waite Hoyt, Rabbit Maranville, and, of course, the Dean brothers (Dizzy and Daffy), to name just a few, all expanded their fame by singing, joking, and "hoofing" on stage in the '20s, '30s, and '40s.[136]

Shows and Sketches Incorporating Baseball-Inspired Dance Routines

The previous section described how theater producers and promoters managed to capitalize on the joint popularity of baseball and dancing by adding genuine diamond stars to the roster of a vaudeville card or a musical revue or even a so-called "straight play." However, the passion for baseball and theater among American citizens also led to the development of theatrical shows, sketches, and revues that featured heavy helpings of baseball without the inclusion of a single practicing baseball professional. Some of these, such as the 1909 comedy *Two Strikes* (written by Thacher Howland Guild) provided a baseball backdrop, with baseball-related scenes, dialogue, characters, and even plots; however, no dancing was involved and, generally, if any music was incorporated, it was merely incidental and/or transitional in nature. These shows were dramas, melodramas, or comedies (or some combination thereof) and relied primarily on *story*.

On the other hand, a number of baseball-centered shows did opt to place the emphasis squarely on dance and music. In this section, we will take a look at three such entertainments, each of which was created for a different "class" of theater. The first of these theatrical pieces is the musical comedy *The Umpire*, which premiered at Chicago's La Salle Theatre in 1905 before being re-staged for many subsequent years throughout the United States; the second is the vaudeville act created in 1911 by renowned choreographer Ned Wayburn for the fledgling song-and-dance team of Fred and Adele Astaire, entitled, "A Rainy Saturday" (or, more commonly, "The Baseball Act"); and the third is the Shubert Brothers' revue, *The Passing Show of 1915*, which, in the very same year mentioned in the show's title, played in theaters across America after extended runs in both New York City and London, England. Each piece blended baseball and dance in a distinctly different fashion and each serves as an effective example of how baseball can inspire a choreographer.

It should be noted that, because of the lengthy discussion provided for *The Umpire*, which represents the category of musical comedy, another baseball-themed musical comedy, *My Cinderella Girl* (produced by William Norris for Chicago's Whitney Opera House in 1910), will not be discussed.[137] *My Cinderella Girl*, which also toured the United States for many months after closing in Chicago, was written by Richard Walton Tully and Robert N. Baker, with music and lyrics provided by William Frederick Peters, C.P. McDonald, and Edward Stevens. The show's musical numbers (which featured dance) were directed by Gus Sohike and, among the various songs performed by actors sporting baseball attire, was the Peters-McDonald ditty, "Put the Ball Over the Pan, McCann." Incidentally, the original title for the show was *Play Ball*, a title that was scrapped shortly before the show opened in April of 1910.

The Umpire (1905)

While umpires always seem to have been viewed by a significant proportion of baseball players and fans as rather bumbling, irksome, incompetent, and even nefarious figures on the ball field, ill feelings regarding umpires probably reached their highest levels from the 1880s through the first few years of the 20th century. Reflections of these contemptuous and volatile sentiments can be observed in such works as Ernest Thayer's "Casey at the Bat" ("Kill him! Kill the umpire!") and Wallace Peck's *A Stitch in Time Saves Nine* ("First in gore, first in pieces, and last in the hearts of his countrymen"), both of which appeared in 1888.[138] In 1905, though, a kind of shift began to occur. On the one hand, 1905 marked the beginning of a "new breed" of umpiring, ushered in by the iconic, future Hall of Famer Bill Klem, who, in 1905, started calling balls and strikes in the major leagues. Klem would continue to umpire for the next thirty-seven years and he is considered by many baseball historians to be the man responsible for bringing respect and authority to the umpiring profession. On the other hand, two artistic offerings strove to reconcile, with great humor, the universal image of the umpire as a maligned figure, fully deserving, in many cases, of the scorn and ridicule (and physical projectiles) hurled at him by furious managers, players, journalists, and spectators, with a new approach that recognized the umpire as an actual, flesh-and-blood human being, with real feelings, who is capable of succeeding as well as failing and who can be forgiven and redeemed.

The first of these humorously conflicted portraits was presented in the form of an article by baseball writer Allen Sangree, published in the September 2 issue of the *Saturday Evening Post*. Sangree's piece, "Why Nobody Loves the Umpire," describes a particularly outrageous call rendered by a California League umpire and the manner in which a pitcher not otherwise known for "swearing" attempts to deal with the unpleasant ruling. The second example was a musical comedy that premiered at Chicago's La Salle Theatre on December 2. The title, appropriately, was *The Umpire*.

With book and lyrics by Will M. Hough and Frank R. Adams and music by Joseph E. Howard (of "Hello, Ma Baby" fame), *The Umpire* became the most successful and longest-running musical to date in the history of the Chicago stage, with over three hundred consecutive performances.[139] The rather zany plot involved yet another controversial call made by an errant umpire (named Johnny Nolan in the show). In this instance, Nolan's call causes so much commotion and inspires so much venom that he is, according to Bordman and Hischak, forced "to flee all the way to Morocco." Happily, though, while hiding out in Morocco, he is able to gain his redemption—and the hand of a lovely young female athlete—as he officiates at, of all things, a football game. The show, which Bordman and Hischak describe as "the first American musical to deal with baseball and football," featured eight new Howard, Hough, and Adams songs, including "The Umpire is a Most Unhappy Man" (often referred to as "How'd You Like to Be the Umpire?"), which, rather surprisingly, regained popularity more than forty years later, thanks to its appearance in the 1947 Lloyd Bacon film, *I Wonder Who's Kissing Her Now*. It also featured a pleasant helping of stage dancing, which was, and continues to be, *de rigeur* for musical comedies. A review in the *Chicago Tribune* on December 4 described the production's primary actor, Cecil Lean, as "an unusually pleasing entertainer," who "sings agreeably, dances well, [and] speaks his lines clearly and with an easy humor."[140] The combination of a popular team of composers (Howard, Hough, and Adams were "box-office gold" in Chicago) and the show's highly publicized baseball core brought in scores of theatrically minded and baseball-crazy fans alike and, in the end, audience members in Chicago and elsewhere had a chance to experience the typically dark and dastardly umpire in a new light as a "bright and spirited" baseball story[141] was conveyed, not only in words, but also in music and dance—an approach, as we shall see, that would be echoed numerous times in the years to come.

"A Rainy Saturday" a.k.a. "The Baseball Act" (1911)

In the minds of most 21st century Americans, the utterance of Fred Astaire's name will immediately conjure up a host of classic screen images: Astaire and Ginger Rogers dancing cheek-to-cheek in films like *Top Hat* and *Swing Time*, Astaire tapping solo to "Puttin' on the Ritz" and "No Strings (I'm Fancy Free)," Astaire in ballroom bliss with such partners as Cyd Charisse and Rita Hayworth, Astaire creating magic with toy drums in *Easter Parade* and a pinball machine in *The Band Wagon*. For the vast majority of people, Fred Astaire is a film star, whose astounding and elegant dance numbers are considered legendary and whose skills as a singer-dancer in movies are consistently placed among the most spectacular in the history of cinema. Yet, prior to becoming a screen immortal in the 1930s, Fred Astaire was a musical comedy and vaudeville star who danced both alone and with a steady partner—a partner who just happened to be his very own sister, Adele.

Fred and Adele Astaire began performing when they were children and were actually appearing in vaudeville shows and touring on the Orpheum Circuit before either had reached the age of puberty. Their act consisted of music and dance, with some comedy tossed in for good measure. Ann Astaire, Fred and Adele's mother, was the pair's manager and, like so many "stage mothers," she was determined to make her children a success.[142] In early 1911, when Fred was nearing his twelfth birthday and Adele was approaching the age of fifteen, Ann was able to arrange for Fred and Adele, who were then living in Highland Park, New Jersey (they were originally from Omaha, Nebraska), to train at the highly acclaimed New York City dance studio of Ned Wayburn, who, at the time, was one of the most sought after and famous choreographers in the United States.[143] According to Peter Levinson, Fred and Adele studied with Wayburn for six months and, in that relatively brief time, learned "more than at any other stage of their early career."[144]

Now equipped with enhanced skills and a renewed vigor, Fred and Adele seemed ready for a new challenge and, in the latter part of 1911, the very driven Ann Astaire made further arrangements to have Wayburn "write and stage a new specialty act" for the Astaire children—an act that would afford them an opportunity to break into the rabidly competitive New York market.[145] The piece that Wayburn wound up creating was given the official title of "A Rainy Saturday," but it was referred to "more familiarly" (in the words of Kathleen Riley) as "The Baseball Act." Wonderful descriptions of this short role-play fantasy are provided by both Levinson and Riley, as well as by Fred Astaire (in his autobiography, *Steps in Time*).[146] Essentially, a rain-soaked Saturday afternoon cancels Fred's scheduled baseball game and both he (playing the part of Robbie) and Adele (as Rosie) are forced to "entertain themselves indoors."[147] Riley explains what happens next: "[T]he children re-enact their parents' marital quarrels, make believe how Rosie's first beau will propose to her, and stage a short series of domestic scenes."[148]

Throughout the twelve-minute routine, which includes two singing and dancing numbers ("You Don't Belong to Me" and "When Uncle Joe Plays a Rag on His Old Banjo"), Fred/Robbie is dressed from head to toe in baseball finery. Riley, in *The Astaires: Fred and Adele*, reproduces a deliciously detailed excerpt from a letter sent by Wayburn to Ann Astaire, revealing just how authentic he wished the baseball outfit to be:

> I want Freddie to wear a gray base-ball uniform the same as the N.Y. Giants traveling uniform at the opening of the act. It is gray with a faint black stripe in it—and it wants a black cap, black stockings, black belt. Across the breast of the shirt have them put THE LITTLE GIANTS in black letters. The shoes should be made by J. [*sic*] Miller, West 23rd Street opposite the Grand Opera House—tell them I sent you. Have them made with gray uppers to imitate base-ball shoes, but the foot and soles must be for dancing and be flexible—so he can do the waltz. Get the uniform made by A.G. Spaulding and Bros., West 42nd Street, near 5th Avenue.[149]

Wayburn managed to secure a one-night premiere engagement for "A Rainy Saturday" at a benefit show being held at the Broadway Theatre. As Riley points out, "The reviews and audience reaction were positive, and the performance sparked the interest of agents."[150] Quickly, a vaudeville run was scheduled at Proctor's Fifth Avenue Theatre, a venue that specialized in "high-class" shows. "A Rainy Saturday" would play for one week, beginning on February 19, 1912. Unfortunately, though, the scheduled week of performances would never happen. After a single, tepidly received installment, "A Rainy Saturday" was cut from the Proctor's line-up and Fred, Adele, and Ann were left to reassess their options. Eventually, "A Rainy Saturday" did find "legs" in what Levinson terms "lower-echelon vaudeville circuits,"[151] thereby allowing Fred, who was a very big baseball fan himself, to once again "don the pinstripes" and, dressed in this extraordinary, near perfect replica of a New York Giants uniform, dance the waltz on stage for the enjoyment of vaudeville audiences across America—at the very same time, it must be remembered, as such real-life New York Giants players as Mike Donlin, Rube Marquard, and Christy Mathewson were drawing huge vaudeville crowds with their own baseball-infused song-and-dance numbers. It was quite a magical time, to say the least, for baseball in the American theater.

The Passing Show of 1915 (1915)

One of the many forms of live theatrical entertainment available to American audiences in the early 20th century was the *revue*. Distinct from both vaudeville and musical theater, the revue is described in the following manner by the New York Public Library for the Performing Arts (in the program that was published in conjunction with the library's 2012 exhibition, *The Great American Revue: How Florenz Ziegfeld, George White and Their Rivals Remade Broadway*):

> What are revues? In our fantasies, fed by nostalgia and Hollywood, they are concoctions of songs, dance, elaborate costumes and semi-nudity…. To historians, they are editorial cartoons, preserving contemporary responses to Suffrage, Prohibition, World War I, and the other topical, political and cultural concerns of their day…. They appeared on Broadway but were not musical comedies or operettas, since those genres were written to character around plots. They respected the specialties of performers, but were not vaudeville, since the selection and order of acts were curated, provided with a consistent vision determined by a producer or director.[152]

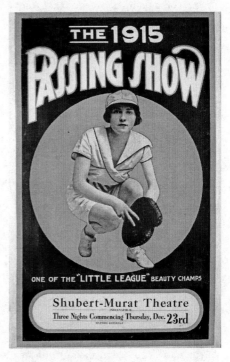

Revues, in essence, were an amalgam of other forms of popular theater that were constructed carefully by a well-organized team of producers, directors, songwriters, scriptwriters, choreographers, set designers, and performers, all working together to devise a spectacular variety show with some kind of topical focus. And, just as there were many forms of live theatrical entertainment available to early 20th century American audiences, the various production teams responsible for creating revues each had their own, idiosyncratic approach to the concept. One of these concepts was the *Passing Show*, which was the product of the famous theatrical impresarios, the Shubert Brothers (J. J. and Lee), and which existed from 1912– 1924. The New York Public Library for the Performing Arts program states that the focus of the *Passing Show* was "[i]ntegrating dance specialties with real life references" to major social and political issues of the day,

Lobby card for *The Passing Show of 1915*, a revue which featured dancing baseball players in a segment called "Summer Sports," or "Fishing" (courtesy Shubert Archive).

The "Baseball Girls" from *The Passing Show of 1915* (courtesy Shubert Archive).

as well as relevant topics that might be morally and ethically "timeless," such as stories and lessons from the Bible.[153]

Each year, the Shuberts' latest installment of the *Passing Show* made its way to Broadway for an extended period before touring the United States and, frequently, the world. *The Passing Show of 1915* arrived at the Winter Garden Theatre in New York for a run of just over four months (from May 29 through October 2) and, as usual, featured a sparkling array of creators, including ballet choreographer Theodor Kosloff of Russia's Imperial Theatre, and veteran stage choreographer Jack Mason.[154] The 1915 show also boasted an extravagant number near the finale that was initially titled "Fishing" and later changed to "Summer Sports." The song upon which the scenario was based was written by the team of Leo Edwards and Harold Atteridge and included the following lines[155]:

> I'm in love with every summer sport,
> I like summer games of every sort,
> Fishing or a baseball game,
> "Summer Sport" must be my middle name.
> You'll find Polo in my book
> Any day at Meadow Brook.

According to *Variety*, three teams of female dancers appeared in "Fishing/Summer Sports," representing the three different sports named in the song: fishing, polo, and baseball.[156] The "Fishing Girls" were led by Leola Lucy; Eleanor Pendleton led the Polo Girls; and an exuberant Rosie Quinn headed up the Baseball Girls (who tossed balls on stage and wore modified baseball uniforms that allowed for ample views of the dancers' "bare legs"). As the *Variety* reporter writes, "It made an active stage picture." The sight of female dancers in baseball uniforms (albeit skimpy ones), miming playing gestures, also highlighted the gracefulness of baseball movement and reinforced the idea that athletics and dance are intertwined (and that playing baseball can be quite sexy). This idea, in fact, was so central to the show that the official poster and advertising campaign for *The Passing Show of 1915* displayed the image of the Baseball Girl (kneeling, wearing a baseball cap and catcher's mitt) above a caption that read, "One of the 'Little League' Beauty Champs."[157] We should also bear in mind that baseball passions, which already were extraordinarily high in the United States, would have been magnified exponentially during the New York run of *The Passing Show of 1915* (taking place, as it did, from late spring all the way to the beginning of the championship season). It is also worth noting, once again, that audiences in 1915 were very familiar with theatrical depictions of baseball and the experience of players dancing on stage in uniform and in dinner clothes. Baseball-playing women, however, likely would have been a curious, surprising, and not-at-all unwelcome sight to witness, for both male and female theatergoers.

Black Baseball and Theatrical Dance

It is important and appropriate to conclude this section, and this chapter, with a brief examination of the Negro Leagues, which—give or take a few years—emerged, flourished, declined, and disbanded within the first fifty to sixty years of the 20th century. Indeed, once the "mid-century" (post–World War II period) arrived and young Negro Leagues star Jackie Robinson joined the Brooklyn Dodgers in 1947, thereby breaking the notorious "color line" of Major League Baseball, the Negro Leagues began to lose both players and popularity and soon faded from existence. However, throughout the entire lifespan of the Negro Leagues, from its nascent stage until its waning days, the relationship between the playing field and the stage was both vital and intrinsic. To quote Donn Rogosin, "The ballplayers became an ingredient, and a major one, of the black entertainment world. In an era when black successes were few, they were among the most applauded of their race ... and strong friendships developed between these two groups of young, male, black achievers."[158]

In terms of dance, as mentioned earlier in this chapter, the most widely visible manifestations of this close-knit relationship could be seen in and around the ballparks of the Negro Leagues. Bill "Bojangles" Robinson and other black luminaries of dance frequently performed before or during baseball games and the pre-game parades that made their way to Negro Leagues ballparks through hometown streets generally featured a myriad of dancers and high-stepping marching bands.[159] In the words of Rogosin, "The arrival of a black professional team created a carnival atmosphere and, in fact, on occasion the Negro League team brought a carnival with them"—a carnival filled with a fair share of dancers and dancing.[160] At the same time, though, dance was a cherished centerpiece of post-game events, gatherings, and celebrations, many of which took place at nightclubs and theaters. Edward J. Rielly writes that "players and musicians [in the 1920s and 1930s] ... frequented each other's places of entertainment."[161] Cheryl Hogan, in her article on black baseball in Louisiana ("The Boys of Summer"), remarks that, following a day of baseball, there "was always a post-game dance at a local bar or club," where the "music and dancing would go on until the wee hours of the morning."[162] Jules Tygiel cites the reminiscences of African American poet and playwright, Amiri Baraka, and Negro Leagues (and, later, major league) baseball star Monte Irvin to illustrate beautifully this post-game music and dance ritual. Baraka, according to Tygiel, reveled "in mixing with the postgame throngs at the Grand Hotel" in Newark, New Jersey, while Irvin recalls that post-game music and dance celebrations at local hotels "presented an opportunity [for fans] to join the ballplayers' special circle," a circle that included "jazz musicians, dancers, actors and actresses, theater and movie stars, and boxers." Tygiel goes on to comment that "a close bond formed between the itinerant athletes and performers."[163]

Moreover, it should be noted once again that not only were many ballplayers and, in some cases, entire teams entertaining Negro League fans with dance steps and comic pantomime routines inside ballparks (before or in the midst of their games), but also many were performing their syncopated steps and routines in clubs and theaters at night, after games were completed and during the off-season. Rogosin discusses this practice at length, particularly in terms of the latter-day teams of the lower echelons of the Negro Leagues, such as the Tennessee Rats, the Zulu Cannibals, and the Miami Clowns.[164] The Tennessee Rats, for example, spent their summers "barnstorming the Midwest … in run-down cars," but, after a day of playing their brand of "comedy/baseball," they would "put on a show in the evening." Teams like the Rats, the Cannibals, and the Clowns certainly were "reinforcing racial stereotypes" in a number of ways with their clowning and sometimes outlandish costumes and vignettes; however, they also were demonstrating incredible grace and precision of movement—and playing some very good baseball. In Rogosin's words, "[T]he Clowns and Zulus were more entertainment acts than baseball teams; nevertheless, Goose Tatum, Dave Barnhill, Buck O'Neil, and other team members went on to distinguished careers" as ballplayers. It is possible to get a flavor of this comic approach to the game in the 1976 film *The Bingo Long Traveling All-Stars and Motor Kings* (which will be discussed in chapter 5), and the subsequent 1985 stage musical *Bingo* (to be discussed in chapter 2).

The demise of the Negro Leagues was concurrent with the dawn of what can be described as the "Mid-Century" or "Postwar Period." The succeeding chapter will begin with a closer look at this period, examining the various ways in which baseball and dance coalesced in the context of the theater. This examination will be followed by a discussion of baseball-inspired theatrical dance in the late 20th century and will conclude with a review of some outstanding 21st century offerings. Clearly, the first half of the 20th century created a tremendously solid foundation upon which to build an even more diverse and expansive body of theatrical dance numbers featuring baseball themes or baseball sensibilities. By the late 1940s vaudeville was dead, the Negro Leagues were disappearing, television was growing in popularity and accessibility, the world was recovering from a long and vicious war, and both baseball and dance in America were continuing to evolve and connect. Much more work was about to begin, ushered in, for the most part, by the widespread, near-urgent, and dichotomous desire, on the one hand, to initiate much-needed social change and, on the other hand, to grasp genuine "meaning" in life and make sense of a world changing at a breakneck pace. Additionally, in this postwar period in the United States, there would develop an even greater interest in telling American stories and capturing the beauty of simple, everyday actions and gestures, as well as exploring "traditional" notions of both gender and sexuality. Reflecting the dance of baseball and illuminating baseball through dance would become a very common, very popular practice over the next sixty to seventy years, and many of these creative efforts would be crafted for Broadway, Off Broadway, Off Off Broadway, and Regional Theater stages. And, as we shall see, the results, in so many cases, were quite exciting and, almost always, interesting, eye-opening, and inspiring.

Interlude

Choreographers on Dance and Baseball—Chris Black, Gail Conrad and Ana Maria Tekina-eirú Maynard

Chris Black, Choreographer of "Pastime"[1]

When I was a child, I did want to be a baseball player. I had a very rich fantasy life about getting to be the first female pitcher for the New York Yankees, which was my dad's team when he was a kid and growing up. So it was sort of my team also, growing up in New Jersey. And being a Yankee fan in the 1970s, there were all sorts of great characters to appeal to a kid and I loved watching them play. But, also, growing up close to New York, I got taken to see the New York City Ballet a lot by my parents and I was also a huge George Balanchine fan. And they were actually kind of complementary, to the extent that the New York City Ballet style is not at all the stereotypical "frou-frou," tutus, pretty-pretty-pretty style of ballet. It's very athletic. The stage at the New York State Theatre, which was built to the specifications of George Balanchine, is huge compared to a lot of the places where ballet companies perform. And so those were my two somewhat conflicting, somewhat complementary interests.

When you were watching dance at an early age, what was it about specific dancers that you admired? Were there similarities between the kinds of dancers that you admired and the kinds of baseball players that you admired?

CB: I think one of the commonalities is that I've always been kind of a sucker for defense in baseball. I mean, I love watching pitching also, but … there's some sort of correlation with dance, I think. Especially outfielders, who have to cover a lot of ground and move really quickly to get to something. Or a shortstop, who has to leap in the air or make a dive all of a sudden. Because there was such an emphasis on speed in a lot of Balanchine's choreography and covering a lot of space in a short amount

Choreographer of "Pastime," Chris Black (photograph by Kegan Marling, used with permission from Chris Black).

47

of time, there was definitely a correlation there. I mean, I was like any kid. Of course, I loved Reggie Jackson and I was a big fan of Bucky Dent, but I have a lot of memories of watching baseball as a kid where I'm not really sure of who I was watching. I was never a kid who went and memorized all of the stats for my favorite player or anything like that. I have a lot of memories, though, of specific *scenes* in my head, but I couldn't even tell you—unless I could pin down the year—which players I'm even thinking of.

Were there specific dancers in the New York City Ballet whom you particularly admired or got turned on by?

Yes. In a way, it was the people you would expect. It was mostly women, interestingly enough. I mean, given Balachine's style of choreography, it makes total sense. Certainly, Suzanne Farrell was just this force of nature and very interesting to watch because it was so extreme. She really gave it her all and I think, again, maybe that was the correlation. It was not a very "careful" company—at least during that era. There was nobody up there dancing in any sort of timid way. It was all about "dive for the ball" type dancing. And certainly Merrill Ashley was extraordinarily fast—she could do all of this *petit allegro* work stunningly, like nobody else. So the two of them were big favorites of mine.

I think one stereotype of "going all out" as a performer is this really emotional, emotive, borderline "too hammy" way of going all out. And I'm sure it was a huge emotional experience for Suzanne Farrell, but it was so physicalized, so it wasn't about acting, especially since so many of Balanchine's pieces are ostensibly abstract. It was really that *physical* all-out. If you look at film of Suzanne Farrell, it sometimes can seem a little "messy" in a way. But that's what's so great about it, because she's pushing it, pushing it, pushing it. Like—how far over can I really go before I'm just going to fall?!

It seems like a lot of the dancers who become really successful and beloved are the ones who are totally fearless. They seem to be the ones who a lot of people really lock onto because they seem to be dancing as if there is no tomorrow. Can you talk a little about the admiration that you had for Ron Guidry, the New York Yankees pitcher? You mentioned this admiration in a Dance Magazine interview a few years ago.

Yes. Again, if you consider what his physicality was like—that sort of lean version of the ballplayer body. Certainly, there's this "dancey" thing in there. And the thing that I really remember was that there was this little "hop" at the end of his delivery, too. A little hop when he landed that's so strong in my mind. I remember just being, like, "Oh, there's that guy!" before I was probably even old enough to really remember his name. And I think, similar to a performer, a pitcher, especially, is just the center of attention. And there's so much wrapped up in a pitcher's motion—everybody pays such close attention to the motion that he goes through to do his job. Obviously, there's a lot of attention paid to how hitters look when they are in the batter's box and their swings and everything else, but it's nothing compared to the way a pitching delivery is going to be analyzed and tweaked. I think there's something, again, about that feeling of almost falling off the mound that goes on with pitchers who throw hard that's kind of related.

Can you talk about your intentions regarding your baseball-inspired dance work, "Pastime"?

I think that my goal with "Pastime," really, was to make something that crossed a lot of borders. I've always been interested in making work that will be liked by people who don't think they like dance. I just find it so satisfying and exciting when somebody comes up to me and says, "My girlfriend dragged me to this show and it was amazing, I had such a good time and, at first, I didn't even want to come!" I love that. I feel that there's plenty of work that is pretty inaccessible to the world at large that I love and that I love watching. But that's not what I'm interested in making. I'm much more interested in trying to communicate with people who don't already go to the theater and pay their money to see weird, avant-garde dance.

I was also hoping to kind of bridge the gap between sports and dance in a very particular way. I think that there's just as much prejudice on each side of that equation at times. Negative attitudes on both sides. I was kind of trying to say that sports is theater, too, and dance, especially, is highly athletic—so can we just stop judging each other and realize where the intersection lies? Beginning with the show that I made before "Pastime," I've wanted to make things that could be performed outside of theaters. So that was part of why I wanted to make that piece to be performed outside, on the grass, in parks, for free, where people could come and watch part of it and leave. They could bring their kids; they could stay for the whole thing, or not. Of course, that also opened up a lot more possibilities in terms of what we could do with it, too. For example, it's much easier to say to a dancer, "OK, you're going to run as hard as you can and then fall down," if they're on the grass as opposed to a wooden floor!

Could you talk a bit about the performances—where and when it was performed and what the experience was like?

Yes. We did three weekends—daytime performances. The start time was—I guess it was 1:15, because that's when the Giants usually start their day games. We had a big banner that we made that had the graphics from the flyer that we had done. We did it in three different locations. There was a park called Precita Park that's very near where I live that was sort of our "home" field—that's where we did all of our rehearsing. So one of the weekends we performed there and then we did another weekend in a park all the way by the Embarcadero downtown—it's called Justin Herman Plaza Park, which is actually right near where the Occupy San Francisco people congregated in 2011. Then the third location was Golden Gate Park, in a space called the Peacock Meadow. I wanted to take it around because I wanted to really have that potential aspect of "accidental." We could have asked to get a permit to do it all three weekends in the same location, but I thought it would be more interesting to move it around a bit more. One of the happiest things that happened for me was the first weekend when we were downtown, this older lady—probably about seventy or so—came up to me afterwards and talked to me about the show. She said, "Oh, I just saw the listing for this and I was so excited because I love dance and I'm a season ticket holder for the Giants and I brought my lawn chair and I went over to the Ferry Building and I got a hot dog and I sat and watched the baseball show while I was eating my hot dog!" It was just so great! I was like, "That's it—that's the perfect thing right there!"

What kind of response did the piece receive?

It was really great—it was really, really satisfying for me. I have these amazing pictures that my photographer took of these kids, these little kids, whose mom actually performs with me sometimes now. God, I think the younger one couldn't have been more than four. And they're just staring super attentively at what the dancers are doing. Then, there are all these grownups who came, too. What was fun was how surprised people were by how much fun it was or, conversely, there were a couple of people who came and said, "You know, I thought it was going to be really silly, but it was super moving in places, too." There were people on both sides of that equation. The dance people were, like, "Oh, I thought 'ugh, sports,' but then I came and it was so great and so fun and I kind of get what the appeal is now." And, as I mentioned earlier, there were people who came up to me and said, "Oh, my girlfriend made me come because I like baseball and she likes dance and I thought it was going to be terrible, but it was so great and I recognized this and I recognized that." A great moment for me was when this older man came up to me and said, "You know, I was there when Bobby Thomson hit that home run." I was like, "Oh, my God—you're kidding me?!" I felt like I had a celebrity at the show, which was lovely.

Gail Conrad, Choreographer of "Beyond the Bases"[2]

Popular culture always has fascinated me because ritual fascinates me. Cultural mores fascinate me. How people like to hang out, play, interact with their environment and interact amongst themselves. The details interest me. So I'm as interested in our daily interactions and in our personal and collective activities as in what we're doing with the other so-called "big" parts of our lives. As for baseball—it's a cultural icon, but it's also a giant American ritual.

Is that what attracted you to it originally?

GC: What attracted me to baseball in particular, say over some of the other sports, at least, is that it's about the teamwork and it's about the individual. It's both huge and it's intimate. The spaces in between the action of the game are as interesting to me as the actual home runs and the winning. This is also how I think about choreography—it's the spaces and transitions between the actual pictures that you see as stills that are fascinating. And it's the details that take my attention.

Baseball is also—so visceral. It's primal to our culture and it's a childhood rite of passage—something that kids get exposed to at a very early age. It's also a great equalizer—cuts across all cultural boundaries and mores and classes and money. It's not like polo or even tennis. You can do it anywhere. I probably played baseball as a kid on just a dead-end street.

So you did play baseball as a child?

Yes, with my cousins. We played all kinds of ball games. I like that it's an activity that seems simple, but it expands in one's imagination with all the intricateness of the action. It's also not a violent game. A ball, a stick, bases—you know, home base. Think of first

Choreographer of "Beyond the Bases," Gail Conrad (photograph © Johan Elbers 2013).

base, second base, third base—how we've used them in our culture as words. Even dating—you got to first base! It's completely infiltrated our language. You're OUT / you're SAFE / you're HOME. And I like that you can look at a game and you get both a still and you get the interior and the exterior feeling of it immediately. Look at TV—today more people just watch baseball on the big screen and it's as much about the players doing these tiny little details, these quirks. Is he scratching his head or chewing gum or…. It's about those little things. It's the pauses, almost, between the game—and it's the meditation of "How is he going to throw the ball next?" and "How is the guy taking the position to bat?" A lot of other games don't naturally slow down as much—they're basically a whirl of action. Baseball certainly has the action, but I think fans like both the panoramic and the almost inherent "zoom in/zoom out" quality of it. I know *I* do.

So what I was portraying in "Beyond the Bases"—well, you never saw a full, actual game. It wasn't literal baseball. It was more about getting into the interior mindset of how these three guys liked to hang out and fantasize, and see themselves enter into this ritualized world and interaction of being "the player." Getting ready. Think of this rite of passage between a father and son, although it could also be father and daughter, brother and sister, or in my case, my older cousins who played ball games with me. So this all seemed like such a big, bold, bright topic. It was as much about the hanging out and the engaging in the whole community of it because, to me, baseball is both communal and personal. I think even people in the stands reflect this. At least at moments, they're quieter at baseball games, wouldn't you say? I like that you can follow it in a slightly different way and that there are real physical bases—not just a goalie at one end. And you follow the lines between the bases. So for me, it's extremely visual and it lends itself to extending beyond the bases—hence the title. The experience transcends the physical sport. It's like dancing. Any good dance goes way beyond the gesture or the boundary of the physical body. What you're sensing is the energy beyond the fingertips, beyond the head, way beyond the actual motion or the running from one side of the room to the other side of the room. The audience and the dancer fill in the gap. You complete it. It's like a good story, where a certain image is given or a certain word and then you fill in the whole picture in your mind or you add your own details to it. "Beyond the Bases" was about *filling in*.

What is it that actually inspired you to focus on baseball?

You know, I knew that you were going to ask me that question and I wish I could tell you the exact moment the idea hit. I can't. But since I'm talking about environments and the tactile nature of dance and the visceral quality of dance and sports—I have as much experience of baseball in parking lots and on dirt streets as I do in stadiums or from viewing it on flat screens. I like that it can happen in almost any environment. I like that you don't need two huge football teams to do it. I like that there could be a whole story just between the catcher and the pitcher. So I think that I thought that I could crystallize it more, in a way, than some other sports. Also, the feeling of it is spring and summer. You get a *sensation* when you think of baseball. Now, of course, people might say that about football. Perhaps, to me, it's more of a dreamy sport—and this was definitely about dreams. It was a dreamy piece—it wasn't an action-packed piece. It wasn't about the competition. For a lot of people, baseball is about winning the game, but I wasn't interested in that part. No one ever won. You would hear crowds cheering at times, but it was more the bonding and the rite of passage of it that interested me. Baseball and ritual seemed like a perfect marriage. What hit me at the time, I don't remember exactly but the pure pleasure from hitting, catching the ball, running bases, and, of course, the physical and symbolic action of returning to home base—that is what I can imagine.

There are so many associations that one has with the sport—when baseball season starts, it's the end of the cold weather and the beginning of the beautiful time of year.

Who doesn't walk by a field of kids playing baseball and not smile? For me, it's a relatively gentle sport compared to some of the others, where you have to beat up people to win. You hear of baseball players pulling their shoulder from batting or throwing, but you rarely hear that another person tackled them so hard that they had concussions. So there's not the same fallout as from some other sports. Or when I think of basketball, for instance, I think of such an action sport. When I think about baseball, I think of the pauses and the silence between the action. So, for me, it has both, and it's more interesting to me in that respect. It's very similar to dance—the stillness and the action. And I appreciate one from the counterpoint and contrast of the other. If I see a dance that is just non-stop action from beginning to end and there are no pauses, I might not enjoy it as much as when I can take in a moment of stillness and then see what activates the subsequent action. That's the fun part—the contrast. The contrast in choreography of movement, style, and dynamics. To me, that's what holds one's attention.

And there's the language—the language of baseball. There's a complete gestural and stylistic vocabulary associated with it and kids—also adults imitate this all the time. Look at the baseball cap—it's infiltrated our culture on every level. We could do an entire study on when, how, and why we wear our baseball caps. Shooting a film, you wear your baseball cap. When you paint, you wear your baseball cap. To advertise a new product, companies put their logos on a baseball cap. And then, of course, we like to tilt them, turn them backwards, flip them up. What happens when you put on your baseball cap? I'd say it does mean something to people—they don this cap, not only for activities, but also in certain moods. So just the baseball cap alone can stand for a mood—a frame of mind.

Ana Maria Tekina-eirú Maynard, Choreographer of "Plena Baseball" and "Boricua Beisbol"[3]

I am the founding director of our Puerto Rican Folkloric Dance and Cultural Center, which consists of educational classes and cultural arts as well as a performing company. As the company and the center grew, I began to study more about my own culture, the corners of my own culture that I didn't know. I began to discover that I wasn't only an artist and a choreographer and a dancer and a musician, but that I was a storyteller. And I enjoyed creating stories that taught people about our cultural traditions from two perspectives: one, to teach people who don't know who we are as a people something about our cultural traditions; and, two, to teach people who are Puerto Rican something about our cultural history that they may not know.

The stories that I create range from cute little unspoken word *estampas*—scenes that are brought to life on the stage through dance and through movement of dance and expression in dance—all the way to the most complex stories that I write, which are full-blown plays with four scenes, live music and dance, acting with a dozen actors on script. And so that's kind of the range there. When I created "Plena Baseball" it was one of those moments where I was inspired to share with the audience something about the love that Puerto Ricans have for baseball. There are certain things that Puerto Ricans are very proud of and very vocal about and very passionate about—boxing, Miss Universe, *patria*, our flag. If you know Puerto Ricans, you know what I mean. And baseball is one of those. And so I wanted to create a story about baseball and the way I remembered baseball growing up in the Bronx. Growing up in the Bronx in a Puerto Rican neighborhood was a very special thing because people all around me really kept their cultural traditions alive. They were all there not because they wanted to leave Puerto Rico but because … most of them were there for economic reasons—they had to leave the island, they had to find a better life, a better job, a better environment to raise their children. And, as a result, they were all very, very homesick and so anything that was Puerto Rican

Choreographer of "Plena Baseball" and "Boricua Beisbol," Anna Maria Tekina-eirú Maynard (photographer: Zera Thompson).

was something that had a lot of value and was always celebrated and was very much kept alive as a cultural tradition, including baseball.

And so the things that I remember as a little girl fed into my "Plena Baseball" choreography. And, of course, I grew up in a very old-fashioned society. My dad was actually a detective on the NYPD Narco Squad and he had a wife and four beautiful daughters and so he was very much "The Dad" and he was very protective and it was a very old-fashioned, traditional family. And there were things that the men did and the men were the ones who would go out and they would play baseball. When I create my stories I like to add a little comedy. You'll never see me write a story that will have a sad ending and people go away, depressed. That's not me. I'm always looking at life and trying to find those joyful moments. And so, as a little girl, I always remember that there were certain things that the men did and sometimes the women were not so excited about it. "Plena Baseball" was a story about how the men would go play and the women thought that they were overly fanatic and the story talked about how they were going to cure the men of their "baseball illness." It's all done with movement and dance. The women come out with candles—big, tall, red candles—and they dance around the men and they're kind of invisible when they're doing it, and the men, all they know is that they feel shock going through their bodies. One minute they're up at bat and the next minute they're being electrified! The women sort of pick off the men one-by-one and each woman takes a man with her until there's no one left on stage. It's a very cute piece.

I can't remember the first year that I created that piece—it was in the late 1990s. Then, in 2009, I wrote a play—one of my musicals—and, in that musical, I actually created a scene that became part of "Plena Baseball." So there was a little more added to it. In 2011, "Plena Baseball" grew into a whole musical. It was called *Boricua Beisbol*. I finally realized my dream of taking that wonderful image presented by "Plena Baseball" and making it a full-length play that had four acts and lasted two hours. It had a lot of traditional dance and music and it was a lot of fun.

I'm curious about the movements and the choreography of "Plena Baseball." Did you incorporate baseball movements in your choreography?

Yes! Actually the opening scene was a re-enactment of a stealing of home plate. I used sound effects of crowds cheering and the ball being hit and all of that. I made it a real comedy—the guys were going in slow motion, stealing the bases and everyone just getting so excited. The audience loved it, they would just get so into it. Of course, the stealing of home plate would happen at the most dramatic moment for baseball—there were two strikes and three balls and then that very last one ends up being that line drive all the way out that no one can seem to get and the guy gets all the way around. So the audience would get very excited about that. I would always have my male dancers as well as the musicians become part of that number and I'd put the musicians in one uniform and the male dancers in another uniform and when they're sort of arguing about whether or not this guy really scored the run, we'd start the plena music. Plena is such an exciting style of music for Puerto Rico and Puerto Rican traditional music. So the plena music would strike up and the guys would decide it's time to go back to playing baseball and that's when the girls would come in with the candles and try to "cure" them.

It's a really fun piece and, like I said, it was a lot of fun, then, to take it from something that stood alone to something that was part of a play. It's always been a crowd-pleaser and is still a featured number in the full-length musical, *Boricua Beisbol*.

Were the costumes in these two works influenced by baseball?

With "Plena Baseball," I went to a real athletic store, a sporting goods store, and I said, "OK, we are a dance company, but I want real uniforms and I want them to look like 1940s, Babe Ruth kind of uniforms and across the chest I want it to say 'PRFDance,' which is our nickname." And they did—they created these beautiful uniforms. I don't know if you've seen the pictures, but they had this little stripe—that edging that the old uniforms used to have. And every guy who was in the company got to pick their own number, their favorite number to put on the back of the shirt. I remember that the man who took and serviced my order laughed and said that these were the nicest uniforms he had made all season and he never would have guessed that the nicest uniforms he had made all season would wind up with a dance company.

Did you keep those uniforms for future performances?

Oh, yes. So that was one of the first things I did—to make it feel really real for the guys. In the original "Plena Baseball," in the late 1990s, we really didn't have a lot of guys so everyone kind of had the same uniform even though that didn't really make a lot of sense—there were two teams on the field but everybody had the same shirt. Back in the late 1990s we were not a live performing company yet, so we did it to recorded music. When we redid it in 2009, I had musicians, so I had more guys. I had to buy more uniforms and I had to create another team. Since we're in Texas and the University of Texas Longhorn is a very famous icon down here, I got T-shirts, really nice, black T-shirts with the emblazoned orange longhorn on the front, and the back said "Texas," and the guys had black baseball caps with the longhorn on the front as an emblem, and the musicians got all over that! In the 2009 version, I let the two different teams take the field separately and come to the front of the stage and the crowd would cheer for them, shouting, "Yay, Texas!"

In terms of teaching people the basics of how to dance plena, it is important to *also* teach how to be expressive. When the women come out with the candles and they're trying to electrify the guys, the guys aren't dancing plena anymore—they're being electrocuted! So how to transition from dance to movement to baseball and to do it within the count but not to make it look like it's mechanical. It's got to look very fluid. But at the same time, it's got to fit with the music. Every time we hear that chorus, that movement that we've seen before has to happen again.

Can you expand on what you were hoping to achieve by staging this piece? I know you've talked a little about this already, but if you have any additional thoughts to share, that would be great.

Down here in Texas, in Austin especially, the majority of the Hispanic population is of Mexican origin. So the local Hispanic population really may not be aware of the Puerto Rican people—who they are and what they are all about. So we have an opportunity to educate people, to show the beauty of our culture, to show the similarities to any Hispanic culture and, yet, the differences that make us a unique people. We also have a lot of Puerto Rican people living here who have never been to Puerto Rico. They grow up in fiercely proud Puerto Rican families; yet, they've never been to the island and maybe really don't know a lot about the traditions. There also are people who maybe grew up on the island and they end up here in Austin for work or college and they find our cultural center. They say over and over again that they learn stuff here with me that they never learned on their own island.

So by staging stories like these that bring to life who we are as a people, what are our traditions, the things that we love, the things that are precious to us—we're teaching people about it in a way that they'll never forget. So that's kind of my goal. Whatever piece we are doing, that's always in my mind. It's really hard to get away from it—to the point that if I put together a dance that's just a dance, maybe I can do one of those in a show or maybe two, but, after a while, it's almost kind of boring. Where's the story? What is the thing that makes this piece special—that people will want to look at for more than a minute? I have so many fond memories of how I grew up, where I grew up, and all of the people around me. Like I said, because I'm always reading and studying and learning, there are just so many stories to tell and I'm not done yet!

2

On Stage II
Theater from the Mid–20th Century
through the Early 21st

The breaking of baseball's "color line" by Jackie Robinson (and, soon after, by Larry Doby of the Cleveland Indians) in 1947, coupled with a "peacetime period" ushered in by the end of World War II, seemed to indicate clearly that a new chapter had begun for America. Very shortly, this mid-century, postwar era would be understood to be the beginning of the "Baby Boom," as well as the era when consumerism exploded, thanks, in part, to an expanded workforce, a reviving economy, astounding (and astoundingly rapid) advances in technology, an almost universal desire to rebuild and to build anew, and an increased interest in social mobility and the achievement of personal prosperity throughout the population. Additionally, the fact that the last decade had exposed a nearly incomprehensible degree of inhumanity and human suffering and that the war itself ended only after two atomic bombs had been used to kill or maim tens of thousands of civilians served to inspire a great deal of individual and societal introspection, not only in the United States, but also around the world. Great changes were taking place and, in general, with great change comes both excitement and fear, as well as a simultaneous urge to embrace the unknown and grab hold of that which makes us feel comfortable and safe. In a sense, a new road was presented and, for many Americans in this period, any kind of progress, fast or slow, required the "traveler" to carry two, well-stocked bags—one filled with the possibilities of the future and one containing the stuff of the past. And, once a destination had been reached and some feeling of accomplishment was induced, a critical question still needed to be asked of oneself: "Is the goal ultimately worth the required effort and cost?"

In terms of the baseball-themed productions that incorporated dance, the dances that were infused with baseball themes and movements, and the dancers who danced during this "transitional" era, this profound question and these societal realities all played pivotal roles. Television, for example, featured a number of clever and timely specials that seamlessly blended baseball and dance (e.g., "High Pitch" from 1955, and "A Man's Game" from 1957), while baseball players *cum* dancers, such as Gene Kelly and Edward Villella, strove tirelessly to shed light on the athleticism and "manliness" of dance and the dance-like grace of movement inherent in baseball. As far as theater was concerned, it may be said that the period between the end of the Second World War and the beginning of America's military involvement in Vietnam was marked by four primary productions that posed some thought-provoking questions about what may be considered "important" and worth seeking in life as they entertained audiences with the glorious spectacle of well-suited, aesthetically pleasing baseball choreography (or movement). In chronological order, these four productions were:

(1) the Harvard Hasty Pudding Club's comic fantasy, *Here's the Pitch,* from 1947; (2) William Schuman's Broadway-laced baseball opera, *The Mighty Casey,* which premiered in full form in 1953; (3) the short-lived 1954 Jerome Moross–John Latouche musical, *The Golden Apple*; and (4) the Broadway blockbuster and future film hit, *Damn Yankees,* which burst onto the American stage in 1955.

Here's the Pitch (1947)

Coinciding with the rookie years of Jackie Robinson and Larry Doby was the mounting of the historic 100th show by the members of Harvard University's Hasty Pudding Theatricals, the stage show-producing wing of the university's comic-minded social organization, the Hasty Pudding Club (founded in 1795). For this landmark show, the Pudding team opted for a musical comedy and recruited Harvard student Craig Gilbert to create the book, while music and lyrics were provided by fellow students Courtney A. Crandall and William M. Scudder. The subject matter would relate to baseball and dance numbers would be included, courtesy of veteran choreographer John Pierce. The director was John Baird and the show was given the title, *Here's the Pitch.*[1]

According to the December 10, 1947, issue of *The Harvard Crimson* (published on the same day that *Here's the Pitch* opened), the basic plot of the show focused on getting what is wished for and then being forced to deal with all of the unavoidable complications that follow the initial spate of good fortune. To quote the *Crimson* preview, "The show deals with a minor sort of intrigue surrounding a ball-club in the 1890's before and after the sale of a magic elixir by a well-meaning huckster." To those who are already familiar with the later and much more widely known *Damn Yankees* (a show based on the 1954 novel, *The Year the Yankees Lost the Pennant,* by Douglass Wallop), this storyline rings at least one or two small bells: the yearning for vigor and success, made possible by a magical or "otherworldly" entity, leading to a crossroads where a fateful decision must be made. For those who enjoy musical comedy, this was a storyline replete with excellent opportunities for the inclusion of humorous music and dance features, interludes, and incidentals. How differently a ballplayer will move when energized and running on a full "tank of gas" than when he is sluggish and "running on empty"— or unwittingly inebriated! A seasoned professional like Pierce was able to handle such scenarios with precision, and the reception for *Here's the Pitch* was laudatory (detailed information about the dances created by Pierce, however, is scarce). After a week-long, sold-out engagement at Harvard, the company embarked upon "an eight-city Christmas road tour" that included a stop at the New York City Center.

Here's the Pitch, which sported three central musical numbers ("So Well So Soon," "Extra-Currickeller Girl," and "Just as Long as I Have You"), looked back to an earlier time to tell a funny story that could be applied quite easily to the issues and mores of the modern age. This desire to look back in order to navigate and reconcile the present was picked up by the baseball-loving American composer (and Juilliard professor) William Schuman in 1951, when he began working on a piece based on the baseball literary classic, "Casey at the Bat." This piece would be completed and finally staged in 1953, an opera—Schuman's first—that turned the famous poem by Thayer into a one-hour epic tale, complete with added characters, a full chorus, and, of course, a variety of segments designed to be performed with choreographed baseball movement. The work was called *The Mighty Casey.*

The Mighty Casey (1953)

In 1952, when William Schuman was questioned by a reporter about the motivation for his latest project, he offered the following response: "I asked myself what I had loved most in my life. It was music and baseball, excluding my personal relationships, of course."[2] Schuman, in fact, was mad about baseball. As Walter Simmons points out, "[I]n his youth he was an avid participant, and even considered seriously a career as a professional ballplayer."[3] Furthermore, like so many of his contemporaries in dance, literature, and painting, as well as music, Schuman was a strong proponent of "Americana"—the artistic movement that sought to tell the stories of its countrymen. It was, therefore, natural for Schuman "to consider a musical adaptation of 'Casey,'" according to Simmons.[4] Indeed, as the *New York Times* noted in 1976, the opera-in-progress that would premiere in 1953 as *The Mighty Casey* certainly provided audiences with a composition that qualified as "authentic Americana."[5] It also would rank as only the third baseball opera or operetta to be produced in the United States in more than sixty years (the first one being the aforementioned 1888 creation by librettist Paul Eaton and composer John Philip Sousa, *Angela, or the Umpire's Revenge*, followed, in 1937, by the operetta, *Brooklyn Baseball Cantata*, with music by George Kleinsinger and lyrics by Michael Stratton).

The story as envisioned by Schuman and his librettist, Jeremy Gury, begins, unsurprisingly, in Mudville, on the morning of what would turn out to be the fateful game against Centerville. With children playing joyfully outside the ballpark fence (jumping rope, tumbling, rolling hoops, playing catch, trading baseball cards) and ballpark workers giddily preparing themselves and their concessions for the big game, the busy corps of townsfolk shout, "Weather's great for baseball, isn't it?" accompanied by spirited, balletic folk dance steps and spins. Amid the exuberant throng appear a pitcher and catcher, two members of the Centerville team, who "secretly" devise a method of quieting the thunderous bat of the Mudville Nine's great slugger, the Mighty Casey: pitch him "high and inside." The pitcher tells the catcher, "Brains, brains, brains is what it takes to win a game of baseball!" The two exit after miming the dance-like motions of their respective positions on the baseball field. Schuman and Gury sought to employ song lyrics, music, and movement to convey the excited anticipation of the game and provide a preview of the action to come.

This approach is continued when the Mudville players are introduced (third baseman, Elmer "Bobo" Blake, the audience discovers, is a vaudevillian by night) and pre-game warm-ups are acted out. Also introduced are Casey's devoted girlfriend, Merry, and the show's narrator, called The Watchman, who perform a powerful expository duet that reveals the importance of the game (there will be major league scouts in attendance to cast judgment on Casey) and the mix of emotions being felt by Merry (she wants the best for Casey but worries that he will leave forever if he is signed). The Watchman also begins to recite from Ernest Thayer's foundational poem and lets the audience know that, although he is aware of the sad outcome of the story (as are most spectators) and despite the certainty that many fans will weep and despair, things may very well wind up working out for the best.

What then follows is the "main event"—the extraordinary rally staged by Mudville, leading to the highly drawn-out at-bat for Casey (complete with a choreographed on-field brawl that extends into the ballpark seats, an umpire's plaintive lament, and more secret conversations between Centerville's catcher and pitcher). A large dose of baseball mime is offered, along with what one reviewer described as "staunch choral numbers, soaring ensembles and brisk orchestral effects." Ultimately, the "Strikeout" does bring tears and cries of desperation; however, there is a hopeful epilogue in Schuman's operatic rendition. Casey leaves the ballpark alone, clearly defeated and ashamed, but he is approached by a young fan who requests Casey's autograph in spite of the terrible disappointment of the day. This child still loves and idolizes Casey and seems to communicate that he, the child, knows that Casey did his best. Once the child departs, Casey picks up a bat and begins to imagine what it would have been like if, instead of striking out, he had belted a home run. More dynamic baseball movement is displayed.

The second bit of redemption comes from Merry, who appears to Casey as he is dreaming of what might have been and "awakens" him to reality. Casey is stopped in his tracks and this awakening is punctuated by an abrupt cessation of the music. A sense of "understanding" then seems to overcome Casey, as he and Merry embrace and walk off together, their love triumphant, their emotional bond stronger than the bond between Casey and baseball. The music rises and the story comes to a close. Casey struck out and lost some of his swagger, yet he learned a great moral lesson and, in the end, made his way safely to "home."

Although Schuman was eager to launch his newly completed opera in Louisville, Kentucky (to be performed by the Louisville Symphony Orchestra),[6] and although he hoped that it would, eventually, find a home on the Broadway stage,[7] the debut of *The Mighty Casey* took place in Hartford, Connecticut, on May 4, 1953. The venue was the Burns School Auditorium at Hartt College of Music, and the show, divided into three acts, clocked in at just over one hour (Douglas Moore's *The Devil and Daniel Webster: A Yankee Folk-Opera* also was on the bill). Reviews were mixed. Harold C. Schonberg of the *New York Times* felt that it was "part sentimentalism, part modernism, but never quite the real thing,"[8] while famed mathematician and "Casey at the Bat" scholar Martin Gardner declared it to be "the most important continuation and elaboration of the Casey story" to date.[9] Another reviewer described the work as "joyous" and pronounced the production to be "first class all around."[10] Still, it was blatantly evident that the show was somewhat confounding to a majority of critics and, regardless of Schuman's relative celebrity status, no New York City dates were scheduled following the Hartford premiere.

Fortunately, though, in just two years, *The Mighty Casey* would "step up to the plate" once again. On March 6, 1955, the CBS television network introduced Schuman's little-known work to tens of thousands of American households by staging a special production of *Mighty Casey* on its *Omnibus* program (an event that will be revisited in chapter 5). Subsequently, Schuman's baseball-centered work, which has been classified alternately as both a "folk-opera" and a "musical pageant," has been restaged sporadically in numerous locations in America and abroad, including an engagement at the National Baseball Hall of Fame in Cooperstown, New York, as well as a City Parks Department-sponsored New York City premiere in 1967 that involved "50 boys and girls between 7 and 20 years of age" who were participating in a special summer "Theater Workshop for Students" program.[11] A prime example of 1950s Americana, *The Mighty Casey* is also timeless and universal in its "message" and effective in its ability to utilize the arts—music, costume and set design, and dance—to reveal the essence of the very game that the creators and spectators of the show revered (and, in the case of spectators, *continue* to revere).

The Golden Apple (1954)

A "sung-through" musical reinterpretation of Homer's *Iliad* and *Odyssey* set in early 20th-century Washington State, complete with county fair pie contests, traveling salesmen, carnival hucksters, and hot-air balloons? An ambitious project, to be sure, but *The Golden Apple*, with its classical roots and full embrace of "Americana," seemed destined to be a hit. As Ethan Mordden writes in *Coming Up Roses*, *The Golden Apple* "wedded" the "glowingly tuneful" music of Jerome Moross with "what may be the most brilliant set of lyrics ever written" by John Latouche.[12] Add to this the expressive, radiant dances of world-renowned choreographer Hanya Holm and what you have is something very special. After an Off Broadway premiere on March 11, 1954, at the Phoenix Theatre in New York's East Village, the show ran for forty-eight performances before being transferred, just one month later, to Broadway. On April 20, *The Golden Apple* opened on Broadway at the Alvin Theatre and, almost universally, critics raved. Mordden cites a few of these wide-eyed proclamations. John McClain of the *New York Journal-American*, for example, referred to the show as "a milestone in the American musical theatre," while Robert Coleman of the *New York Mirror* declared it to be "a magnificent achievement," and John Chapman of the *New York Daily News* stated in no uncertain terms that *The Golden Apple* was "the best thing that has happened in and to the theatre in a very long time."[13] In spite of this nearly unanimous critical acclaim, *The Golden Apple* lasted only 125 performances at the Alvin before closing on August 7, 1954.

It is difficult to understand precisely why *The Golden Apple* did not achieve greater success on Broadway (explanations range from over-sophistication of content to poor theater ventilation) and the likely conclusion is that a variety of factors were responsible. Still, it continues to confound that, in addition to the show's overall creative quality and undeniable originality, a musical with such vivid, familiar American imagery and such close ties to the Americana movement would not attract a greater field of ticket buyers and supporters. The story depicts soldiers returning home to the imaginary town of Angel's Roost, Washington, after the life-altering experience of the Spanish-American War. The returning soldiers yearn to be home and to enjoy the simple pleasures of peace and small-town life; yet, the war has changed them in many ways and adjustment is not always as easy as they would hope and expect. Ulysses, in particular, loves his dedicated wife, Penelope, and longs to be reunited, but also aches for more adventures, which, like Homer's Odysseus, he will need to undertake (and *suffer*) before he is able to realize fully just how deeply he misses (and needs) the security and comfort of his home and loving family. Certainly, some elements of *The Golden Apple* were unconventional and even moderately controversial (the sexuality exuded in the musical number, "Lazy Afternoon," and the possible questions raised about American values—albeit in subtle ways—throughout the show are two examples); however, in terms of scope, *The Golden Apple* was very much "of the period"—a true post–World War II, 1950s musical. To quote Mordden, it was "another show that embodie[d] fifties energies—in its experimental nature, its heavy dance component, its array of new performing talent."[14]

Above all, *The Golden Apple*, even with its Homeric roots, was a steadfastly American tale—a portrait of life in a typical turn-of-the-20th-century American town, reflecting pleasures and sorrows, leisure and work, affection and jealousy, dreams and realities. And, of course, baseball. At a critical point in act I, after the returned soldiers have settled into what seems to be at least an approximation of hometown "normalcy," a fair takes place, and Helen, the beautiful wife of town leader, Menelaus, is seduced and whisked away by a mysterious and attractive out-of-towner named Paris. As this occurs, the townsfolk are busy enjoying the fair and playing games. Just as Helen and Paris depart, Ulysses and his pals (minus Menelaus) enter, sporting baseball outfits and gear, readying themselves for an exciting afternoon game on the town diamond. Menelaus, at this point, is informed of the "abduction" of his wife by an "outsider" and, along with the town elders, implores the group of ballplayers to aid him in Helen's recovery. The original stage directions read as follows: "The boys try to nonchalantly continue their ball game (Play ball! Play ball!) while Menelaus and the old men remind them of their promise and urge them on to vengeance. Eventually, Ulysses, who has resisted the most, agrees to lead the fight."[15] Baseball, in this case, is used as a "shorthand" symbol of the American ideal of home and security. The movements of the game are carried out on stage convincingly, as one would expect with a choreographer like Hanya Holm at the helm (Holm, one of the pioneers of Americana, whose work will be discussed again in the next chapter, was one of the first dance-makers in America to use baseball imagery in her concert dance creations).

Coincidentally, the signature song of *The Golden Apple*, "It's the Going Home Together," is a moving, Americana-soaked ballad that links beautifully with the "home and hearth" compositions that appear in both *The Mighty Casey* and *Damn Yankees*. And what, after all, is the essence of baseball, if not "going home"?

Damn Yankees (1955)

When producer, director, and writer George Abbott made the bold decision to convert Douglass Wallop's Faustian 1954 novel, *The Year the Yankees Lost the Pennant*, into a Broadway musical comedy, he lit a fuse that would soon ignite the most successful and spectacular baseball-themed, dance-studded theatrical creation of any era, the enormous 1955 hit show, *Damn Yankees*. Countless words have been written about this now-classic Broadway musical, to say nothing of the massive number of pages that have been devoted to discussions of the equally successful 1957 film (that, very interestingly, featured the almost identical stellar cast as the original Broadway show and, as theater historian, Ethan Mordden, points out, was exceptionally faithful to the original show in just about every way, save the elimination of a few songs).[16] Moreover, the "staying power" of *Damn Yankees* has been phenomenal, with productions being staged regularly throughout the world, often headlined by show business giants. With songs by Richard Adler and Jerry Ross, a book by Abbott and Wallop, costumes and sets by Jean and William Eckart ("imparted with complete authenticity" to baseball, according to Lewis Funke of the *New York Times*),[17] and choreography by one of the most respected and talented dance-makers in the history of theater and film (and a big baseball fan, to boot), Bob Fosse, the show is a veritable *juggernaut*.

As far as the present study is concerned, *Damn Yankees* may be viewed as "textbook." The story is pure baseball fantasy: a middle-aged fan of the Washington Senators makes a pact with the Devil to be transformed into a youthful baseball star who will lead his beloved, but perpetually beleaguered, Senators to a pennant victory over the perennially victorious New York Yankees in exchange for his soul. The simple, albeit (to quote Mordden) "implausible" tale[18] is then conveyed with dialogue and lyrics that are at once funny, snappy, witty, and sorrowful; music that is memorable and stylistically diverse; and dance that is exhilarating, often stunning, and dabbed carefully and repeatedly with brilliant strokes of baseball move-ment—movement, as the *New York Times* revealed in a preview piece on April 17, 1955, that Fosse "patterned ... after the actual movements of baseball."[19] What we have is a baseball-themed musical with dance numbers that are either staged in the context of a baseball-related scene or else inspired and informed by the dance-like skills, physical idiosyncrasies, and ath-letic grace (and/or struggles) of the players, non-playing personnel, fans, and other observers of the "National Game."

After the show opened on Broadway on May 5, 1955 (at New York City's 46th Street Theatre), there was an instant outburst of widespread praise from both critics and audience members alike. Lewis Funke raved, "As shiny as a new baseball and almost as smooth," adding that "Mr. Fosse ... is one of the evening's heroes," with "dance numbers ... full of fun and vitality."[20] Examples of such song and dance routines included "Heart," "The Game," and "Whatever Lola Wants," all performed in the clubhouse of the Senators. However, if an award could have been granted for the most rousing, anthemic, baseball-spangled, baseball-rooted, baseball-drenched number in the show, there is little doubt that it would have gone to "Shoe-less Joe from Hannibal, Mo.," a "splendid hoedown"[21] that took place on the field, as the entire Senators' squad engage in the familiar practice of warming up. Sliding, swinging, pitching, throwing, catching, running bases, and general pre-game activities, all choreographed exquis-itely and breathtakingly by Fosse to the high-octane rhythms provided by Adler and Ross. In later years, dance documentarian Ann Barzel would remark that this "baseball ballet," deemed the show's "identifying number" by Mordden,[22] was perhaps the "most exciting" scene in the musical[23] and it is likely that most viewers would agree. It is difficult to imagine anyone observing this number and not being left with a feeling of conviction that many ele-ments of dance are present in the typical movements associated with the game of baseball.

It is also important to note, as Mordden writes, that "for all its baseball background, [*Damn Yankees*] is a love story"—and not just *any* love story.[24] For, instead of desiring to cling to his youth and glory and falling under the spell of the sexy temptress sent to him by the Devil, the young Joe—Joe the baseball hero, whose presence on the ball field at the eleventh hour could bring the Senators that much-longed-for championship—yearns to be his older, middle-aged self once more, so that he may resume his life with the woman he loves, his wife. In effect, much like Schuman's Casey (and in a similar fashion to the main character, Ulysses, in *The Golden Apple*), Joe realizes that "home" is what is most desirable, that love and comfort, compassion and loyalty, are the greatest possessions and virtues. It is, once more, the expression of a potent 1950s sensibility that uses baseball to assist with the delivery of the thematic payoff.

Of course, at the same time, *Damn Yankees* is a love letter to baseball itself, a celebration of the characters and characteristics of the game, a portrait of the beauty found within even the most insignificant-seeming gestures and the indescribable pleasure that baseball brings to its vast legion of disciples and true believers. The show's publicity and marketing team was well aware of this fact, which is why it did such a remarkable job of "playing up" the base-ball angle. Opening night tickets, for example, were "printed to resemble those of baseball, containing the usual rain check provisions, gate numbers and the game being played."[25] One would expect that a sizable percentage of audience members came for the baseball and got magnificent dance and music (and a scantily clad singing and dancing Gwen Verdon) as a happy dividend—an approach and technique that would be repeated with great frequency and success in the years to come, not only in the theater, but also in the dance world and at ballparks. Certainly, Gene Kelly and Edward Villella (as well as Fred Astaire, Mabel Hite, William Schuman, the Shubert Brothers, and Ned Wayburn) would applaud—and, undoubtedly, such methods would be actively employed by other baseball-minded choreographers in the very near future. *Damn Yankees* pointed to the past and clutched the present, but—with its sexuality, its infusion of contemporary jazz dance and jazz sounds, and, as Mordden states, its inclusion of unconventional characters and subjects—it also looked furtively ahead.

* * *

Thus, we are transported from the highly "transitional" postwar 1940s and 1950s to the restless, often volatile, socially and politically transformative period of the 1960s through the 1980s. Interestingly, as we make this period shift and advance to the next section of this chapter, we are forced to note that, although the ignominious Major League Baseball strikes of 1981 and 1994 actually would wind up playing at least a small role in the initiation of two of the most prolific and innovative periods of baseball-inspired dance, theater, film, literature, and music in American history, the more immediate decades of the 1960s and the 1970s, by contrast, would turn out to be marked by a dramatic, unmistakable dearth of baseball-related performance pieces. In the 1960s and '70s, an occasional television special, comedy, drama, or variety show would feature some baseball theatrics and/or a few observations about the similarities between the movements of baseball and ballet. Here and there, too, a 1960s or '70s concert dance event would include a work that, in some way, was linked to baseball (generally, as we shall see in chapter 3, with regard to gender and sexuality). However, with the exception of one new show that brought fan frolics to the forefront (*Bleacher Bums*), one new show that offered audiences a lone baseball-inflected dance number (*You're a Good Man, Charlie Brown*), and occasional revivals of *Damn Yankees* (football Hall of Famer Joe Namath played Joe Hardy in a 1981 Jones Beach production) and Schuman's *Mighty Casey*, the theater universe in the 1960s and '70s busied itself with other topics and pursuits, along with new approaches to the entire concept of the "musical." Exciting times for the convergence of baseball and dance, though, were just around the corner and the 1980s,'90s, and early 2000s would more than make up for the veritable "baseball-dance desert" of the previous decades.

1960s to the 1980s

On television, Tommy Davis, Don Drysdale, and Sandy Koufax donned tuxedos and danced on a Bob Hope special in 1964, while Edward Villella compared ballet to baseball in a 1968 documentary and taught ballet steps to sportswriter Oscar Madison (Jack Klugman), in a 1974, season 4 installment of *The Odd Couple*. In arenas of dance, Eliot Feld, in 1974, and Dianne Hulburt, in 1978, borrowed baseball movement vocabulary to inform their own choreography and, in baseball stadiums everywhere, team mascots jitterbugged, fans boogied to pumping music, and both Max Patkin and Morganna the Kissing Bandit executed their trademark bumps and grinds for players and fans. Yet, in live theaters across America during the 1960s and '70s, baseball, by and large, was a forgotten subject. By the same token, the dawn of the 1960s signaled a shift in the use of dance in musicals. As Ethan Mordden observes, "[T]here [was] suddenly a lot less dancing" in the shows of the 1960s and, when dance movements were incorporated, they were, generally speaking, not "stylized," but, rather, "placed strictly within the action" (Mordden cites the parade of waiters in *Hello, Dolly!* and the famous "bottle dance" in *Fiddler on the Roof* as examples of this choreographic shift).[26] Indeed, with sporadic exceptions, musicals as a whole in the 1960s were, in Mordden's words, "becoming more serious,"[27] reflecting the seriousness and changing fashions, attitudes, movements, and mores of the times. Baseball fans still flocked to ballparks and tuned into games religiously on television and radio, playwrights and composers continued to create comedies and musicals (many with dance numbers) for American stages of all shapes and sizes, and American children still went on spending their summers pitching and hitting in organized leagues or with friends on makeshift fields. Nevertheless, theatrically speaking, baseball—at least for the time being—was out.

This trend spilled over into the 1970s, a decade whose first five to six years were consumed almost entirely by the ongoing war in Vietnam, the Watergate fiasco, a Presidential resignation, and the plight of American cities. Yet, as the tail-end of the 1970s arrived and drifted into the early 1980s, a new "appreciation" of baseball and a fresh respect for its historical and cultural significance seemed to pervade the American psyche. Artists, including choreographers, began to re-embrace the images, traditions, and stories of baseball and refused to shy away from uncomfortable, controversial topics, such as racism, sexism, homophobia, cheating, greedy owners, and substance abuse. It seemed as though an attempt was being made in society at large, and in the artistic and journalistic communities in particular, to reaffirm the belief in baseball's uplifting nature, its physical and spiritual beauty, and its important place in American life and culture, while striving, at the same time, to understand the morally problematic elements present in the overall picture (writers such as A. Bartlett Giamatti and Roger Angell offered examinations that were especially eloquent and elegant).

It can be said that the sad and disruptive 1981 Major League Baseball strike, which halted all games from June 12 until August 9, served as a kind of psychological "wake-up call." Over one-third of the baseball season was lost and, for the most part, the blame was placed squarely and angrily on the shoulders of team owners and baseball executives (although, in the minds of many observers, the players themselves shared some of the responsibility). The strike led many fans and sportswriters to question the game and ponder its future. What had become of the great National Pastime and what was to be its fate? Simultaneously, the strike forced supporters and detractors alike to reconsider the essence of the game. What was it that made baseball so attractive in the first place and why did it mean so much to the people, history, and culture of the nation?

Furthermore, in 1980, a wave of nostalgia for "Americana" began to spread throughout the United States, and American voters elected a decidedly pro-business president whose most popular television commercial urged the country's citizens to imagine a new "morning in America" and whose speeches emphasized "traditional" American values and a return to an image of the United States as a "shining city on a hill." Additionally, after boycotting the 1980 Summer Olympics in Moscow (along with sixty-four other countries), the United States served as host of the 1980 Winter Olympics (held in Lake Placid, New York) and a baseball-loving choreographer, Moses Pendleton, was hired by the United States Olympic Committee to create sports-based dances to help commemorate the event. Moreover, in 1984, the United States also was awarded the Summer Olympics (boycotted, tit-for-tat, by the Soviet Union and its political and ideological allies) and a major Olympic Arts Festival was held immediately prior to the Games in the host city of Los Angeles—a festival that included dance concerts and a sports-themed theater showcase that featured one piece entitled, *Mickey Mantle Ruined My Life*, which told the tale of a professional ballet dancer who never recovered from a childhood love of baseball (to be discussed in more detail later on in this section).

Whatever the reasons, the 1980s were awash in literature, film, and performance that probed, glorified, dissected, sampled, and celebrated the game of baseball (in frequently remarkable and unusual ways). Consider, for example, that landmark baseball motion pictures such as *The Natural, Bull Durham, Eight Men Out, Major League,* and the hugely influential *Field of Dreams* all were released between 1984 and 1989. And recall that the Smithsonian Institution's expansive and pioneering touring exhibition "Diamonds Are Forever: Artists and Writers on Baseball" was launched in 1988. Very much in keeping with this widespread trend, a return to baseball themes could be found in the theatrical productions of the 1980s and, as one might expect, the interest in capturing the intrinsic, aesthetically delightful, wholeheartedly dance-like movements of the game inspired producers, directors, and choreographers to display real—or nearly real—baseball action on the stage.

What follows is a review of eight theatrical creations from 1960 through 1989 that presented viewers with images and storylines linking baseball with dance, dance with baseball. The review begins with the aforementioned *You're a Good Man, Charlie Brown* and *Bleacher Bums* and proceeds with short descriptions and discussions of six pieces from the 1980s, in chronological order: *1919: A Baseball Opera* (1981), *The First* (1981), *Diamonds* (1984), *Mickey Mantle Ruined My Life* (1984), *The Dream Team* (1985), and *Bingo!* (1985).

You're a Good Man, Charlie Brown (Off Broadway: 1967; Broadway: 1971)

In 1966, a young television composer named Clark Gesner contacted Charles M. Schulz, creator of the popular syndicated comic strip, "Peanuts," and asked for permission to record a series of songs inspired by the comic strip's "characters and situations."[28] Schulz provided his consent and Gesner managed to work out a deal with MGM Records. Soon, an album was recorded and released and, very quickly, the album aroused the attention of two theatrical producers, Arthur Whitelow and Gene Persson. Discussions were held and the idea to turn the "concept album" into a stage show was born. A creative team was assembled, a cast of six was selected (Gary Burghoff and Bob Balaban, both in the nascent days of their acting careers, landed the roles of Charlie Brown and Linus, respectively), and, by February 1967, the show, now called *You're a Good Man, Charlie Brown*, was ready to "go live." New York City's Theater 80 St. Marks, a tiny, historic, Off Broadway venue in Manhattan's East Village, was secured and, on March 8, 1967, the curtain was raised for the first time. The result? Rave reviews, huge ticket sales, a run of 1,597 consecutive Off Broadway performances, the dispatching of numerous "offshoots" to theaters around the world,[29] a Broadway transfer in 1971, and, perhaps most important of all, a profound effect on the minds and lives of countless theatergoers.

One member of the original creative team was choreographer (or "musical stager") Patricia Birch, a former Broadway dancer who would go on to contribute choreography to a dazzling array of films, television shows, and, of course, theatrical productions. In general, like many stage shows of the 1960s, the dance numbers in *You're a Good Man, Charlie Brown* were short and sporadic and, when dance was featured, it was, in keeping with Mordden's observation, placed constantly "within the action." The lengthiest and most rousing dance routine, for example, was reserved for Charlie Brown's wise and "splendidly churlish" pet beagle, Snoopy, who, to quote *New York Times* critic, Walter Kerr, "does more than sing" for his supper once he is given his "red dish" filled with the "evening's savories."[30] Here is how Kerr describes what could be referred to as the "Dance of the Dog Food":

> Mr. [Bill] Hinnant [the actor who played Snoopy] … is leaping in loops all over his sunbaked roof, slithering to the floor in slavering ardor and taking directly off into a cake-walk of floor-show proportions as he warbles composer Clark Gesner's most bubbling tune, "Suppertime."[31]

On a less flamboyant note, but significant in the context of the present study, a series of choreographed baseball movements was executed during another segment of the show. As Charlie Brown composed a letter to his pen pal, recounting the sad events that transpired earlier in the day on the baseball field, a kind of "flashback" to the action was presented and the entire cast assembled to belt out Gesner's rally song, "T.E.A.M. (The Baseball Game)." Baseball gestures were displayed, along with a smattering of dance steps. Overall, a very slight dance affair, but a definite nod to the notion of baseball as ballet—a notion that Charles M. Schulz, in all likelihood, would have endorsed emphatically. Schulz, after all, was a huge baseball fan who peppered his comic strips with baseball storylines and baseball lingo as much as possible.[32] In fact, as reported by Vincent Canby in the March 9, 1967, edition of the *New York Times*, Schulz attended no rehearsals of *You're a Good Man, Charlie Brown*, missed opening night, and let Canby know that he was not planning to get his first glimpse of the show until late April 1967 (almost two months into the run)—all because, in addition to his "Peanuts" work, he was thoroughly engulfed in the new baseball season.[33]

When *You're a Good Man, Charlie Brown* moved to Broadway in June 1971, the raves turned to rebukes, primarily due to a new cast and new venue that most critics seemed to agree were equally ill-suited to the show.[34] The musical, though, has become a "modern classic" and is performed constantly all over the globe (it is a special favorite of high school and college drama classes and departments). In 1999, a new Broadway production was mounted, with choreography supplied by Jerry Mitchell, and the critical response was much more favorable than that of 1971. Some new songs and characters were added and the new staging was considered much more appropriate for a Broadway theater; however, the core of the show was left intact, including the motivational, bittersweet baseball number, "T.E.A.M." Audience members continued (and continue) to be treated to a slight but memorable depiction of the unifying spirit, the dance-like grace, and the humanity of the favorite sport of the show's mastermind.

Bleacher Bums (1977)

There were few professional sports teams in the second half of the 20th century that had as much hard luck as the Chicago Cubs. By the time 1977 rolled around, the Cubs had not played in a World Series for more than thirty years and had not been World Champions since 1908—a drought of nearly seventy years. Faced with this fairly dismal history, one would be hard-pressed to believe that a typical Cubs fan would be anything but deflated and dejected. But, as any baseball lover knows, adversity very often breeds extreme passion and, in spite of the allergy to the post-season with which the Cubs seemed to be afflicted, hordes of loyal, emphatic fans came out to see the team play and watched or listened religiously to broadcasts of their games from spring training to season's end. At Chicago's Wrigley Field, perhaps the *most* emphatic (and certainly the most storied) fans were (and remain) the slightly zany denizens of the bleachers that lie above the ivy-walled outfield—the fans known far and wide as the "Bleacher Bums." In 1977, the Chicago-based actor, director, writer, producer, and future national star of stage and screen, Joe Mantegna, conceived of an idea that would pay theatrical tribute to these rollicking, die-hard fans. Mantegna and his cutting-edge Chicago troupe, the Organic Theater Company, worked improvisationally and then molded the smorgasbord of ideas that emerged, with the help of writer Dennis Paoli, into a brand new, nine-inning comedy that was honored with the name of the group that provided original inspiration, *Bleacher Bums*.[35]

Although *Bleacher Bums* could not be classified as a musical and while no specific choreographer was hired for the show, *Bleacher Bums* turned out to be one long dance, from start to finish. In this case, it was the movements and actions of the "motley crew" of fans that were on full display.[36] The ninety-minute show, in fact, took place over nine innings, with the Cubs playing host to the Cardinals, and included a seventh-inning stretch and ballpark food (consumed by actors and on sale in the theater), meaning that audience members got the complete picture of a day at the game as experienced by the men and women who occupy the "cheap seats." There was even a screaming character known as "The Cheerleader," described by a reviewer in later years as the wild, frequently shirtless fan whom "you do not want to sit next to."[37]

Bleacher Bums opened on August 2, 1977, at the Leo A. Lerner (or Uptown Center) Theater in Chicago, directed by Stuart Gordon, featuring a multitalented cast headed by Mantegna and Dennis Franz. The show was an instant sensation. Chicago theater critic Richard Christiansen referred to it as a "masterpiece"[38] and Joe Hughes, in the arts section of the Illinois Institute of Technology's *Technology News*, was beside himself with praise: "To say that 'Bleacher Bums' is a hit would be an understatement. A more proper term would be a 'home run,' and the audience is definitely the winner."[39] Beginning in 1978, the company rode its wave of triumph into cities across America, including New York, where a three-week run at the Performing Garage turned into a six-month "residency," and Los Angeles, where *Bleacher Bums* opened at the Century City Playhouse on April 24, 1980, and went on to become the longest-running show in the city's history (finally closing on April 28, 1991).

In 1979, the Public Broadcasting System's Chicago television affiliate, WTTW, aired a live performance of *Bleacher Bums* (which eventually earned an Emmy Award) and, in 2002, *Bleacher Bums* was re-created as a television movie (directed by Saul Rubinek, with Peter Riegert and Charles Durning in major roles). In between, in 1989, the show had a much-anticipated, gala return engagement in Chicago, at the Buckingham Theatre, staged once again by Mantegna and the Organic Theater Company and kicked off by a memorable opening-night benefit performance that featured special guest appearances by Cubs heroes from the 1960s, including Glenn Beckert, Ken Holtzman, Randy Hundley, Ron Santo, and Billy Williams—a fantasy come true for Cubs fans.[40] Over the years, the improv-based fan comedy has been restaged repeatedly by large and small companies all over the United States. Tellingly, one 2010 production, which took place at the Cotuit Center for the Arts on Cape Cod, was actually directed by a professional choreographer named Michele Colley. The Cotuit production was reviewed by Kathi Scrizzi Driscoll in the June 10 issue of the *Cape Cod Times*, and Driscoll, who interviewed Colley and various cast members prior to the premiere, described the process of putting together the show as "a crash course in baseball choreography."[41] One actor, Christopher Cooley, made the relevance of dance in *Bleacher Bums* crystal clear: "When I first read the script, I thought, 'How are we going to block it' ... I don't think anyone could [direct] it except a choreographer."[42]

1919: A Baseball Opera (1981)

Scandal and human tragedy, in most cases, make for great theater, which is why the young composer Rusty Magee was dumfounded when he discovered, sometime around 1980, that no theatrical production existed which made an attempt to tell the story of the notorious "Black Sox Scandal" of 1919, that "grimly beguiling episode in American lore," which saw an entire World Series compromised as a result of organized crime infiltration and bribery.[43] "As far as we know," said Magee in a 1981 *Sports Illustrated* article, "there has never before been an opera or a ballet or anything theatrical based on the Black Sox scandal, which seems astonishing."[44] Being a baseball fan himself and itching to begin work on his first musical, Magee was convinced that this was the project for him.

Magee found a collaborator named Rob Barron and a brand new show, entitled, *1919: A Baseball Opera*, was born—precisely in time for the 1981 baseball season. Ironically, the premiere—held on June 24 at the Yale Repertory Theatre Summer Cabaret in New Haven, Connecticut—wound up taking place in the early days of the aforementioned 1981 Major League Baseball strike, signaling a kind of weird stellar alignment. Without question, the production could not have been more timely and, perhaps predictably, the response was quite positive. Robert W. Creamer, in *Sports Illustrated*, reported that the audience on the night that he attended "repeatedly broke into applause, and at the end there was an ovation of such length that the company decided to present *1919* again later in its season."[45]

Creamer also described some of the staging and chose to make the following observation: "There is no dancing as such, but the lively movement of the characters on stage seems almost choreographed." In other words, an impression of dancing conveyed by the depiction of baseball's physicality—very much like watching an actual baseball game on stage and, as the gestures and motions are taken in and processed, recognizing the presence of genuine physical art and the beauty of the movement being witnessed.

Later in the 1980s, the Black Sox Scandal would be revisited in literature and in cinema (with Eliot Asinof's novel, *Eight Men Out*, and its subsequent film adaptation) and Magee and Barron would have their 1981 baseball opera restaged from time to time for short runs on small stages. As of yet, though, the larger dream of Magee, who died at the age of forty-seven in 2003, and Barron—"to move the opera onto a full-size stage and expand its scope"—has not been realized.[46] One can only imagine how much livelier and expressive the baseball movements in *1919* would be in a bigger space. As Creamer says, "It will be worth watching for."

The First (1981)

Rusty Magee had a kindred spirit in Joel Siegel. Siegel, a popular film and theater critic in the 1970s and 1980s for Channel 7, ABC Television in New York City, was perplexed to discover in the late 1970s that a compelling and important, real-life baseball story had never been brought to the stage as a dramatic play or musical in New York City or elsewhere.[47] In Siegel's case, the story in question was that of Jackie Robinson and his monumental breaking of Major League Baseball's so-called "color line" in 1947. Yes, a famous film biography, starring Robinson himself, had been produced in 1950 and re-released in a colorized format for television in 1974; yet, it disturbed Siegel to think that this extraordinary American hero was fading a bit from America's collective memory. Siegel, a native New Yorker and lifelong Robinson admirer, decided to take matters into his own hands. Despite a lack of playwriting experience, Siegel began work on a story outline and was able to share his idea with theater producer Zev Bufman, along with one of the biggest names in the New York theater scene, Martin Charnin. Bufman and Charnin were sold and agreed to lead the project. Thus, *The First* was born.

As the work got underway, hopes were high. Charnin, a Broadway luminary, who had danced in the original stage production of *West Side Story* and who was the creative force behind the smash hit musical *Annie*, organized a talented team of veterans and newcomers. The story was to be told as a musical, with book by Siegel and Charnin, music by Robert Brush, lyrics and direction by Charnin, and choreography by the widely known and lavishly praised Peter Gennaro. The role of Jackie Robinson was given to a recent graduate of the Yale Drama School and a member of the school's softball team, David Alan Grier,[48] while singing sensation, Lonette McKee, was cast as Robinson's wife, Rachel, and Darren McGavin, a popular television and stage actor, was recruited to play the role of Branch Rickey, the owner of the Brooklyn Dodgers, who helped to instigate and facilitate Robinson's jump from the Negro Leagues to the major leagues.

Sadly, though, setbacks began to occur almost immediately. As reported by Eleanor Blau in the November 4, 1981, issue of the *New York Times*, *The First* did not enjoy "an out-of-town run before performances started" at the Martin Beck Theatre on Broadway.[49] This meant that editing and refining based on "trial run" feedback could not take place, which was unusual for new Broadway shows. Then, two key team members, Peter Gennaro and Darren McGavin, departed while the show was still in pre-performance production.[50] Gennaro and McGavin were quickly replaced by choreographer Alan Johnson and actor David Huddleston; however, much regrouping needed to be done in a very short time. Opening night was postponed three weeks and, when the show finally opened on November 17, the response was disastrous. While dispensing praise to Mr. Grier and the show's "baseball sequences,"[51] the three major New York City newspapers were otherwise uniformly ruthless in their criticism; the prime television network reviewers were equally negative. Some publications, such as *Sports Illustrated*, offered more positive comments and questioned the harsh reaction of other media outlets.[52] At the same time, audiences, which grew increasingly scant after the slew of bad reviews, seemed to enjoy the production. Still, the outcome was clear: doom was inevitable for *The First*. Sure enough, after thirty-three previews and thirty-seven performances, the show was pulled on December 13, 1981.

Interestingly, although *New York Times* critic Frank Rich complained on November 18, 1981, that "like the other three musicals to open on Broadway in the past week, 'The First' has virtually no dancing,"[53] Rich's colleague at the *Times*, Fred Ferretti, actually seemed to glow when he described the show's "baseball ballet." To quote Ferretti:

> Because it *is* the sport that so many theatregoers are familiar with, there was a need for the stuff of baseball to appear convincingly on stage. Players bat with bats and catch with gloves, a portion of a baseball ballet

is precisely like a second baseman pivoting on a double play. The actor-players slide, they leap, they feign catches against the outfield fence.[54]

What Rich may have missed but Ferretti picked up on was the "dance" that was being displayed as the so-called "actor-players" performed the typical movements of the game. Furthermore, Ferretti devoted considerable column space to a description of a spring-training workout scene, overseen by an actor playing the role of Leo Durocher. Players, working as hard as they can to limber up winter-stiffened legs and flatten stomachs bloated by the ample meals and physical inactivity of the off-season, make the exhausting effort to "pump their legs in the air" and carry out the grueling regimen of exercises required to reach "playing shape." A very neat visual trick is employed to demonstrate the physical transformation. As Charnin explains in Ferretti's article, "We outfit the chorus with inflatable girdles…. Then, as they exercise, the air gradually is forced out and they gradually get thinner and thinner, so that by the end of *our* spring training, the team is thin."[55] Simple, but supremely clever. And, once again, indicative of the connections between baseball and dance, not only in terms of movement, but also in terms of training and preparation for performance and the "new season."

On a happy note, one of the relatively rare viewers of the original 1981 production of *The First*, Kary M. Walker, went on to produce the first professional revival of the show—twelve years later, in 1993.[56] Walker had seen a performance of that 1981 show without any prior knowledge of the dire reviews, and loved it. When he did get wind of the bad press and learned that the producers already had scheduled a closing date for the show, he was aghast and made a vow to bring back *The First* at some point in the future. Not long afterwards, Walker became the producer for Marriott's Lincolnshire Theatre, just outside of Chicago, and made good on his promise. At long last, *The First* was given a second chance.

Diamonds (1984)

On December 16, 1984, a brand new baseball-themed musical revue, *Diamonds*, premiered Off Broadway at the Circle in the Square Downtown theater. On the day after opening night, the *New York Times* published a review by its theater critic, Frank Rich, that contained the following opening passage: "An all-star team takes the field in 'Diamonds.' … The roster of songwriters reads like a hall of fame of the present-day musical theater; the sketches are by such literary sluggers as Roy Blount, Jr. and John Lahr; [and] the veteran director is Harold Prince, who, in an early season of his career, co-produced the all-time champ of baseball musicals, 'Damn Yankees.'"[57] *Diamonds*, in other words, seemed to be destined for greatness. Critical response, though, turned out to be mixed (the *New York Times*, for example, panned the show, while the *Christian Science Monitor* referred to it as a "small gem") and, even with such an "all-star" lineup of creative contributors, *Diamonds* failed to garner enough support to propel a transition to Broadway.[58] On March 31, 1985, the show closed after a run of 122 performances.

Still, *Diamonds*, released in the same year as the highly acclaimed and influential baseball film *The Natural*, did manage to inspire a legion of spectators and performing artists. As a revue, the show presented a rich menu of styles and formats—an "alphabet soup" of approaches to the blending of baseball, music, and dance on stage. Indeed, *Diamonds* boasted an abundance of all three elements and made use of lavish costumes and a multiplicity of special effects (including filmed interviews with cultural icons, such as Casey Stengel and Ronald Reagan), as well as an award-winning, stadium-style set by Tony Straiges, to add even more sweetness and spice to the "pot." This cornucopia of ingredients—these many variations on the idea of celebrating the National Pastime in song and movement—meant that audience members and performing artists alike had plenty to digest and consider, much to draw from and, of course, reinterpret and use. The logic was straightforward: more than thirty different sketches driven by nearly twenty different songs added up to a smorgasbord of templates or models for future reference.

The show's choreographer, Theodore Pappas (fresh from his recent work on the Broadway adaptation of the film *Zorba*), was not treated kindly by Frank Rich (Rich, in his December 17 review, called Pappas's work "routine"); however, the nature of the show meant that versatility was key and Pappas seems to have responded to such a difficult task with skill and aplomb. There was a gospel number ("He Threw Out the Ball"); there was a retelling of "Casey at the Bat" in the style of *kabuki* theater, complete with "lion dancer and samurai" ("Ka-Si Atta Bat"[59]); there was a look at baseball at the turn of the 20th century, featuring a ragtime "dancing vocal ensemble" ("Hundreds of Hats"[60]); there was a "joyous, anticipatory ode to spring" and the beginning of the new baseball season ("Winter in New York"[61]); and there was even a version of "Take Me Out to the Ball Game" performed with an "ersatz French accent" by an actor (Chip Zien) imitating Maurice Chevalier ("Escorte Moi").[62] As John Beaufort stated in his *Christian Science Monitor* review, "*Diamonds* covers its subject from Little League parents to the childhood of George Steinbrenner, the impetuous owner of the New York Yankees."[63] Pappas, in turn, was called upon to design dances that could capture the mood and illustrate the specific music of each piece, making sure to keep baseball front and center all along the way. It was baseball seen from many angles and through multiple lenses, providing everyone involved—creators, performers, and observers—with a wealth of ideas and a ballpark full of inspiration.

Mickey Mantle Ruined My Life (1984)

As the host city of Los Angeles made ready for the 1984 Summer Olympic Games, an announcement was made that, in conjunction with the magnificent international sports spectacle, the city would be sponsoring what was referred to as an "Olympic Arts Festival"—a city-wide initiative that would celebrate both the upcoming summer games and the culturally rich and diverse Los Angeles arts community. Many different individuals, organizations, companies, groups, and venues were chosen to participate in an "official" capacity, including the historic Ensemble Studio Theatre (EST). Once selected, EST let it be known that its program would consist of a series of short, sports-centered plays, each penned by a different author.[64] The unified title of the production would be "Sporting Goods" and none of the plays presented would exceed twenty minutes. EST also intended to transform the theater into a veritable sports palace, with "bright banners and flags," "stadium music," costumed staff, and anything else that might reinforce the sports connection with a certain degree of "pizzazz." EST director, Jenny O'Hara, made it clear: "We want this to be not just an evening of short plays, but an *event*."[65]

The number of plays selected for "Sporting Goods" wound up being nine—a very baseball-friendly number, to be sure. Each play had a theme that related to one Olympic sport, such as shotput or boxing, although, interestingly, it turned out that two of the nine plays actually dealt with baseball. Perhaps even more interestingly, one of the two baseball-themed plays set its sights directly on dance. This play, written by Roy London, was given the declarative title, *Mickey Mantle Ruined My Life*, and, as Janice Arkatov reported in the *Los Angeles Times*, the action concerned "a male ballet dancer still grudging old dreams of a base-ball career."[66] Despite the fact that the male dancer, Stefan (Charley Lang), and his "impatient" female dance partner, Gloria (Lisa Robins), were situated in a dance studio throughout the single, extended scene, not a great deal of baseball-inspired dance movement occurred. Instead, *Mickey Mantle Ruined My Life* was, at heart, a two-pronged rumination on life choices and notions of sexuality, gender, and identity in American society. In this way, the piece was very much in keeping with other works being created at the time for stage and screen, such as the concert dance pieces "Football" by Christopher Chadman (1980) and "Beyond the Bases" by Gail Conrad (1985), as well as the hit film *Flashdance* (1983), Mark Bermin's base-ball stage drama *Lady of the Diamond* (1980), Richard Harris's musical comedy *Stepping Out* (1984), and yet another short play contributed to "Sporting Goods," Jane Anderson's *Shot-put*.

Los Angeles Times critic Dan Sullivan pointed out that, in the end, Stefan "belatedly real-izes that Mickey actually turned his [Stefan's] life around by making it okay for him to hate baseball."[67] The story, as a whole, gave audiences another opportunity to experience the many ways in which baseball and dance converge and diverge. Stefan's life story, without question, was very different from the real-life "ballplayer-turned-dancer" stories of people like Joe E. Brown, Gene Kelly, Jim Morrow, Tom Redway, Ron Thiele, and Edward Villella. Yet, in certain ways, there would be a fair amount of commonality (e.g., presence of external and internal pressures, coming to terms with proficiency or lack thereof, the never-ending battle between self-knowledge and self-doubt, the pursuit of excellence, the desire to be accepted, etc.). Clearly, such stories increase our understanding of the connections between dance and base-ball and our acute awareness of how we and our fellow members of society feel about the very nature of each discipline.

The Dream Team (1985)

For most people who were alive in 1992, especially those residing in the United States, a reference to the "Dream Team" would almost certainly inspire thoughts of basketball heroics and that year's Barcelona Olympic Games. The famous 1992 "Dream Team" was the nickname of perhaps the most spectacular collection of basketball players ever assembled in the history of the universe—the powerhouse troupe led by Charles Barkley, Larry Bird, Magic Johnson, Michael Jordan, and Karl Malone that represented the United States in Barcelona and, for lack of a more accurate word, *annihilated* all opposing national squads. It is probably not at all risky to suggest that very few individuals, upon hearing a reference to that majestic team, would harken back to a one-month period in 1985, when a musical play of the same name graced the stage of the Norma Terris Theatre in Chester, Connecticut.

Still, from April 23, 1985, until May 26, 1985, Goodspeed-at-Chester's Norma Terris Theatre *did*, in fact, feature a new musical play called *The Dream Team*. And, by coincidence, the theatrical *Dream Team* also was sports-based. The sport, however, was not basketball, it was baseball. With a book by Richard Wesley, music by Terry Tierney, lyrics by John Forster, and choreography (as well as direction) by Dan Siretta, *The Dream Team* turned out to be the first of two brand new stage productions in 1985 that used music and dance to tell a story about the Negro Leagues and the early introduction of black ballplayers into the previously all-white major leagues (the second production, *Bingo!*, shall be discussed next). In this case, the action involved two brothers, Cal and Luke Davenport—both baseball players in the Negro Leagues at the tail-end of the 1940s. When the color line of Major League Baseball is broken, Cal is pursued by a formerly all-white club, while Luke remains unrecruited.[68] Faced with this new reality, each must make a critical decision about the future and, as expressed in *The Day*, a newspaper published in New London, Connecticut, both "brothers must look more closely at their lives and their loyalties."[69]

Ballplayers danced in *The Dream Team* and the well documented, astonishingly acrobatic antics performed by many members of the Negro Leagues were displayed with verve and style on the Terris stage, thanks to the carefully crafted work of Siretta. The dance, along with period music and historically accurate costumes and uniforms, worked in unison to "paint a portrait of the era," according to *The Day*.[70] The show succeeded in shining another bright spotlight on black baseball before and at the time of the integration of the major leagues, leading to even more interest in celebrating the achievements and the stories of the players of the Negro Leagues. Surprisingly, *The Dream Team* did not re-emerge on a bigger, more prominent stage once its Goodspeed-at-Chester run came to a close on May 26, 1985. Nevertheless, in the fall of the same year, the Negro Leagues, once again, became the focal point of an ambitious musical play, complete with lively and historically accurate music and dance.

Bingo! (1985)

In 1976, William Brashler's 1973 novel of life in the Negro Leagues, *The Bingo Long Traveling All-Stars and Motor Kings*, was transformed into a successful, star-packed film that managed, refreshingly, to maintain the integrity of Brashler's honest, entertaining, and often hilarious book. To quote Mel Gussow of the *New York Times*, "The 1976 movie ... dramatized the exuberance of black baseball teams in the late 1930's without overlooking the despair of marvelous athletes playing our national pastime far from the limelight."[71] The film, which will be discussed more fully in chapter 5, employed a jazzy, bluesy soundtrack to effectively season its images and depicted with authenticity the madcap, perfectly choreographed on-field routines of the players, as well as the typical nightclub activities that regularly followed ball games and the promotional gimmicks utilized by team personnel and local businesses to drum up enthusiasm and ticket sales (including long processions to local ballparks involving marching bands, raucous songs, and continuous dancing). The fact that Brashler based his fictional story on a series of in-depth interviews conducted with one of the great figures of Negro League baseball, Cool Papa Bell, lent an even stronger feeling of authenticity to the book, which transferred quite successfully to the film version.

This feeling of authenticity was retained when, in 1985, writer/director/actor Ossie Davis opted to re-create Brashler's book yet again, this time in the form of a musical play called, very simply, *Bingo!* (one-word, first name show titles like *Annie*, *Evita*, and *Zorba* were all the rage in this era). Davis directed the show and co-wrote the book with Hy Gilbert. Songs were by Gilbert (lyrics) and George Fischoff (music), while choreography was created by one of the true masters of tap and jazz dance, Henry LeTang. A small but upbeat preview article, written by Richard E. Shepard, appeared in the *New York Times*[72] and the show made its debut at the AMAS Repertory Theatre in New York on October 24, 1985. Unfortunately, once more, even with such an "A-list" team of creators, reviews were decidedly mediocre and, after the show closed its short run at the AMAS on November 7, no producers were enticed enough to pick up *Bingo!* and bring it to Broadway (unlike other AMAS productions, such as *Bubbling Brown Sugar* and *It's So Nice to Be Civilized*).

    Bingo!, though, was brimming with bright, effervescent dance numbers—as one might expect with Henry LeTang at the helm. The stage at the AMAS was tiny, but LeTang met the challenge head-on, producing a joyful assortment of nightclub and ball field routines.[73] As in the 1976 film version of *The Bingo Long Traveling All-Stars and Motor Kings* and reminiscent of the days of vaudeville, when the spectacle of hoofing baseball players—like Mike "King" Kelly and Germany Schaefer—was so common, stylish dance steps performed by graceful infielders, pitchers, outfielders, and catchers were front and center. The intimate connections between baseball and dance were on grand display in *Bingo!* Furthermore, *Bingo!* carried on the struggle being waged by other dance-infused, baseball-themed theatrical productions of the 1980s (*The First*, *The Dream Team*, and even *Diamonds*), to bring greater attention to the nearly forgotten teams and players of the Negro Leagues. There is no question that these efforts played at least a small part in helping to inspire the establishment of the Negro Leagues Baseball Museum in 1990, which, in turn, prompted the National Baseball Hall of Fame to step up efforts in 1995 to open its own doors to more stories and stars of the Negro Leagues.

*   *   *

    As the 1980s drew to a close, it was clear to see that baseball-themed or baseball-inclusive theatrical productions could be, at once, entertaining and serious, light and complex. Thorny social issues and darker moments in baseball history were no longer off limits and some unpleasant notions about the game itself began to permeate the American psyche: the purity and perfection of baseball becoming tainted, the innocence of baseball gradually corrupted, the beauty of baseball increasingly tarnished, the child-like nature of baseball thrust ignobly into the seamier realm of adulthood. These thoughts would deepen in 1994, when an even more jarring Major League Baseball strike would take place, resulting in widespread disillusionment and, in many cases, outright rejection of the game by formerly dedicated fans. America, as a whole, was grappling with a worsening economy, a drastic reduction in arts funding, growing instability in the Middle East, and a major health crisis that was finally being acknowledged by government after almost a decade of neglect. Moreover, the end of the century and the beginning of a new millennium loomed, prompting much reflection and re-evaluation—and making the history of baseball in America a very ripe topic for review and discussion. It was, in a very real sense, only natural for the theater to respond. And, in the year that ushered in the new decade, 1990, a powerful first note on the trumpet was sounded, marking the beginning of a new—and thrillingly prolific—era for baseball and dance in America.

1990 to 2013

    At the very start of the previous chapter, it was stated that another "golden age" for the marriage of baseball and dance would occur in the period between 1990 and 2013—a nearly non-stop barrage, lasting more than twenty years, of baseball-infused choreography, ballplaying performers, and dancing baseball players, umpires, mascots, cheer squads, and fans appearing on the concert dance stage, on television, in music videos and film, inside baseball parks and stadiums, and, of course, on theatrical stages of every conceivable dimension. In terms of theater (and, as shall be revealed in the chapters that follow, with regard to concert dance, television, videos, and movies), baseball's past would become a focal point and baseball would be seen as an effective tool for exploring a wide range of historic and contemporary realities. At the same time, re-examining the beauty of the game itself would become a common pursuit, as would making use of the game's movements to probe human thought, behavior, and emotion—or, quite simply, to provide a few moments of amusement and sheer fun.

The very first theatrical work of this period to offer baseball choreography, William Finn's 1990 musical *Falsettoland* (which morphed into *Falsettos* one year later), demonstrates this expansive, multifaceted approach in a brief and seemingly lighthearted, but extraordinarily poignant, quietly devastating manner.

Falsettoland (1990) and *Falsettos* (1991)

In 1978, playwright and composer, William Finn, premiered the first installment of what, eventually, would become known as the "Marvin Trilogy." The work, a musical play, was entitled *In Trousers* and the subject matter could not have been more timely: a young married man—Marvin—coming to terms with his true self and his true sexuality.[74] The gay rights movement was blossoming, a sense of liberation was in the air all across America, and the play's humor, honesty, and genuine exuberance spoke volumes to theatergoers who flocked to New York City's popular Off Broadway theater laboratory, Playwrights Horizons, after reading effusive reviews or getting an emphatic tip from friends. Just three years later, in 1981, Finn continued the saga of Marvin and his new-found self with *March of the Falsettos*, a funny, painful whirlwind of a musical about love and passion, self-interest versus concern for the well-being of others, and the consequences of our choices in life. The basic plot: Marvin leaves his wife, Trina, and their *bar mitzvah*-aged, baseball-playing son, Jason, in order to be with his male lover, Whizzer, while Trina becomes involved romantically with Marvin's psychiatrist, Mendel, who just happens to be the man responsible for providing Marvin with relationship advice. Critical acclaim was even louder and, once again, the show presented a convincing snapshot of this still, relatively "carefree" era—an era that would be changing in tragic ways all too soon.

It would take Finn another nine years to complete the third and final chapter of the trilogy, *Falsettoland*, which picked up the story in 1981, almost exactly where *March of the Falsettos* left off. The nine intervening years, though, had a profound effect on the direction of the plot. In *Falsettoland*, a new main character was AIDS. As Glenn Collins remarked in the July 23, 1990, edition of the *New York Times*, "In this play, as in the real New York of the time, the appearance of that malady, which we now know to be AIDS, inevitably changes everything." After Whizzer and Marvin split up, it is revealed that Whizzer has contracted AIDS, which, in 1981, remained an unnamed source of immense mystery and fear. At the same time, all of the principal characters. to quote Collins, are "busily engaged in a witty musical-comedy battle over the bar mitzvah of Marvin's son, Jason." Jason, initially baffled by his father's sexual orientation and hateful of Whizzer in *March of the Falsettos*, becomes understanding and accepting of both his father and Whizzer in *Falsettoland*.

This growth and enlightenment inspires Jason to invite Whizzer to watch Jason play a baseball game in the park, unbeknown to either of Jason's parents, who also are scheduled to be in attendance. When game day arrives, Marvin, Trina, and Mendel sit with a group of anxious parents in bleacher seats on stage, singing the song, "Watching Jason Play Baseball (The Baseball Game)." Soon the group is joined by Whizzer, referred to by Trina as "my ex-husband's ex-lover," who adds his own proud, wistful, enthusiastic voice to the song. It is clear that he and Jason have formed a real bond and that Whizzer's feelings for Jason are fatherly and deep. There is cheering and lamentation, fist-pumping and hand-wringing, and we observe Jason, wearing baseball shirt and baseball cap, holding his bat, taking batting practice swings, and getting hitting tips from Whizzer. It is deceptively simple and light baseball choreography, but baseball choreography nonetheless. Later on in the show, after Whizzer's illness worsens rapidly and he is forced to seek treatment and comfort in a hospital, Jason makes a decision, in the words of *New York Times* critic Frank Rich, to "celebrate his manhood by having his bar mitzvah in the dying Whizzer's hospital room"—an act that "gives the show its most inspiring burst of hope."[75] In context, therefore, the funny and superficially uncomplicated baseball number in *Falsettoland* is at once poignant, revealing, and bold. Rich astutely describes Jason's emotional "journey" as "heroic"[76] and it can be said that a significant part of this heroism is expressed in the generous and loving act of extending to a man who is openly gay and infected with the AIDS virus an invitation to come to a baseball game and be a member of Jason's immediate family.

Falsettoland was transferred from Playwrights Horizons to Lucille Lortel Theater on September 28, 1990, where it ran for 176 performances. In October of 1991, the Hartford Stage in Hartford, Connecticut, produced a "unified" version of *March of the Falsettos* and *Falsettoland* that was given the title, *Falsettos*. This version turned out to be, in the words of Frank Rich, not only "larger than the sum of its parts but … also more powerful than any other American musical of its day."[77] Not surprisingly, the new, two-act *Falsettos* quickly made its way to Broadway, opening on April 29, 1992, at the John Golden Theatre and closing on June 27, 1993 (after 23 previews and 487 performances). Of course, "Watching Jason Play Baseball (The Baseball Game)" was retained and continues to be a major part of both *Falsettoland* and the second act of *Falsettos* whenever either of these "startling" musical plays is revived.[78]

Damn Yankees (1994 Broadway revival)

The first Broadway revival of the "granddaddy" of baseball musicals featured an all-star cast (including Bebe Neuwirth and Victor Garber, as well as Garber's replacement, Jerry Lewis) and new choreography contributed by Rob Marshall. With the 1994 Major League Baseball strike in full swing, the show's opening on March 3, 1994, could not have been timed more perfectly. Audiences certainly responded favorably, as the Broadway revival of *Damn Yankees* ran for 533 performances at the Marquis Theatre, ultimately closing in August 1995, by which time Major League Baseball was back and those "damn Yankees" were on their way to a post-season playoff appearance for the first time in fifteen years.

The Golden Apple (1995 fully orchestrated revival)

The 1954 Jerome Moross-John Latouche "ballet ballad," discussed earlier in this chapter, had very few revivals following its initial departure from Broadway on August 7, 1954, and no revival had ever attempted to re-create the full orchestrations, stage directions, and choreography of the original show—until 1995. Under the direction of Dominic Missimi, the Pegasus Players and Light Opera Works of Chicago embarked upon a project to restage *The Golden Apple* in its entirety. To ensure accuracy, Missimi and Light Opera Works brought in the set designer who had worked on the original 1954 production (as well as the original 1955 production of *Damn Yankees*), William Eckart.[79] Songs and musical sections left out of previous revivals were re-incorporated according to the original score and dance parts contributed by Hanya Holm were carefully reproduced and reinterpreted based on stage directions from the original script (by Chicago choreographer Nancy Teinowitz).[80] The show was performed from August 19–27, 1995, at Northwestern University's Cahn Auditorium (located just outside of Chicago, in Evanston, Illinois), and each performance found Ulysses and his "band of brothers" back out on the village green at the end of act 1, playing what would turn out to be a joyfully animated, but sadly abbreviated, game of baseball.

Batter Up (1996)

On the heels of the rancorous, aforementioned 1994 Major League Baseball strike—at a time when America's faith in the sanctity of the game was in serious jeopardy—it seems only natural that the full backstory and true motives of even the most sacred fictional baseball icon, the Mighty Casey, would be subjected to intense scrutiny by at least a few of America's shell-shocked baseball lovers and detractors. By the mid–1990s, Ernest Thayer's legendary poem, "Casey at the Bat," had been recited and reinterpreted in a myriad of ways: dramatic readings of "Casey" in vaudeville and on the radio by trained actors and moonlighting baseball players (readings which, in some cases, were captured on film and screened in cinemas); dance treatments by well-known American choreographers (such as Bentley Stone and Lisa de Ribere); poetic sequels, prequels, and adaptations by other poets inspired by Thayer's work; and, as described in the early portion of the current chapter, an operatic version by one of the most respected 20th-century American composers, William Schuman. In 1995, an Alabama-based playwright named Chuck Puckett decided to approach the "Casey" story from a slightly different angle.

Puckett's completed musical, *Batter Up: A Musical about Baseball*, had its world premiere in May 1996 at the Princess Theatre in Decatur, Alabama.[81] The show featured a frisky lineup of Puckett's songs (including "Shortstuff," "We Can Do It," and the eponymous, "Batter Up") and a generous helping of lively dance numbers, some of which take place inside the ball park and some of which are staged within the cozy confines of the team locker, à la *Damn Yankees*.[82] And, speaking of *Damn Yankees*, very much like the 1994 revival of the 1955 Adler, Ross, Abbott, and Wallop show, *Batter Up* benefited from excellent timing (the strike being a fresh memory and the brand new baseball season still in its infant stage). Unfortunately, after the show closed in 1996, it would take another thirteen years before a revival was staged—this time at the Renaissance Theatre in Huntsville, Alabama (from May 15–23, 2009).[83]

Chuck Puckett promised a possible answer to the "mystery" behind Casey's famous strikeout, along with "a constellation of tunes" and a bevy of dance numbers, adding up to "a full evening's entertainment for the whole family"—and he definitely delivered.[84] *Batter Up* was a good, old-fashioned showcase for baseball's folklore, rhythms, musicality, and balletic athleticism.

Ragtime (1996, 1998, 2009)

The nostalgia trend and the growing interest in re-examining America's complex and controversial social history continued in 1996 with the adaptation of E. L. Doctorow's sprawling 1975 novel, *Ragtime*, into a blockbuster, Broadway-bound musical of the same name. The equally expansive show was produced by the Toronto, Ontario-based theatrical organization, Livent, for Toronto's Ford Centre for the Performing Arts. As was the case with Doctorow's book, the musical theater version of *Ragtime* looked back to America at the turn of the 20th century, the "ragtime" period in American musical history. Change was rampant as the 19th century receded, although frequently bloody battles would need to be fought before some less than savory "old ways" were left behind. The musical, like the book, attempted to look at many facets of social and political life in order to present as complete a picture of the era as possible. One such facet was baseball, America's most popular and indigenous sport. Baseball, too, was undergoing rampant changes in the early 20th century, very much in keeping with societal shifts, and the creators of *Ragtime*—Terrence McNally (book), Stephen Flaherty (music), Lynn Ahrens (lyrics), and Graciela Daniele (choreography)—understood that this element needed to be included in the production.

The result was the musical baseball number "What a Game"—a song and a scene that shines a bright light on the growing populism of baseball and the way in which this populism is perceived by an "old school" spectator (nostalgia, of course, is present in every period of history). The singers are the fans in the stands—rooting and cheering, brawling, spitting, arguing, razzing, and following the ball and the action (both on- and off-field) at all times. There is constant movement, non-stop activity—even some footwork that may be easily interpreted as tap dance. This is the "dance of the crowd," pointing to the fact that the so-called "ballet of baseball" exists in the bleachers as much as it does on the base paths.

Ragtime made it to Broadway in 1998 and opened—very successfully—on January 18 at New York's own Ford Center for the Performing Arts (currently known as the Lyric Theatre). It played for 834 performances and then had a sixty-five-show revival run on Broadway in 2009 (at the Neil Simon Theatre).

You're a Good Man, Charlie Brown (1999 Broadway revival)

It took twenty-eight years, but *You're a Good Man, Charlie Brown* finally found the fortunate timing to bring the "Peanuts" gang back to Broadway. Choreography, this time, was supplied by Jerry Mitchell and a youthful, energetic cast was headed by future stars Kristin Chenoweth and B. D. Wong. The show opened at New York's Ambassador Theatre on February 4 and closed on June 13, 1999, after 149 performances—or, in baseball terms, after 149 more opportunities to watch Linus and Lucy, Sally and Schroeder (and, of course, Snoopy) throw and field and provide much needed pep as they belted out the rally song, "T.E.A.M. (The Baseball Game)."

Curse of the Bambino (2001, 2004, 2007)

With baseball history, nostalgia, and folklore serving as the inspiration for so many theatrical productions, film scripts, and dance pieces in the 1980s and beyond, it was only a matter of time before the fabled Boston Red Sox would become the focus of a show. The inevitable finally occurred in 2001, when composers (and baseball fans) David Kruh and Steven Bergman joined forces to create *Curse of the Bambino*, a musical theater journey that opens and closes with the tragic 1986 World Series loss to the New York Mets.[85] In between, the show traces the life and generally disappointing (but always hopeful) times of the Sox (and their fans), beginning with the cataclysmic sale of Babe Ruth to the New York Yankees in 1919. Kruh contributed book and lyrics, while music and additional lyrics were provided by Bergman. Songs, cleverly, were composed in the styles of the period with which they were associated (swing in the 1940s, psychedelic rock in the 1960s, disco in the 1970s, and so on) and both costumes and hairdos shifted accordingly.[86] Choreography, designed by Ilyse Robbins, was ever-present and all choral numbers were performed by a small fan ensemble ("fan dancers"?) referred to by Kruh and Bergman as the "Royal Rooters."

The original production took place in front of "packed houses" from April 25 through June 3, 2001, at the Lyric Stage in Boston, and response was favorable. Boston audiences were delighted to have a show of "their own"—a show that celebrated glorious Red Sox moments and helped lighten the load of nearly a century of missed opportunities and misfortune. Then 2004 happened. As the baseball season progressed, it was evident that the Red Sox were genuine contenders for the Eastern Division title and the American League playoffs—but tragedy was never far off in the minds of Red Sox supporters. The time seemed ripe for a revival of *Curse of the Bambino* and, in September 2004, just one month before Red Sox fans would know the fate of their perennially snake-bitten team, Theater to Go, in Stoneham, Massachusetts, gave audiences an opportunity to prepare for the worst by restaging Kruh and Bergman's bittersweet show. A new choreographer, Elizabeth Sheeran, was brought on board and reviews were upbeat. Roger Bentley, of New England's *Theater Mirror*, applauded the singing and dancing of the Royal Rooters, exclaiming, "The Rooters had some very difficult music and choreography to handle but they did [so] with gusto and enthusiasm. Bravo!"[87]

Miraculously (or so it would seem), just after the run at Theater to Go ended on October 2, 2004, the Red Sox barreled their way to an American League Championship and their first World Series victory in eighty-six years. The dreaded "curse" had been lifted and, appropriately, Kruh and Bergman began work on a revised version of *Curse of the Bambino*. This updated version, featuring a new ending set in 2004 rather than 1986, was posted online on December 1, 2004, and rechristened, *The Curse is Reversed!* Three years later, in 2007, when the Red Sox, once again, were racing to the pinnacle of Major League Baseball, *The Curse is Reversed!* had its stage premiere at the Abbott Memorial Theatre in Waltham, Massachusetts (performed from May 11–26 by Waltham's Hovey Players). New choreography ("all the right moves," according to *Theater Mirror* critic, Beverly Creasey) was supplied by Linda Sughrue and a grand guest appearance was made by the new Red Sox theme song, Neil Diamond's "Sweet Caroline."[88] An incredible culmination for a musical that not only documented but actually lived through the agony of the "curse" and the ecstasy of its banishment.

The Summer King (2007, 2012/2013)

In 2003, Daniel Sonenberg began work on an opera, *The Summer King*, based on the life of Negro Leagues star Josh Gibson, possibly the most powerful hitter in the entire history of American baseball.[89] According to a 2012 press release issued by the University of Southern

Maine, where Sonenberg was employed as an associate professor and resident composer, Sonenberg, having "been captivated by the story of Negro League baseball" as a child, knew that "one day he would write an opera about Josh Gibson."[90] To Sonenberg, Gibson was an "ideal opera character"[91]—a player with talents that surpassed almost all contemporaries, but whose physical and mental health declined with great speed, resulting in his tragic death at the age of thirty-five in 1947, just months before the color barrier in the all-white major leagues was destroyed.[92]

For Sonenberg, this would not be his first baseball-inspired musical endeavor. In 1999, he composed a haunting, five-song cycle for high lyric baritone and piano, entitled "Baseball Songs," which included the recorded voices of New York Yankees' announcer, Phil Rizzuto, and former Kansas City Royals' pitcher Dan Quisenberry.[93] One song in the cycle, "Prayer for the Captain," contained the profoundly moving comments made by Rizzuto as he reflected, in 1979, on the recent death of New York Yankees' catcher Thurman Munson, just thirty-two and still in the prime of his career. Another song, "Old (G)love," was driven by the recitation of an original poem written in tribute to a cherished baseball glove by Quisenberry, a much-admired player—and published poet—who died at the equally untimely age of forty-five in 1998, just one year before "Baseball Songs" was completed. Clearly, the triumphs and tragedies of baseball stirred Sonenberg. Through music, it was possible for him to mourn and celebrate great players and important stories—stories that were in danger of being distorted or altogether forgotten. The Josh Gibson story, therefore, was a natural pull for Sonenberg. While illustrating the life of Gibson, the Negro Leagues as an institution—its own life and legacy—also could be examined.

The first components of the opera were completed by Sonenberg, with assistance from librettist Daniel Nester, in 2007, and a "workshop" production of the first two scenes from act 1 was presented in New York City on March 18 at the Manhattan School of Music's Opera Index.[94] Stage direction was handled by film and theater veteran Seret Scott, who, among her many tasks, was responsible for putting together a convincing and aesthetically pleasing bit of baseball pantomime in scene 2. As barbers and customers talk baseball in a local barbershop in 1957, one barber recalls the miraculous moment, on September 27, 1930, when Josh Gibson, then a member of the Homestead Grays, hit the home run that many believed was the only fair ball ever to sail completely out of Yankee Stadium. The barber describes the event in detail and, as the story unfolds, the action is replayed on stage—a projected memory—by three of the story's pivotal characters: a ball park announcer, a pitcher, and, wielding his ferocious bat, the awe-inspiring figure of Josh Gibson. Like the choreographed baseball movement in Schuman's *The Mighty Casey*, the pantomimed Gibson at-bat serves to heighten the drama and intensify the emotions already stirred by the music of Sonenberg and Nester. It is also possible to connect this scene to iconic photographs and paintings, featuring such immortal sluggers as Hank Aaron, Lou Gehrig, Reggie Jackson, Mickey Mantle, Willie Mays, Babe Ruth, and Ted Williams (photographs and paintings, it should be noted, that also influenced and continue to influence the work of many concert dance choreographers, including Chris Black, Christopher Fleming, Moses Pendleton, and Peter Pucci). Needless to say, the first two scenes held great promise for what was to come.

In the summer of 2007, the two-scene sampler of *The Summer King* was brought to the streets and parks of Brooklyn, thanks to American Opera Projects (AOP), a not-for-profit organization that decided to lend its support to the development of Sonenberg's baseball opus.[95] AOP, along with Sonenberg, believed that *The Summer King* was an excellent "vehicle for outreach into communities that don't usually come to the opera house"[96]—a work of relevance and appeal that might either help introduce opera to members of the public whose knowledge of the art form is nonexistent, or else help to change the perception of opera in the minds of those for whom opera is believed to be old and stodgy or boring and silly. Three performances were staged from late August through early September, including two at Fort Greene Park (as part of FortGreeneFest) and one on the sidewalk in front of the Five Myles Gallery in Crown Heights (as part of the eighth annual St. John's Place on Stage mini-festival). As AOP executive director, Charles Jarden, stated, "This is our first chance to get this music out to neighborhoods and communities that we believe will connect strongly with the material … [and who] might be seeing live opera for the first time."[97] Once again, baseball and recognizable movement functioning as "connective tissue" for the public at large and a performing art form that might be either misunderstood, unfamiliar, or generally inaccessible.

Sonenberg finally completed *The Summer King* in 2012 and had four arias from the newly finished work presented at the Black Cave Contemporary Music Festival in Portland, Maine. Christopher Hyde, in the *Portland Press Herald*, reported that the arias were a "highlight" of the festival and commented enthusiastically that "a full staging of 'The Summer King' would be well worthwhile."[98] Hyde would get his wish in May 2013, when *The Summer King*, in its entirety, would have its world premiere at the first-ever "Frontiers" program of new musical works, sponsored by the Fort Worth (Texas) Opera. New scenes, taking place in nightclubs frequented by Gibson and other players from the Negro Leagues (reminiscent of *Bingo!*), were added and Sonenberg's scope broadened to include much more content about the world of black baseball in the era before and after Jackie Robinson.[99] According to Sonenberg, "My opera celebrates both Josh and the countless others who were unable to cross over."[100] Through music, words, and movement, *The Summer King* helps to keep the memories, accomplishments, realities, and lessons of the past very much alive and serves to inspire listeners and viewers to learn more.

Bleacher Bums (2010 revival)

As described earlier, this 1977 improv-based comedy was created in Chicago by Joe Mantegna and the Organic Theater Company. The setting is Chicago's Wrigley Field and the action takes place entirely in the bleachers over the course of nine innings. The show has been—and continues to be—revived quite regularly in Chicago and in cities and towns throughout North America. The 2010 restaging at the Cotuit Center for the Arts in Cotuit, Massachusetts, is particularly notable, however, for two primary reasons. First of all, the show was directed by a choreographer (Michele Colley) and, secondly, Colley's original intention was to relocate the action of the show from Wrigley Field to Fenway Park, which would have resulted in a "double-header" of Red Sox-centric shows playing on Massachusetts stages in June 2010 (the other being *Johnny Baseball*, which will be discussed next). It also would have meant that three different full-length theatrical productions highlighting the trials and tribulations of the Red Sox organization and fans would have been presented in Massachusetts since 2001 (the third being the aforementioned *Curse of the Bambino*). This occurrence, though, would remain unrealized. Colley's request for permission to alter the setting of *Bleacher Bums* was denied by the original producer and director of the show, Stuart Gordon (who also owned the show's production rights).[101] As a result, the Cotuit Center production of *Bleacher Bums* was once again set in Wrigley Field. Still, Colley was given permission to make one slight but significant alteration. Instead of a 1970s game between the Cubs and Cardinals, the fans in Colley's version of *Bleacher Bums* were witnessing a 1998 face-off between a Sammy Sosa-led Cubs squad and a powerhouse Cardinals team commanded by super slugger Mark McGwire.[102] Definitely a game to remember.

Johnny Baseball (2010)

When Diane Paulus, in 2009, accepted the artistic director position at the American Repertory Theater (ART) in Cambridge, Massachusetts, she had a clear mission: "to create populist theater with integrity."[103] Paulus's goal, in other words, was to attract new audiences by producing quality shows with engaging and, insofar as theater is concerned, unconventional themes and settings that might have wider appeal and familiarity to people whose experience with theater is limited or close to nonexistent. Speaking of Paulus's first year as artistic director, *Variety*'s Frank Rizzo had this to say: "Paulus has opened up the playing field, producing shows that attract a wider, younger and nontraditional crowd with works that please and provoke."[104] It made perfect sense, therefore, that Paulus decided to bring *Johnny Baseball* to the ART stage in 2010. As Paulus explained to Joan Anderman of the *Boston Globe* just before *Johnny Baseball* had its premiere on May 16, "This is exactly the kind of show we should be doing.... Part of what we do in theater is keep our stories alive and keep our history present. And so much of what I've been interested in this year has been kind of enlarging what we call the [theatrical] experience."[105] *Johnny Baseball* was popular entertainment with sophistication and a message—a baseball musical unafraid to take on some serious social issues and the historical warts of a beloved team in its very own backyard.

A "time-leaping" musical theater history of the Boston Red Sox, from the post–Ruthian 1920s through the "Curse-busting" 2004 World Series victory, *Johnny Baseball* was described in an ART press release as "a thoughtful investigation of the issue of race in Major League Baseball as a mirror of American societal attitudes through the 20th century."[106] For the creators of the show—Richard Dresser (book), Robert Reale (music), and Willie Reale (lyrics)—there seemed to be no better way of conducting this "investigation of race" than by using their own favorite team, the Red Sox, as a representative specimen. The Red Sox, after all, were the last Major League Baseball team to open its doors to non-white players following the destruction of the "color line" in 1947 (the Red Sox finally added Pumpsie Green to the roster in 1953). Also, there was that damned "Curse" that hovered over the team for eighty-six years, only to be broken when the team was fully integrated and many of its on-field heroes, including its biggest slugger and most spectacular pitcher, were people of color and/or foreign born.

Also fully integrated in *Johnny Baseball* was the choreography.[107] Peter Pucci, one of America's most experienced blenders of dance and athletics, was selected by Paulus to direct stage movement and make the baseball segments look authentic, natural, and beautiful. Pucci, who played baseball as a young man in Baltimore and who, for his own dance company, created a full evening of athletic dance called "Pucci: Sport," carried out extensive research to prepare for the show, looking at "period" pitching, batting, and fielding styles from the major leagues and Negro Leagues throughout the 20th century and, in the case of the Red

Sox, into the 21st century.[108] According to Pucci, even when baseball movement was brief, "authenticity" was paramount.[109] Pucci also included a short but humorous cheerleading segment that may not have been "period," but certainly managed to capture the correct spirit and added a few moments of lightness to the production. Rizzo, in his *Variety* review, chimed, "Paulus, an expert at ensemble helming ... shows her stuff again, this time with a staging assist from choreographer Peter Pucci.... [T]he entire show is grounded in natural speed, ease and grace."[110] Using expert "movement direction" and "musical staging," Pucci made the baseball action and related choreography look seamless and made *Johnny Baseball*, as a whole, seem even more convincing and carefully constructed.

During the run of the show at ART's Loeb Drama Center, Paulus and Pucci and the entire *Johnny Baseball* team managed to present theatergoers with what Nancy Grossman called "a total baseball experience," including a stadium setting and the availability of ballpark food inside the performance venue.[111] And Paulus, ultimately, did achieve what she had intended: the ability to "lure" audience members "who would otherwise be more inclined to spend the evening at a sports venue than in a playhouse."[112] Frank Rizzo felt that *Johnny Baseball* possessed the ability to "draw—and satisfy—fathers and sons, not exactly your target musical audience."[113] This allure, of course, was quite true; however, Paulus and Pucci would have disagreed with Rizzo's "target musical audience" remark. To them, and to countless other theatrical producers and choreographers, the "target musical audience" was and is precisely those who might not place theater and dance on their lists of favorite things. As we have seen and as we shall continue to see in the pages to come, baseball can be a magnificent vehicle to use in pursuit of this democratic goal.

Johnny Baseball played at the Loeb Drama Center in Cambridge, Massachusetts, from May 16 through July 11, 2010 (after being extended from the original closing date of June 27). On August 12, 2012, the show was performed as a staged reading at Seattle's Village Theatre (as part of the 12th annual Village Originals Festival) and there is little doubt that more revivals and re-stagings—and more chances to hear renditions of such tunes as "God Bless the Boston Red Sox," "Worcester Boosters Fight Song," "Brotherhood of Bastards," and "Not Rivera"—will be presented in American theaters in the years to come.

National Pastime (2010, 2011, 2012)

What happens when two friends and lifelong baseball fanatics, one of whom is a librettist and the other a composer, decide to collaborate on a new theater project? In the case of Tony Sportiello and Al Tapper, what you get is a baseball musical called *National Pastime* that makes its theatrical debut in 2010 at the National Baseball Hall of Fame in Cooperstown, New York.

For Sportiello and Tapper, baseball certainly was "in the blood." Sportiello, a playwright and librettist who "grew up as a Baltimore Orioles fan living in Brooklyn and New Jersey,"[114] transferred his passion for baseball into a one-act, baseball-themed play in the early 1990s. This play, entitled *Contract Time*, was performed at the National Baseball Hall of Fame in 1992, thereby lending some Hall of Fame "cred" to Sportiello prior to his collaborative work with Tapper nearly twenty years later.[115] For composer Tapper, a former financier and die-hard Red Sox supporter, the baseball passion was intense enough to inspire a museum-worthy baseball memorabilia collection, containing such jaw-dropping artifacts as the cap worn by New York Giants' outfielder Bobby Thomson when he hit the famous "Shot Heard 'Round the World" off Brooklyn Dodgers' pitcher Ralph Branca in 1951; the home plate from opening day of the original Yankee Stadium in 1923; and what Tapper considers his "most prized possession," the spikes worn by his childhood hero, Ted Williams, in the very last game played by Williams at Fenway Park in 1960—a game that Tapper actually attended (and recalls with great clarity and emotion).[116] Trying to imagine a more appropriate team to join forces on the development of a "new screwball musical comedy" about baseball would be a difficult task, indeed.

National Pastime is as much an homage to the mellifluous baseball radio broadcasters of the 1930s and '40s as it is a tribute to the game itself. The story, set in 1933, describes the herculean efforts of a once-popular, but currently struggling, radio station in Baker City, Iowa (WZBQ), to recapture its former glory—and, thus, save itself from dissolution—by broadcasting the thrilling but thoroughly fictitious games played by a wholly invented team called the Cougars.[117] It is up to the announcers, through their incredible powers of imagination and their captivating, exhilarating vocal stylings, to bring the games to life and create a Cougar frenzy in Baker City. The fact that the team seems to be on a perpetual "road trip" does wind up presenting some major problems, leading to even more comic diversions, "kooky characters," and zany plot twists.[118] Along the way, music and dance pay regular visits, not surprising when one considers Tapper's outlook on the nature of baseball. In Tapper's mind, baseball is not only "musical," but also a "ballet."[119] As Tapper stated to a number of reporters, including Fern Siegel of the *Huffington Post* and Brian Scott Lipton of TheaterMania.com, "There's a certain ballet when someone hits a ground ball or single, and watching everyone on the field all move together—and move beautifully."[120] What both Tapper and Sportiello consider to be "truly magical" about baseball—the game's musicality and balletic core—could not help but be reflected in the action of their collaborative baseball stage ode, *National Pastime.*[121]

The infant show came to the stage of the National Baseball Hall of Fame's Grandstand Theater on May 1, 2010, as a "one-day-only," work-in-progress presentation, just in time to help "kick off" the new baseball season.[122] At the time, the vision for *National Pastime* was an initial regional run (during which time the show could be honed and tweaked), followed by a stint on Broadway. Plans, though, are subject to immense change when it comes to the theater and, after the show was greeted with mediocre reviews once it had its world premiere as a fully realized musical in Washington, D.C. (performed by the Keegan Theatre Company at the Church Street Theater, from April 9–May 14, 2011), *National Pastime* was reworked and made ready for an Off Broadway trial run in 2012. Kurt Boehm, the choreographer for the Keegan production, was replaced by Chip Klose and, on August 8, 2012, the revised show opened at the Peter Jay Sharp Theater at Playwrights Horizons in New York City. Reviews, sadly, turned out to be lukewarm once again and, upon the show's closing on August 25, no immediate transfer to Broadway was scheduled. There is no reason to doubt, however, that *National Pastime* will make a comeback. In baseball and dance, comebacks are common and fans are always primed to cheer for a true "gamer."

DC-37: *The Roberto Clemente Story* (2011, 2012, 2013)

With the exception of Ana Maria Maynard's 2001 dance work "Plena Baseball" (to be discussed in chapter 4), the impact of Latin America on the game of baseball in the United States was not at all a prime subject of scrutiny in theater or dance, either in the late 20th century or in the first decade of the 21st century. In spite of the increasingly popular theatrical and choreographic trend of examining baseball's history and the ways in which this history reflected and affected American society, as well as the corresponding, equally popular theatrical/choreographic trend of spotlighting baseball players and personnel who helped to bring progressive change to the game (and despite the fact that so many baseball-themed and baseball-inspired theater productions and dance pieces were created between 1980 and 2010), Latin America and its players were rarely, if ever, addressed. In 2011, though, this rather gaping hole would begin to be filled when writer/director Luis Caballero, composer/musical director Harold Gutierrez, and choreographer/musical stager Luis Salgado (the creative force behind the hit Broadway musical *In the Heights*) lent their talents to the development of a new bilingual musical celebrating the life and legacy of the Pittsburgh Pirates' Hall of Fame outfielder Roberto Clemente. The show, produced in cooperation with the Society of the Educational Arts (SEA) and Manuel A. Moran, was given the title, *DC-7: The Roberto Clemente Story*, in commemoration of Clemente's tragically heroic death—a plane crash that occurred in 1972, as Clemente was in the process of delivering humanitarian assistance to victims of a catastrophic earthquake in Nicaragua. Its world premiere took place on November 11, 2011, during the sixth annual "BORIMIX: Puerto Rico Fest," held at Teatro SEA on New York City's Lower East Side.[123]

DC-7 begins with Roberto Clemente's funeral. To quote Juan-Jose Gonzalez, as "three of the most influential characters in Clemente's life [his brother, wife, and closest friend] … share their memories" about the Pirates' star, the action shifts, in flashback, to Clemente's childhood in Puerto Rico.[124] These childhood scenes are followed by depictions of Clemente's minor and Major League Baseball career, with close attention paid to the civil rights movement in America and how this influenced both Clemente and Major League Baseball, as well as American society in general. Throughout the show, music and dance are abundant, an interpretation that at least one actor in the show, Modesto Lacen (who played the role of Roberto Clemente), felt was not merely appropriate, but truly *necessary*. In an interview with Julian Garcia of the *New York Daily News*, Lacen had this to say: "Doing the research, I found out that Roberto did dance; he was a good dancer…. And he also wrote music and played music. So doing a musical about him is not that far from how he was."[125] Dance, therefore, was integral and the creators of *DC-7* intended the show to be a joyful and moving remembrance of "a hero," in the words of Gonzalez, "whose extraordinary life continues to inspire and touch" others.[126] The movements of *salsa* and *meringue* and *plena* blended with the movements of baseball in *DC-7*, introducing a whole new, long overdue chapter to the story of baseball and dance on the theatrical stage.

DC-7 closed its short run at Teatro SEA on December 4, 2011, and moved to a larger, Off Broadway space at the Puerto Rican Traveling Theatre in New York City, where it played from February 14 to April 8, 2012.[127] The show also was picked up by Washington, D.C.'s GALA Hispanic Theatre for its Spring 2013 season (performance schedule: April 18–May 26), allowing the National Pastime and Latin American dance to shine on stage in the shadows of the U.S. Capitol and White House.

Broadway, Baseball and Beer (2012)

Like dancers Jim Morrow and Ron Thiele, along with fellow stage actor Shuler Hensley, Broadway musical star Patrick Ryan Sullivan managed to reach a high level of organized baseball before deciding to shift gears and follow a different career path. For Morrow and Hensley, who each entered college on a baseball scholarship, the change of direction occurred before graduation. Thiele and Sullivan, on the other hand, were toiling in the minor leagues, dreaming of a major league call-up, when a decision was made to bid farewell to the diamond in order to pursue a different kind of performing career.

Sullivan, in fact, made it all the way to Triple-A (as reported by Brian Scott Lipton) before abandoning his baseball dream.[128] His choice, ultimately, proved to be a wise one and his acting, singing, and dancing skills were able to take him all the way to Broadway, where he landed featured roles in such productions as *42nd Street, Beauty and the Beast,* and *Titanic.* An avid and talented writer as well as a stage performer (on his personal website, he says, "In recent years I have found myself wielding a pen more often than a baseball bat.... I've hit many home runs with both"),[129] Sullivan created an autobiographical, one-man show in 2012, *Broadway, Baseball and Beer,* which featured stories, songs, and movement. Interestingly, Sullivan's show bore a striking resemblance to the vaudeville and music hall shows from the early 20th century, when baseball stars entertained audiences with a theatrical *paella* of song-and-dance routines, humorous anecdotes, recitations, and touching vignettes. A remarkable "full circle" in many ways and, by coincidence, taking place almost precisely 100 years after New York Giants' pitcher Rube Marquard appeared for the first time in a show with stage partner and future wife, Blossom Seeley (*Breaking the Record; or Nineteen Straight*).

Patrick Ryan Sullivan's *Broadway, Baseball and Beer* was performed on June 22, 2012, at the Engeman Theatre in Northport, Long Island (New York). It is difficult to say with certainty, but there is every reason to believe that, had Sullivan's show been produced in 1912, it would have been a main act at Hammerstein's, perhaps squeezed in between a ballet *pas de deux* demonstration and a slapstick comedy sketch.

1990 to 2013: Beyond the United States

Shadowball (Great Britain, 2010–2012)

Perhaps the perfect theatrical showcase for the connection between baseball and dance, as well as the perfect theatrical vehicle for helping audiences develop a deeper appreciation for both disciplines, was created outside of the United States. As reported by Neil McKim of the British Broadcasting Company's online music magazine Classical-Music.com, in 2010, as London and all of Great Britain prepared for the 2012 Summer Olympics and Paralympics, the director of a community-based music education organization in London, the Hackney Music Development Trust (located in the ethnically and racially diverse, working-class neighborhood of Hackney), began searching "for a project to engage children in Hackney about sport and music."[130] Of course, the fact that the director, Adam Eisenberg, was a born-and-raised New Yorker might have had an effect on the direction of the search to a small degree; still, the project ultimately selected would prove to be brilliant not only in its ability to engage, but also in its capacity to educate, entertain, and inspire. Eisenberg's idea was to explore and reveal the links between black baseball and jazz music in the United States.[131] An educational production, involving a large segment of young people in the community, could be developed and, as participants examined the issues of racial segregation and discrimination and were taught about a critical period (the 1920s through the 1950s) in U.S. history, they also would have an opportunity to learn (and play) a relatively unknown sport and listen to a music form that was equally "foreign." Ambitious? Yes. Possible? Absolutely!

In order to get this rough blueprint off the ground, Eisenberg approached a talented, respected, experienced, and education-minded songwriting team. Julian Joseph, a jazz composer, pianist, and radio personality, and Mike Phillips, a librettist and historian, had worked together in the past, composing, in 2007, a jazz opera, *Bridgetower—A Fable of 1807*, about George Bridgetower, a 19th-century black violinist.[132] Joseph and Phillips signed on, agreeing to compose a new jazz opera focusing on the connections between the teams and players of the Negro Leagues and the black bandleaders and performers of the "jazz age" in America, many of whom were actual owners of all-black baseball teams and some of whom even played ball in the Negro Leagues. A production crew was assembled and a massive education outreach campaign was launched. When the jazz opera was completed, the Hackney Music Development Trust (HMDT) and its education wing produced extensive curriculum materials and the implementation of the program in Hackney schools began, with Jubilee Primary School and Kingsmead Community School leading the way,[133] soon to be joined by nearly twenty additional schools and, over the next two years, extending to schools in many other parts of England, including Birmingham, Manchester, and Sheffield, as well as many other boroughs of London.

The show was given the title *Shadowball*, based on the pre-game warmups and exhibitions commonly held by players in the Negro Leagues, involving the use of an imaginary ball to carry out a "pantomime" or a "mock game" for the entertainment of fans and fellow players. As Eisenberg, Joseph, and Phillips understood, and as the HMDT website pointed out, even though Negro League players may not have realized it at the time, the game of "shadowball" would serve as an "apt metaphor for the exclusion of [b]lacks from Major League play in America."[134] The game of shadowball also was a magnificent example of baseball choreography and is certainly one of the highlights of the film and stage versions of William Brashler's 1973 novel, *The Bingo Long Traveling All-Stars and Motor Kings*, as mentioned previously. As one would expect, the exquisite pre-game pantomime is well represented in the HMDT production of *Shadowball*. In terms of dance, though, *Shadowball* goes much further. At its core, jazz music is dance music and any discussion of jazz history and the men and women who inhabited the world of jazz in the mid-20th century would be incomplete without a heavy dose of dance. Accordingly, *Shadowball* is filled with movement, from the nightclubs to the ball fields, and the stage—"laid out around a baseball pitch"—features a non-stop array of jitterbuggers, steppers, and sliders.[135] McKim, in his Classical-Music.com piece, remarked that the young actor (Samson Adeola) playing the role of Cab Calloway at one 2010 production "almost has enough dance moves to steal the show!"[136]

Young actors, in fact, turned out to be the driving force of *Shadowball*, which is precisely what Eisenberg had intended. For its initial production, ninety-five children (between the ages of nine and eleven) were involved, representing each of the targeted primary schools.[137] Only one adult was featured, a popular jazz singer named Cleveland Watkiss, who played the part of Satchel Paige, the legendary Negro Leagues pitcher. Otherwise, all roles—from Josh Gibson and "Cool Papa" Bell to Bill "Bojangles" Robinson (who danced on dugout roofs during baseball games) and the aforementioned Cab Calloway—were handled by pre-teens, sporting 1940s garb, along with baseball uniforms replicating those of the Kansas City Monarchs and other famous Negro Leagues teams.[138] Students and schools participating in the program were treated to a full, unique educational and cultural experience. HMDT provided "specially designed lesson plans," as well as "composing workshops with Julian Joseph, residencies, performances, and baseball activities"—activities which included "six weeks of baseball training from Baseball/Softball UK."[139] The premiere engagement took place at London's Mermaid Theatre on June 29th and 30th and one critic from *The Guardian*, John Fordham, described the show as "undeniably a thrilling and illuminating venture for its young participants" and spoke in bright tones of the music composed by Joseph and Phillips, with "astute deployments of gospel ... and blues," in addition to the "elegant mutations" of 1930s and '40s jazz themes.[140] An educational marvel, *Shadowball* attracted much attention beyond the borough of Hackney, winning the esteemed "Inspire Mark" award from the Organising Committee of the Olympic Games and earning the endorsement of Major League Baseball.[141] The Hackney schools and Mermaid Theatre performances were only the beginning.

For the next two years, through the summer of 2012 (when London played host to the Olympic and Paralympic Games), *Shadowball*'s arm extended throughout the country, reaching dozens of schools, hundreds of school children, and thousands of spectators. The HMDT website noted that interest in and knowledge of both baseball and jazz increased and a greater understanding of the issues of prejudice and discrimination was achieved in those areas of the country touched by *Shadowball*. At the same time, the project was successful in its mission to "inspire confidence" and "teamwork" among participants and to *engage* young people in an exhilarating educational adventure.[142] Julian Joseph, the show's composer and tireless promoter, had this to say about *Shadowball*'s message: "*Shadowball* is a story of triumph in the face of adversity. It demonstrates the greatness of a people denied their civil liberties. How do you thrive in an unjust system? Baseball and jazz."[143] It is exciting, indeed, to think of baseball, music, and dance in such powerful, liberating terms. Exciting, too, to realize that, with *Shadowball*, the world now had two 21st century jazz-oriented operas (*The Summer King* being the other) based on the Negro Leagues and the history of black baseball in America. New theatrical avenues and new windows to the past were continuing to open up, with new insights and new lessons—and baseball and dance, once again, in the spotlight at center stage, illuminated.

Burning Up the Infield (Canada, 2011)

Stories about minor league and semi-professional baseball often are filled with a blend of pathos and humor that is particularly profound. There are quirky fans and outlandish marketing schemes, odd mascots and endless bus rides, struggling old-timers seeking another moment of glory and scrappy young players hungry to advance to the next level. And everything—the hilarity and the boredom, the sadness, the joy, and, above all, the hope—is set against a backdrop of small towns and cities, containing a slew of rooming houses and motels, offering a constant supply of fans and detractors of every stripe who, at times, may bring derision and cruelty, but, far more frequently, will dispense enthusiasm, loyalty, and love quite freely and openly. In literature, cinema, and even theater, there are many such stories—some of which have been described in this and previous chapters (and some of which will be described in the chapter devoted to film, television, and video). Less common, however, are stories about the minor and semi-professional leagues that take place outside of the United States, especially in countries where baseball takes a back seat—or even a ride in the trunk—

Members of City Stage New West (New Westminster, BC, Canada) perform *Burning Up the Infield*, 2011 (used by permission of the photographer, Renee Bucciarelli).

to pastimes that are far more popular and deeply ingrained in the fabric of the culture. Perhaps even more rare are stories about teams that existed for what may seem like an instant—a single season or two—before shifting affiliations or moving to a new town or simply disappearing from the face of the earth. This is why the 2011 production of *Burning Up the Infield* in New Westminster, British Columbia, Canada was, at once, so familiar and so remarkable.

The story upon which *Burning Up the Infield* was based goes back to 1974, when the Class A Northwest League added a team in New Westminster, a small, primarily blue-collar city located just southeast of Vancouver. Dubbed the New Westminster Frasers, after the historic and vitally important nearby river, the team was provided with a home field (Queen's Park Stadium) and uniforms, a schedule of games, a typical mixed roster of aging and novice professionals, and precious little else. A full, generally unsuccessful, season was played, with total home attendance registered as the "lowest that year in organized baseball," and, just eight months after the Frasers began their shaky but hopeful flight, the plane crashed and the team disintegrated—presumably vanishing from history forever.[144] But, much like the Seattle Pilots, their similarly short-lived neighbors to the south, the Frasers managed to muster enough character and bizarre panache in their brief existence to keep the memory of their single year of life "burning" bright in the minds of at least a handful of dedicated boosters.

Two of these loyal fans were Ken McIntosh and Rod Drown and, in 2010, McIntosh (a sixty-two-year-old former New Westminster police officer) and Drown (a New Westminster-based writer and historian) collaborated on a commemorative book about the Frasers, which they called *Burning Up the Infield*, a reference to one of the typically strange incidents that occurred during their single season (in order to hasten the evaporation of rain puddles on the infield dirt in Queen's Park Stadium, the players and ground crew retrieved some old, discarded tires and, after scattering them around the infield, set them ablaze—an activity that attracted the attention and disbelief of the local fire department, as well as the local media). Eventually, thanks to a chance meeting in a local coffee shop, McIntosh and Drown's funny and fascinating remembrance came into the hands of Renee Bucciarelli, the American-born artistic director of New Westminster's City Stage New West, and the idea for a new project was born. As Lowell Ullrich reported in the *Vancouver Province*, Bucciarelli "somehow saw the merits of a theatrical performance about a slapstick baseball team" and set about the task of constructing a working script, with full cooperation from McIntosh and Drown.[145]

The bulk of the play was completed by March 2011 and City Stage New West was invited to present selections from the book and the play-in-progress at a World Theatre Day event held on March 27, 2011, at the New Westminster Public Library (the event, quite fittingly, was called, "From the Page to the Stage").[146] Response was positive and, following the March 27 show, Bucciarelli continued to develop and refine the work, adding music (by George Ryan) and movement. On June 12, 2011, a staged reading of the full play, complete with Ryan's music and Bucciarelli's simple choreography, was presented at Douglas College's Laura C. Muir Theatre (in New Westminster). Again, response was favorable and Bucciarelli commented that, while the theatrical version of *Burning Up the Infield* may not have been "Pulitzer Prize-winning" material, it certainly was "charming enough to tell this very funny story." According to Bucciarelli, "This is New Westminster's *Bull Durham*."[147]

In terms of physicality, Bucciarelli concedes that, because the June 12 performance marked the "first workshop staging," there were no full-fledged dance numbers. However, the entire production was "set up … like a series of baseball games, using the movements of the players as the key dynamic—or slowing down for effect, or focusing on the ballet of a single spit and chew pitch."[148] Baseball movement as ballet was an ever-present notion for Bucciarelli and a driving force. "Even in the writing of the piece," says Bucciarelli, "the movement of the game is what inspired much of the dramatic action."[149] Additionally, there was a routine reminiscent of the Keystone Cops (used "to illustrate the constant trades going on between a handful of [Northwest League] teams") and a physical comedy segment depicting a bus ride back to New Westminster after a road game, featuring "drunken players singing, draped over the bus seats, rolling in the aisles trying to get some sleep."[150] Even if no routine in the June 12th staging of *Burning Up the Infield* could be compared to, say, "Shoeless Joe from Hannibal, Mo." from *Damn Yankees*, there is much to praise in Bucciarelli's effort to use choreography to express such baseball realities as player trades and road game journeys. Bucciarelli has remarked, "If we ever did the show again (and someone [has] expressed interest in the story for a short film), I do think we'd have even more choreography, and probably a professional choreographer!"[151] Any such future production would have a fabulous set of ideas from which to draw, thanks to the skilled and inventive groundwork of Bucciarelli, McIntosh, Drown, and the 2011 City Stage New West crew.

"Take Me Out to the Opera" and "Opera in the Outfield"

"When the fat lady sings … her audience will be eating peanuts and Cracker Jack."[152] This is how Lisa Leff began her September 28, 2007, *USA Today* article about a plan hatched by the San Francisco Opera, in cooperation with the San Francisco Giants baseball club, to broadcast a live performance of Saint-Saens' *Samson and Delilah* on the center field scoreboard of the Giants' home field, A.T. & T. Park, at the tail end of the 2007 baseball season. The program, christened "Take Me Out to the Opera," was part of an effort by the San Francisco Opera to connect with new audiences by "opening up the walls" of San Francisco's War Memorial Opera House and bringing opera to less conventional venues, thereby providing spectators with a completely different kind of experience and, hopefully, a greater appreciation and understanding of the art form. According to the general director of the 2007 San Francisco Opera, David Gockley, himself a baseball fan, the intent was to "democratize" the opera company— to "make it more accessible to new patrons, particularly young people."[153] As for the content of the show, Gockley was enthusiastic: "We are going to have fun. We are going to sing 'Take Me Out to the Opera.' We are going to have tailgate parties, load up on garlic fries, get our blue bloods here clotted up."[154] In the end, the show was a success, with thousands of fans in attendance, munching on hot dogs on the field as Olga Borodina belted out arias, and members of the San Francisco Opera performed choreographed movements on the jumbo screen.

The 2007 "Take Me Out to the Opera" program contained no baseball-inspired dance pieces; however, it proved to be the first joint venture by an opera company and a Major League Baseball team to simulcast an opera performance live from the opera house stage on a video screen inside a baseball stadium, which meant that *theatrical dance*, too, was being promoted. Because dance and choreographed movements are so integral to opera, fans at A.T. & T. Park were being treated not merely to soaring sopranos and booming baritones, but also to a steady diet of *chassés*, *passés*, and *port de bras* positions. Like tea or coffee with sugar and cream, or a red plastic cup of cola flavored with vanilla or cherry, the opera and dance came as a blend—directly from the concert hall stage, to be consumed by a crowd resting on blankets laid atop outfield grass and infield dirt.

One year later, in 2008, the Washington National Opera and the Washington Nationals baseball team launched a similar effort, called "Opera in the Outfield," which would turn into an annual free event, attracting tens of thousands of spectators to a new production each September at Nationals Park. In fact, "Opera in the Outfield" would take the initiative one "giant" step further, by adding a sparkling bill of pre-opera activities and performances to the celebration, all tied tightly to the Washington, D.C., community. In 2011, for example, several local performing artists were invited to showcase their talents before the live broadcast of Puccini's *Tosca*, including the S.I.T.Y. Stars double dutch jump rope squad from Greenbelt, Maryland, the Yorktown High School Marching Band from Arlington, Virginia, and Washington, D.C.'s own Tarabitu Pan-African Step Dance Team—altogether, a true dance extravaganza, especially when combined with the dance on display by the Washington National Opera.[155] A new feature, "The Fly Ball," a free pre-show party held in the Stars and Stripes Club at Nationals Park, was introduced in 2012 as an incentive to attract even more young attendees, offering show-goers an opportunity to meet and mingle over food, drink, music, and, of course, dancing.[156] Add to this the ritual "donning of the Washington Nationals baseball caps" by members of the Washington National Opera during all "Opera in the Outfield" curtain calls (which are taking place physically on the stage of the Kennedy Center in Washington, D.C.) and you are presented with a striking demonstration of collaboration in its most clear-cut form.[157] It is difficult to imagine departing Nationals Park without feeling a strong sense of interconnectedness between baseball, music, and dance.

There is no doubt that similar collaborative ventures will take place in the years to come and every reason to believe that baseball field simulcasts of concert dance performances soon will be as common—or, at least, *almost* as common—as on-field mascot races and choreographed ground crew exhibitions. Steve Cohen, general manager of the Brooklyn Cyclones of the Class-A New York-Penn League, has stated that he would love to produce a collaborative baseball and dance show called "Craig Swan Lake," honoring the former New York Mets' pitcher, with choreography set to the world famous ballet music by Tchaikovsky.[158] It is hard to imagine that such a delightful and delicious idea would not be actualized at some point in the not-too-distant future. Anyone for "Donnie Baseball Quixote"?

*   *   *

Before concluding our extended, though not exhaustive, discussion of baseball-infused and baseball-themed theatrical dance and commencing our equally grand exploration of the connections that exist between baseball and dance in the realm of what is referred to commonly as "concert dance," it is impossible to resist remarking on a relatively recent publication that possesses a pedigree that would likely be sanctioned by both Major League Baseball and the American Theatre Wing. Indeed, if any measure of skepticism about the connections that exist between theater and baseball might have lurked in the mind of any general observer prior to this book's release, it seems fairly inconceivable that such skepticism would not be quashed wholeheartedly following the 2011 publication of Peter Filichia's comprehensive and entertaining study, *Broadway Musical MVPs 1960–2010: The Most Valuable Players of the Past 50 Seasons* (Applause). A press release for the book states the following:

> Musicals and baseball have many commonalities: both have runs, hits, and errors; both have cheap seats that aren't so cheap and overpriced concessions; both have stars with high salaries; and both have awards at the end of the season. But baseball does have what the Tonys, Opera Desk, and Theatre World awards don't offer: an annual Most Valuable Player award given to the single individual who made the most impact either for his team or the season. What if musical theatre did choose an MVP?[159]

Filichia himself has commented that "both baseball and musicals require teamwork" and that each season in baseball and on Broadway has its share of winners and losers.[160] In the book, therefore, Filichia covers the best and the worst of each of the fifty years in question, bestowing a wide range of baseball-inspired awards upon the standout (for better or worse) plays and players. Barbra Streisand, for example, is cited as 1961–62 "Rookie of the Year" for her "splashy debut" in *I Can Get It for You Wholesale*, while a supposedly fading Vivien Leigh is presented with the "Comeback Player of the Year" award for her 1962–63 work in the musical *Tovarich*. Filichia is well aware of the fact that baseball and theater share a very real, rather intimate relationship and it makes perfect sense to learn that the seed of Filichia's awareness was planted at a very early age—way back on July 26, 1961, to be precise, when Filichia had the great fortune to attend "his first Broadway musical" (*My Fair Lady*) in the afternoon, proceeded by a journey to the Bronx, where he sat in the stands at Yankee Stadium to watch a double-header between the Yankees and Chicago White Sox.[161] The light bulb inside of his head must have been blazing as he rode the subway back home, fresh from a miraculous day of music, dance, and drama inside both the theater and the ballpark.

Interlude
Choreographers and Dancers on
Dance and Baseball—Louis Kavouras,
Peter Pucci and Nick Ross

Louis Kavouras, Choreographer of "The Baseball Dance"[1]

My dad always wanted to be a baseball player, so he put both of his sons into baseball. I grew up in Florida, and even in summers, when I kind of wanted to be at the beach with my friends, I'd be practicing baseball. I even had private baseball lessons. I wasn't the best player at it. I probably had pretty good form, which probably comes from my dancer side. Later on, I think I translated that into dance—the form of the movements that I could do. I played and watched baseball constantly and then kind of put it away for a little while. Then I started college as an engineering student and, after a while, I got bit by the dance bug. I continued to take dance classes and then switched my major from engineering to dance. In the midst of the dance classes, I took a choreography class and we were given an assignment called "Second Function Costume Dance"—"Second Function" meaning that it was not just pure movement (which would be "First Function"). Second Function meant that it had representational references to something else. So I just pulled out an old baseball uniform and that was the impetus for this baseball study. It was a solo and everyone in the class really liked it. I started with the pitcher and basically what I did was take choreographed movements that the pitcher would do, including all of the little idiosyncratic things that they do with the hat and the leg and everything in preparation for throwing the ball. The whole three- or four-minute solo was about him throwing the ball. And really drawing it out, because what's interesting about baseball is that the pitcher is sort of the "kingpin" of the field and everyone just waits for him to throw the ball.

So that's what I did at first with the piece. It was 1986. It was one of my first choreographic pieces. Afterwards, I kept being asked to do various little concerts and, frequently, I'd be asked to do that solo. So I would drag it out and over and over again I kept refining it. About two years later—around 1988—I was working on my MFA and I had to do my thesis and when I was thinking about what pieces I wanted to make, I realized that I wanted to expand that baseball piece because I knew that there were other characters that I could draw on and I could create a bigger piece than just this one little solo. And that's when I started developing the batter. I made a solo for the batter and then also I brought in an outfield. And I sort of stopped there. Rather than do all of the bases and the catcher, I cut it to six characters. Some of the movement for the catcher and some of the bases I could do with that outfield and I guess I put the shortstop in with the outfield. So I ended up with six. The piece wound up

93

being about twenty minutes long. It was choreographed and first presented in February 1989. It was a really fun piece. And there were some other interesting things about it.

When I made the solo for the pitcher—the pitcher was in silence and there were all these different rhythms with the feet and different meters of time. Most dances are standard 5–6–7–8 time, but there were 3s, there were 4s, there were 7s. I was really manipulating the time of the dance phrases and the dance movements. What ended up happening is that it made it really difficult when I needed to find music for the bigger piece. The solo I had always done in silence and there was even some clapping and sometimes the fist would hit the other hand. I never had a ball in the piece and I never had a bat and I never had a glove—I didn't have the props, so an open hand would act as the glove and the other hand would hit it and you'd get that sound. And there were the sounds of the feet. That's what I did with the solo.

When I ended up expanding the piece, I needed music because I thought that twenty minutes of silence was just too much. I recruited an audio engineer and we recorded the sound of a ball hitting a bat—the crack of the bat. We recorded the sound of a ball hitting a mitt. We recorded the sound of a shuffle of footsteps. We sampled these sounds and then we created a kind of score of these sounds. It was an interesting score of these pops and clicks and whistles and even exasperated breath. With the batter, I ended up recording the footsteps of all the shuffling in—digging the foot into the dirt on both sides. All of that "getting ready." I sort of treated it like a tap dance, like a contemporary tap dance of the positions and really getting the bat into the correct position, waiting for the pitcher. Then there were the three strikes, so the whole thing was waiting for the batter to hit the home run on the third pitch. It turned out to be a really interesting score for the whole thing. I also recorded some sounds of crowds cheering, things you would hear at baseball games—the organ sounds and so on. Creating the sound was an interesting project. The only piece of music that I used was "The

Choreographer of "The Baseball Dance," Louis Kavouras (photograph courtesy Louis Kavouras).

Blue Danube" for the last section, when they play the game and you see all of the characters interacting. It was a little bit abstract—it was just divided into sections and was not a pantomime of a game.

I've set it on various groups and it's turned out to be kind of a popular piece. Every so often it gets a little bit of a resurgence. I'll pull it out and do it again or I'll find another group of people. It's been done for a group of high school guys in a theater class who didn't count and had to learn all these rhythmical counts and it's been done by a professional dance company in Ohio, to name just two.

When I made the piece, I didn't want it to be a bunch of dance movements with baseball uniforms on. So what I did was—I spent probably the whole summer of 1988 going to Cleveland Indians baseball games and watching the Indians on TV and watching other baseball games on TV and I started recording every movement that I thought was done in baseball that could have been a dance movement. What I found was really fascinating. Like the baseball pitcher picking up his leg—it's almost into like the ballet dancer's *passé* position. There would be *chassés*, there would be these movements that were kind of *battements* of the leg that were really similar—there was some overlap. So what I tried to do was take movements that were in baseball, that baseball players were doing, and stylize them into more of a dance form. What I kind of realized is that movement is movement. We're using the same body and the bodies move in similar ways, so there was a connection between how a baseball player moved and how the dancer moved, although the results and the purposes were different. I also found it really interesting how, when you looked at the different pitchers, there were different forms. Some of them were far more stylized than others in how they did the wind-up, how they brought the leg up, how they followed through on the throw. I didn't want it to just feel like this was a gimmick for a dance—I really wanted to use authentic movement from baseball. And some of that is what I was getting from being a kid who played baseball—I was using that training to influence the dance.

When you were growing up, did you ever envision that you would be moving into the dance world?

   LK: You know, I didn't. When I was doing the baseball piece, I always thought, Well, this is a dance for my dad. I couldn't be the baseball player that he wanted me to be, but this was a dance for him. My past took me in a different direction than maybe what his dream might have been for me. But that was also what was interesting about it. Something about it felt kind of right—that there was a purpose. There also was a purpose for all that training. I could use it and that was really wonderful. Also, as a young choreographer, I was able to make use of all of the "research" that I had done on the baseball field when I was ten, eleven, twelve years old.

Did you find that dance came somewhat naturally for you?

   I did. In the dance world, I'm considered having started late. I started when I was fifteen or sixteen. So it was late. But, you know, movement is about coordinating the body, and so is baseball. I've never really thought of it so much. I always thought I was more of a natural mover and that's what most of my teachers would say. But perhaps the baseball had a way of connecting. Some of it, I think, is also … baseball really does use the entire body—the upper and the lower body. It connects those two things. And that's one of the more difficult things in dance—having people learn how to connect the upper and the lower parts of the body so that they work in concert. I think that baseball players do that all the time. I also think about that sense of the "center"—baseball pitchers throw the ball from the center and, when you bat, you swing the bat from your center, from your core. And that's what dancers work at. So there's a similar idea of "center" and being centered. I even think in terms of being psychologically centered. There is that same kind of focus and attention that is in a lot of the game of baseball that is also in the focus and the attention of the dancer or any athlete.

Is it true that the piece was performed at Jacobs Field in Cleveland when it first opened?

   Yes, it *was* performed at Jacobs Field when it opened! There was a company called the Repertory Dance Company in Cleveland, Ohio, and, when I left Cleveland to come out here [Las Vegas] in 1991, they asked if they could put the piece into their repertory. And they performed the piece in quite a few places. Then, when Jacobs Field opened, they did it on the field! And this was just perfect for me—I was like, "Oh, this is just fantastic!" Here we are—it comes full circle back to baseball! I had already left to come out here [to the University of Nevada at Las Vegas], so, unfortunately, I didn't have a chance to see the performance at Jacobs Field, but, God, I wish I had! Susan Miller was the artistic director of that company and she might have some photos of that. I have photos of other performances—I think I have a couple different casts. Some of the best photos I have are from 1999, with the dancers in UNLV uniforms. That's always another fun thing—deciding what uniforms we're going to use when we do the piece. It's always fun to go to the athletic department, especially if there are women doing the piece, and ask what are the smallest baseball uniforms that you can get. There's no set team for the piece, which I kind of like. It can be appropriate for whatever the crowd is or whatever the school is. It was done at Southwest Texas State, which is now Texas State University. It's had some legs!

In terms of the connections between baseball and dance—the main ones are the ones we've talked about. There are similarities if you look at the movements: the batter *pliés* down to hit the ball and creases the hips; the pitcher winds up and moves into *passé*. There are such similar movements that are used. Also that similar sense of how we use the center. And even the psychological focus, I think, is quite similar. I might have started late as a dancer at fifteen, but my training as a baseball player might have helped me move further along. In the dance, I had always been called a "natural mover," which accounted for my quick progress. I think some of that natural movement is what baseball is all about. I think as a sport, too, baseball [requires] a kind of naturalism—of using the body correctly, of using the body the way that it is designed, getting the most out of the body. I don't think that it's quite as aggressive or breaks the body down as much as a sport like football. Thinking about that now is quite interesting. Dance is really about form and about building movement forms. I think that's what I saw in those baseball players—that there were forms that they followed, that they developed, that had a purpose. I think that any dancer—ballet or modern or jazz—seeks the same thing with form.

Peter Pucci, Choreographer of "Pucci: Sport" and *Johnny Baseball*[2]

I was born in Baltimore, Maryland, and I started playing baseball and other organized sports when I was seven or eight years old. That's what I did as a kid—I played sports. I didn't really start dancing until I was in college. I had exposure to social dance through recreation center dances on Friday nights—things like that. My sisters and my brother and my mother were good dancers, so social dancing was always sort of in my life. But modern dance and ballet were not on my radar until I got to college. My earliest memories are really all sports related.

Since I grew up in Baltimore, I followed the old Baltimore Orioles. I was a Junior Oriole. In those days, for ten bucks you could get general admission and gifts and all kinds of things. I used to go to Memorial Stadium—which is long gone, unfortunately—and watch the Orioles. The team at the time was Brooks Robinson and Frank Robinson and Boog Powell, Jerry Adair, Luis Aparicio, Dave McNally—those kind of guys. They were great teams. In those days, the Orioles had a special way of playing and they were pretty successful for a very long time. I'd ride my bike across town to go watch the Orioles and through high school I would

always drop in on games late in the day—
I'd come in after everybody was in and I
got to know some of the ushers and I'd
drop into games just to watch. As a kid, I
had, like, probably at least six different
ways to get into the stadium. I used to
make my way into a group of kids whose
fathers had tickets and they would send all
of the kids in and I would sneak my way
in. I would climb under a fence. There
were a number of ways to get into the stadium. I didn't have very much money and
a lot of us guys would just go and stand
out in front of the stadium and wait for
someone to give us a ticket or whatever.
We always found a way to get in. Sometimes, in those days, the ushers would get
to know you and they would let you come
in after a certain inning. I think a lot of my
baseball memories are definitely linked to
the Orioles and playing from an early age
on pretty consistently.

Choreographer of "Pucci: Sport" and *Johnny Baseball*, **Peter Pucci (used with permission from the
photographer, Michael O'Neill).**

*When did you begin thinking about the connections between sports and dance (and, in particular,
baseball and dance) and consider combining the two in a piece that you would create for the stage?*

PP: The first sports-related piece I started working on was in 1997. I began playing
with the idea of doing a dance with basketballs and I called it "Basketball Jones" after the
Bill Cosby cartoon character. It premiered on Broadway at the New Victory Theatre in 1998.
It was part of a show we did there and it became such a big hit. It got a rave review in the
New York Times. Then we got interest from around the country. I think Nike's advertising
firm on the West Coast—Wieden & Kennedy—tracked me down and asked for videotapes.

That's how it started. I started with basketball. And then it was so successful and got
such great response from the basketball and dance people that I decided to do an evening of
sports. I played baseball and knew the vernacular of it, all of the stylistic ways that baseball
players move. Everything that you saw in that piece was based on true movement of players.
Then I started doing boxing and I had a hockey piece and surfing and badminton and did a
football segment and I just started auditioning people who had sports ability and who could
also dance. Some of the dancers in my company could play basketball, some couldn't; some
had played baseball and some hadn't. I basically had to teach them how to use the glove, how
to do a backhand, all of that kind of stuff. It took some time to do that. "Baseball" was always
done to "The Four Seasons" by Vivaldi—a very well-known piece of classical music. It was
a very conscious choice to connect the classics with baseball stylistically and put it in the
framework of a spring-training season and a playoff. It is what the three sections of the piece
are all about.

I had been wondering if there was a definite, conscious decision to connect baseball to classical music because you felt that the sport lends itself to that association.

Having played all of these sports, there was a familiar connection for me to the movement. I always liked to play the infield in baseball and I loved watching great players like Brooks Robinson and Luis Aparicio and always picked up on how smooth and fluid those guys were and I tried to play that way. There is sort of a dance in that—how they moved and what kind of ease they had in fielding and throwing the ball and running and hitting. I took that idea and tried to put it into dance and thought that it would be a really good juxtaposition to use classical music because baseball is such a traditional American game and I thought that choosing something popular would be a safer choice. So it came out of that—that wanting to look at the beauty of how players move in the moment. There is a lot of standing around in baseball, waiting for something to happen—but when it happens, it happens quickly and there is a fluidity in how players move and how they throw and slide and glide and so on.

You were able to incorporate even these tiny movements that a lot of people either don't pay attention to or take for granted—the kinds of movements that you wouldn't necessarily expect to see in a dance piece. Little gestures, like the touching of the cap or the smoothing of the hair…

That was all intentional. That's all part of the vernacular of baseball. That's the connective tissue. That is just what players do: they grab their crotches, they rub the brims of their hats, pat their gloves, spit in their hands, pick up dirt. All of that stuff is part of the vernacular and I figured that anyone who knows baseball is going to get this. I tried to really be true stylistically, movement-wise, to what happens on the field. That came very naturally to me because I did it! It wasn't a stretch for me. But for my dancers, I had to kind of teach them…. I had to make them look at baseball games and take them to baseball games so that they could say, "This is what we're doing." And I had them watch baseball games on TV. We would also throw a ball around in the studio because they had to know what it's like to actually catch and throw.

I forgot to mention that I also did a dance with baseball bats to "Take Me Out to the Ball Game"—a modern, sort of poppy version that a composer friend of mine made. I had ten people dancing with baseball bats and I was able to incorporate that into "Sport." I started the whole program with "Baseball"—that was usually the opening number—and I decided to "bookend" the program: start with gloves and catching balls and then I thought that we needed to do something at the end with baseball bats, so I got ten baseball bats and we danced with the bats. They were steel bats—the wooden ones were too heavy and too pricey.

How was the piece received when it was originally performed at the Joyce Theater in New York City?

It was received really well. I had a set designer named Fred Schwartz, who's a friend of mine, do the floor. We taped the floor to evoke all of the different sports. There's a baseball diamond on the floor that's taped—that's the set design. We had popcorn that was sold in the lobby. There were sandwich boards out in front. It was like a ten-inning event and we called it "extra innings." We had Astro Turf on the rugs out front and we had opening day bunting in the theater and cheerleaders cheering in between some of the sports. So it was a real take on all of these sports in a way that was fun and kind of wacky and serious and all that—because I did all the sports and had a personal relationship to them. That was a whole other side of my life that I put aside once I started dancing professionally. So it was sort of like coming back to it and revisiting it and when you learn how to play a sport or handle a bat or a lacrosse stick or a glove, you usually don't lose that.

I had to find the right personnel. I did a lot of auditions because I had to find people who knew how to play—in basketball, for instance, people who could bounce a ball and who just had that natural ability. You can tell in two seconds if someone can bounce a ball. Otherwise you can look at it and say, "No, no, no, nope, you don't have it." Someone can put on a glove and you can throw a ball to that person and see how they catch it and you can tell in about five seconds whether or not someone can play baseball. So I had to search around and get people who were dancers but who were also multifaceted as far as their sports ability was concerned. I had a Division III scoring champion hockey player, Tony Guglietti, who was in "Sport." He played hockey in college and he was an amazing skater. We did this piece where he was on rollerblades or inline skates and I gave him a couple of hockey sticks and we had a female "puck" on skates. Later on, one of my guys was Nick Ross, who played baseball in college, and he was very accomplished as a baseball player, so it wasn't a stretch for him.

Were there any professional athletes ever involved in the piece?

I think in Kansas City we had a former ballplayer come on and do a cameo role. I can't remember who it was, but I know he was a professional ballplayer. I've also had people do guest singing whenever we took the show on the road. We would always have someone come in and sing the national anthem live at the beginning of the show. That was part of the piece—just like they do at the ballpark. We'd open up the whole show with people standing on the baseball diamond with their hats off and have a live singer sing the national anthem. Anyone in the audience with any kind of connection to sports would get it right away and would get a kick out of it. We'd turn all the house lights up and ask everyone to stand for the national anthem. It's not normally done in a theater. We'd try to get guests or ballplayers or celebrities to do little cameos on stage, or we'd have someone throw out the first ball or something crazy like that.

It seems as though you have an interest in attracting a wider range of people to dance performances. Is this a motivation for you?

Yes! That was a reason why "Basketball Jones" was so popular back in 1998. It tapped into a whole other audience—people who had an interest in sports. That was a way for them to come in and see dance. And that's why I pursued a whole evening of sports. And it turned out to be very, very popular around the country. We did it on tour until late in 2006. I've always felt like I wanted to make dance that reaches out to the masses and becomes accessible to people who don't normally come to the theater. That was a way to get new audiences in to see dance and if you get people into the theater when they don't normally come, then, hopefully, they'll come back and see something else. That was part of my effort as a choreographer, to reach as many people as possible. The "Sport" piece was a way to do that.

That show was played in parks and many other unusual venues. We played on the 9th Avenue Bridge going over to the new stadium in Pittsburgh. As people were on their way to see the Pirates, we were on the bridge, doing the show. I think I have a video of a police motorcycle riding right through the middle of the show at one point, which was ridiculous. We've done it in gymnasiums, we did it in parks around New York City…. I think over the summer we did it in about ten or twelve different venues and we got a lot of coverage from the news media. CNN showed up and we attracted really big crowds just because people thought it was such a great idea to combine sports and dance and perform in the parks and on tennis and basketball courts, in recreation centers, and so on. The show really could be adapted to getting people to see it. Not a lot of dance companies do that and not a lot of work can be done that way. There's more of it done now. But back then we were doing a kind of show that no one else was doing and putting it out there in a lot of different places.

We did a half-time show at Madison Square Garden where I had seventeen people with basketballs and for six minutes we had fourteen thousand people watching us bounce basketballs, which was pretty cool. It was during a New York Liberty game. (It's on my website—if you go under "Concert Dance" and you look down, it says "Madison Square Garden.") So the "Sport" show has had a lot of permutations, in different venues.

Regarding Johnny Baseball, *can you talk about the project?*

I was just sent the script because the word out there was that I was a choreographer who had a sports background and on my website you can see the dances I've made to baseball. The producers were looking for someone who had that history. So I read the script and I met with the director, Diane Paulus, and I told her that this was something that was in my back pocket—baseball. I could teach an actor how to throw or how to handle a bat or how to field. The piece takes place in the '20s and the '40s and it travels across several decades, beginning with Babe Ruth in 1918, the last time the Red Sox won a World Series before breaking "the curse" in 2004. So I had to do a lot of research about period baseball—finding out how people held the bat, how they pitched, gestures of the time. It was basically a love story about a white character, Johnny Baseball, who falls in love with a cabaret singer who happens to be African American. At that time, in the '20s, this kind of relationship was taboo. Babe Ruth is a character in the musical because he plays for the Red Sox and this kid was a phenom and he was going to be the next great Red Sox pitcher, but he runs up against the Red Sox management and their wanting him not to be involved with a person of color. Basically, he's shipped off and his career goes down the tubes because of that relationship, and Babe Ruth is shipped off to the Yankees. The whole premise of the musical is the institutional racism that existed in baseball and in the Red Sox organization for so many years. The Red Sox were the last team to integrate—with Pumpsie Green—in 1953. They looked at Willie Mays, they looked at Jackie Robinson, and neither was signed. Robinson hated the Red Sox for many years because they just didn't treat him nicely; they turned their backs on him when he auditioned. A lot of it is based on truth. So it's a long story involving this interracial romance that butts up against that history of the Red Sox. Actually the piece was originally called *Red Sox Nation*, but, apparently, they couldn't get the rights to that so they changed it to *Johnny Baseball*. It was a big hit up in Boston. The guys who wrote it … two of the guys were Yankee fans and one of the guys was a Red Sox fan, so they really knew their baseball. When I read the script, I could tell that whoever wrote it and wrote the songs really knew what they were talking about as far as baseball was concerned. So when I interviewed for the job, it was obvious to the director that I knew baseball and I knew that *they* knew baseball, so that was one of the reasons I got the job.

Can you describe the choreography?

It wasn't really much choreography—it was mostly what they call "musical staging." The baseball stuff was pretty straightforward. I used period pitching styles that I had researched. One of the characters is a Negro Leagues player and I had to look into pitchers from the

Negro Leagues, like Satchel Paige, and the kinds of styles they had. There were a lot of moments where people had to catch, there was a catcher involved, and I had to get people into the right stances. So there were really brief moments of baseball throughout, but they had to look authentic and "period." It was really what they call "movement direction" or "musical staging." There was not much choreography, but there was this very funny, short thing I did with three cheerleaders, which meant that I took a few liberties, since you don't really have baseball cheerleaders. They changed the musical to make it work and, in the end, there were three cheerleaders rooting for the Worcester Boosters. All in all, a lot of the ideas for the movements came out of my research.

Do you have some general thoughts about the connections between baseball and dance?

They both take a lot of education and a lot of hard work. You have to be highly disciplined, you have to take care of your body, you have to keep up on the training. Dancers are very similar to athletes in how hard they work, how dedicated they are to what they do. They are both professions that are short-lived—they're like thoroughbreds. Some people can only dance for ten years or so and some players are only in the league for that long. So both of them are very demanding professions physically, especially in today's sports world where these guys are so regimented and there is science behind everything that they do. And the medicine and training are so advanced now. And, in the same way, in dance there is so much great research that has come out about how to heal dancers and how to properly maintain their bodies and stretch them, and new techniques and Pilates. And so many different ways to train. I think that there are similarities in terms of gracefulness. In baseball, some players are beautiful movers and, of course, you have that in dance as well. Baseball players make it look effortless in the same way a dancer does. When you look at people on stage, you're looking at someone who's trained as hard and as long as a ballplayer and they make it look easy in a different kind of context.

Did you find that your training and experience in sports paid off in terms of your training for dance? Was there a natural transition or connection?

Oh, absolutely. All the discipline and all of the hard work that I put into athletic endeavors paid off tremendously. I had a lot of great coaches who worked us hard and I knew just how hard it is to be really good at something. That kind of discipline and focus that you have in sports was really just a natural transition into dance. You need to have that same kind of laser vision as far as being good at something—in that sense, it is very, very similar.

Nick Ross, Dancer, Choreographer and Company Director[3]

I've been playing baseball most of my life—I guess since I was about four years old. I played in the back yard with my dad, throwing me the ball. I played organized baseball—Little League and everything, all the way through college. And I still play in men's leagues and stuff like that—I'm still very involved. And I am coaching in high school. So it's definitely a part of me.

As far as the dance goes, I had been introduced to the performing arts when I was younger. I took some dance classes and musical theater and did some acting and some plays when I was little and then broke away from it and then came back to it when I was about fifteen or sixteen. I got back into it in high school—they needed a couple of guys to do some partnering for a show, so I kind of got suckered into that. They were doing a *Saturday Night Fever* piece and they needed some John Travolta–esque guys. From there, it developed into studying dance, taking ballet classes, and I ended up finding my way to SUNY-Purchase to study dance. I was introduced to a lot more modern dance and, ultimately, I became a working dancer. So you never know which path you're going to take, but this is the path that I'm on—both sports and dance together.

When you got invited to do the Saturday Night Fever thing in high school, you already were involved in theater to a certain extent, correct?

NR: Correct. It was more actual drama—acting in plays, as well as reading Russian literature and Russian plays. They were doing that piece for a spring concert and a girl I was dating was a cheerleader and she was in that piece and she said, "Oh, Nick, would be good for this!" Suddenly, with very few rehearsals, I wound up on stage and, from there, it kind of trickled along.

So what was it about dance that turned you on?

I don't know. I think I always saw the athletic side of it. I saw it was a challenge. I liked being around the girls. When you're a teenage male, I think you're like, Oh, I spend enough time in the locker room with the guys, it's kind of fun to be around the girls. So that's kind of where it went. There weren't too many guys involved—at least where I was from—and there were a whole lot of girls! So, socially, it was not a very hard decision. And I found some teachers who really took me under their wing and saw that there was potential there. I think it was just a different way to express yourself. The social reasons were probably a lot more prominent at the beginning and then it turned into more finding a different way to speak and to interpret. Both of my parents had been artists, had been musicians originally, and my aunt was a singer. My grandmother had taken me to opera when I was little. So the arts were definitely a big part of the family and I definitely was cultured when I was growing up.

But dance was also something you were thinking about?

Yeah, I think I had always liked.... I mean, I had seen ballet—I had been taken to the ballet when I was younger, as well, and I had seen Baryshnikov dance and I had seen

Dancer, choreographer, and company director, Nick Ross (photograph courtesy Nick Ross).

how high these guys could jump and the athleticism involved and I thought that was pretty cool. So I got to see that. And I was a huge football fan when I was growing up and I knew that guys like Herschel Walker were amazing running backs and pro athletes, but they were also dancers, so I think I definitely always saw that and knew that this connection existed.

As you were doing this, did you find that your athletic training was helping your dancing and did you find that dance training was a help in your athletics?

Definitely. As far as my dance training was concerned, I was always used more as a partner in pieces because I was very reliable and I was very strong. The girls trusted me. Everything that came from that, the work that I put in, allowed me to become a performer on my own, but it all kind of stemmed from my ability to partner and then everything else was just gravy on top. In terms of the benefits to my athletic ability, right away I saw differences in my flexibility and my agility and my ability to make plays that I could not make previously. Also, as your body's maturing and you're growing up, you see that there's a little bit of a difference. It definitely helped me improve.

Did you find that some of the exercises and warmups that you were doing in sports weren't sufficient and that the players could have benefited from dance exercises and training?

Absolutely. In terms of flexibility and strength, I think definitely they could have. I think the other thing that the dance helped me with was my ability to take corrections. You have to apply corrections from your coaching staff to be a very good athlete. In dance, I had very old-school teachers and the corrections were very hard—there was no sugarcoating or anything. The teachers were very direct; they were very "to the point." Athletics is a very result-driven field, and dance is as well. So I think it helped my ability to take that criticism and use it in a positive way and be able to learn faster and apply the corrections, both on the field and in the classroom. You have to be a quick learner. I'm not taking dance class anymore, but the people who are actually training can tell you that your ability to learn happens very quickly— you need to be able to learn things at a very rapid pace. When you step away from the classroom and the dance training, you tend to lose that a little bit. I felt that my athletics showed that as well. I always was able to take that correction and apply it to the batting cage or whatever I was doing. My muscle memory. I knew my body better than any other athletes I was around. Body awareness is kind of the key.

In terms of discipline, I think it's a trait that you have or you don't have and I think that I had that trait. It doesn't really matter what I'm working at, I just think I have that drive and that discipline. Most good athletes and most good artists have to have that—that's something that they share, even though it might be a different type of discipline, they all have to have that discipline.

Rejection also is a big issue—how you deal with rejection. In the dance world, rejection is huge. People go to audition after audition after audition, never getting a job. In the world of athletics, as you go up the pyramid, there's rejection involved there, too—otherwise, we'd all be professional athletes! So I think it's how you deal with the rejection that makes you stronger. Both things played a part in my life and helped me push myself to go further. I think I was told first that I couldn't be a dancer, then I was told that I couldn't be a baseball player, and then I was told again I couldn't be a dancer! So it kind of went back and forth. That's the thing that builds your character, so I was okay with it. I was told this by coaches and by dance teachers—by dance teachers first and then by coaches. And even one current major league coach who will remain unnamed—he's currently a manager of a major league team—he told me it was time to hang up the cleats. This was after high school and I was very serious about baseball. It was a good eye-opener. When you're eighteen years old, you'll pretty much jump at anything. I think it was a big wake-up call to tell me to go to college and take care of things and get a degree and go play baseball in college versus going down the baseball path right away. It was the summer after high school—a summer rookie ball league. I had a dream to go further and suddenly I was hit with the realization of stopping. It was a good experience and, when you're young, you can have those kinds of experiences. And I had many dance teachers along the way tell me that I wasn't going to make it, either, and that I should consider going on other paths and think about what else I could do. It's all about perseverance. For everybody. You definitely have to have a strong constitution for both.

Can you talk a bit more about the connections and similarities that you see between baseball and dance?

I think that there's a connection in terms of the "groundedness" and the transfer of weight. To be a good athlete, you always talk about being in a good "athletic position." Whether it's basketball or hockey or tennis or baseball or football—there's this athletic position that you want to be in. It's about being aware of your structure—your muscular structure and your bone structure. I think dance has that same thing and when you're aware of that and when you're able to use it, I think that you're able to move effortlessly. Things that look hard to the audience or the crowd, you are able to do effortlessly. We see that every day in sports— you see the highlights on *Sports Center* of the "Top Ten Plays." Well, dance performance, to me, is the *Sports Center* "Top Ten Plays" all put together to music and with a different concept or idea, whatever it is you want to talk about or show—whatever kind of feelings that I'm having when I'm creating the piece. I don't really make statement pieces, but I definitely leave the audience thinking how that piece applies to their everyday lives. Maybe one person sees one thing and another person sees another thing and that's okay because they've both been inspired. But that poetic quality of movement that's driving the piece is always there.

I think there's definitely that balance between things that look hard but are really effort- less and things that look effortless but are really hard! My dancers will tell you that they work really hard. I hope that it looks effortless and that there's a freedom of movement. I think everybody in the audience realizes at a certain point, even though it looks effortless, just how much effort is being put in—how high they jump and how far they fall in that suspension. I like showing that suspension of the body in the movement. The ability to use different level changes—on the ground, standing, in the air.

I think there are lots of connections between baseball and dance. It's not just one. It's kind of a web that's intertwined and if you choose not to see it, and a lot of people do, then that's okay. But, if you open up your eyes, I think you can see that there are a lot of things that transfer between professional dancers and professional athletes and their work ethic and ability. There are a lot of similarities, and I think that there will be a lot more athletes who find their way to dance as we go on.

3

On Stage III
Concert Dance in the 20th Century

As noted in this book's introduction, there is, for most Americans, at least some recognition of the link between baseball and dance in the varied forms of the Broadway musical, motion pictures, television, and even ballparks of major and minor league baseball teams. On Broadway and on stages throughout the world, *Damn Yankees* (as we have discussed) continues to enjoy revival after revival; film buffs are still treated to screenings of *Take Me Out to the Ball Game*, featuring Gene Kelly and Frank Sinatra as singing and dancing baseball players (to be examined at greater length in chapter 5); modern television viewers are able to get a glimpse of infielders *en l'air* by tuning into *Smash* or *So You Think You Can Dance*; classic TV aficionados can watch countless reruns of episode 1 from season 6 of *I Love Lucy*, also to be discussed further in chapter 5, in which Lucy, Ricky, and special guest Bob Hope, perform a rousing rendition of "Nobody Loves the Ump," and innumerable ballpark denizens have observed and continue to marvel (or simply gape) at the gyrations of dancing groundskeepers, cheerleading squads, manic mascots, spirited fans, music-driven players, specialty performers (such as Morganna the Kissing Bandit and player-acrobat, Jackie Price), and baseball clowns like Max Patkin, Al Schacht, Germany Schaefer, and Nick Altrock.

However, when it comes to "concert dance," or dance created exclusively for performance by a dance company or in a dance venue, the connection is much less widely known. Indeed, the vast majority of Americans would likely find it difficult to identify even a single example of such a baseball-themed or baseball-inspired work of concert dance. And, yet, the astonishing truth is that baseball and concert dance have been close partners for nearly a century.

In the United States, concert dance choreographers, those who make dances for the concert stage, have been attracted to baseball for four primary reasons: (1) the sheer beauty of movement and the physicality of the game; (2) the symbolic nature of baseball as an "icon" of American culture (or the ultimate form of "Americana"); (3) the inherent issues relating to gender and sexuality; and (4) the interest in connecting with greater numbers of people, developing new audiences, and making dance more accessible to the general public. Frequently, it is the case that all four reasons play equal roles in the choreographer's thought process and art. On the other hand, a certain choreographer may be motivated by only one or two of these reasons. As we examine the sampling of baseball-themed or baseball-inspired concert dance pieces created in America (or by a choreographer with American influences) over the past eighty-plus years, what should become very clear is that, regardless of the period in which a particular dance was crafted, at least *one* of the "reasons" listed above is always at the heart of the work.

Along these lines, it is worthwhile to begin this two-chapter section with a brief review and discussion of the Americana movement—from its emergence in the late 19th century through its early to mid–20th century flowering. It is, of course, also valuable to look first at some of the earliest examples that may be found of baseball being woven into the fabric of a work designed for the concert dance stage. Focusing initially on such early works not only makes it possible to gain a broader historical perspective on American dance in general, but also affords us the opportunity to see them at play, in all their glory.

(Please note that some of the material that follows appeared earlier in this book and is being repeated for the sake of clarity and context.)

Baseball and Dance in the United States: Americana

In his landmark book, *Baseball: The Early Years*, Harold Seymour and Dorothy Seymour Mills writes, "By the turn of the [20th] century, baseball had thrust itself sharply onto the American scene."[1] Seymour and Mills then quote a line from an article which appeared in an 1891 issue of *Sporting News*, declaring that "no game has taken so strong a hold on Americans as base ball."[2] As to the source of this growing popularity (or even *obsession*), baseball historian, Steve Riess, in *Touching Base*, states, "The public identified [baseball] with certain basic American concepts."[3] Baseball was seen as a true American game: a glimmering spoke in the wheel of genuine American culture.

Simultaneous to the rise of baseball's popularity and influence was the growth and expansion of a movement in the arts that is referred to quite simply as "Americana." Germinating in the late 19th century, this movement reached full flowering in the 1920s. Social historian Studs Terkel described it in the following manner: "The 1920s was [the] time for new subject matter, new themes. This country felt wonderful about itself. So the themes we drew on sprung from our daily lives, our deep feelings about our growing national consciousness. The result was…. Americana."[4]

Operating at the very center of this movement was *dance*. After years of being tied, almost suffocatingly, to European forms and forebears, American dancers and choreographers began to free themselves from these ties by looking within and without and experimenting with *new* forms and styles, developing vocabularies and expressing themes that were distinctly American. Isadora Bennett, in an article about the history of modern dance that appeared in a souvenir program for the modern dance team Winslow-Fitz-Simmons, had this to say about the shift in outlook among American dancers and choreographers in the late 19th and early 20th centuries:

> Isadora Duncan … ventured a prophesy on what the new dance would be in America. It would be different from any form on the continent. It would be "long-legged" and "athletic." It would be free-born. Growing out of a native culture and a native taste, it would be, in short, American.[5]

Along the same lines, Ruth Page, another one of the true pioneers of this American revolution in dance (and whose own baseball-related concert dance works will be discussed shortly), talks at length about this extraordinary transformation in her autobiography, *Page by Page*: "What spurred us on to look in our own backyards for the treasures hidden there? Why did we desert the swans, the bluebirds, and the fairytale princesses? Well, we were young and venturesome, and we wanted to strike out on new paths."[6] Moreover, as Page states in an interview with Terkel, what she wanted to reflect in her dances were "the realities of life."[7]

Of course, if a choreographer or dancer intended to reflect the actual "realities of life," this meant that Page and her cohorts would be required to exhibit struggle as well as triumph, pain as well as joy, and the pursuits and pleasures not just of the elite, but also of the common, working-class citizen. In a very real sense, then, what the promoters of Americana were vitally interested in was a celebration of everyday movement—the actions and activities of the ordinary American. Additionally, by focusing so intently on the average American citizen and the images, themes, and subjects that would be recognized and understood by most Americans, choreographers and dancers in America were, both consciously and unconsciously, connecting more intimately and forging more powerful bonds with their fellow countrymen and women. It is, therefore, not at all surprising to

Members of Ruth Page's touring troupe, Les Ballets Americains, 1950. Kenneth McKenzie is shown in front as the baseball player from Page's "Americans in Paris." Standing (from left to right) are Bentley Stone, Ruth Page, Jose Limón, and Pauline Koner.

discover that, by the 1930s and 1940s, American dance was, in the words of Walter Sorell, definitely "coming into its own," becoming wildly popular, and that the dancers and choreographers of the United States were "leading America toward the forefront of the dance world."[8] John Briggs, in a 1946 *Dance Magazine* article, went even further, declaring, "There is little doubt that New York, not Russia or France, is currently the [world] center of ballet."[9]

It would seem quite natural, then, that sports would be an extremely enticing subject area for American choreographers to explore and illustrate. And they most certainly did— and with great passion, delight, and invention. Helen Tamiris, born and raised on New York City's Lower East Side and provided with free dance lessons at the Henry Street Settlement House, found beauty in the physicality of boxing[10]; Ted Shawn, who helped create what is known commonly as modern dance and who, in the words of Walter Terry, tried to build "a way of movement for American men, for athletes," displayed basketball players, fencers, and gymnasts in his 1938 piece, "Olympiad"[11]; and both George Balanchine and William Dollar, respectively, in "Alma Mater" (1935) and "Juke Box" (1941), following Ruth Page's groundbreaking 1926 effort, "The Flapper and the Quarterback," thrilled audiences with depictions of soda shops and the excitement of a college football weekend.

In this period, though, the favorite sport of Americans was *baseball* and, from the 1920s to the 1950s, with Americana advancing at full force, the subject of baseball made its way not only into numerous theatrical and cinematic dance works, but also into a substantial number of pieces created for the concert dance stage. What follows is a discussion of six of these pieces. This discussion will be proceeded by an examination of some of the many baseball-inspired and baseball-infused concert dance works created in the last third of the 20th century. In the next chapter, this examination will advance to the 21st century, with a closer look at some of the most recent examples of baseball-related concert dance.

"Americans in Paris" (1936)[12]

It is fitting to "lead off" with Ruth Page. Page, a true pioneer of American dance, whose decidedly American dances dealt frequently with easily recognizable and pressing social issues, opted to create a piece in 1936 that made use of the contemporary George Gershwin composition, "An American in Paris" (which Gershwin himself characterized as a "rhapsodic ballet"). In Page's dance treatment, however, it was an American woman—not a man—who made her own way to the city of her dreams, only to find herself homesick and yearning to return to her native land. The work premiered at the Cincinnati Zoological Gardens, as part of the Cincinnati Summer Opera Festival, on August 2, 1936, with Page and popular tap dance artist Paul Draper in the lead roles. A few months later, on November 13, Page and her troupe of dancers staged an indoor revival of "Americans in Paris" at the Chicago Civic Opera House (this time with the lead male role danced by Bentley Stone).

Page also created a modified version of the story in 1950, retitled "Homesick Blues," featuring four women on a journey, pursued by their lovelorn and jealous boyfriends. In the original story, the lonesome traveler, feeling sad, encounters, in a dream and in reality, a wide range of fellow Americans, also on a journey. Included among this group of somewhat iconic American figures is a baseball player, dressed, fittingly, in a rather exaggerated rendition of a New York Yankees uniform, created by costume designer Nicholas (also known as Nicolas and Nicolai) Remisoff. What, after all, could better represent America, or be more familiar to the majority of Americans, than the figure of a baseball player from the most popular baseball team in the United States? Needless to say, "Americans in Paris," which Page and her dance troupe brought to cities and small towns throughout the country, was a hit.

"Americans in Paris" also demonstrated Page's unrelenting courage and her disdain for all varieties of discrimination and inequality. Non-white dancers were featured in the ballet—indeed, a group of men representing the "Ghosts of Harlem" were depicted in nostalgic terms, representing the land longed for but left behind by the central character. Although by no means unheard of (the New Dance Group, for example, founded in 1932 and based in New York City, was a racially and ethnically diverse company), the presentation of an integrated concert dance cast was not particularly common at the time and Page's decision to include a quartet of black dancers in "Americans in Paris" proved to be a kind of precursor to the decision made by George Balanchine to invite the great African American *danseur* Arthur Mitchell to join the New York City Ballet in 1955. The color barriers that existed in professional dance companies and Major League Baseball were then being breached, thanks to enlightened and ethical women and men, like Page and Balanchine and Branch Rickey.

"Metropolitan Daily" (1938)[13]

Hanya Holm, another pioneer of modern dance, emigrated from Germany to the United States in 1931, where she remained, becoming one of the prime proponents of Americana in the world of dance. Indeed, Holm achieved fame as a choreographer for such memorable Broadway musicals as *Kiss Me Kate, Out of This World, Camelot,* and the musical discussed at length in chapter 2, *The Golden Apple.* Prior to her Broadway career, however, Hanya Holm created groundbreaking pieces of concert dance and, in 1938, just two years after Ruth Page's "Americans in Paris" (as well as Ted Shawn's "Olympiad"), Holm's wit, inventiveness, and interest in all things American were displayed with brilliance in "Metropolitan Daily." In essence, the piece is a newspaper brought to life—seven sections of a daily newspaper, from front-page headlines to the closing sports section, illustrated on stage by Holm's exuberant company of dancers.

Of course, it is in the concluding "Sports" section when the subject of baseball is addressed. In the original 1938 production, which debuted at the Bennington Festival in Bennington, Vermont (in the month of August), the dancers Louise Kloeper and Harriet Roeder performed the baseball variation, which, in and of itself, was startling. Baseball, after all, was considered to be a sport for men. The sight of Kloeper and Roeder expressing the beauty of pitching and hitting could not have failed to raise at least a few male eyebrows (while simultaneously delighting female members of the audience).

In any case, "Metropolitan Daily," like "Americans in Paris," proved to be a great success and, thanks to extensive touring, audiences throughout the United States were given an opportunity to watch Holm's dynamic company perform its ode to baseball. Moreover, as critic Ruth Franck commented in a review of the piece in the *Swarthmore Phoenix,* it "accomplished Miss Holm's purpose—to increase the number of admirers of the modern dance."[14] Hanya Holm's interest was in making dance more accessible without sacrificing any degree of quality or creative sophistication (a reason why she found it so easy to transition to the Broadway stage).

The interest in accessibility and making dance more popular was also demonstrated a year later, in 1939, when "Metropolitan Daily" became the first work of concert dance ever to be broadcast on television.[15] Visitors to the New York World's Fair on May 31, watching Holm's company enthusiastically perform "Metropolitan Daily," experienced Kloeper and Roeder executing choreographed baseball movements to an original American musical score (composed by Gregory Tucker)—all thanks to the National Broadcasting Company and the new technological "miracle" known as "live TV." It was an almost perfect blend of Americana, gender bending, arts expansion, and the promotion of the close relationship between baseball and dance. And, of course, it would be only the beginning of a long tradition of televised dance.

"Casey at the Bat" (1939)[16]

Two other early proponents and promoters of Americana in dance were Walter Camryn and Bentley Stone. From the 1920s through the 1950s, Camryn and Stone were associated closely with fellow Chicagoan Ruth Page, with whom they shared an intense interest in the stories of America and the everyday lives of its citizens. Camryn, Stone, and Page, in fact, danced and choreographed together with great frequency in the 1930s and '40s, even forming a dance company that was called, variously, the Page-Stone Ballet and Page-Stone-Camryn Ballet. Camryn and Stone also performed with and choreographed for Ruth Page's own company, while Page did the same for the Stone-Camryn Ballet. Like Page, Walter Camryn and Bentley Stone created dances with distinctly American themes, inspired by popular folk tales and songs, familiar poems, memories of childhood, and the American landscape, as well as the many inhabitants of the broad country they called home. Each also took traditional, European and non-Western dance ideas and infused them with an American sensibility, as if to show audiences how a genuine culture had evolved from the ancestral roots and cultures of America's immigrants. For example, a pre–World War II piece that Walter Camryn choreographed with Ruth Page, entitled "Valse," began with a Viennese waltz and concluded with a jazzy, all–American jitterbug.

In early 1939, Walter Camryn was invited by the Goodman Theater in Chicago to present a show of new works, and Camryn, wishing to present a range of styles and ideas, asked his good friend Bentley Stone to assist by creating a couple of dance pieces for the performance. Stone consented, and, in keeping with the interest that he and Camryn shared in the exploration and presentation of American themes, designed a funny and engaging solo for Camryn based on Ernest Thayer's exceedingly well-known baseball poem, "Casey at the Bat" (with original music by the Chicago-based composer Lora Aborn). The dance premiered on February 5, 1939, and was greeted with enthusiastic praise.[17] Camryn, in a baseball uniform, performed a winning rendition of a cocky slugger, strutting up to the plate with obvious zeal and self-confidence, ready to be the big hero, only to fall flat on his face and out of favor thanks to his monumental fanning at the game's pivotal moment. *Dance Magazine* called the piece "hilarious" and observed that the audience was clearly entertained.[18] Just three months later, when Camryn performed at the Chicago Dance Council's annual May festival (also held at the Goodman Theater), "Casey at the Bat" made a second appearance and, once again, the piece proved to be a genuine "crowd pleaser." The *Chicago Daily Tribune* declared Camryn's May 2nd performance of "Casey at the Bat" to be "as delightful as was Bentley Stone's choreography."[19]

Subsequently, "Casey at the Bat" was revived on many occasions, in many different venues, by an interesting assortment of soloists. Dance historian Ann Barzel (who filmed and documented many rehearsals and performances of works by Camryn, Page, and Stone), remarked that Stone's "Casey at the Bat" proved to be "enduringly popular,"[20] a testament to the choreographers' ability to interpret the poem in a manner that was true to the movements and spirit of the game. More than fifty years later, in 1990, the Casey story would be revisited and reinterpreted for the concert dance stage by Lisa de Ribere and the Pittsburgh Ballet Theatre; it is safe to say that new interpretations and renditions will appear in the coming years. Undoubtedly, Camryn and Stone, along with Ruth Page, would be pleased to know that the tale of the Mudville Nine has become, in many ways, as important for American choreographers and dance companies to explore as *Giselle, Don Quixote, Swan Lake, The Nutcracker*, and other French, Italian, Danish, German, and Russian concert dance classics.

On a side note, it is worth pointing out that Walter Camryn choreographed a piece in the 1940s that was given the title, "The Singing Yankees." In the context of dances that contain baseball themes and/or elements, the possibilities that such a title presents are quite thrilling. Unfortunately, the content of the dance bore absolutely no connection whatsoever to the world-famous New York baseball team. It is, however, a very entertaining image to contemplate!

"Sports Newsreel" (c. 1945)

Like Hanya Holm, Meta Krahn and Otto Ulbricht were skilled European modern dancers who, after embracing and then relocating to the United States, quickly became prime proponents and driving forces of the Americana movement in dance. Krahn and Ulbricht, both hailing from Switzerland, first experienced the United States as members of the Swiss-based Trudi Schoop Dance Company, also known as Trudi Schoop and Her Dancing Comedians. Talented and highly trained professionals, Schoop and her company rejected the excessive seriousness and remoteness of some newer dance forms and specialized, instead, in satire and humor, which many contemporary writers and spectators referred to as "exotic" or simply "comic" dance. In 1937, the Schoop troupe made its first appearance in America, which turned out to be a great success. Following the tour, however, Krahn and Ulbricht, a married couple whose gracefulness, speed, and incredible comedic sensibility and timing won many accolades all across the continent, made a decision to strike out on their own as a comedy dance team. They dubbed themselves "Mata and Hari," with Krahn taking on the stage name Ruth Mata and Ulbricht transforming himself into Eugene Hari.[21]

In just two short years, they were genuine theatrical stars, performing extended engagements in major theaters, either on their own or alongside some of the greatest artists of the day (including Imogene Coca, Jack Cole, Agnes deMille, Danny Kaye, and Jerome Robbins). The press adored them and the public flocked to their shows (which were "designed for the eye, ear and imagination") in droves.[22] Phrases and terms such as "high comedy at its best," "marvelous," and "incomparable" were used frequently and with accuracy in response to their madcap, but intelligent and beautifully executed, routines—routines that good-naturedly spoofed some of the most familiar and recognizable elements of American culture, such as Hollywood films, circuses, art galleries, classical music recitals, ballet concerts, and socializing on the street corner.[23]

One of the most beloved and frequently revived pieces presented by Mata and Hari was "Sports Newsreel," a lighthearted, playful, 1940s cousin of Holm's "Metropolitan Daily" (and perhaps even Shawn's "Olympiad"). Using pantomime, Mata and Hari re-created the images, structure, and pacing of the common cinema newsreel, complete with typical newsreel musical accompaniment, using the "gamut of popular competitive games" as their focal point.[24] One of the many "games" enacted in "Sports Newsreel" was baseball, enabling Mata and Hari to mimic the great batters and pitchers and fielders of the day and demonstrating to audiences from New York to Spokane that a home run swing, a double-play pivot, a race to steal second base, and the wind-up required to hurl an effective fastball all represent the "dance of the ball field." Said Mabel Watrous of the *Spokesman-Review*, "As creative artists in pantomime this duo is unchallenged."[25]

"Billy Sunday (or Giving the Devil His Due)" (1946/1948)[26]

The subject of baseball materialized once again in a work by Ruth Page in 1946. "Billy Sunday (or Giving the Devil His Due)" was based on the fire-and-brimstone evangelist who began his adult life as a professional baseball player. Following Sunday's eight-year career, playing for three different teams (including the 1883–1887 Cap Anson-led Chicago White Stockings) and stealing more than seventy bases in a single season on two separate occasions, the spiked baseball shoes and flannel uniform were replaced by a pulpit and a preacher's suit. Page found herself unable to resist exploring this expressly American tale in dance.

As Page revealed in a 1946 lecture, the idea for a ballet based on the life of Billy Sunday

germinated in the early 1940s, after she succeeded in reading the Bible "from cover to cover." Page believed that the stories of the Bible could be given an American twist and translated into a full-length dance piece if someone like Sunday—a popular, dramatic, controversial, and fascinatingly enigmatic figure—could be used as a focal point. Right away, Page considered Kurt Weill to be "the *ideal* composer" for the project and offered him the commission.[27] Unfortunately, according to Page, Weill declined, citing the fact that "he had just finished [Max] Reinhardt's *Eternal Road*" (an opera created with librettist Franz Werfel) and was not prepared just yet to plunge into another biblical-themed creation.[28] Apparently, writer John Latouche (librettist for *The Golden Apple*) was also approached as a potential collaborator, but could not sign on because of his service in World War II, which forced him overseas for more than two years.

Billy Sunday, Chicago White Stockings, 1887, Goodman & Company/Old Judge baseball card (Library of Congress Prints and Photographs Division).

"I know the fast pitches of the Devil!" Image from the earliest version of Ruth Page's concert dance piece, "Billy Sunday (or Giving the Devil His Due)," 1946.

Page then turned to Chicago-based composer Remi Gassmann, who had helped to create the successful "Composers Concert Series" at the University of Chicago, which "brought the creators of modern music to Chicago to talk of their own music before it was excellently played."[29] By 1946, an "extremely rough first draft" of "Billy Sunday" was ready to be shared with audiences and Page arranged for the work-in-progress to be staged at the University of Chicago's Mandel Hall. For the next two years, Page and Gassmann continued to craft and refine the piece and, after much revision, the completed "Billy Sunday" premiered at The City Center in New York on March 2, 1948, performed by the Ballet Russe de Monte Carlo, featuring a dynamic cast that included Frederic Franklin, Alexandra Danilova, and Ruthanna Boris.

Following the engagement at The City Center, which was received with a mixture of excitement and confusion (the piece contained subject matter and movement that was slightly unconventional, particularly in the world of ballet), Page and her own company, Les Ballets Americains, took "Billy Sunday" to Europe. Once again, audiences everywhere were stunned by the content and amazed by Ruth Page's skill as a choreographer and her ability to stage such a complex and ambitious work.

As far as the structure of the ballet was concerned, Page chose to incorporate dialogue and, as a result, the topic of baseball is expressed through both movement *and* sermon. Sunday, who was portrayed in the original production by Franklin, uses continuous baseball metaphors to rail against sin and the Devil. At one point, for example, Sunday winds up and throws in the manner of a pitcher as he exclaims, "I know the fast pitches of the Devil! Oh, he's quite a pitcher! Strictly Big League stuff. And it's amazin' the fellas he strikes out. Steee-rikes them out!" Page noted in her 1946 lecture that Sunday, in his barn-burning sermons, often compared the Devil to both a pitcher *and* a batter. Said Page, "Billy Sunday was always having terrific bouts with the Devil and his language was so graphic that the audience actually *visualized* 'Old Nick, Star Hitter of the Brimstones,' as Billy liked to call him."[30]

Towards the end of the work, a group of dancing devils is brought on, as the sounds of the song "Take Me Out to the Ball Game" can be heard in the background. The dancing devils are dressed in stylized baseball uniforms, colored a bright Devil red. And, at the very end, Sunday screams as the *corps* of dancers makes pitching motions, "So swing the bat of righteousness! Swing the bat of faith! Hit a home run and knock that Devil right out of the box!"

Interestingly, in 1983, the Cincinnati Ballet chose to revive "Billy Sunday," and the revival was captured on film—it

Billy Sunday in front of the White House, February 20, 1922 (Library of Congress Prints and Photographs Division).

was part of a television special, in fact, that was narrated, appropriately, by Johnny Bench, Hall of Fame catcher of the Cincinnati Reds. The special included a clip of Bench hitting a home run in game 5 of the 1972 National League Playoffs and features Bench describing the connections between baseball and dance. Bench also discusses the creation of "Billy Sunday" and what Ruth Page may have been thinking when she choreographed this baseball-infused work. "Taking the idea of one of Billy's sermons against temptation, Ruth Page made a ballet she felt was in Billy's style: vernacular, athletic, fast-paced, comic." And, it could be added, peppered with dance movement (according to Page, Sunday called himself "The Gymnast for Jesus" and drove home his sermon themes by not only climbing on furniture and standing on his head, but also doing dance steps as he displayed his own brand of baseball "choreography"). Once again a deliberate mix of elements and ideas that all point directly to the "four reasons" expressed earlier. And, without question, a stunning example of Americana.

"Rooms" (1955)

Anna Sokolow, who, like Helen Tamiris, received her introduction to dance and her earliest dance training at neighborhood settlement houses, was a major force in the modern dance world for many decades. During the 1930s, Sokolow, based in New York City, was associated with modern dance pioneer Martha Graham and then with Louis Horst of the Neighborhood Playhouse. Sokolow's skills as both a dancer and choreographer were honed at this stage and it was not long before she branched out, forming her own company, choreographing for Broadway (in the tradition of both Tamiris and Hanya Holm), and becoming a master teacher of both dance and drama. In the midst of all of this activity, Sokolow also contributed many pieces of choreography to the New Dance Group (NDG) of New York City, a dance and choreography collective that was formed, according to the NDG manifesto, for "the purpose of developing and creating group and mass dances expressive of the working class and its revolutionary upsurge."[31] It was, in other words, an organization devoted to promoting social change and celebrating the working people (and oppressed) of both America and the world through dance and "dance activism."

Among the works created by Sokolow for NDG was "Rooms," choreographed in 1955 to a commissioned score for jazz ensemble by noted American composer Kenyon Hopkins (best known in later years for such film scores as *Baby Doll* and *12 Angry Men*). "Rooms," conceived as a study of alienation and solidarity (or community), portrayed young members of American society in search of some kind of connection and identity, danced to a highly contemporary jazz score (the veritable "soundtrack" of a generation).[32] In the piece's opening segment, a young man in everyday clothing (casual windbreaker over a T-shirt and chino pants) performs a jagged, wrenching, "cool" but slightly awkward solo. Seeming as though he is struggling to figure out who he is and unable to perform any movement on his own with any consistency (which communicates a feeling of internal confusion and uncertainty), the young man "experiments" with an assortment of gestures and guises, possibly in an attempt to find the one that is right for him, which may reflect a nearly overwhelming mass of influences and impulses that cloud his mind and judgment. For a few seconds, there is a flurry of boxing jabs, as well as a brief mime of dribbling and shooting a basketball. Then, not once but multiple times, the young man runs and slides, an unmistakable baseball reference that expresses a desire to safely reach a destination that, at present, is unclear.

In somewhat different contexts, such choreographers as Dale Lee Niven and Peter Pucci would make use of this partially metaphorical image of the baseball slide in their own work in the latter part of the 20th century. Moreover, the idea of portraying the alienation and community of American youth and, at the same time, the culture and sensibility of modern America through a jazz dance ensemble piece (danced by young dancers clad in hip, contemporary street clothes) would be reflected in the very near future in the work of Jerome Robbins (in the Broadway musical *West Side Story* and the concert dance piece "New York Export: Opus Jazz"). The baseball movement in Sokolow's "Rooms" was limited, but the impact left by the inclusion of this movement was definite and long-lasting.

* * *

In the years following the works of Ruth Page, Hanya Holm, Mata and Hari, Bentley Stone, and Anna Sokolow—and, particularly, since "Billy Sunday" was revived by the Cincinnati Ballet in 1983—dance and baseball have been relatively familiar partners on the concert dance stage. In the next section, some of the most noteworthy examples of such works will be described briefly, proceeded in the next chapter by an examination of the remarkably large number of early 21st century baseball-themed and baseball-inspired concert dance works that have been created in the United States. What is strikingly clear is that the game of baseball continues to attract a wonderfully diverse set of choreographers and dancers—dance artists who come from every corner of the nation, representing and working with dance companies of all sizes, styles, backgrounds, and skill levels. Truly, to borrow a phrase used by Ruth Page as a title for a 1937 dance piece, an "American pattern."

Baseball-Themed and Baseball-Inspired Concert Dance

"The Real McCoy" ("The Blues" segment) (1974)[33]

Passionately interested in exploring American themes and the mythology of America, choreographer Eliot Feld, in the 1970s, had his eyes set firmly on populism and audience broadening. A piece entitled "Half-Time," for example, displayed drum majorettes and cheerleaders dancing to the marching band music of American composer Morton Gould. Not surprisingly, it was during this period—in 1974, to be precise—that Feld created "The Real McCoy," which featured a segment called "The Blues" that consisted of a ballroom dancing couple surrounded by a group of male dancers wearing straw hats and carrying canes. As the lush, soulful American songs of George Gershwin played in the background and the movie-image couple danced in the foreground, the group of male dancers could be observed using their canes like baseball bats, striking poses that certainly allude to the swing of a batter (the baseball uniform-like trousers they wear only serve to reinforce this allusion). It is, to be sure, a wholeheartedly American extravaganza, with iconic American music blended with iconic American movement, seasoned heavily with baseball.

"The Real McCoy," incidentally, premiered at Joseph Papp's Public Theater in New York City on December 1, 1974.

It is also worth noting that, in order to publicize his company and attract a wider audience, Feld, in the 1970s, produced "collector cards" (containing photos of his Feld Ballet dancers) that were distributed to the public by mail and by placement inside concert programs. It is hard to imagine that the popularity of baseball cards and the belief that his dancers were part of a genuine "team" did not influence Feld's decision to undertake such a marketing scheme. Recall, if you will, the famous words uttered by Lucy Van Pelt to pint-sized concert pianist Schroeder in the 1965 television cartoon special, "A Charlie Brown Christmas": "Beethoven wasn't so great…. He never got his picture on bubblegum cards, did he? … How can you say someone is great who's never had his picture on bubblegum cards?" By Lucy's standards, the Feld Ballet dancers rose to a level of greatness once their images and "stats" were stamped on small cardboard rectangles and shared with dance fans, albeit without the usual bubblegum.

Interestingly, this concept was repeated in 2007 and 2008 by Matthew Murphy on the online dance blog, *The Winger*. Murphy, a former dancer with the American Ballet Theatre (ABT), designed a series of "Dancer Trading Cards" for the blog, which served to call attention to a number of ABT's "rising stars," such as Blaine Hoven and Jacquelyn Reyes. With photos and snazzy graphics on the card face and personal statistics and anecdotes on the flip side, Murphy's cards were meant to resemble traditional baseball cards in every way. They could not, however, be purchased in candy stores—a computer with Internet access and a good printer were needed to create physical copies of Murphy's "collector set." Again, no free bubblegum, either.

"Womensports" (1976)[34]

In 1976, picking up on the approach introduced a half-century before by choreographers such as Hanya Holm and Helen Tamiris, Dianne Hulburt, a graduate of the Juilliard School, created "Womensports," an examination of the sporting world performed exclusively by female dancers (members of Hulburt's Workwith Dancers Company). Divided into five segments and executed by eight muscular, athletic women, "Womensports" included a lengthy component that focused entirely on baseball. Following the introduction of each dancer by an unseen announcer, in the manner of a baseball game (even going so far as to describe the group of performers as being part of "today's lineup"), Hulburt's baseball section is launched by way of the playing of an actual broadcast from a game between the New York Yankees and Kansas City Royals. As the broadcast continues to be heard, the dancers emerge in baseball caps and essentially present the audience with a choreographic soup of baseball movements that comes to a halt only when the inning being broadcast also reaches its climax.

Hulburt's piece, performed at the Jim May Studio in New York City, was captured on videotape on May 17, 1976, by videographers Eva Maier and Kate Parker. In later years, Hulburt became known as Dunya McPherson and introduced a Sufi-inspired style of dance called "Dancemeditation."

"Jocks 'n' Socks" (c. 1978–79)[35]

Like many of her fellow dancers and choreographers, Dale Lee Niven, a native of the Midwest, embarked upon a journey to the Pacific Northwest in the late 1970s in order to take advantage of a burgeoning dance scene and receive additional training from the magnetic master teacher Bill Evans (who had set up shop in Seattle after a number of years as a kind of "roving educator" in the United States). Two kindred spirits, Gail Heilbron and Jesse

Jaramillo, each followed similar paths (from Cleveland, Ohio, and Abilene, Texas, respectively) and wound up creating a new, Seattle-based modern dance "collective," which they called Co-Motion. When Niven arrived in Seattle, Co-Motion was just beginning to "take off" and Heilbron, Jaramillo, and company were busy formulating a full educational component of their own (complementing their performing wing). The core of Co-Motion's educational work involved school residencies and one-time lecture demonstrations, all of which necessitated the inclusion of entertaining and interactive dance works to engage, excite, and instruct student participants. Fortunately, both Heilbron and Jaramillo (who just happened to be a former Abilene High School baseball star) were choreographers as well as dancers, enabling them to create pieces that were suitable for classrooms as well as concert dance stages. Nevertheless, if a piece of choreography created by another member of the collective or by a non-Co-Motion dance maker could function well as an educational tool, particularly in relation to boys ("boy appeal" in education being all-important), Heilbron and Jaramillo were very much open to incorporating it into their educational program.

Niven, as it turns out, had just such a piece.

A mutual friend alerted Heilbron and Jaramillo, at the tail end of the 1970s, that Niven had choreographed a fun, lively, and genuinely participatory work, inspired by sports, called "Jocks 'n' Socks," and suggested that this work might be ideal for Co-Motion lecture demonstrations. Once Heilbron and Jaramillo had a chance to view "Jocks 'n' Socks" in action, they agreed wholeheartedly and received permission from Niven to add it to their educational repertoire. It remained a staple of Co-Motion school lecture demonstrations for more than five years and, in general, was featured as a closing number due to its unbounded energy and high level of accessibility.

Three sports were showcased in "Jocks 'n' Socks," including football and basketball. Baseball, however, provided "Jocks 'n' Socks" with its most memorable imagery—the safe slide into "home plate" at the very end of the dance. In the baseball section, five dancers were showcased, representing a pitcher, batter, catcher (doubling as umpire), and two fielders. Baseball-inspired costumes—baseball caps, along with baseball-flavored "Co-Motion" inscribed T-shirts—were worn, and high-octane, choreographed baseball movements (leaping, diving, swinging, throwing) were on full display. The purpose of the piece was as clear as the sound of a ball hitting the "sweet spot" of a Louisville Slugger: there is dance in sports and sports in dance. Young people attending a Co-Motion workshop and witnessing "Jocks 'n' Socks" were able to experience a pitcher's wind-up, a batter's follow-through, and an umpire's arms, hands, and fingers in a decidedly different light.

It is interesting to note that another dancer-educator, Patricia Hruby, also was making effective use of baseball in her dance teaching in the mid- to late 1970s. Hruby, co-founder of the One Plus One Dance-Music Theater of Champaign, Illinois, was hired by the Indiana Arts Commission as an artist-in-residence in 1976 and taught dance to students in two Indianapolis public schools. Her work, based on the theory that "everyone can move," was documented in a film called *In the Beginning*....[36] In the film, Hruby describes the importance of using familiar, everyday activities in her dance workshops to motivate and enlighten students. One such activity is baseball and the film captures a portion of Hruby's baseball-themed dance lessons, which include a pitch-catch-pitch-hit sequence. Hruby explains, "We've made phrases of the serial movements in baseball." Undoubtedly, Gail Heilbron, Jesse Jaramillo, and Dale Lee Niven would wholeheartedly support these efforts by Hruby, as would Theresa

M. Purcell (later Theresa Purcell Cone), who introduced a baseball dance "learning experience" in her book, *Teaching Children Dance*, in 1994.[37]

"Football" (1980)[38]

Christopher Chadman, whose work as both a dancer and choreographer is most familiar to Broadway audiences, presented a New York City concert workshop in 1980 that showcased a somewhat autobiographical piece which included movements taken from ballroom dance, football, and, as one may expect, baseball. At its core, Chadman's piece was a study of masculinity, sexual orientation, and the individual's wrenching struggle to reconcile the pressure to conform and be accepted with the inner need to follow a path that may lead to alienation and rejection (or worse) within one's peer group (and, possibly, one's own family). In other words, the struggle to be true to oneself. With baseball and football players representing accepted masculine pursuits (and, at the same time, heterosexuality) and ballroom dancers symbolizing the internal desire to move in a different direction, Chadman was able to demonstrate that both sides share much and that it is not merely possible for these two sides to co-exist, but also to enrich one another.

It should be mentioned that Chadman's baseball players, dressed in New York Yankees baseball jerseys and caps and carrying baseball bats, dance their steps to a disco beat, while the football players (clad in helmets and jerseys, toting footballs) perform their patterns to the drum roll of a marching band. Once again, decidedly American-style rhythms fueling a dance rooted firmly in American soil.

"Vortex: Life in America and Far Beyond" (1984)[39]

Another exploration of baseball movement, this time without any accompanying sound, was crafted by the mime performance group, Mime X Two, in 1984. Choreographed by Neil Intraub and Paul Rajeckas and presented at the Riverside Dance Festival's "Mime Choreo Showcase" in New York City's Riverside Church, "Vortex: Life in America and Far Beyond," in its baseball section, concerned itself with the drama of a single at-bat. A tobacco-chewing pitcher, a wily catcher, a forceful umpire, a determined batter, a skilled fielder, and a desperate runner are all involved. What makes this rendition especially remarkable, though, is the fact that all characters are portrayed by the same performing artist (Mr. Intraub) and a particularly effective sequence occurs when this performer lapses into slow motion to show the exquisite beauty of a pitch and a swing. Anna Kisselgoff of the *New York Times* observed that "body agility as well as facial expression" were "vital" to the work of Mime X Two,[40] a characteristic also apparent in the work of the aforementioned comic mime dancers, Mata and Hari, to whom Intraub and Rajeckas owe a great debt. Like Mata and Hari, Intraub and Rajeckas at the core, were dancers whose years of rigorous training equipped them with the technique, physical awareness, and discipline necessary to achieve a high level of success in the world of mime.

"Beyond the Bases" (1985)[41]

Pushing and bypassing boundaries, probing the relationship between that which is shared and that which is kept private or hidden, and delving into the complex and frequently murky realms of myth, ritual, dreams, fantasies, and memory are some of the paramount pursuits of choreographer Gail Conrad. Born in Brooklyn and raised in New Jersey by a show business family (her parents were ballroom dance entertainers), Conrad learned multiple dance forms in her youth and, from an early age, was interested in making use of the varied styles available to create something new and, in some ways, difficult to categorize. Still, in the 1970s and 1980s, Conrad was known primarily for her tap dance prowess, developed through years of training with legendary tap master, Charles "Cookie" Cook (of the equally legendary tap team the Copacetics). The name chosen for her dance troupe, the Gail Conrad Tap Dance Theater, reinforced this tap identity; yet, the addition of the word "theater" to the company name indicated that strict, "by the book" tap dance was not necessarily part of the program. Conrad was fully capable of performing and choreographing what may be termed "conventional" tap and tap routines; however, she was interested in broadening the conventional and using the all-important fundamentals as a foundation for, and stepping stone to, new and sometimes startlingly unconventional platforms. "Gail Conrad is a brave soul," wrote *New York Times* dance critic Jennifer Dunning in 1985, adding that Conrad was fully aware of the unwritten but almost universally observed "rules" of traditional tap dance choreography and performance (for example, utilizing "familiar" jazz and pop music), but did not allow these expectations and presumptions to dampen or inhibit her creative process.[42] "Miss Conrad," said Dunning, "breaks those rules."

Dunning's declaration was expressed in her review of a brand new dance work that Conrad and her Tap Dance Theater had just premiered at the Marymount Manhattan Theater in New York City. The work was entitled "Beyond the Bases," and, while the content of the piece was unconventional by tap standards, even the subject matter turned out to be quite surprising in terms of Conrad's output heretofore. "Beyond the Bases" was a dance about baseball. Or, more precisely, it was a piece of choreography that used baseball as a launching pad or backdrop for an artistic "meditation" on a wide range of complicated and thorny topics, including the collective versus the personal, the nature of friendship and bonding, hope and regret, reality and imagination, longing and despair, comfort and confusion, joy and pain, freedom and restraint, and the innocence and timelessness of youth versus the supreme consciousness and foreboding that may characterize adulthood. A tall order, to be sure. Yet, Conrad recognized that all of these elements, all of these dichotomies, also happened to be integral to the game and culture of baseball, making the sport a nearly perfect vehicle to employ in this artistic endeavor. Moreover, she

David Parker in Gail Conrad's "Between the Bases" (photograph © Johan Elbers, 2013).

appreciated the ritualistic details of the game—on-field and off—and the beauty not only of the more extreme, obviously dance-like movements, but also "in the quiet, in-between movements of the sport." Finally, she understood that baseball, for so many Americans, gives rise to a flood of feelings, associations, and images that, in some cases, may be expressed and shared in a communal setting or, in others, may remain the exclusive property of the individual. And, once more, that unique aspect of baseball, referred to by Conrad as "the physical and symbolic action of returning to home base," proved to be extraordinarily attractive to contemplate and include. Despite the fact that it was an unexpected subject in the minds of many of her critics and audience members, baseball as a centerpiece seemed to have it all for Gail Conrad.

The action of "Beyond the Bases" does have a "beginning, middle, and end" structure; however, Conrad has noted that she did not intend to present a "literal" story. Instead, the three sections of "Beyond the Bases" form a kind of "dream quilt," connecting the interior and exterior lives of three men meeting socially for a leisurely picnic. What was fascinating for Conrad was "how these three guys liked to hang out and fantasize and see themselves," all of which could be linked in some way to baseball. Conrad's choreographed tap steps could be explosive and complex or "stretched out" and sporadic, following the ebbs and flows and occasional open spaces of Ernest Provencher's original score, seeming, at times, almost like danced dialogue or, as Dunning points out, the soundtrack of dreams and deeply felt personal images.[43] The baseball fantasies grow as the piece progresses, with each man "raising the ante" of expression and delving further and further into his own interior world. At one point, a group of three shadowy, sneaker-clad women enter (described by Conrad as a "sort of enhanced vision of the men's minds"), adding another element to the overall sense of mystery and introspection. The women, who often appear to be "apparitions," float in and out of the scene, as the men continue to harvest their baseball-saturated memories. The picnic blanket becomes a baseball diamond and baseball bats materialize. Television-perfect, slow-motion movements are displayed as lights and music continually shift, accented by Conrad's off-kilter tap designs. Finally, in the piece's third section, a thunderstorm threatens to interrupt the action, but the three "players" keep right on playing. The fantasies are too strong for any delay or postponement. At this stage, according to Gail Conrad, neither rain nor thunder can destroy the game.

Following its run at Marymount Manhattan Theater in the winter of 1985, "Beyond the Bases" traveled to Germany and other parts of Europe, where it encountered receptive audiences. The piece also received praise from baseball fans, including one gentleman, recalled twenty-five years later by Conrad, who was especially impressed by the accuracy of the work's iconic gestures. For Conrad, the project was thoroughly enjoyable and satisfying. Furthermore, it reinforced the close connection between baseball and dance. To quote Conrad: "When I think of baseball, I think of the pauses and the silence between the action. So, for me, it has both.... It's very similar in that way to dance—the stillness and the action.... I think that you appreciate one from the counterpoint and contrast of the other.... That's the fun part—it's the contrast. The contrast in choreography of movement, of style or vision. All of that stuff is what gets one interested. That's what I imagine."

"The Baseball Dance" (1986)[44]

For most professional dancers, dance training and the setting of a professional dance goal begins at a very early age—quite often in the pre-teen years. For Louis Kavouras, who was named "Best Soloist in New York" by a panel of New York City dance critics in 1997, a possible dance career did not reveal itself until college. After entering Cleveland's Case Western Reserve University in 1984, Kavouras, a native Floridian and longtime baseball fan and practitioner, decided to take a few dance classes and, just about instantly, became hooked. Kavouras then changed his major from engineering to dance and started preparing himself for a radically different life. In 1986, Kavouras took a choreography class and was given an assignment to create a work based on principles discussed in class. Kavouras drew from what he knew best, which was baseball, and designed a solo based on the movements of a pitcher. The three-to-four- minute piece was greeted with praise and Kavouras was asked to demonstrate the work on many subsequent occasions over the next two years by fellow students and faculty members.

Then, in 1988, as Kavouras was working towards his MFA in dance at Case Western (he received his bachelor's degree in 1987), he decided that the time had come to expand his solo, which had become known as "The Baseball Dance." Kavouras spent the summer of 1988 attending Cleveland Indians games and watching as much baseball as possible on television, noting and recording the quirks and commonalities of the players and absorbing all elements of the baseball game atmosphere. When he resumed work on "The Baseball Dance," a batter was added, as well as a catcher and three fielders, six characters in all, and new variations were choreographed, extending the piece to nearly twenty minutes. Kavouras also added music, reasoning that "twenty minutes of silence was just too much." An audio engineer was brought on board and both he and Kavouras recorded an assortment of sounds, such as the crack of a bat hitting a ball, a thrown ball smacking into a glove, and footsteps shuffling in the dirt. These sounds were spliced in and used to accent the dance. Some ballpark-style organ rolls (featuring occasional riffs lifted from "Take Me Out to the Ball Game") also were tossed in, along with portions of "The Blue Danube" waltz and snippets from Beethoven. By February 1989, the revised and expanded version of "The Baseball Dance" was performance-ready and Kavouras staged the piece at Case Western, to much acclaim.

Since the premiere of "The Baseball Dance" in its longer form, the work has been danced "on many stages ... before many audiences, even one in Russia." As Barbara Cloud points out in *UNLV Magazine*, "The Baseball Dance" has "become part of the repertory of dance companies in several [U.S.] cities"[45] and Kavouras has staged the work using not only professional dancers and dance students, but also athletes and physical education majors (reminiscent of the approach used by the great dancer, dance ambassador, and high school baseball letterman Edward Villella). In fact, "The Baseball Dance" is one of the few pieces of baseball-themed concert dance choreography ever to be performed inside an actual Major League Baseball stadium. In 1995, at the recently unveiled Jacobs Field in Cleveland (which became Progressive Field in 2008), the Cleveland Repertory Dance Project was added to the lineup of opening day, pre-game performers and, in honor of this very special occasion, showcased "The Baseball Dance." Undoubtedly, Kavouras, whose father had dreams of seeing his son play big league baseball someday,[46] must have been overjoyed and quite proud.

It also should be noted that, in 1996, Louis Kavouras became a principal dancer and soloist for the Erick Hawkins Dance Company and a faculty member of the Erick Hawkins School of Dance. Kavouras also danced in the company of another sports-inspired choreographer, Peter Pucci, and joined the faculty of the University of Nevada at Las Vegas (UNLV) in 1992. In 1994, Kavouras was named UNLV dance department chair. He has created more than fifty dance works since the first iteration of "The Baseball Dance" and his choreography has been performed throughout the world, from Canada to China. Kavouras's own company, Joe's Universe, was launched in 1999.

Clarence Teeters and Dancers/ American Dance Festival (1986)[47]

Teeters, a choreographer and dancer who has worked with numerous companies and performers throughout the United States and who has used American jazz and soul music to drive his creations, contributed a piece to Duke University's American Dance Festival in 1986 which incorporated excerpts from an actual Major League Baseball game broadcast (complete with beer and dog food commercials) into the soundtrack. As audience members listened to an announcer describe a base hit by Harry Spilman and a subsequent error by Ken Griffey, Sr., they watched the student dancers on stage present what seemed to be the scene of an exercise or dance class veering rapidly into chaos, disturbed, perhaps, by the excitement of the game.

"Scarecrow" (1989)[48]

Henry Yu is considered to be "the founder of modern dance in Taiwan" and is recognized in his native country as "the first local dancer to leap onto the international stage."[49] After studying dance in Taiwan in the 1950s and '60s, Yu departed for Spain in 1968 in order to study classical ballet. In 1970, he continued on his educational journey and settled in New York City, where he joined the Eleo Pomare Dance Company. Then, in 1974, Yu was invited to dance with Martha Graham's company and, after accepting the invitation, remained a Graham dancer until 1982, at which time he returned to Taiwan to start his own dance ensemble.[50]

Accordingly, although Yu's baseball-infused work, "Scarecrow," was created in 1989 for his Taiwanese troupe of dancers, it is included in this section because of his extensive American influences and experience. Yu's unique style blends Taiwanese, Chinese, and Western forms and many of his choreographic themes, including "Scarecrow," are saturated with Western flavors and sounds. "Scarecrow," in fact, features the music of Leo Delibes and Yeh Chi-Tien, in addition to a Chinese-language baseball game broadcast.

In truth, Yu's work is an exaltation of baseball from beginning to end. Nine dancers, a perfect number by baseball standards, dressed in costumes that closely resemble baseball uniforms, execute balletic baseball movements to the heavenly melodies of Delibes's "Coppelia," followed by segments of a baseball game broadcast, leading to a dynamic exhibition of baseball choreography that may be viewed as almost "cubist" in nature: each dancer, representing a different player on or off the field (a relief pitcher, for example), carries out movements that demonstrate what that particular player would be doing, from all angles, at a given point in the game. There is a seventh-inning stretch embellished with Taiwanese music and a climax that marks the ecstatic return of the nine whirling performers, powerfully reprising their steps, one by one, until the "game" is finally over and a single dancer is lifted in the air by his eight celebratory teammates, who raise their arms in victory as the lights go down. Yu's work, like Yu himself, turns out to be a smooth, ornate bridge between East and West and there is no question that "Scarecrow" would be appreciated by followers of dance or baseball in Taipei or Toledo.

A videotape of "Scarecrow," recorded on December 12, 1989, at Taipei's National Theatre, is available for viewing at the Jerome Robbins Dance Division of the New York Public Library for the Performing Arts.

"The Mighty Casey" (1990)[51]

As a member of the New York City Ballet in the 1970s and the American Ballet Theatre from the late 1970s through the mid–1980s, Lisa de Ribere had the astounding good fortune of being able to work directly with choreographic icons George Balanchine and Jerome Robbins, as well as the world-renowned *danseur* and dance-maker Mikhail Baryshnikov—experiences that not only benefited de Ribere's work as a dancer but also helped to influence her decision to become a choreographer. After retiring from performing in 1984, de Ribere devoted herself to creating dance and, because of the lyricism and strong musicality (as well as accessibility) of her choreographic work, many companies in the United States and abroad began clamoring for her services. One such company was the Pittsburgh Ballet Theatre (PBT), the same company that made a strong connection at almost the same time with former American Ballet Theatre principal dancer (and baseball fanatic) Marianna Tcherkassky. In 1988, by which time de Ribere already had done "a couple of works" for PBT, the PBT administration approached her about creating a new, evening-length story ballet, with children's appeal. At a meeting shortly after the offer was made, a number of suggested ideas were discussed (including something related to the Marvel Comics superhero Spider Man and a ballet with a *Star Wars* theme). De Ribere was not overly excited about most of the suggestions; however, one idea did appeal to her: a ballet based on the poem, "Casey at the Bat." She excitedly responded, "Wait a minute! I think I can probably do something with that!"

Realizing that there needed to be more than a straightforward retelling of the events laid out in Ernest Thayer's classic baseball poem, de Ribere hunted for something that would provide the well-known story with a bit of a twist and, at the same time, allow for a few storytelling liberties here and there. Once she discovered Martin Gardner's anthology of Casey-related poems, *The Annotated* Casey at the Bat: *A Collection of Ballads about the Mighty Casey*, the pieces started falling into place. In particular, a poem written and published in 1908, to commemorate the twentieth anniversary of Thayer's landmark effort, provided a wealth of inspiration. The author of the poem was Clarence P. (or C. P.) McDonald and the poem itself, originally published in the *San Francisco Examiner*, possessed two titles: "The Volunteer" (which was its title on July 26, 1908, when the *Examiner* shared it with newspaper readers) and "Casey—Twenty Years Later." It would be possible, in de Ribere's mind, to choreograph a two-part story, with a joyful ending, allowing Casey to redeem himself in later life (thereby honoring the original story, as well as the aforementioned approaches of Bentley Stone and William Schuman, but taking things one intriguing step further).

The new story, as crafted by Lisa de Ribere, would begin in 1908, with Casey—now twenty years older and married to his sweetheart, Betsy—attending (as a spectator) a big baseball game between hometown Bugville (no longer Mudville) and the familiar arch-rival team, The Other Nine. It is the bottom of the ninth inning and, with Bugville behind and in need of a couple of runs to win the game, an injury to a player and an absence of any additional team members leaves the team one man short. In search of a suitable replacement, Casey comes out of the grandstands, is handed a Bugville cap and a bat, and steps up to the plate as a pinch hitter. With the drama unfolding, the action shifts backwards in time to Mudville in 1888. Yet, with cleverness and great effect, de Ribere does not immediately confront us with the legendary game described in Thayer's poem. Instead, we watch a different game between Mudville and The Other Nine, one of which occurred a few days before. In this game, we are able to see Casey in all of his splendor—the true "Mighty Casey," who could strike fear in the hearts of opposing teams and whose fearsome bat could send pitched balls soaring into the distant bleachers and beyond. In essence, de Ribere provides us with a powerful prologue—a fascinating way to make the portrait of Casey even more complete and the legend of Casey's remarkable prowess even more believable.

Following this excursion, the action shifts again and we are transported to Mudville "a few days later," when Thayer's "big game" is taking place. The basic storyline is the same; however, the famous third strike does not complete the tale. In de Ribere's version, there is a fourth scene (and, in effect, a "second act"), in which Casey is able to have another chance to deliver a winning clout and, this time, Casey does connect. There may not have been joy in Mudville, but there is plenty to celebrate in Bugville.

Lisa de Ribere's new balletic telling of the Casey story was titled "The Mighty Casey," and had its premiere at the Benedum Centre in Pittsburgh on October 6, 1990. As she was developing the piece, de Ribere devoted herself to the intricate study of baseball players and games, carefully observing and noting activities on and off the field. She also understood that her dancers needed to look and perform like real baseball players; this led her to reach out to the Pittsburgh Pirates and ask if a member of the team could assist with baseball training. "I wanted to have somebody come and work with [the dancers] because I wanted [the dancers] to get really authentic movement," said de Ribere in an interview with Bill Geist on CBS-television's *Sunday Morning* in 1991.[52] The Pirates responded by sending over first base coach (and former player) Tommy Sandt, who worked wonders with the dancers, some of whom already possessed baseball knowledge and considered themselves fans (such as PBT's Brian Bloomquist, the original Casey in de Ribere's new production) and some of whom had neither witnessed a baseball game, nor picked up either a bat, ball, or glove in their entire lives.

When the show opened, the dancers were well prepared in every way and, thanks to de Ribere's creativity, numerous parts existed for both men and women in the PBT company. It turned out to be a lavish production, with period costumes (including stunning turn-of-the-20th-century baseball uniforms) and sets. The music, from start to finish, was purely American. Michael Moricz, the PBT Orchestra conductor, composed an original score that revealed traces of Aaron Copland, as well as popular folk tunes, parlor songs, and music hall numbers. Moricz also opted to incorporate familiar pieces by John Philip Sousa and Stephen Foster, including "Beautiful Dreamer," which served as the theme for Casey and Betsy. Additionally, "Take Me Out to the Ball Game" made a grand appearance as a sing-along following the final curtain call.

Lisa de Ribere's choreography also provided the audience with a true taste of Americana. Ballet steps were blended with folk and ballroom dances, as well as comic gestures and, of course, a veritable country picnic of baseball movements, many of which made use of bats, balls, gloves, and the umpire's brush as props. Fans and sweethearts were fully integrated into the on-stage action and there were appearances by food vendors, policemen, and a barbershop quartet (providing musical narration, complete with harmonized lines from Thayer's poem, to the tune of "Oh! Susanna"). Beginning with ballpark food being hawked in the theater and a rousing "Play ball!" shouted by a baseball cap-wearing Moricz from the orchestra pit through the final strains of "Take Me Out to the Ball Game," this new version of "The Mighty Casey" managed to present audiences with a total package of baseball and dance.[53] Geist, in his news report, remarked, "They're not doing 'The Wave' yet at the ballet—but just about!"

"The Mighty Casey" has been revived repeatedly over the years, in Pittsburgh and in cities and towns throughout North America. At various times, professional baseball players, such as pitchers Kent Tekulve and Tug McGraw, joined the cast (generally in the non-dancing role of the Mudville coach) and, on many occasions, professional players have attended performances and made themselves available to sign autographs at the end of the show. As one may imagine, de Ribere's baseball-centric work also has proven to be a fabulous education and outreach tool for PBT and all other companies that have chosen to stage "The Mighty Casey." Clearly, Lisa de Ribere knew precisely what she was doing when she said "yes" to the idea of creating a ballet based on "Casey at the Bat." "I'm a choreographer," said de Ribere, "so movement is really important to me" and the fact of the matter is that "there are a lot of similar movements" in baseball and ballet.[54] The idea, therefore, of combining these two extraordinary disciplines, according to de Ribere, was "a natural."

"Bat Habits" (1992) and "Baseball" (1994)[55]

The phenomenon of recruiting new audiences to the world of concert dance through baseball may be observed vividly and with powerful effect by considering the contributions of choreographer Moses Pendleton, whose passion for baseball was described in the opening passages of this book. Pendleton, a Red Sox rooter and former Little League and Pony League player, has claimed that his dance troupe, Momix, was established essentially to turn "people who don't normally go to dance" shows into dance supporters and even dancers. For Pendleton, expanding dance audiences and making concert dance more accessible is a primary motivating factor.

Yet, even with the notion of accessibility lurking constantly in the background (or at the core), what drove Pendleton (as well as Chris Black, as we shall see in the forthcoming chapter) to warmly embrace baseball as a theme was something more complex and, at the same time, even more elemental. In essence, it was baseball's beauty, and it was baseball's intimate connection to American culture, and it was also baseball's symbolic and simultaneously ritualistic nature. Insofar as being a good subject for dance, Pendleton—like Louis Kavouras and Gail Conrad, Lisa de Ribere and Christopher Fleming, Chris Black and Ana Maria Maynard—believed baseball to be just about perfect.

Choreographed for Momix in 1994, "Baseball," in actuality, evolved from a shorter piece, called "Bat Habits," that Pendleton created in 1992.[56] Working with Momix in Scottsdale, Arizona, during the time that the Smithsonian Institution's traveling baseball exhibition, "Diamonds Are Forever," was on display at the Scottsdale Center for the Arts, Pendleton received permission from the San Francisco Giants, who were in the midst of spring training, to have his dancers train with the baseball team. Soon, "Bat Habits" was born and, subsequently, many members of the Giants—often encouraged by then-batting coach Dusty

Baker—attended performances of Pendleton's piece at the Center for the Arts, following an exhibition game or a day of workouts and practice. For many players, it was their very first experience with concert dance. (Baker, who has become a highly successful and respected major league manager, has been known to recommend ballet lessons to players in need of becoming more limber.)

The success and pleasure that resulted from this relatively modest effort then inspired Pendleton to envision something much more expansive—and much wilder. He began to construct an evening-length work that would trace the origins of baseball to primitive times ("In the beginning, it was

Moses Pendleton's "Baseball," performed by MOMIX (used with permission from the photographer, John Kane, and Momix).

just a game") and feature living, breathing baseball gloves, rolling human baseballs, and spinning beer cans with arms and legs. He imagined a pulsating soundtrack, splattered with American funk and rally chants and advertising jingles and the familiar voice of Casey Stengel. A true baseball spectacular, joyfully casting a panoramic view on the real and the fantastic, all the while expressing a sincere love of Pendleton's own favorite sport.

Eventually, of course, "Baseball" did emerge and, much to the delight of Moses Pendleton, succeeded in attracting more than simply a few fans and players. The fact that the premiere of "Baseball" in 1994 (at the Joyce Theater in New York City) happened to coincide with the infamous 1994–95 Major League Baseball strike only served to enhance interest in Pendleton's labor of love and he made sure that the public's sense of uncertainty about baseball's future was reflected on some level in the work. It was a case of odd but fortunate timing and, as Pendleton has said, while "people were wondering if they should follow baseball at all," his own piece served to provide fans with an opportunity to "re-think, re-new, re-see ... something

Promotional photograph for "Baseball," choreographed by Moses Pendleton and performed by MOMIX (used with permission from the photographer, John Kane, and Momix).

that's gone a bit awry, a bit stale, gone a bit corrupt, lost some kind of perspective."[57] "Baseball" proved to be a kind of elixir, as well as a torch that, for many, helped to re-kindle an old passion and, for many more, ignite a new appreciation for a hitherto unknown art form.

Once the 1994–95 strike ended, Pendleton modified a few images to correspond to the overall shift in public sentiment about the future of the game and, since its premiere, "Baseball" has been staged all over the world, including a two-week run in Rome, Italy, that played to nearly sold-out houses every night.[58] While on tour, one especially memorable moment occurred in Toronto, when Pendleton was invited to throw out the first pitch at the Skydome, before a game between the hometown Blue Jays and their cross-border rivals, the Cleveland Indians. With fifty-thousand fans in attendance, Pendleton took the mound, executed a graceful wind-up, and fired "some high heat" at the catcher's mitt. Unfortunately, the ball did not reach its desired destination. Instead, it veered about twelve to fifteen feet wide, in the direction of the Indians' dugout, and came close to colliding with slugger Albert Belle, who happened to be standing on the field. According to Pendleton, "The guy who was catching ran and made a diving catch and he got a big cheer out of that." The pitching skills that Pendleton honed as a boy in Vermont may have been compromised by nerves, but the exciting play that transpired, in the words of Pendleton fifteen years after the fact, was "a thrill anyway for me." Leave it to Moses Pendleton to give a major league catcher a chance to demonstrate some improvised dance moves right on the baseball field, in front of a sell-out crowd.

"Out of Season (The Athletes Project)" and "Out of Season, or Eating Pizza While Watching *Raging Bull*" (1993)[59]

From the 1960s through the 1980s, the number of male athletes who got converted to the dance profession after taking a single dance or movement class in college (often their first experience with formal dance instruction) is, quite frankly, staggering. Even more astonishing is the fact that a large percentage of these baseball players-turned-dancers went on to form their own—largely successful—dance companies. In this chapter, we have already met three members of this extraordinary group: Jesse Jaramillo, Louis Kavouras, and Moses Pendleton. Peter Pucci, another dancing ball player, was introduced in the previous chapter and will make a follow-up appearance in the coming pages.

One more name to add to this esteemed circle is David Dorfman. After winning letters in both football and baseball at Niles West High School in Skokie, Illinois, Dorfman entered Washington University in St. Louis with the intention of earning a degree in business.[60] At one point during his tenure as an undergraduate, Dorfman took a leave of absence and returned to the Chicago area, where he decided to enroll in a dance class—his first—at the University of Illinois. Like Pendleton, Kavouras, Jaramillo, and Pucci, the experience was transformational and Dorfman was hooked. He did return to Washington University, got his business degree, and, following graduation, even took a job as an assistant manager at Saks Fifth Avenue in Chicago.[61] However, the "dance bug" proved to be much too powerful and, within two years, Dorfman's career path had switched entirely.

By 1985, Dorfman had his own company, David Dorfman Dance, and was committed to making dance not only universally accessible but also *achievable*, as well as desirable as an activity and a source of pleasure and expression for "everyday people."[62] Being a man with a "non-traditional" (i.e., stocky and thick) dance body and coming from a blue-collar back-ground, in which dance was basically non-existent, Dorfman was sensitive to the need for dance to find ways to attract a broader audience and encourage diversity in all forms. At the core of his dance credo is the notion that dance is not something reserved for a coterie of technically superior, predominantly young beings, whose physiques conform to a set of stan-dards unattainable by most people of any age. As Suzanne Carbonneau explains, "In insisting on the pleasures of watching seemingly ordinary people dance, Dorfman does much to dispel the notion that there is some kind of ideal, or that there is only one way to look and be."[63] Even more revealing is the title of an article about Dorfman composed in 1997 by *New York Times* critic, William Harris: "An Eccentric Who Likes to Make Things Accessible."

In 1993, David Dorfman put this idea of "dancing for all" into genuine practice by embark-ing upon a series of "projects made for people with no previous dance experience."[64] The first of these projects drew directly from Dorfman's early life, which was affected substantially by athletics and athletic training. The project, fittingly, was called "Out of Season" and Dorfman decided to approach the work in two ways, both of which were realized on the concert dance stage in entirely different but steadfastly related forms. Each of the two versions, one a solo and one a collaborative group piece, appeared almost simultaneously in early 1993. The solo was given the title, "Out of Season, or Eating Pizza While Watching *Raging Bull*," while the name of the group work served to hammer home the sports link: "Out of Season (The Athletes Project)." Baseball proved to be a major source of inspiration in both cases.

In the solo piece, Dorfman uses visual and verbal humor (movement is carried out while Dorfman recites a slightly off-kilter monologue) to raise questions about and explore such topics as fear, personal choices, sexuality, and the relationship between the performer and his or her audience (both general spectators and media critics). There is plenty of parody (particularly of "confessional performance art," as Lewis Segal of the *Los Angeles Times* pointed out) and, at the same time, an almost overpowering sense of concern about the perils of the external world.[65] When Dorfman enters, he is forced to step over the body of a man lying on the floor. We then encounter a performer who is decked out, head to toe, in protective athletic attire—attire referred to quite astutely by Miriam Seidel of the *Philadelphia Inquirer* as a kind of "jock exoskeleton."[66] On Dorfman's head is a vintage, early 20th century football helmet, matched by a set of exposed shoulder pads, a baseball catcher's shin guard on his left leg, a batting glove on his left hand, and two baseball helmets dangling from his waist. After announcing that he is Superman through an on-stage microphone, the lights go off and on, revealing a figure weighed down with even more external protection, including a standard baseball umpire's chest protector. Dorfman is then pelted by ping pong balls (flung in unison by audience members and Dorfman's own musical director), which forces him to use the chest protector as a shield. When the balls cease flying, Dorfman resumes his monologue, ruminating on a wide range of topics and shifting his body into poses that resemble a catcher squatting behind home plate and an infielder stretching for a ground ball.

Clearly, there are numerous possible interpretations to be had. Considering that the piece was created and produced in the midst of the AIDS crisis and that Dorfman only recently had choreographed two works that referred to AIDS in a much more direct way (1987's "Sleep Story" and "Dayenu" from 1992), it is possible to assert that the solo version of "Out of Sea-son" was influenced by the obsession with protection and the fear of infection and death that had become all too rampant in American society (especially in the arts community). At the same time, the obsession with protection could relate to human interaction in general and the fear of being damaged by others (including dance critics and spectators), either physically, emotionally, or psychologically. Along the same lines, the self-equation with Superman may refer to the widely held belief in or perception of athletes (and, not uncommonly, dancers) as "super human." The Superman persona also could relate to masculinity and the sense of invulnerability and power present in many male minds. Whatever the case may be, Dorfman's solo version of "Out of Season"—with its many sports images, references, and clothing accessories—uses sight gags, bizarre humor, and a combination of movements designed to be both familiar and startling to command the attention and motivate analysis.

The "collective" variation, "Out of Season (The Athletes Project)," had its debut at the Flynn Theatre in Burlington, Vermont, in January 1993,[67] and was created by Dorfman for the express purpose of "blur[ring] the lines between sports and dance and challeng[ing] the audience's perceptions of who shall and shall not dance on stage."[68] Dorfman spent November 1992 recruiting athletes of all ages and specialties (and, for the most part, with no prior dance experience) from the Burlington area (he actually posted advertisements throughout the city which read "WANTED: Athletes") and, once the recruiting was completed, devoted three full weeks ("three hours a day, six days a week") to providing intense dance training and developing a brand new dance work with the full collaboration of all participating athlete-dancers.[69] The result was something totally unique, thoroughly unconventional, utterly breathtaking, deeply moving, and, according to Elizabeth Zimmer of the *Village Voice*, actually "important to American life" and even "mythic."[70] The piece was groundbreaking enough to inspire a lengthy, glowing review in *Sports Illustrated* (an achievement shared with Lisa de Ribere's "The Mighty Casey" and Moses Pendleton's "Baseball"[71]) and prompted David Dorfman himself to declare it a "macrocosm of my artistic desires," citing it as a project that was "central to his creative vision" of "rawness and inclusiveness," honesty, "unfettered" performing, and the challenging of stereotypes and preconceptions.[72]

"Out of Season (The Athletes Project)" was restaged repeatedly in the subsequent fifteen months (in Helena, Montana; New York City; Lincoln and Omaha, Nebraska; Chicago; and St. Louis). On each occasion, the same process was followed: recruitment of local athletes, three weeks of intense training, development of brand new choreography based on "the experiences the different athletes [brought] to each residency," and a series of mind-blowing shows.[73] In the *Sports Illustrated* article, Dorfman is quoted as saying, "Athletes and dancers have so much in common…. Yet you always have athletes calling dancers fairies and dancers calling athletes Neanderthals."[74] In Dorfman's eyes, his own responsibility as a dancer with "one foot planted on the playing field" is to "bring the two camps together."[75] In other words, make it abundantly clear to all that dance and a sport such as baseball are much more similar than they are at odds with one another—and that the dancer and the ballplayer, in reality, are splashes of differently hued paints on a single canvas applied by a common brush.

Dorfman's ensemble piece for athletes continues to receive commissions from cities, towns, and arts centers throughout North America. Notably, in the summer of 1997, the work was brought to Jacob's Pillow, site of the famous Massachusetts dance festival. When the call went out for volunteer athletes, one of the responders turned out to be Jim Bouton, author of *Ball Four* and former pitcher for the New York Yankees, Seattle Pilots, and Houston Astros.[76] Though Bouton was fifty-eight years of age at the time of the production, he was welcomed enthusiastically by Dorfman and contributed mightily to the choreography. His years of baseball experience and understanding of the physical and mental requirements of the professional athlete, as well as his sharp wit, multilayered sense of humor, and respect for both dance and dancers were invaluable. When asked by *Hartford Courant* reporter Frank Rizzo about his approach to becoming proficient on the dance floor, especially given his somewhat advanced age and lack of previous dance training, Bouton offered an eloquent response: "To me, [dance] is a different kind of sport…. You're trying to get your body to do something that it doesn't know how to do, and then, when you figure out the right way to do it, learn how to repeat the action successfully. Once you've learned how to do it on a technical level, you then need to release the technical approach and then do it instinctively. That's when you have a really good art or athletic performance."[77] By applying the lessons of baseball to his newly adopted "sport" of dance, Bouton was confident that he could meet the challenge and, "win or lose," deliver a performance of which he could be proud.

Jackie Robinson Tribute/Jackie Robinson School Tap Dancers (1997)

The year 1997 marked the fiftieth anniversary of Jackie Robinson's 1947 debut with the Brooklyn Dodgers. In order to celebrate this historic event, the New York City borough of Brooklyn declared May 21, 1997, to be "Jackie Robinson Day" and a special Jackie Robinson Day Committee was created by Brooklyn Borough President Howard Golden to help plan the day's schedule of events. In addition to a "gala parade," a commemorative exhibition at Brooklyn Borough Hall, and a guest appearance by Jackie Robinson's widow, Rachel Robinson, the Jackie Robinson Day Committee enlisted Vernetta Johnson, a teacher at Jackie Robinson Intermediate School 320 and director of the Jackie Robinson School Tap Dancers, to work with her students on a dance tribute to the groundbreaking Dodgers star.[78] The result was a joyful and moving performance of tap dance artistry that added spark, light, and grace to an already-festive day. The event, held on the plaza in front of Borough Hall, also was attended by Joe Torre,[79] current manager of the New York Yankees and a Brooklyn native, who likely recognized the similarities between the skillful footwork of the young tappers and that which could be seen on a regular basis on the field of Yankee Stadium, displayed by such lithe and elegant players as Derek Jeter and Bernie Williams.

"Pucci: Sport (Baseball Section)" (1999)[80]

Baseball has played a major role in the life of choreographer Peter Pucci since he was a child in Baltimore, listening to Orioles games on the radio and cheering for favorite players like Brooks and Frank Robinson at Memorial Stadium (sometimes sneaking into the park during the late innings of a game). As mentioned earlier in the chapter, Pucci, while in college, also became a member of the surprisingly large "club" of athletes whose career paths shifted dramatically after deciding (or, in Pucci's case, being forced) to take a dance class as an undergraduate. A physical education major, Pucci was required to enroll in a modern dance class (called "Rhythmic Analysis") and—like Moses Pendleton, Louis Kavouras, and David Dorfman—quickly became intrigued enough to want more. Soon, he found himself in the university dance company and, not long after that, was rapidly honing his skills in the intensive dance training programs offered by the Dallas Ballet Academy and the North Carolina School of the Arts. Once he was in his mid-twenties, Pucci departed North Carolina and headed for the mecca of modern dance, New York City (carrying "fifty bucks and a duffel bag"). In fairly short order, Pucci found a job with the eclectic and athletic modern dance company Pilobolus (whose membership still included Moses Pendleton) and, in 1980, the professional dance career of Peter Pucci was underway. With Pilobolus, Pucci would have ample opportunities to exercise and expand his abilities as a dancer. Additionally, he would have a chance to explore a related area for which he was beginning to develop a passion: choreography.

In 1986, while still a member of Pilobolus, Pucci, who had been performing solo works in New York City since 1981, decided to start his own company, which would enable him to showcase his own work and delve into new styles and dance forms. Pucci and Pilobolus then parted ways permanently in 1989 and Pucci's troupe became a major force in the world of modern dance. By the mid–1990s, Peter Pucci Plus was performing in sold-out venues all over the world and Pucci's work was being commissioned and borrowed by numerous outside dance companies (and, as we have seen in the previous chapter, even theatrical producers began to take notice and seek collaboration). Pucci, for his part, continued to find inspiration everywhere and maintained a powerful interest in making dance more accessible to the general public, both in terms of subject matter and location. Accordingly, it was inevitable, considering Pucci's sports background, that Pucci would wind up setting his creative sights at some point on athletes, athletics, and athletic arenas.

By 1997, the "athletic spark" ignited and Pucci began work on a basketball-related piece called "Basketball Jones," inspired by a Bill Cosby comedy routine. By 1998, the work was completed and, after a robustly lauded premiere run at the New Victory Theatre on New York's 42nd Street,[81] Pucci began to envision a full evening of sports-based dance, which could serve as a multipurpose "vehicle for outreach, dance education, and just plain fun."[82] Pucci—in the tradition of Hanya Holm, Ted Shawn, Mata and Hari, Dianne Hulburt, and Dale Lee Niven—imagined a series of dances highlighting the physical artistry present in a multiplicity of athletic pastimes, with each segment choreographed to a different, carefully matched piece of music and a fair helping of humor added for good measure. He also was determined to avoid neglecting the "wow factor": it would be important for the various segments to show off both the athletic prowess of dancers and the extraordinary grace and aesthetic beauty of the sports player. As Pucci's own website expresses, Pucci was seeking to create a work that would serve as "[a] showcase for professional dancers and athletes, bringing together national talents from both worlds in a celebration of the joy of making sport."[83]

After a year of development, "Pucci: Sport" debuted at New York's Joyce Theatre in June 1999 and the piece's very first segment was devoted to baseball. As the national anthem was broadcast over the loud speakers, dancers appeared on stage in baseball uniforms, in a diamond formation, filling the audience with the familiar feeling of being at the ballpark (or perhaps watching the start of a baseball game on television). When the anthem ceased playing, the crack of a baseball bat and the cheering of a stadium crowd could be heard and four "fielders" proceeded to entertain the concert dance audience with typical baseball movements executed in exquisite rhythm, with true balletic elegance (toting baseball gloves and decked out in full baseball finery): stretching, sliding, leaping, throwing, rolling, spinning, hopping, and sprinting. It was spring training and baseball players were performing/dancing their workouts to the strains of Vivaldi's "Four Seasons." Two more movements followed, tracing the progress of the baseball season, and the piece came to a close with a championship victory,

dancer-players rejoicing and cheerleaders punctuating the triumph with
delighted leaps and pom-pom rattles.

Other sports—such as hockey,
tennis, surfing, and even Frisbee tossing—were given their moments in the
spotlight, but Pucci made a conscious
decision to return to baseball in the
piece's concluding moments, understanding the need for a "baseball
bookend." This time, instead of "Four
Seasons," Pucci made use of a newly
arranged version of "Take Me Out to
the Ball Game" and had ten of his
dancers entertain the audience with a
baseball bat dance. In the beginning,
there was baseball and it is baseball
that will "take you home."

"Pucci: Sport" became an unmit-

Promotional photograph for the "Baseball" section of
"Pucci: Sport," choreographed by Peter Pucci (used with
permission from the photographer, Michael O'Neill).

igated hit. Television news stations did feature stories on the show and Pucci's education and
outreach team arranged to have the work performed in a vast number of atypical venues,
including streets, playgrounds, and parks in cities throughout the United States.[84] At various
points, professional athletes would join the cast and, on one occasion, a performance was
carried out on the surface of Pittsburgh's Ninth Avenue Bridge, as fans were busy making
their way to Three Rivers Stadium to see a Pirates game. Moreover, the "Baseball" segment
of "Pucci: Sport" was—and continues to be—commissioned and performed as a "stand-
alone" by American dance companies. The State Street Ballet of Santa Barbara, California,
for example, selected Pucci's "Baseball" for its 2006 "American Legends" dance series, which
was created, in the words of the Santa Barbara Independent's Elizabeth Schwyzer, to "celebrate
and glorify the realities of modern America."[85] Once again, the spirit of Americana and the
bounty of American culture extolled by a baseball-infused work of choreography, danced by
an American dance company dedicated to "bringing a decidedly American approach" to its
performance art.[86]

Interlude
Choreographers and Dancers on Dance and Baseball—Lisa de Ribere, Christopher Fleming and Marianna Tcherkassky

Lisa de Ribere, Choreographer of "The Mighty Casey"[1]

"Mighty Casey" came about because I had done a couple of works for Pittsburgh Ballet Theatre. The board and whatever "powers-that-be" at PBT decided that they wanted to do a kid-oriented program that would appeal to both adults and children. I guess at that point everybody started realizing that it's easier to get funding if something is directed at education and children. Pat Wilde at PBT called me up and said, "We want you to do this program, but we don't know what it is right now." So I went into her office and she had this list that the Board members had suggested. One of them, interestingly, was Spider Man! Another was *Star Wars* and all of this crazy stuff. This was around 1988—that's when the discussions started. And I'm, like, "Oh my God," and we're both rolling our eyes. So there are about fifteen or so suggestions and then Pat said, "And this one—I don't know what this person was thinking: 'Casey at the Bat.'" And I looked at her and said, "Wait a minute— I think I can probably do something with that!" She said, "What?! Are you kidding me?!" I don't know— it felt as though the light bulb just went on for me!

So I said, "Let me do some research, but this sounds like something." I found the original poem and reacquainted myself with that and then found a book of "Casey at the Bat" spin-off poems. Things such as "Casey's Three Daughters" and "Casey in the Garden"—all based on the same format as "Casey at the Bat," with the same meter and everything that many different people had written. I went through the whole book and found the one that I actually wanted to use, to add to "Casey at the Bat." "Casey at the Bat" is pretty brief, it's pretty spare and they wanted a forty-five-minute piece and I thought that the original poem alone wouldn't be enough. The one I chose was "Casey Twenty Years Later," which

Choreographer of "The Mighty Casey," Lisa de Ribere (photograph by Rosalie O'Connor; used with permission from Lisa de Ribere).

133

was about Casey's life twenty years after the famous at-bat. Casey is married and he's going to see the local baseball team play. It's the Bugville team. Then all of these injuries start occurring. One of the players falls down and hurts his knees, so he can't play. And then they send in another guy and then more and more people get injured until they're down to eight men. Casey, old Casey, is sitting up in the stands and the captain of the team says to him, "Come on, Casey, we need you!" So he comes down and saves the game. The ballet starts at that point. Then there's a flashback to young Casey and the whole original poem. Of course, I had to embellish—I had to basically create a libretto, a book. It's a full story and it's long enough to sustain the time that they needed, forty-five minutes. Casey has a girlfriend and she has her friends. It's sort of an old-fashioned story ballet. That's how it came about.

Did you want to duplicate baseball movements in the choreography?

LDR: I did. In fact, there are two "games" that are very abbreviated. There are bases and they use bats. A lot of the dancers played softball anyway—they had teams in Pittsburgh and they played softball. So we actually would go out and have games, with me knowing nothing. One time I was the umpire and everybody was furious with me because I was, like, "Okay, that was a strike." They would turn around and look at me and say, "It's not this serious—it's just a softball game!" I would say, "He's out!" and they would give me these looks—because I take everything very seriously when I'm working!

Until I started working on "Casey," I probably had seen some baseball on TV, but I had never been to a game. My very good friend Daphne Hurford wrote for *Sports Illustrated* and her husband, Sandy Padwe, was an investigative reporter for *Sports Illustrated* for years. Daphne said to me, "Lisa, I think it's time for you to go to a baseball game." So she took me to see the Yankees one afternoon and I got a lot of stuff out of that. We got there early and they were warming up and that just fascinated me. A ballet dancer's idea of warming up and a baseball player's idea of warming up are just like night and day. Ballet dancers stretch and do all of this stuff and then there's a whole series of exercises that build their way up to the big stuff and it goes on for a long time. So I'm watching these baseball players out there— they come trotting out, they throw themselves on the ground, and they start bouncing, which is a way that you should never, ever stretch! If you bounce, you actually shorten your muscles rather than lengthening. And I'm going, "What are they doing?! Somebody has to tell them not to do that!" It was hilarious. And then they would do this thing where they're running backwards. I said to Daphne, "What are they doing?" She said, "You know, sometimes they have to field balls and they have to be ready." So that went into the ballet—they're all running backwards in lines. Coming in as a novice, I caught everything. Someone who has been watching games for years just takes this for granted and after a while it doesn't even hit your radar screen. It was really funny.

After that, I went to see the Pirates play and it was really cool because some of the players were brought in to help the dancers with things like getting the right stance for batting (because even though a bunch of the guys had played baseball, some of the guys had never played or even watched baseball). So the Pirate reps came in and coached the dancers in actual batting and pitching and all that stuff. I'm not going to remember all the names, but there were some really famous players who sometimes came in and one coach, Tommy Sandt, worked with the dancers a lot. In the various companies that staged "Casey," there were many different players who came. I remember that Tug McGraw came in at some point and a lot of other kind of legendary people. In Milwaukee and in Tulsa and whatever, these people showed up. And some of them were actually in the ballet. There was a role that I created just for that purpose, to have a cameo appearance. It was the captain of the Mudville team and it was a non-dancing role. The companies would bring in some famous older baseball player and some of them were really good. It was a really good P.R. thing and we would have baseball signings at the end, where all the kids would be running up with their baseballs. It was marketed very well and all of the companies handled it in the same way. It was this kind of self-perpetuating thing. I think maybe the baseballs were made available by somebody—maybe the company that made the baseballs. It was understood that people at the end would have this opportunity. And the ballplayers who were involved had to rehearse with the company. There was also the role of the Team Manager—that was a role that could be done either by a dancer or a celebrity walk-on. Also, at the very end, when the ballet is finished, everybody sings "Take Me Out to the Ball Game" and the dancers are singing and everyone in the audience is encouraged to sing along, which was always a lot of fun. The dancers come out and bow and then the orchestra starts playing "Take Me Out to the Ball Game" and everybody sings.

It was quite an experience and it was so interesting to work with four different companies and see what each dancer made of the Casey role and the role of Casey's girlfriend, Betsy. The guys in the corps on the teams were really great because they really got into the characters and I made a separate character for almost everybody. There were eighteen in all—nine and nine. It was very literal. It wasn't just "this is sort of a baseball team." There was a whole team over here and a whole team over there. Mostly men, but in some companies there weren't enough men. In Pittsburgh, I think that there were two women who were on the "Other Nine" and a couple of companies had one woman on the Mudville team and a couple on the "Other" team. Having eighteen men for companies that size is unusual, so we had to have women play the parts of men on the teams. Then the women had to learn how to act like men. Fortunately, though, they didn't have to get the fine nuances of being a man! They had scruffy beards and so on. I think everybody had a lot of fun. In fact, I'm on the faculty of the School of American Ballet and one of my fellow teachers came up to me when I first started teaching and said, "I don't know if you if you remember me, but I was the Batboy in 'The Mighty Casey' in Philadelphia with Pittsburgh Ballet Theatre." The Pittsburgh Ballet Theatre toured it. I was pretty shocked and said, "Oh my God! Nice to see you again!" It was very funny. So there are all of these adult dancers now who were in "Casey" as children years ago and they come out of the woodwork every once in a while!

While you were watching baseball, did you identify actual dance steps in the movements of the players?

Yes! When they were fielding a ground ball, for example, there's this thing that they do which is like a *chassé* to the side, that's not turned out. In fact, when one of the coaches from the Pirates came in to teach the dancers how to move when you are playing baseball, he was talking about fielding a ground ball and he used the term "sashay," which is the same root and the same kind of movement: not turned out. I said to him, "Wait, what did you call that?" He said, "A sashay," and I said, "Do you mean a *chassé*?" and he said, "Whatever." Basically, it's this gliding step that moves laterally. You step and then you do almost like a little sliding skip in the same direction. And I said, "Oh my God—that's a ballet step!" But, of course, whoever it was who invented baseball was not thinking, "Oh, I'm going to put this ballet step in there." It's a thing that happens naturally—you just physically do that. I mean, anybody who has to catch a mouse running across the ground is going to have to do something like that! So that was totally fascinating to me. I'm a choreographer so movement is really important to me.

If you had the opportunity to talk to the baseball players whom you were watching, what would you say to them about warming up?

I would have told them how to stretch differently. Stretching is something that you have to do in increments. You stretch and then you gently retract and then you can go a little further. What they were doing was bouncing. Joggers do this all the time. They come running out of their brownstones and they throw their legs up on the wall and then they're bouncing. When I see that, I think, "Oh, my God!" What happens is you bounce and then the muscle gets tighter and tighter and tighter. Then they go out and jog and the next thing you know, they have hamstring injuries. What you have to do is do it slowly and you go to just beyond what's comfortable, then you hold it and release. And then you do it a little bit more. There are different ways that you can do this. You can lay down and have a Thera-Band or a towel around your foot and you can pull your leg up. There are all kinds of positions. But you have to do it slowly. You have to do it and then hold it and it's a little bit painful at first. Then it starts to release and then you let it go and then the next time you do it, you go a little bit further. It's good to be warm when you're doing it, although I've stretched when I was cold many times. But you have to be really careful. If you don't do it that way, then you can get more injured than if you never had stretched at all. So that was the first thing that hit me—that they were not taking care of their bodies at all! They just didn't know how to do it!

Did you feel that "Mighty Casey" was able to attract new audiences to watch dance?

Absolutely. I mean the kids were coming, but we started finding that the *dads* were bringing them! "Casey" was a forty-eight-minute piece and there was always some other, balletic piece on the program, because the program has to be about one-and-a-half to two hours long. So the dads were coming in to see the baseball game, but now they're seeing excerpts from *Swan Lake* to start or something like that. And then we started hearing this feedback, like, "Wow, this isn't what I thought it would be at all—this is really beautiful and it's really hard!" It really brought a big awareness to whatever community it went to. It was a baseball ballet and it was pulling in guys. Not that all these guys were saying, "Oh, let's go see the baseball ballet," but their kids wanted to go and sometimes Mom couldn't do it, or whatever. So I think that maybe they thought, "Well, maybe it's interesting—it's baseball, so maybe I'll venture into the ballet performance." And then we'd find people saying, "Gee, this is not what I thought it was." Ballet has, in the past, had a huge stigma. Homophobes, preconceptions about what it is—fancy prancing around. Then they go and see it and realize that it's incredibly difficult and athletic. Plus, the ballet dancers aren't out there huffing and puffing and spitting into their hands—they're actually making it look like it's so easy. They're six feet in the air and they land quietly and they're not galumphing around and people are going, "Wow, what is this?" People who would never, ever come to the theater to see this. I don't know, but I would venture to say that the companies that did "Casey" at that time probably started to see differences in their audiences. Then everything became much different. Now, when I go to the ballet, it's not what it was like in the '70s and '80s. It's not just ballet fans. You see all sorts of people at the ballet—it's cool to go to the ballet. And then you have a movie like *Black Swan,* which gives you some other perspective, whatever that perspective is! But it creates a stir. I saw something on the Internet which was saying, "Ballet is hot! Everybody wants to go to the ballet now! Everybody wants to see *Swan Lake*." It's so weird!

Christopher Fleming, Choreographer of "Playball!"[2]

Baseball is something that is easily recognizable to almost all Americans. Even women, especially with the advent of slow-pitch and fast-pitch softball. More and more of the population has picked up a ball at some point and has played some form of baseball. When I was a kid in New York, we used to play in our schoolyard at P.S. 111 on 53rd and 10th, and it was all concrete. We played softball because hardball would have been a little too tough. But we played on concrete. There are people in America who can't fathom what that means. We sometimes played in the mornings before school started. I was watching and playing baseball all the time as a kid.

Oddly, down in Florida, where I went to middle school, baseball wasn't as big. And you could play it all year long there. Football seemed to be the big sport in Florida. I just kept looking at them and saying, "Yeah, okay, this is fun—August, playing in the heat with your pads on. Yeah, this is a good time, guys—way to go." I think it might have just come from the huge popularity of the college football teams—Florida State and Miami and the University

of Florida. In the beginning, the schools recruited a lot of kids from Florida. They would even convert kids from basketball to football. It's true!

So you played a lot of baseball when you were growing up?

CF: I had a first baseman's mitt and we played a lot of softball. With a baseball in the schoolyard, things could get broken, so we stuck with a softball. But we were pretty avid. I remember reading all kinds of baseball books that I got in my elementary school library—biographies of Willie Mays and Duke Snider and the story of the Gas House Gang and Dizzy and Daffy Dean. It was all really interesting. I remember my uncle took me to a Mets game in the early 1960s and I wound up getting hooked on the Mets. I still have the program from that game somewhere. It was actually kind of

Choreographer of "Playball!" Christopher Fleming (**photograph courtesy Christopher Fleming**).

cool to be a Mets fan because they sucked for so long! And then 1969 was just amazing. They finally got the pitching together and they had a pretty solid team all around. I can still remember the players on that team and you only remember those things if you're an avid fan. If you're collecting baseball cards and reading the programs—I mean, we used to know how to score. You'd go to the game and get your program and your scorecard and you'd keep score.

Did you go to a lot of games?

Yeah, yeah. Back in those days you could get coupons if you bought Borden orange drinks—they were on the containers and you'd have to cut them out. Then, once you got enough, you could exchange them for tickets to games and be able to sit in the bleachers. The Mets were terrible and no one was going to the games, so they had to do these promotions.

We were pretty wrapped up in baseball. We all collected baseball cards and we figured out games to play with the cards every morning. And my friend Steve and I used to make cards for the different kids in our class and play at recess. Steve was the big Yankees fan and I was the Mets fan and we were always the team captains. We were lucky—we had some nice teachers who would take us on field trips once in a while to the park on 12th Avenue and we would play ball. And, like I said, we played on concrete all the time.

On weekends—I lived uptown, on 75th Street—we'd go to Central Park. You had your glove on your bicycle handlebars and your ball in between the two bars under the seat and off you'd go. You had a ball and a glove and you were ready. And someone always had a bat. We played on the big softball field in the park. I mean, really, we *lived* there.

I moved down to Florida after sixth grade and was there through ninth grade and then I wound up coming back to New York as a dancer. I played one year of Little League in Florida, and it was miserable. The new fields were under construction. They're near my mom's house now. But when I was playing, they were still under construction. I was a first baseman, but I got moved to the outfield because there was a ninth grader playing first base when I got there and there was no way I was going to dethrone him. So like any good team player, I said "Okay" when I was asked to play the outfield. The bad part was that, since the sod on the field still hadn't been laid, the outfield was just sand. It really made the term "sandlot" come to life. If you're in the outfield and someone hits a line drive into that Florida sand, it's doesn't bounce. You don't "play it"—you have to go and dig it out. I remember standing out there one time—and I'm basically a city kid—and I'm waving my arms and yelling, "Could we stop for a minute?!" And everyone was like, "Oh, not him again. What?" I said, "I think there's a coral snake out here." As far as I know, this is the most poisonous snake in America. "Could someone come out here with a bat?" And, sure enough, it was a coral snake. They're small, but if you get bit by one, you're dead. I was thinking, this is rolling right by me and if I go chase something and I fall or dive and I come up and there's a snake in my face, I'm a dead man, so we need to do something about this now.

Years later I went back to that field because it is near my mom's house. It was actually when I was putting together this baseball ballet. So I sat and watched the Little League games there. It was great fun. It was 1999 and Major League Baseball had changed so much. I felt that I needed to go and watch Little League games because it seemed as though I wasn't going to get the kind of enthusiasm in baseball that I was looking for my ballet unless I watched kids play. So I went and just watched for the whole day. I'm sure some of the parents were giving me weird looks and thinking, "Who are you and why are you here?" After a while, though, I started talking to the parents who were there and they were cool with everything, although they still thought it was a little strange that I was there to get some inspiration and ideas for a ballet.

I then went to see the minor league team, the Orlando Twins, play and I sat by this older guy who was retired. He was originally from New York City and had a career in the insurance business. I started to watch the game and began to talk to him about my ideas for the ballet I was putting together and it turned out that he kind of liked the idea. He thought it would work well. He said that he wasn't a big ballet fan, even though his wife dragged him to *The Nutcracker* a few times. But he thought that the ideas I was expressing were good ones. A *chassé*, for example. It's more visual than anything else. If a guy is on first base, you'll see that guy take a few steps off of the base and then he'll *chassé* back. It's kind of a side scoot where your feet come together and then your feet go apart again. That is a ballet *chassé*. And I remembered watching this television special that featured the second baseman Joe Morgan. It was on PBS and they were trying to show the similarities between dance and sports. So they had Joe Morgan doing those three steps off the base and then he was in this big second position—where your legs are spread and your weight is kind of balanced in the middle—and then he would either take off or he would shoot back to first base. But he was doing a lot of *chassés*. I thought, "Okay, we can do that, too."

And then with pitchers. If you're a pitcher, you're doing *developpés* at a pretty quick speed. You're bringing your leg up to *passé*, you're kicking it out, you're stepping forward into an *attitude* position, and throwing your arm forward into third *arabesque*. This is shown very clearly in the "Pitching Section" of the ballet—those are all ballet steps.

Is this how you explained things to your dancers?

You know, I didn't have to describe a lot to them. On the first day of rehearsal for this ballet, the director went out of town for a conference or something and the ballet master was a bit lazy. So I said to him, "Instead of rehearsing today, I'm going to take everyone to a little baseball field outside and we're going to play some baseball, so you have the day off." I took the dancers over to the field and I conducted what was kind of like a Little League "tryout." You know, where everyone has a chance to bat and then you let all the kids pick their positions and they have a chance to try out and you shag flies and hit ground balls and so on. Well, that's sort of what I did with the dancers. By the way, this was the Dayton Ballet and, interestingly, the director of the company, Dermot Burke, was a standout high school baseball player and he was also trained in ballet by my aunt and by my mother. He was also really supportive of the idea of a baseball ballet. In fact, that company still has my old first baseman's mitt!

So we all went out to the field. We had one hardball and some softballs and, at one point, when the various dancers were getting up to bat, I said to them, "Any of you who have experience playing ball, take it easy now because we're going to be using a hardball and if you hit it to someone who hasn't played much, it could be tough." Well, there was this one dancer who had played before and, as soon as he got up to bat, he just laid into one and sent it over the fence and into the street and into the sewer. And, as it turned out, it was a baseball of mine that I had caught in the stands at a Mets game! I wanted to kill him. So I made him the catcher in the ballet and there's a scene, "The Base Stealer's Waltz," where the catcher gets trampled by the other players, and that's why. Don't get mad, get even. I remember him looking at me in rehearsals and saying, "You know, I'm really sorry about the ball," and I said, "I told you, I told you not to do it." We still laugh about it today.

What was the actual inspiration for the ballet? What made you want to do it in the first place?

Well, if you make ballets, you're always coming up with different ideas. For example, in Tampa, Florida, we just did a two-act pirate ballet about Jose Gaspar. Since 1907, Tampa has had a "Gasparilla" festival in February and it's kind of the equivalent of Mardi Gras, except with pirates. So, when I was there in the 1990s, I thought that we should do a ballet about this. Why can't we do things that relate to the community? I used to work for George Balanchine and Jerome Robbins, and Robbins did a ballet called "Fancy Free," which was about three sailors on leave in New York during World War II, chasing girls. That's America. Agnes deMille did "Rodeo." That's America. Baseball is an American anomaly that has become really popular in many places throughout the world. In fact, I'm talking to someone now about the possibility of taking "Playball!" to Taiwan, since baseball is so big there at this point—I think they'd love it over there.

If you think about the old ballet classics, most of them are based on folk tales and fairy stories from other parts of the world. *The Nutcracker* and *Swan Lake* and *Giselle* and *Sleeping Beauty*—these are all stories that originated in other countries. We should have our own stuff, based on our own stories here in America. And what's more American than baseball? And then, around that time, the movie *A League of Their Own* came out. Actually, I knew Penny Marshall [the film's director] from when I was dancing. She used to call me her "little ballet buddy." She's great—she's exactly like the way she acts. She was dating a friend of mine who was a rock and roller and I got them tickets to the ballet and after that, whenever I'd run into her at restaurants, she would say, "Chris! My ballet buddy! Get over here!"

So when *A League of Their Own* came out, I thought, "Wow, hold on, now we can add girls!" I mean, if it hadn't been for *A League of Their Own*, I probably wouldn't have come up with the idea because baseball, to me, had always been a male thing. So how do you do an only-male ballet when most companies actually have more females than males. Once I saw *A League of Their Own* it actually seemed possible to make this happen. The whole premise of the piece is what would happen if the guys had played the girls once they came back from the war.

The similarities between dance and baseball are huge. That's why it was so easy to do. Making it was flat-out fun, the dancers had a good time, and they never knew what the hell I was up to. Each inning starts as a game and then dissolves into some kind of chaos. Even the no-hitter. With Little League teams, long fly balls are not as common and, in the outfield, sometimes there is nothing to do and you might find yourself daydreaming a bit out there. Except for the chatter—and the outfielders in professional ball don't really chatter too much. Most of the time, they're just trying to avoid getting hit by a bottle.

I remember the very first game I went to—it was actually a Yankees game, even though I was a Mets fan. The father of a friend of mine had been in the Tigers organization for a while and he wound up taking us to Yankee Stadium one day. I just remember walking into the stadium and thinking, "Wow!" It was almost surrealistic, especially for us city kids. Just seeing the bright green grass and how huge the place was. It was just beautiful and it's something that you never forget. So, as a choreographer, there's no way you're not going to wander back to that at some point. Because it's the "big show" and what do you do? You make shows. Also, when you do a ballet like this, which is comedic, you have no clue about whether or not it's going to work until you get it in front of an audience. You know what a comedian must go through. All of those famous comedians say that they honed their skill while doing stand-up over and over again. It's because the only way that you know you've succeeded is by the reaction of the audience. Yeah, your friends will tell you it's great, your director will like it, you'll be thinking that it's fun, but you could get out there and tank. I mean, if it's just a regular ballet, it's about aesthetics, it's about all kinds of things, moving the audience. With this, we're not only making a baseball ballet, but we're kind of making fun of the National Pastime a little bit, too. Like Lou Piniella kicking dirt on the umpire's shoes.

I mean, really, if you think about it and you break it down into the mental states that are involved, most of these sports are pretty comical. I remember when I was in Bogota, the Super Bowl was going to be broadcast. At that point in my life, I didn't understand the whole commercial aspect of the Super Bowl. This was around 1989 and I think it was the game where the Redskins won by some ridiculous score, like 52–3. So I invited all of these Colombian friends who were used to soccer, which just moves. Well, when they re-broadcast the game, Colombian television didn't fill up all of the commercial slots, so you'd see players on the field, staring at the big screen and waiting for the commercials to be over. And it sort of took the whole thing and put it into perspective. I was thinking, "Oh, I get it—this is just a show. It's a violent show and it requires lots of skills, but, man, this is a show." Or if you think about the fact that basketball players run up and down the court and toss a ball into a little basket. I mean, it's one thing to watch an Olympic high jumper or an Olympic runner or an Olympic marathoner, but these competitive sports that we have are kind of silly. I'm not making fun of the players or their skills. If someone threw a 100-mile-an-hour fastball at me, all that would be left would be my shoes. So there is this amazing skill level that's involved.

But I think that baseball is a sport that more Americans have probably tried. It's a gentler game and, I think, because of that, it lends itself better to dance than any other sport—except for maybe volleyball. I remember the first time I watched a little documentary about an Olympic volleyball team practicing and I was like, "Oh, my God!" They were diving and rolling and jumping—stuff that you really didn't think about. A lot of us have played volleyball, but we weren't going to kill ourselves to get the ball, but these guys were diving on hardwood to get that ball. Another thing that would be close to ballet would be the original Olympic sports—things like wrestling and running and jumping.

Most artists draw from what they know, so it makes sense that I did this ballet. You'll hear Bruce Springsteen songs, where he writes about some town in New Jersey or some guy in a bar talking about his "glory days." Well, Springsteen probably knows that town and he probably knew that guy. So that's where most of that inspiration comes from for this ballet. I grew up knowing and loving baseball.

There is one final story I would like to relate. Back in 2000, when I was at the Rock School in Pennsylvania, the Philly Pops had heard that we had this baseball ballet and were interested in doing it because at that time the Phillies were celebrating the twentieth anniversary of the last time they won the World Series. So we put "three innings" of "Playball!" together and it was performed on stage, right in front of the orchestra. Believe it or not, I wasn't able to be there—I was choreographing a ballet in the Czech Republic—but it turned out that Tug McGraw, the great relief pitcher, was recruited to read "Casey at the Bat" before the dancing began. It was pretty thrilling for those die-hard Phillies fans who had been waiting twenty years for another championship team. Tug was a mainstay here in Philadelphia after he was traded to the Phillies by the Mets and he was a big part of that 1980 team. It was sad that I didn't get to be a part of it, but I'm really happy it happened.

Marianna Tcherkassky, Dancer, Teacher, Ballet Mistress[3]

I grew up in an artistic family. My father was an opera singer, as was his mother, for whom I'm named. My mother was a professional ballet dancer. She danced primarily in Europe, with the Ballet Russe de Monte Carlo. My father also worked for the Ballet Russe as part of management and that's how they met. So I grew up with classical music, opera, and ballet in the house. My mother was my first teacher and, from as early as I can remember, I was exposed to ballet.

I was not really exposed to sports. I do have an older brother who did some track and field in high school, but we just didn't grow up with sports. However, I did play a little bit of softball in seventh grade when I attended public school. I then went to the Washington School of Ballet, where I received my dance and academic education. From there I went to New York on scholarship, where I attended the School of American Ballet for dance, and the Professional Children's School for academics. But I will just do a little sidebar, because it was one crowning moment that I'll never forget. In playing seventh grade softball, I hit a home run! It was towards the end of the girls' athletic period, and all the guys were already coming in from their period when I hit my home run. I hit the ball, which was really a hard grounder, through the middle of the center fielder's legs, but I was pretty fast and I was able to make it all the way around the bases. I just remember that everyone was cheering me on, and it was very exciting. I impressed the guys and then for a little while after that they all wanted me on their team. It was really for one year and then I went into The Academy of the Washington School of Ballet, and that kind of ended my sports days.

Dancer, teacher, and ballet Mistress, Marianna Tcherkassky (photograph by Nicholas Coppula; used with permission from Marianna Tcherkassky [Orr]).

I joined American Ballet Theatre, ABT, in 1970 and became a principal dancer in 1976. I met my future husband, Terrence Orr, at ABT. He was from San Francisco, an All-American guy who got into dance because of beautiful women, but that's another story! He was very interested in sports, and as I started spending more time with him, I began to pay attention to sports, too. It was 1977, I was now a principal dancer with ABT and a guest artist for the Eglevsky Ballet, while other young, up-and-coming students performed beside me. I was performing Swanhilda in *Coppelia* and Terrence came to the performance with his closest friend, Byam Stevens. Byam is now the artistic director of a theater company in Chester, Massachusetts. Not to get off the subject, but there is a single- or double-A ballpark near Chester, in Pittsfield, Massachusetts, where we really enjoyed going to games. It was a very small, family-oriented ballpark, a true piece of Americana. I can remember home runs being hit out of the park, and then going to get the car and saying, "It's a good thing we parked far away," because there were windshields that were smashed and baseballs hitting in the front seats.

Anyway, back to *Coppelia*: Terry and Byam came to see the performance. Usually, after the show, they would come backstage or come to the dressing room, but they were nowhere in sight. So I took my makeup off and cleaned up and I still had no idea where they were. Somebody said that they may have seen them outside. So I went outside and they were sitting in the car, with the radio blasting. I came over and they were wide-eyed, talking about this "Reggie Jackson" and how he was making history. I had no idea what they were talking about, but I ended up sitting with them, listening to the game. I don't think Reggie had hit his third home run yet, but you could feel the energy over the airwaves. The sportscasters were amazing, with the sense of excitement that they were able to generate over the radio. I can remember thinking, Okay, this must be something that's pretty monumental and historic. Then I guess I said to Terry and Byam, "Did you guys even see the performance?" And they never really confessed. They said, "Oh yeah, yeah, yeah, it was great." But I was not convinced. After that I was watching the rest of the World Series on television, which was fine by me.

That's a pretty incredible coincidence—that your performance happened on the same day as Reggie Jackson's three home run game. That's a great kind of "marker."

MT: Very much so—totally memorable to me! Then my husband realized, if you're living in New York, you have to go to Yankee Stadium at least once in your life. So the following year, in 1978, he took me to my first live baseball game. It was the game where Ron Guidry broke the strikeout record for left-handed American League pitchers and during that game I fell in love with him. I thought he was just beautiful to look at—artistically, what he did with his pitches, but then, also, physically, as an athlete, the way he moved, his agility, his grace. A kind of refinement, in a way. Also, it was my first time being in that kind of atmosphere and just being swept up by the excitement of something. I felt the energy in the stadium, and found myself involuntarily screaming my head off and standing up and yelling, simply swept up by the moment. It was such a wonderful release and such a contrast from the world in which I existed.

Yet I could also relate to the similarity between ballet dancers and baseball players, where the actions are more physical and about timing and not so vocal. For me, it used to be an opportunity to kind of disappear in a crowd and have all this emotional release, which I found to be an interesting balance to my vocally silent, ethereal world of dance. Maybe that's why I gravitated towards baseball to begin with, a real contrast, but as I got more into it, I started perceiving similarities.

Nineteen-seventy-eight was just such a banner year for the Yankees. Guidry went on to win the Cy Young Award. I started to observe the other players. They called Graig Nettles "The Vacuum Cleaner" at third base. It was just amazing how nothing got by him, and to look at the dives and the leaps! They were pretty amazing athletes! As in baseball or dance, the more agile and flexible you are, the better performance you can give.

What were some of your other thoughts and observations at that time about the game and about the similarities to dance?

After that, I don't know how many games a year we went to. That very first game, I was just mesmerized by Guidry in general—his prowess on the mound, how quickly he moved, reacted to balls, and was off the mound and over to cover first base. I was hooked—I really had a crush on Guidry. So then I would ask, "Okay, when is the next game that Guidry is pitching? Can we go?"

What also happened was that, through a mutual friend, we met a great gentleman named Roger McCann, who worked for the Yankees front office. Sadly, he has since passed away. He was a basketball coach and I'm not even sure what he did in the Yankees front office. He used to get us tickets and, eventually, blocks of tickets to Yankee games. We'd trade ballet tickets for Yankee tickets, which was great fun. Of course, the ratio might have been fifty Yankee tickets, which back then cost a lot less, for twenty-five tickets to ABT at the Metropolitan Opera. We used to take big groups from our administrative office, as well as dancers. I never found out who from the Yankees organization actually came to the ballet. Once, to my surprise and excitement, Roger arranged to get my name put up on the scoreboard. The board read, "The New York Yankees welcome American Ballet Theatre ballerina Marianna Tcherkassky."

So, as a dancer, I started keying into the ways in which players moved. Sometimes we would go early just to watch pre-game warmups and drills. As I watched the short sprints and these bouncy, little calf stretches and side-steps, I thought, I don't know what else their regimen is, but that would never do for ballet dancers! It all seemed like those exercises would shorten and tighten the muscles. For dancers, you want to lengthen your muscles and build strength. You don't want to build bulk. It's a little different in baseball, of course, but I still thought it didn't look sufficient to really get warmed up enough to suddenly take off after a ball, to dive, or do unexpected moves. When I think about it now, of course, I didn't really know what their entire regimen might have been. I only saw their pre-game drills.

I'm sure that there's a lot more cross-training in baseball these days. In dance today, there's so much more cross-training and Pilates is a huge addition to the ballet regimen for building core strength. When I danced with ABT we toured for two to three months at a time, then returned to open our New York season. You had to be really diligent in maintaining a personal regimen. Cross-training wasn't as accessible as it is now, where most major ballet companies and schools have in-house Pilates instructors and equipment at their disposal. If you wanted to cross-train or do Pilates, you had to really seek those things out.

In my early days at ABT, we would do our training in the fall. We would have the summer months off and then we'd go through this two-month period of getting back in shape and preparing the repertoire for the year. It was very much like baseball spring training. Going through those basic drills, the fundamentals, and honing our technique so that when we went into performances, we didn't have to think about executing the technique. It should be second nature, allowing the dancers to focus on conveying art, and hopefully expressing the music and movement. Baseball players also go over their fundamentals so it becomes second nature. When a ball comes to them, their reflexes become more natural, with their sense of timing, coordination, and how they react to the moment.

Dancers are used to always having something hurt, they must identify the pain as something they can work through or the kind of pain that will cause an injury. You need to understand when your body is telling you that you need to slow down or stop for a little bit. It's probably very much the same dilemma that baseball players and their managers have. You just have to be so in tune with your own physicality.

Were there occasions when you went on stage even though it seemed as though your body was telling you not to?

Yes, there were. Currently, at American Ballet Theatre, there is an on-site physical therapist. When I first started out, there wasn't one. Now, the minute that dancers feel something wrong, they can go to the on-site therapist, have it looked at and assessed to get some direction and guidance. When I started at ABT, we had to either seek out a recommended therapist or make the decision to work through the pain.

I had a chronic problem with my left foot. It used to become inflamed, so I took an anti-inflammatory medication for it. It wasn't until much later, when I had a back injury and they were doing various tests, that it was revealed that I had a "stress fracture of undisclosed age" in the left foot. I had become accustomed to it hurting, but with taking medication and being immersed in a performance, I forgot about the pain. I didn't even know about stress fractures at that point. Now, one of the first signs of stress on a bone is often on the shins, for example, and may feel like a shin splint. If there's a little bump on the shinbone an early diagnosis might be a "stress reaction," which is the precursor to a stress fracture. Now doctors will order MRIs right away and, if there is a shadow or something odd, they'll put you in a boot and tell you that you are off for so many weeks.

There have been so many talented dancers who seem to have been plagued with injuries. It is difficult to gauge pain because the mind and will can be stronger than the body. Obviously, one is afraid to cancel out of a performance because there is always someone waiting in the wings, and then you have to work a lot harder to prove your reliability and value.

For dancers in the U.S., there is no job security at any level, which is different from the government-subsidized European companies. So there is a lot of competition. A big part of the job is trying to keep yourself physically at your optimum and prevent injury. Of course, accidents happen, but sometimes it seems as though there are some dancers who are more injury-prone. Some dancers may be born with certain physical attributes which allow them to not have to push their bodies as hard—their bodies just naturally form those aesthetic lines and shapes for classical ballet. Then there are the ones for whom dancing is a passion and they want to do it more than anything, which allows them to overcome their physical shortcomings. I certainly didn't have the perfect ballet body. This means that you have to work a lot harder to "hone your instrument." That's where great coaches really come in, to help dancers confront and overcome their weaknesses and capitalize on their strengths.

It's not unlike ballplayers who find their niche as great catchers, pitchers, outfielders, or infielders. With dancers, there are some who will excel in the realm of the classics while others find their brilliance in the more contemporary repertoire. There are the ones who move quicker, and those who are more adagio or lyrical dancers. You do find your niche.

That's very interesting. Certainly, in baseball, you find a lot of players who start off in a certain position and then someone—usually a coach—sees that they might be better suited to a different position and they make the switch and, in general, it works out for the best. Sometimes it doesn't, but more often it does.

I think about the coaching. For me, as a dancer, I actually loved the process in the studio.

I love the relationship, the one-on-one with partners and coaches in developing roles, creating things, trying to create magic and the intimacy of that process. Definitely, if you find a good coach who just brings out the best, who has that eye that you trust, it is pretty amazing.

Is it true that you used to listen to baseball games when you were doing warmups?

I did. Yeah, I had my radio on in the dressing room while I was doing my makeup and then I'd have to go and do my warmup before performances, and if the game was really exciting, I would take the radio with me and listen with earphones. I didn't want to miss anything! If I was performing *Giselle* or something like that, where I had to have my head in a different place, I probably didn't do it. But if it was something lighter, maybe a repertoire piece where I felt really confident, or if I felt I needed to get away from the music for a bit, I would listen to the game. Somehow it would clear my mind and help me approach a performance in a fresh way. If it was a really exciting game it would get my adrenaline going, which was helpful for high-energy ballets. Of course, I can't remember if I ever listened to a game where the Yankees lost, which would have made me really depressed! Then, fortunately, I had my ballet to help me forget about it.

Do you happen to know of any other dancers who were baseball fans or who were influenced and inspired by baseball?

I know that you spoke with Lisa de Ribere and she choreographed a charming ballet for Pittsburgh Ballet Theatre that was based on "Casey at the Bat." I know there were other dancers at American Ballet Theatre, like Victor Barbee (who was a principal dancer and a good friend), who used to come with us to games at Yankee Stadium. I also remember that there were a few dancers who played softball in the Broadway Show League. Victor did a few stints on Broadway and I think he talked to a couple of the male dancers at ABT and some of them went and played.

When we were in San Francisco, an ex–ABT soloist, Paula Tracy, introduced me to Tony LaRussa and his wife, whose daughters were taking ballet. I was still dancing, so it was probably in the late 1980s. I just remember him coming to watch a few rehearsals. He was a wonderful guy and I remember watching some games on television where he was actually wearing a San Francisco or Oakland Ballet sweatshirt, which was great exposure for ballet.

Also, early on, one of our soloists at the American Ballet Theatre, Kristine Elliott, was featured in a poster with Bucky Dent. She was in a tutu and he was in his Yankee uniform and they were standing in Yankee Stadium. I remember feeling a tinge of jealousy and wishing it was me.

The friend I was telling you about, Roger, who worked for the Yankees, was able to get me a signed photo of Ron Guidry and two autographed baseballs—one from Dave Winfield and one from Don Baylor. Both of them say "To Marianna"!

I should also mention that my husband did a new *Nutcracker* for Pittsburgh Ballet Theatre in 2002 and he really tried to make it a whole Pittsburgh-focused production. One of the doll dancers in the first act does a pirate dance and is made to look like the pirate in the Pittsburgh Pirates logo! There is also a big penguin in the battle scene that is meant to pay tribute to the Pittsburgh Penguins. In the latest edition, our Fritz makes his first entrance with a football in hand and wearing a replica, early-20th-century Steelers leather helmet.

Regarding the dance and baseball connection, is there anything you'd like to add?

I think about how many little girls dream of being ballerinas and how many little boys dream of being baseball players. Both are passions and disciplines. There are those connections—the necessary discipline and focus, the pursuit of excellence, the perseverance required. Both teach some great life lessons, whether or not you become a professional. Learning that discipline at an early age is so important and valuable. Also, having a chance to experience the thrill of the rewards of all of this hard work is so wonderful. For me, performing, in a way, was like the icing on the cake. I really loved the process in the studio. You really delve into things—the discussion and the action. I really remember having absolutely magical moments in the studio—and sometimes more so than on the stage. There are probably a handful of experiences on the stage where everything seems to come together and you go to some other place. That's kind of what keeps you going, because you always want to achieve that feeling again once you experience it. In sports, I think that there are similar feelings. The players who experience those magical moments and the teams that achieve that glory—there is always a desire to feel or experience that again.

Also, in both baseball and dance, you can really sense the performers who have the passion, who seem to be really loving what they are doing and giving their all. Baseball is about winning and losing, but more than that it is about the team spirit, camaraderie, and the sheer love of playing the game. And, for sure, there are also lots of very passionate baseball fans and dance fans!

Finally, I just want to say that a goal of mine for a long time has been to see a baseball game at every major league ballpark. I still might do that!

4

On Stage IV
Concert Dance in the Early 21st Century

In looking carefully at the first fifteen years of the 21st century—beginning with 2000's "Playball!" Christopher Fleming's crowd-pleasing "nine-inning ballet, "Playball!"—it is possible to observe a definite acceleration in the use of baseball themes and steps in concert dance. In some cases, of course, the baseball image or gesture that a choreographer chooses to inject into a work may be characterized as "minor" in the context of the overall dance piece. In other instances, baseball, without question, forms the heart and soul of a choreographer's creation. What is constant is the ability of baseball to motivate choreography and to somehow navigate its way into the minds of dance-makers who represent a true diversity of styles and approaches—resulting, quite often, in some very happy surprises. If the first fifteen years of the "new millennium" is any indication of what lies ahead for the relationship between baseball and dance on the concert dance stage, it is quite clear that the next eighty-five years will bring plenty of excitement, generated by a veritable army of new voices, bearing a robust and variegated arsenal of imaginative and often breathtaking conceptions, perspectives, and styles.

Male fielders in Fleming's "Playball!" with the Dayton Ballet (photograph by Susan Kettering; courtesy Christopher Fleming).

"Playball!" (2000)[1]

Baseball films have been produced almost since the medium of motion pictures came into being. Yet, it is possible to say with a fair amount of conviction that, with respect to the sheer volume of baseball films released within a certain space of time and the percentage of these films that proved, ultimately, to be both influential and popular, the period that lasted from the mid–1980s through the early 1990s was particularly remarkable. Consider, for example, films such as *The Natural* (1984), *Bull Durham* (1988), *Eight Men Out* (1988), *Field of Dreams* (1989), and *Major League* (1989), all of which fared well at the box office and all of which were designated as "classics" by baseball fans almost instantly. Another such movie, of course, was the 1992 historical comedy *A League of Their Own* (which, as shall be described in the next chapter, had its own connections to the world of dance). Directed by Penny Marshall and featuring a lively, star-studded cast that included Geena Davis, Tom Hanks, Rosie O'Donnell, and Madonna, *A League of Their Own* brought renewed recognition to (and interest in) the long-ignored All-American Girls Professional Baseball League (AAGPBL), which functioned during the World War II years, when so many professional male baseball players were performing military service.

Female team members explode during a big rally in Christopher Fleming's "Playball!" (photograph by Susan Kettering; courtesy Christopher Fleming).

In some ways, Marshall's funny, bittersweet film had an especially far-reaching effect, since the increased fascination with the history of the AAGPBL that *A League of Their Own* generated in late-20th century American society helped, to some degree, to influence the National Baseball Hall of Fame to install a new, permanent exhibit that would be devoted to the past and future roles of women in baseball. At the same time, the film's release served to motivate a certain populist-minded American choreographer named Christopher Fleming. Fleming, a former New York City Ballet dancer who had graduated from performance to leadership roles in the dance world, had played baseball while growing up in New York City and Florida and had always dreamed of making a baseball ballet. He was reluctant, though, because of what he saw as the dearth of substantial female roles in such a baseball-centric piece. However, once *A League of Their Own* appeared in movie theaters, Fleming understood how the baseball ballet of his dreams could be realized. To quote Fleming:

> When *A League of Their Own* came out, I thought, Wow, hold on, now we can add girls! I mean, if it hadn't been for *A League of Their Own*, I probably wouldn't have come up with the idea because baseball, to me, had always been a male thing. So how do you do an only-male ballet when most companies actually have more females than males? Once I saw *A League of Their Own*, it actually seemed possible to make this happen. The whole premise of the piece is what would happen if the guys had played the girls once they came back from the war.[2]

Accordingly, Fleming set his piece, which was choreographed originally for Ohio's Dayton Ballet in 2000 and given the title, "Playball!," in the post–World War II era, a time when American society was undergoing massive changes. In order to illustrate this sense of transition and the seismic shifts that were taking place in every corner of American culture, Fleming created a genuine "nine-inning ballet" that featured a confrontation between a baseball team comprised of men and one made up entirely of women (dressed in uniforms that recalled those of the AAGPBL). Every section of the piece was meant to highlight different idiosyncratic (and highly balletic) elements of the game, such as infield play, baserunning, pitching, the offensive rally, the battles between players and umpires, and the quiet moments in the

outfield. With plenty of physical humor (such as a hapless catcher being literally run over by players racing across home plate and a female fan flirting with a lonely left fielder), announcements from an off-stage announcer, a seventh-inning stretch rendition of "Take Me Out to the Ball Game" (led by a 1940s-style vocal group), and the tossing of bags of peanuts and popcorn to the audience by company members acting as ballpark vendors, "Playball!" managed to be simultaneously true to the game and true to the dance form.

Moreover, although the piece was not based on a specific story in the manner of "The Mighty Casey," there was a clear and unmistakable *cohesiveness* to "Playball!" One "inning" felt connected to the next and every movement felt deliberate but natural—and at all times accurate. The touching of a cap or the rubbing of hands, the kicking of "dirt" or the pounding of the glove were gestures that could be spotted throughout the ballet and were depicted in a graceful, non-caricatured manner that might appeal to

Base stealer humiliates catcher in Fleming's "Playball!" with the Dayton Ballet (photograph by Susan Kettering; courtesy Christopher Fleming).

the avid baseball fan and novice watcher alike. Fleming's own passion for both the sport and the performing art was strikingly present and on full display and the concluding segment, featuring a line of men sliding in between a line of women swinging baseball bats, was exhilarating and masterfully arranged—a sumptuous cocktail infused with the best of the ball field and the conservatory. It also seemed to consolidate the concepts that Fleming and his troupe were tossing around from the moment that male and female dancers in full uniform lined up on stage at the very start of the show to sing the "Star-Spangled Banner" with everyone in the auditorium. Indeed, during the course of "Playball!" as dancers batted and scooped up grounders, leaped and executed pirouettes in their baseball regalia, viewers, it could be said, were witnessing a clash of sexes that was relevant not only in the context of American social and cultural history, but also in terms of the ballet universe.

Since its 2000 premiere, "Playball!" has been performed regularly on stages across the United States. According to Christopher Fleming, "Since I first made the piece, it's been done somewhere every year," either in full-length form or in a shortened version that may highlight only two or three "innings."[3] In addition to the U.S. national anthem and "Take Me Out to the Ball Game," "Playball!" is made up entirely of familiar classical compositions that have "public domain" status and that serve to enhance the ballet's accessibility and reinforce its creator's own populist sensibilities.

"Plena Baseball" (2001)[4]

"Nothing brings family, cultural pride and a love of sports together in Puerto Rico like baseball," remarked Nancy Flores in the *Austin American-Statesman* in a 2011 article. This reality was prominent in the mind of Ana Maria Maynard, founder of the Puerto Rican Folkloric Dance Company (PRFD) of Austin, Texas, when she created the dance piece "Plena Baseball" for her youthful troupe in 2001. Maynard, who grew up in a Puerto Rican household and neighborhood in the Bronx, New York, had vivid memories of playing and watching baseball as a child and understood the sport's importance to her family, her neighborhood, and her culture. According to Maynard, "There are certain things that Puerto Ricans are very proud of and very vocal about and very passionate about ... and baseball is one of those."[5] Taking into account the dual "mission" of PRFD (i.e., to "teach people who don't know who we are as a people something about our cultural traditions" and "to teach people who are Puerto Rican ... something about our cultural history that they may not know"),[6] Maynard realized that baseball would be an ideal subject for a culturally significant and vastly entertaining dance work.

What Maynard needed was a storyline and, as she recalled the fanaticism that could overtake men in her family and neighborhood when it came to baseball, she began to consider a different kind of "clash of the sexes"—one in which the very strong women in the story band together to try to "rid" the baseball-crazed men of their "illness," which caused them to ignore their families and responsibilities. Puerto Rican plena music would be used to fuel the dance and women would set out to retrieve their distracted husbands, bearing tall, culturally recognizable red candles that possessed almost supernatural powers. The candles would serve to "shock" or "electrify" the wayward men into submission, thereby "curing" them of their baseball-induced malady.

Maynard added hefty doses of humor to the piece as she created the choreography and made sure that baseball movements shared the stage with the more traditional movements associated with plena music. A local sporting goods store was contacted and real, "1940s-style" baseball uniforms, bearing the name "PRF Dance" on the front of the uniform jersey, were commissioned (with each company dancer given permission to select a personal uniform number). On June 24, "Plena Baseball" debuted at Austin's State Theater and, based on its success and its ability to attract new audience members (of whom *many*, in all likelihood, had made a decision to give concert dance a try for the first time in their lives), Maynard's energetic and elegant piece was revived in 2009, this time with a live group of musicians who doubled as dancers (which necessitated the commission of a second set of uniforms). With "Plena Baseball," a new and vibrant panel was added to the ever-expanding mosaic of baseball-inspired dance work—and, for Ana Maria Maynard, this achievement proved to be an inspiration for yet another piece of choreography that explored and celebrated the importance of baseball in Puerto Rican culture and history. (That second choreographic adventure will be described in greater detail later in this chapter.)

"Decadance vs. the Firebird" (2004)

In 2004, Jennifer Weber and her artistically eclectic, kinetically electric Decadancetheatre, an all-female, Brooklyn-based dance troupe that uses hip-hop as a building block for what the company terms "mashup" performances, premiered a highly original version of the Russian folktale and ballet classic *The Firebird*. Weber dubbed the piece, "Decadance vs. the Firebird," and the title role was performed by red-haired Keely Wright, whose performance as the "blazing" Firebird was described as "phenomenal" and "gorgeous" by Tim Cusack, a critic for the website nytheatre.com.[7] Wright's dancing incorporated ballet and jazz, along with Weber's signature hip-hop movements, and her Firebird, like the classical Firebirds of the past, was a spectacular, glittering creature. Although now "sparkling scarlet sequins"[8] and a gleaming avian fringe, designed by costumer Gentry Farley, were matched with a hip-hop (and National Pastime) wardrobe staple: the baseball cap. The sports connection continued as Weber tossed in an "intricately choreographed" basketball sequence ("complete with referee making elaborate hand signals"),[9] underscoring the overall athletic nature and sensibility of the dance. Even the title of the piece was meant to evoke the image of a sporting contest.

"Decadance vs. the Firebird" was performed on two occasions in 2004—at the Connelly Theater in New York (as part of the New York International Fringe Festival) and at the Jacob's Pillow Dance Festival in Massachusetts.

"Pastime" (2007)[10]

Like Christopher Fleming, Ana Maria Maynard, Moses Pendleton, and so many other dance makers and dancers in the United States (many of whom have been discussed at length in this book), choreographer Chris Black has considered the recruitment of new concert dance fans and the whole idea of making dance more accessible to be of paramount importance as she sketches out and, ultimately, creates new dance works. Rather than focusing on choreography that might appeal exclusively to seasoned followers of dance, Black has stated quite openly that she is "much more interested in trying to communicate with people who don't already go to the theater."[11] "I just find it so satisfying and exciting," remarks Black, "when somebody comes up to me and says, 'My girlfriend dragged me to this show and it

Dancers perform Chris Black's "Pastime" in San Francisco's Precita Park, 2007 (photograph by Will Waghorn; used with permission of Chris Black).

was amazing. I had such a good time and, at first, I didn't even want to come.' I love that!"[12] Still, although the idea of creating something "accessible" is a constant source of motivation for Black, when she decided to direct her choreographic attention to baseball in 2007, it was not the only motivating factor. To be sure, along with the burning desire to reach new audiences, the other forces that drove Black to embrace baseball were acutely similar to those forces that helped to ignite the creative passions of Moses Pendleton—namely, baseball's beauty, baseball's innate connection to American culture, baseball's iconic stature, and the simultaneously symbolic and ritualistic nature of the game. Once again, the Great American Pastime seemed to be an almost perfect subject for a thought-provoking and entertaining dance experiment.

Chris Black grew up in New Jersey and found her early inspiration not only in the breathtaking choreography of George Balanchine, the precision and prowess of New York City Ballet star Suzanne Farrell, and the athletic footwork and suave but muscular technique of Gene Kelly, but also in the style, poise, and determination of New York Yankees' pitching ace Ron Guidry, and the graceful play of shortstop Bucky Dent.[13] As *Dance Magazine* pointed out in September 2007, Black's dream had always been to somehow combine her two great loves, dance and baseball.[14] Up until the time she entered high school, Black played soccer and a bit of softball, rooted for the Yankees, attended as many New York City Ballet performances as possible, and "bounce[d] in and out of dance classes."[15] In high school, though, her interest in dance increased. At long last, Black was introduced to more athletic forms of dance that seemed to suit her and she was given opportunities for the first time to actually *make* dances—to try her hand at choreography. She was enthralled and, after graduation, attended Cornell University, where she found even greater inspiration and more chances to choreograph in the school's exceptional dance department. Baseball, however, was a bit of a casualty, due to the time-consuming nature of her studies.

After a couple of years, though, Black's relationship with baseball was rekindled when she began reading and falling in love with the writings of Roger Angell that appeared regularly in *The New Yorker*. These masterful features, bursting with baseball-based philosophy and brimming with Angell's delightfully brilliant observations of the game, brought baseball back to Black, this time for good. Eventually, Black made her way to San Francisco and, ultimately, she formed her own company, the Potrzebie Dance Project (named after a term borrowed from *Mad Magazine*). Black became a devoted Giants fan and, much like Roger Angell, she continued to be a keen observer of the world around her and was able to identify many connections between the wider world and the more finite world of baseball. At a time when the United States was mired in a terrible and bloody war in Iraq and the images from this war were flashed repeatedly in the media, Black considered the joy of baseball and its own extraordinary images and felt, finally, that it was time to realize her deep, long-standing dream of blending dance and baseball. It was time to celebrate something beautiful, something that might induce warm feelings, something that Americans of every stripe could enjoy together. And so "Pastime" was born.

Although conceived, in the manner of Christopher Fleming, as a piece to be performed over the course of nine "innings," "Pastime" was not at all intended by Black to be a straightforward representation of a baseball game in dance. Instead, to quote Black, "I wanted the choreography to function more the way memory does, as a series of images that are not necessarily experienced in linear order."[16] References, sometimes subtle and sometimes more familiar, to iconic poses (such as the swing of Willie Mays or the pitching motion of Juan Marichal) would be scattered throughout. The movements of "players" would consist of a collage of coordinated "snapshots," rather than a single, smooth follow-through.[17] "Pastime" most certainly would describe a game, but a game as it might look if filtered through the lens of an artist like Pablo Picasso or a writer such as Marcel Proust—both a revelation and a meditation, filled with color and light and moments of clarity and confusion, heavy traffic and complete stillness.

Children in San Francisco's Precita Park watch Chris Black and her dancers perform "Pastime" in 2007 (photograph by Will Waghorn; used with permission of Chris Black).

Moreover, in order to truly fulfill Black's desire to reach "people who wouldn't otherwise go to see dance but were interested in baseball" (and in order to reinforce the feeling of actually witnessing a game, impressionistic as it may be), Black arranged for "Pastime" to be performed outdoors, on grass, all around San Francisco—from Golden Gate Park to Herman Plaza Park to what Black refers to as the "home field" of Potrzebie, Precita Park in the Mission District.[18] Audience members could dress in baseball jerseys and caps, pack a lunch (or buy a hot dog), spread out a blanket, and watch the Potrzebie dancers leap, slide, brawl, and get completely covered in dirt over the course of a lovely San Francisco afternoon. Original music by local composer Erik Pearson was blended with the familiar sounds of the ballpark and the booth, including "Take Me Out to the Ball Game," the national anthem, and a recording of the famous words screamed by announcer Russ Hodges as he witnessed Bobby Thomson slug the "Shot Heard 'Round the World" in 1951, "The Giants win the pennant!"—and all audio (pre-recorded) was generated by a CD player hooked up to a short-wave FM transmitter, allowing spectators to hear "the game" on the radio (attendees, in fact, were encouraged to carry portable radios to each performance location, which helped to generate what Black termed that "nice, fuzzy tinge"—the kind of sound that her father's tiny transistor radio used to produce when he listened to New York Yankees' games during Black's childhood).[19] Black, in "Pastime," was able to fuse baseball and concert dance and transport the creation directly to the turf of the everyday American citizen. The sometimes contentious, but undeniably intimate and altogether natural relationship between baseball and concert dance in America could not find a better vehicle of expression than "Pastime," nor a more passionate messenger than Chris Black.

Coincidentally, Black recalls that one of her most memorable moments during the 2007 performance run of "Pastime" was when an older gentleman came up to her at the end of one show and said, "You know, I was there when Bobby Thomson hit that home run." Black was thrilled, deeply moved, and honored. Later on, she observed, "I felt like I had a celebrity at the show, which was lovely."[20]

"Opening Day at Fenway" (2007)

Less than one year after the Boston Red Sox finally broke the infamous "Curse of the Bambino" by winning the 2004 World Series, a member of the championship Red Sox team, pitcher Bronson Arroyo, recorded and released a rock 'n' roll album called *Covering the Bases*. Among the twelve tunes that appeared on the record was a raunchy version of Ed Cobb's popular 1966 song (written originally for The Standells), "Dirty Water." Arroyo's treatment of this well-known song featured a trio of 2004 teammates as backing vocalists (outfielder Johnny Damon, pitcher Lenny DiNardo, and third baseman Kevin Youkilis). As the guitar, bass, and drums barreled along in the forefront, Arroyo, singing the muscular lead vocal, and his baseball pals jawed with one another over and under the beat, coalescing only when it was time to scream the rousing chorus line, "Oh, Boston, you're my home!" With its slightly raucous sound and its off-kilter celebration of the city in all its gritty beauty, "Dirty Water" was a near-perfect match for the 2004 Red Sox team, whose players fostered a kind of "rebel" image, complete with unkempt beards and scruffy hair. Damon, in fact, even coined the term "the Idiots" to refer to himself and his scraggly BoSox stablemates, a nickname that, somehow, endeared the club even more to the long-suffering, increasingly energized "Red Sox Nation."

By 2007, Arroyo had departed for the Cincinnati Reds (and even two-thirds of his backing choir were no longer commanding Red Sox roster spots). Nevertheless, Arroyo's rendition of "Dirty Water" and the spirit it reflected lived on in the hearts (and record collections) of many Red Sox devotees. One such fan was Samantha Kacos, a student at the University of Southern California (USC) and a member of the USC Repertory Dance Company. Kacos, who had choreographed two pieces for the company's 2006 production, "Peter Pan: Dancing through Neverland" (and performed in a few others), was recruited to contribute additional choreography to the 2007 "Step into Spring" program, scheduled to take place at USC's Bing Theatre on April 26 and 27. Kacos responded by collaborating with a few fellow members of the troupe on two pieces, while creating one piece entirely on her own.[21] Taking into account the "spring" theme and considering her own passion for the Red Sox (and her active memory of the 2004 World Series triumph), Kacos settled on a very appropriate subject to serve as her driving force—and a very appropriate tune to ignite and inspire her choreography. The result was a dance work entitled, "Opening Day at Fenway Park," and the music selected by Kacos was none other than Bronson Arroyo's version of "Dirty Water."

The piece, which utilized ten members of the USC Repertory Dance Company (including Kacos herself), opened with three dancers wielding and swinging baseball bats at the front of the stage. Kacos opted for a jazz style that incorporated movements used by cheer squads. Baseball bats functioned as props throughout the performance and, on occasion, seemed to take the place of poles as the dancers gyrated and extended in the fashion of pole dancers. From start to finish, the choreography was energetic and athletic and Kacos made constant references to baseball along the way, as company members displayed swinging, sliding, and pitching motions at various times, including one moment when a dancer, playing the part of an umpire, signaled that another sliding dancer was "safe." It was a fitting tribute to a cherished ball club and served as a kind of good luck charm, as well. After all, it was in 2007 that the Red Sox made their second trip to the World Series in four years and, once more, earned a championship crown for the city celebrated in the song that inspired a dance work by Samantha Kacos at the very beginning of the baseball season.

It is worth noting that, following her time at USC, Samantha Kacos returned to the Boston area to attend the Massachusetts Institute of Technology (MIT), where she continued to dance and choreograph for the MIT Dance Troupe.[22]

"Baseball Dance" (2009)[23]

Comic dance ensembles are relatively rare; however, those companies that do choose the path of physical comedy very often draw their themes from popular culture. In the previous chapter, we discussed the piece, "Sports Newsreel," created and performed by the mid-20th-century comic dance team Mata and Hari, which featured a lively and humorous section devoted to baseball. In the early 21st century, another dance group that sought to infuse their choreography with comedy was the Brooklyn-based, all-female Cocoon Central Dance Team, a self-described "energy packed dance group ready to wet your pants." Cocoon Central, whose members actually met as students at Boston's Emerson College, formed as "house dancers for The Moon Comedy Variety Show," held at the Brooklyn club, Union Pool. On July 28, 2009, Cocoon Central presented what was described as a "Baseball Dance" for the evening's entertainment. The piece featured three dancers (Sunita Mani, Tallie Medel, and Eleanore Pienta), sporting baseball caps, sneakers, black tank tops, athletic shorts, and striped tube socks resembling baseball stockings. After jogging onto the stage, the dancers came together in a huddle, with arms draped around one another's shoulders, as a recorded, barely audible voice began warbling the opening lines of "Take Me Out to the Ball Game." Soon, the voice was replaced by a surging dance beat and the dancers broke out of the huddle and proceeded to perform a series of movements and steps for the next three minutes that repeatedly referenced the more obvious and more subtle movements of baseball, including the swinging of the batter, the wind-up and follow-through of the pitcher, the flashing of signals by both the catcher and third base coach, the use of the bat to knock dirt out of the batter's spiked shoes, and the use of hands to adjust wayward athletic supporters.

In the end, certain audience members may have viewed Cocoon Central's rapid-fire piece as an amusing trifle and even, perhaps, a gentle spoof of the rituals and common gestures of those "actors" who inhabit the baseball diamond. However, some may have considered Cocoon Central's "Baseball Dance" to be much more of a spotlight on the innate presence of dance in the actions of the players and the rhythms of the game.

"Forever" (2009)

Described by Deborah Jowitt of the *Village Voice* as "taut and turbulent … witty and beguiling,"[24] and by Tom Phillips of danceviewtimes.com as "a pleasure to watch,"[25] the high energy dance work, "Forever," which premiered in 2009 at Dance New Amsterdam (DNA) in New York City, was not about baseball and did not include any overt movements taken from the game itself. Still, the performance of choreographer Laura Peterson's abstract, "candy-colored,"[26] cheetah-fast piece prompted critic Phillips to reference baseball in his February 19, 2009, review. Remarking on the performance of one particular dancer from Peterson's company, Phillips wrote, "Watching Christopher Hutchings run, fall, roll, and shake himself off is like watching a good ballplayer do his work on the diamond."[27] Later in the review, Phillips once again harkened back to baseball, stating, "The sound is loud and funny, with many references to the rough rhythms of everyday life, such as the repeated 'boom-boom WHOMP' that sounds like the old applause machine at Shea Stadium."[28] Although Phillips conceded that "Forever," with its avant-garde score by Rob Erickson and its multiple stylistic influences, was able to "remind you of anything," it was quite telling that the clearest association brought to the mind of Phillips himself was baseball—a sport that has been described by multitudes of fans and admirers as "timeless" and one that inspired an art exhibition and a corresponding book that bore the name, *Diamonds are Forever*.

"Uptown" (2009)

In 2009, Matthew Rushing, then a dancer with the Alvin Ailey American Dance Theater, presented the Ailey company with a brand new choreographic work. The piece was called "Uptown" and its source of inspiration was the Harlem Renaissance. Only the second piece of choreography contributed by Rushing to the Ailey company in his seventeen-year career, "Uptown" was big and ambitious and, given its subject matter and scope (the Harlem Renaissance's multitude of facets, its major personalities, and its profound cultural impact), almost iconic.[29] Part meditation and part celebration, "Uptown" featured period costumes and music, authentic spoken word recordings, historic images, and, as one might expect, movements adapted from the era's most popular dances. In what could be viewed as a subconscious nod to baseball, Rushing divided "Uptown" into nine sections (commencing with "No More Auction Block" and culminating with "Cotton Club") and used a different historic and carefully selected recording and/or series of photographs to set the tone for each section and help drive the action.

Among the many images flashed onto a screen set behind the stage was a particularly striking one from the early 1930s of the New York Black Yankees baseball club, a team that attracted many dedicated supporters from the African American entertainment world, including the great dancer Bill "Bojangles" Robinson (who actually wound up co-owning the team in the latter part of the 1930s).[30] The ballpark and the stage maintained an intimate relationship during the Harlem Renaissance and many of the leading cultural figures in New York's black community spent a substantial portion of their leisure hours cheering on the team at Yankee Stadium, as well as at other baseball fields in the New York Metropolitan area. Indeed, many performing artists, including dancers, entertained spectators before and during ball games. The link between black baseball and black culture was quite obvious to even the most casual observer and, like the team's two immediate predecessors, the New York Lincoln Giants and the New York Harlem Stars, the New York Black Yankees were a source of pride and a powerful unifying force in the Harlem Renaissance era. It is no wonder that Matthew Rushing made a decision to display a team photo of the Black Yankees alongside images of such Harlem Renaissance giants as Josephine Baker, W. E. B. DuBois, Duke Ellington, and Zora Neale Hurston. The Black Yankees *mattered* and, just as the team's on-field play helped to inspire musicians, writers, and dancers of the day, so did the work of the day's black artists provide inspiration to the Black Yankees and the legion of black baseball clubs that thrived in this pre-integration period.

Since premiering in 2009, "Uptown" has become a regular part of the Alvin Ailey Company repertory and, thanks to the Ailey Company's extensive and rigorous touring schedule, spectators throughout the world have had an opportunity to experience the brilliant juxtaposition of baseball and the jitterbug, the Lindy hop, and other representative dances from the heyday of the Savoy Ballroom, the Audubon Ballroom, the Cotton Club, and the Apollo Theatre.

"Boricua Beisbol" (2011)[31]

Ten years after her first choreographic meditation on the place that is held by baseball in the history and culture of Puerto Rico and the Puerto Rican people, Austin, Texas–based choreographer Ana Maria Maynard chose to return to this theme in celebration of and tribute to the great Puerto Rican baseball players of the past, including the magnificent Roberto Clemente, a member of the National Baseball Hall of Fame in Cooperstown, New York, and the man who is considered by many to be the greatest Puerto Rican baseball player of all time. As she did in "Plena Baseball" (her 2001 composition), Maynard, in "Boricua Beisbol," focused on family to tell a larger tale. In the case of "Boricua Beisbol," the tale is recognizable to all. A young man, Emilio, is a member of his town's baseball team in Puerto Rico; however, he is not prepared to pursue the sport as a career. Then, in a crucial game at the end of the season, Emilio succeeds in hitting a home run that results in a victory for his team and a trip to the thrilling league playoffs. This experience causes Emilio to reconsider his plans and this new sense of uncertainty provokes a series of strange encounters with a set of "inspiring and unexpected advisors" drawn from the annals of Puerto Rican baseball history.[32]

Maynard selected her accompanying music, performed by live musicians, to represent the "diverse musical palette" of the island.[33] As critic Nancy Flores points out in her December 13, 2011, *Austin American-Statesman* review, in "Boricua Beisbol" Maynard "showcases everything from salsa to the more traditional music of the Puerto Rican mountains."[34] According to a press release issued by Maynard's Puerto Rican Folkloric Dance company (PRFD) on November 4, 2011, "Each year, Sembrando Herencia [the name given to the series of musicals produced annually by PRFD] seeds an awareness of often-forgotten elements from Puerto Rico's rich heritage—bringing history to life for … the audience and the dancers, musicians, and performing arts students who share in the experience."[35] History and the "shared" experience of an entire culture, indeed, were brought "to life" in "Boricua Beisbol." Using bilingual dialogue as well as dance and music, Maynard's joyful work was able to shine a clear light on the complex and painful decisions—and resulting struggles—that are faced by so many who are given an opportunity to pursue what may be a "better life," but who never wish to lose their identity or

Publicity photograph for Ana Maria Tekina-eirú Maynard's "Boricua Beisbol," featuring members of the Puerto Rican Folkloric Dance troupe, Austin, Texas, 2011 (photograph by Zera Thompson; courtesy Ana Maria Tekina-eirú Maynard).

Puerto Rican Folkloric Dance ensemble in "Boricua Beisbol," 2011 (photograph by Zera Thompson; courtesy Ana Maria Tekina-eirú Maynard).

their connection to "Boricua." And driving the production from beginning to end was Puerto Rico's own National Pastime, the game of *beisbol*.

"Boricua Beisbol" premiered on December 4, 2011, in Austin at the Rollins Theatre at the Long Center for the Performing Arts.

"A History of Ballet in Nine Innings" (2012)[36]

Although a full discussion of the vast, multi-layered topic of "dancing at the ballpark" shall be reserved for a follow-up book, it is important to mention a few instances where dance companies and baseball clubs collaborated on an event held on the baseball field, in front of hundreds, thousands, or even tens of thousands of fans in attendance primarily to watch a baseball game. Two of these collaborative ballpark dance programs—the performance of Louis Kavouras's "Baseball Dance" by the Repertory Dance Company at Cleveland's Jacobs Field and the staging of segments from Moses Pendleton's "Bat Habits" and "Baseball" by Momix at the SkyDome in Toronto, both having taken place in the 1990s—already have been described. It is also important to cite the 1997 pre-game show by the Streb/Ringside dance ensemble, led by choreographer Elizabeth Streb, at Minnesota's Metrodome (in advance of a game between the hometown Twins and the New York Yankees),[37] as well as the demonstration of Navajo powwow dancing at Phoenix's Bank One Ballpark, home of the Arizona Diamondbacks, on Native American Day in 2002.[38] Additionally, in the summer of 2010, New Jersey's ICON Dance Complex excited minor league fans of both the AA-level Trenton Thunder (at Arm & Hammer Park) and the Class-A Lakewood Blue Claws (at FirstEnergy Park) with fully charged numbers choreographed by director Beth Hubela.[39]

One event, though, merits a slightly lengthier discussion in the context of this book, due principally to the careful and rewardingly collaborative manner in which the two parties in question were able to plan the program and cooperate on its successful execution. Early in 2012, the Brooklyn Ballet and the Class-A minor league Brooklyn Cyclones, both relatively fledgling entities and each seeking wider exposure and stronger community ties, made a decision to initiate a joint, mutually beneficial venture, to be held inside of Coney Island's MCU Park during the baseball season. Taking advantage of the extravagant, eclectic, and bounteous promotional efforts designed to lure and reward Cyclones rooters, as well as the creative, copious, and unbounded outreach efforts carried out year-round by the Brooklyn Ballet to connect with younger and older citizens of Brooklyn, the two upstart, Brooklyn-based organizations came up with the idea of a midsummer "ballet night" at the ballpark, to be held at a time when the children enrolled in Brooklyn Ballet's summer dance program also could be involved in the on-field performance. The date selected was Monday, July 23, when the Cyclones were hosting the Aberdeen IronBirds, and arrangements were made for tickets to be sold at the box offices of both the Cyclones and the Brooklyn Ballet. A decision also was made to provide any fan wearing a tutu with a voucher for a free hot dog and soft drink.[40]

Using a diagram of MCU Park in the rehearsal studio, Brooklyn Ballet director, Lynn Parkerson, and her enthusiastic artistic assistants crafted a full evening's worth of dance, to be presented in small, two-minute sequences and to be linked to the histories of both ballet and baseball. To quote Parkerson, "We decided it would be great to show five transformative historical moments in the evolution of both ballet and baseball ... great coinciding events in the history of baseball and ballet"—with a decidedly New York City focus—that would be clarified further for fans through projections "on the Jumbotron at the ballpark," as well as through brief descriptions offered by ballpark announcers.[41] The title chosen for the program was "A History of Ballet in Nine Innings," which reflected the desire to demonstrate the many connections that exist between the two disciplines. Performances of the short dance sequences would take place during pre-game warmups, in between innings, and as fans rose for the seventh-inning stretch. Dance segments selected by Parkerson, by and large, were taken from the repertory—first of all, in order to illustrate the historical events being commemorated (e.g., a portion of *The Nutcracker* was danced after fans were informed that, historically, the premiere of George Balanchine's *Nutcracker* and the World Series victory of the Brooklyn Dodgers over the New York Yankees occurred just one year apart) and secondly, in order to reduce the tension level for the dancers, for whom a relatively unknown and unpredictable performance area already would be a source of stress. In other words, familiar pieces and movements would be much easier to handle and would allow the dancers to relax and focus on the performance rather than worrying about learning and remembering new steps.

At the same time, though, Parkerson did arrange for one brand new piece of choreography to be created—and this new work did manage to sprinkle some baseball movement into the mix. Michael Fields, also known as Mike Supreme and director of the hip-hop program at Brooklyn Ballet, put together an original, baseball-infused dance number for his hip-hop students—a number which would be unleashed during the seventh-inning stretch, at which time the coinciding historical events being celebrated would be the birth of the Cyclones in 2001 and the inaugural year of Brooklyn Ballet, which occurred in 2002.

In the months leading up to the show, various collaborative promotions were arranged, some of which involved the two Cyclones mascots, Sandy the Seagull and PeeWee, dressing in tutus and performing ballet steps at Brooklyn Ballet performances. Finally, when July 23 arrived and the "Baseball Meets Ballet" extravaganza was finally realized, media coverage was substantial and a mix of baseball fans converged on MCU Park. A lengthy rain delay interrupted the game and performances at one point and the Cyclones wound up on the losing end of the game; however, the joy and excitement of the collaboration were not at all dampened. Mike Supreme and Sandy the Seagull traded hip-hop moves while the game was delayed, ballerinas "danced on the crisp green grass," and ballplayers and spectators alike gaped at the artistry and "graceful athleticism" (in the words of Eric P. Newcomer of the *New York Times*) of the Brooklyn Ballet team.[42] Steve Cohen, General Manager of the Cyclones, advised fans in a press release that this would be "a night you won't want to miss."[43] Cohen explained that "fans who come to MCU Park tend to expect the unexpected … but seeing a *grand battement* instead of a grand slam, or *sautes* instead of stolen bases … is going to be a completely different experience."[44] Of course, he was absolutely correct—but in a very positive way. The feeling of success, perhaps, was described best by King Henry, a Cyclones "on-the-field promoter," whose real name is Guy Zoda. As Newcomer reveals in his *New York Times* article, when asked by Newcomer to describe the event, King Henry very astutely commented, "Win, win, win, win."[45] And both Parkerson and Cohen, in their own ways, echoed this comment, with each expressing a strong desire to make this collaborative venture, this melding of baseball and dance, an annual tradition.

Carmen (2013)

The 2013 North Carolina Dance Theatre production of *Carmen* is a wonderfully fitting way to round out this review of baseball-inspired concert dance in the early 21st century. Australian-born associate artistic director, Sasha Janes, opted to transport this classic, uni-

versally known story of "passion and betrayal" from 19th-century Seville, Spain, to North
Carolina in 1934, with its even more familiar musical score slightly rearranged and augmented
by the more local sounds of (live) bluegrass music.[46] Instead of a Spanish cigarette factory,
Janes placed the center of the action in a North Carolina textile mill, where Carmen was
employed and which, based on actual historical events, was in the midst of a volatile workers'
strike. Moreover, Janes, in his research of the period, learned that, in the 1930s, there existed
something called the Carolinas Baseball League, which consisted of teams composed of local
millworkers. In his desire to keep the story rooted firmly in North Carolina soil, Janes concluded that a star Carolinas League baseball player (and fellow millworker) would be the
ideal illicit love interest for Carmen, substituting for the traditional toreador character featured
in Georges Bizet's opera.[47] Thus, a baseball element was added to the story, which meant that
baseball choreography, created by Janes, would be required.

The final product, which premiered at the Knight Theater in Charlotte, North Carolina,
on October 17, 2013, revealed a baseball player, portrayed by Pete Leo Walker, whose movements exploded with power, grace, and sensuality. Melissa Anduiza as Carmen could not
help but be seduced by the spectacle of masculinity that was tempered by sensitivity of spirit
and delicacy of form. It was bold and beautiful and thoroughly attractive—impossible to
ignore. And, thanks to Janes, it proved to be a glorious example of Americana—a newly
begotten, exceedingly close relative of "Mighty Casey" and "Billy Sunday," a performance
piece that transformed Old World rudiments into something distinctly American, oiled and
richly seasoned by the game of baseball. Incredible, of course, is the realization that the North
Carolina Dance Theatre's production of "Carmen" turned out to be—to expand on the
thoughts of Rebecca Ritzel of the *Charlotte Observer*—"a Spanish story, written by French
composer, set in North Carolina,"[48] choreographed by an Australian transplant, danced by
an international cast of performers, and featuring a main character who happens to be a star
baseball player. Sasha Janes managed to make a piece that drew from the past, celebrated the
present, and pointed happily and anxiously to the future.

*   *   *

Finally, before our extended examination of the manner in which baseball has permeated
the world of concert dance comes to a close, it seems important (and rather appropriate) to
devote a few lines to the topic of dance school recitals and the corresponding impact of the
Internet. For decades, dance schools throughout North America have used baseball as a tool
in dance education. Working from the concept of using the movements associated with familiar subjects and activities to teach young people the fundamental techniques of dance, American, Latin American, and Canadian dance educators have drawn heavily from simple, basic
baseball vocabulary when working on creative movement with children. A wonderful and
striking example of this approach can be seen in the 1976 educational video, *In the Beginning…*, which highlights the work of dance educator Patricia Hruby, who is filmed during a
"serial movement" class while working with kids in an Indianapolis elementary school on
"phrases" and "combinations" based on pitching, catching, and hitting. According to Hruby,
"We're making combinations of movements out of those familiar baseball movements because
all kids know how to play baseball."[49]

Another excellent example may be found in one of the standard texts used by North
American dance educators, *Teaching Children Dance*, by Theresa Purcell Cone and Stephen

L. Cone. In the book's section on "Learning Experiences for Third, Fourth, and Fifth Grades," the authors describe in great detail a "Baseball Dance," which is presented as having three primary objectives: (1) To help young students "perform movement sequences based on baseball skills"; (2) To train young students to "move in unison with others to the same rhythm"; and (3) To make students aware of the fact that "dance can be used to celebrate an event."[50] And the song that Cone and Cone suggest that teachers use when working with kids on the "Baseball Dance"? Why, "Take Me Out to the Ball Game," of course!

Along these lines, it should come as no surprise to learn that, in addition to pirates and sailors and animals and sweets, baseball is a relatively common subject for dance pieces that instructors create for school recitals. And this is where the impact of the Internet is demonstrated in a striking and significant manner. Prior to the 21st century, it was not very common for homemade tapes of dance recitals (usually recorded either by family members of the young dancers or by the dance schools themselves) to be available to anyone beyond those with some connection to a given dance academy. Parents, for example, might share tapes with friends or relatives, school directors might offer tapes for sale to the friends and relatives of students, and dance teachers might screen tapes in class for instructional and/or entertainment purposes. In recent years, however, thanks to such Internet video sharing sites as Vimeo and YouTube, these hitherto "limited edition" tapes may be posted and shared with the entire world. This ease of access has made it possible to view numerous recordings of school recitals that take place all over the North American continent, many of which feature baseball-inspired routines, including a "Take Me Out to the Ball Game" number performed in 2009 by students from the Panorama School of Dance of Surrey, British Columbia[51]; a National Dance Day performance by the teen and pre-teen members of the Dance Factory "tour team" prior to a 2010 baseball game in Bridgewater, New Jersey (choreographed to the Pat Benatar song "Hit Me with Your Best Shot"[52]); and two different dance pieces, choreographed for end-of-term recitals in 2008 to John Fogerty's "Centerfield" (one featuring students from the Susan Winter School of Dance, located in Massachusetts, and one capturing the baseball moves of children being trained at the Experimental Movement Concepts dance center of Maryland and Pennsylvania).[53]

Of course, videotaped dance recitals turn out to be only one of many types of recorded dance works that are accessible to viewers via the Internet—and the Internet itself is merely one vehicle, albeit an exceedingly large (and growing) one, that can provide a viewer or potential viewer with access to recorded performances and images. In the next chapter, we will explore the universe of the recorded performance and the recorded image and discuss at least some of the many instances where baseball and dance have intersected over time in motion pictures, on television, and, more recently, in video format (which is generally designed to be shared and accessed electronically). Once again, it will become clear that if a medium is invented or created that makes it possible to showcase dance or baseball, dance and baseball will find a way to intersect very early on. As Howard Good comments so eloquently in his study of baseball films, *Diamonds in the Dark*, "There is an artistic potential in baseball that isn't found in other major sports."[54] Film and television choreographers, as well as producers of works for the "screen" (in all its forms) have attempted for decades (and continue to attempt) to capture this quality (or "potential") on film and/or tape. The end product is an impressively large, open-ended catalog of recordings that shed even more light on the intimate connections that exist between baseball and dance.

Interlude

A Physical Therapist, a Ballet Company Volunteer Coordinator, a Dance Company Director and a Baseball Executive Talk about Dance and Baseball—Dean Caswell, Joan Quatrano, Lynn Parkerson and Steve Cohen

Dean Caswell, Physical Therapist[1]

When you train as an athlete, you go to practice all the time and what do you do at practice? You repeat and repeat and repeat skills until they become *habit*. Anyone who has been an athlete really has that mindset about what it takes to be excellent. If you really want to be the best, you had better practice and you had better practice it hundreds and hundreds of times. And this is true of dance as well. It's the same concept with both: to get the motor skill acquisition so that it becomes automatic. You have a mindset and knowledge that you've got to just do it over and over and over again. I would drive my parents crazy with kicking a soccer ball off the wall: left foot, right foot, left foot, right foot, left foot, right foot, left foot, right foot, pattern, pattern, pattern, pattern, reaction, reaction, reaction, reaction. I didn't have to think about it—my feet would just do it. My brain didn't have to go, "Okay, I'm going to do this, this, this, and this." It just did it.

Let's say someone comes in with a neck problem. The best question to ask right away is, "What aggravates your neck?" And then the patient may tell you, "Well, it bothers my neck to have to look to my left" or "to change lanes" or "to reach." Then I will say, "Okay, do that for me," and I will watch the patient move. Does he move in a pattern that explains why he is potentially driving that pain pattern to happen? If you don't look at that and you only look at the things in individual components, you're going to miss something because the body doesn't work in individual pieces. It works in very large, global pieces, with small pieces having to stabilize, other pieces having to move you, etc.

Let's say you have a baseball player or a dancer come in and tell you that they have back pain or shoulder pain, I will ask right away, "What aggravates your pain, what movement aggravates your pain?" With the dancer, "What part of the dance choreography are you having problems with? Can you demonstrate that for me? Let me see it." With the baseball player, "Let me see how you throw, let me see what your throwing mechanics look like." What are they doing? You start really looking at how the movement is influenced and what adaptive behaviors potentially have to kick in because of the pain or the strain or the sense of instability that they're describing.

164

So that's kind of where my approach comes from. I have this background of my own and then I started to really get exposed to just observing and seeing—and especially observing sports and physical activities that I hadn't done myself. I realized that I needed to understand them better in order to treat the practitioners better. The Rockettes, for example. When the Rockettes were in town, I took care of their dancers—I was going to say "athletes," because, to me, athletes and dancers are kind of in the same category. Before they started coming in, I asked them if I could come and observe one of their practices (I'm going to call it a practice). And, just like with baseball players, they were doing their pre-performance routine, their warmup. So I went in and watched them do a warmup and then I

Physical therapist, Dean Caswell (photograph courtesy Dean Caswell).

watched them do their show, without anybody there, so I could see the physical demands and what conditions they were working in. For example, the floors. The floors in some of these old theaters are horrible, so what is the reverb that is coming through the floor, up their joints? They're dancing on three-inch heels, so what kind of disadvantage is that overall to their skeletal system? It's putting them outside of neutral and they are having to control that; yet, they're jumping and bouncing and doing high kicks. They had a portion of the show where they did this jump, leap, down into a split, hitting smack-dab onto the floor. That's a major trauma. There was another part of the show where they leaned up against each other, slid their arms through each other's arms, and then did this lean-back while they were on their heels and they were holding each other up through this massive core, massive trunk strength, all the way down. Many of the girls would come in and they had bruises on their triceps from where the person's weight was sitting against them, and bruises on their biceps from the weight of the person in front of them because that person was under their armpits and all that weight was sitting back on them as they were in this line. And the people in the back of the line had bigger bruises than the people in the front. And so they had this chronic bruising from just holding that pose. I wouldn't have understood that unless I had seen the show.

So it's that same concept. It's a huge advantage if you take the time to look at movement. I think that the tendency to break things down into pieces that are too small is probably one of the biggest errors that is out there in many cases with people who are trying to set up programs and treat cases. Yeah, you have to break it down into the specific tissue that is injured, so that you can help to heal it, but you have to look at the *cause and the factor behind the breakdown of that tissue*. Sometimes it's really complex because it could be something that is really far away from the injury site that's creating the problem.

I've worked with some professional baseball players, but the professional world has really enclosed itself at this point. Professional teams really keep things in-house, which is at least partially a result of wanting to protect themselves and the athletes on the team. News gets out fast and the next thing you know it's being reported in the paper. So they've really tried to create a "team network" environment and a lot of teams have really developed a great health and wellness team. They have their team of doctors, trainers, PTs, massage therapists, and acupuncturists, all built around the athletes. It's all right there, which is a much better avenue than what existed in the past. It's really improving and they're more aware of what they need to do to keep people healthy.

This approach focuses not only on dealing with injuries when they happen, but also on preventing injuries from happening in the first place. How do you make it so that in the grind of a 162-game season and in the grind of a dance season, where you might have six to eight shows that demand body movements and muscular needs that may be completely different from one show to the next—how do you keep these ballplayers and dancers healthy so that they can be on the field or on the stage, performing?

As far as the work that I have done with dancers is concerned, it comes down to location and experience. The work with the Rockettes, for example, took place when they were performing here in Seattle. They were looking for a specific type of group and they were looking for a PT/ATC kind of combination. They are very much like athletes when it comes to their approach to performing. Athletes and dancers get used to performing with things that are not 100 percent. It's life. I mean, I have played many games with a sprained ankle that was nowhere near 100 percent; yet, I was out on the field with a taped-up ankle, playing. When you're grinding two shows a day on weekdays with one day off somewhere and then three shows a day on the weekend and rehearsing all the time, things are going to be sore. You're going to have sore stuff. So you're also dealing with a little bit of just maintenance. They've got something going on and they need it worked on, just to keep it loose because it keeps wanting to tighten up because they're performing tons and tons of repetition. This ankle needs to be taped, this hamstring's got a little bit of a strain, but can you keep it as healthy as possible and keep it going so that it doesn't become a bigger strain?

So they're looking at that triage of keeping people on the field, keeping them as healthy as possible when they're performing as much as they are. And, simultaneously, there is the PT front: What can you give them, as well, to potentially make this go away even though they're still performing, or to provide improvement so that it doesn't get worse? Or how can you change something that is potentially negatively influencing the situation? You're looking at a lot of different things at once.

Recently, I went with my daughters to see *Cinderella* performed by the Pacific Northwest Ballet and, for the whole show, you just sit there amazed, watching the performers and seeing how fluid and easy and simple they make it look. And, yet, I know how *not* simple and easy it is—how hard it is on their bodies to be doing what they're doing. Yet, they make it look so graceful and smile the whole time. It's pretty amazing.

Can you talk a bit about the issue of training regimens and warmups?

DC: Dancers seem to do a nice overall combination of stretching to actively performing some of the skill tasks that they're going to be doing, kind of preparing their bodies for the performance. Besides that, it just seems as though they're able to set up their nervous systems to be ready to go. The biggest similarity that I've seen with baseball and dance is that they both really require a huge amount of *deceleration strength*. The ability to slow something down. When you swing a bat, the opposite muscles of those that created the swing have to slow you down or you go past a point and then you have to reaccelerate. The shortstop who goes into the hole and has all of his momentum going in one direction but he's got to throw in the opposite direction—he's got to be able to decelerate himself enough to then reaccelerate to make the throw. A dancer who goes into a leap has to land and then decelerate all of his weight because what is he going to do next? He has to then change direction and create acceleration elsewhere. They do lots of rotational motions. To make it look beautiful they have to accelerate into it but then they have to control it. Those other muscles have to decelerate it to keep it in control, to ensure that they don't keep going forward and that they land where they're supposed to.

I would say that there is one other major difference that is important to point out in terms of warmup and training and it really has to do with the different ways that dancers and ballplayers approach "in-between" time. What do ballplayers do in between each inning? They sit. Dancers never sit. They have no time to sit. So you have a ballplayer who needs to be in this active position and then in the middle of the inning, he sits—it's these flexion postures. It is just completely opposite of what you're going to be asking your body to be doing in a few minutes. All of a sudden I'm going to go from sitting on the bench … so, yeah, they swing the bat, but what have they done? They've just totally cooled down any warmup they may have done for their hamstrings and everything else by sitting. And then they have to go and get upright and then completely extend by swinging the bat and then completely extend the sprint. But they do this over a four-and-a-half-hour period: sit, stand on the field, sit, stand on the field, sit, stand on the field. That's really hard on the body because you're going into this kind of flexion concept but then your entire sport is extension focused. I mean, there really isn't anything else to say. That's a very difficult thing to be coming in and out of, especially if you have a long inning. Think about that pitcher who has been sitting on the bench for so long and then he has to go up and completely reopen his body to throw the ball.

Dancers will collapse for a little while, but then they'll get up and immediately start stretching and moving again. What would you suggest for ballplayers?

There should just be more movement. Stay upright, do some walking around in the dugout, just keep moving. Same thing for pitchers. Even without resistance, just some light movement with the arms—and you'll see them doing that sometimes with bands, where they're just kind of keeping things warmed up, keeping the arms moving. Again, get upright, walk around a little bit, try not to sit for long durations of more than a couple of minutes at a time and then move. That's why you hear about so many designated hitters who go back into the clubhouse and spin on the bike and try to move around and they get on ellipticals and they do things to keep their bodies active and moving. There's a reason for it. It's hard to swing a bat after you've just been sitting.

Overall, in both cases, it primarily comes down to training. No matter how well you warm up or stay warmed up, if your body is not trained to accept or generate the forces that you're going to ask of it—speed, power, agility—eventually it's going to break down. So on the warmup versus the training, I still think it really comes down to the training. You can warm up in the best possible way, but if you're not trained up for it…. I mean, I can go warm up right now for skiing. But I haven't been on the slopes all year and no matter how well I warm up, I have a chance to strain my muscles if I go ahead and ski because my muscles are not in shape for skiing. So it's that concept. Warmup can have so many variances to it and it's important to have it, but if you're not trained up for the amount of force you're going to apply to your body, the chance of an injury is there. It's a question of singular plane, power work, speed work, agility work, acceleration vs. deceleration, but then also where based on watching the function of the sport or dance or activity that you're going to be doing, integrating pieces of it together as part of your training so that you're doing things in coordination with the activity that you're going to be doing.

In terms of characteristics that dancers and ballplayers or dance and baseball have in common, what are your thoughts?

If you are considering mental and psychological and physical characteristics, I think that you have some clear similarities and differences. If we take things by position, we can correlate things a little better. Outfielders and dancers, middle infielders and dancers—they probably have body types that are more similar. A little more lean, quick, agile, and, at the same time, powerful and skilled. There are probably some third basemen and pitchers who would be in this group as well. But definitely not all! And, on that same flipside, you will find most catchers and first basemen. With pitchers, you're going to have many who are pretty heavy or stocky and solid or not necessarily in the greatest shape—many who just don't have that kind of body type. At the same time, though, you see some kind of overall similarities. When you get to a professional level, most of these people have some blessed skill set. Coordination—hand/eye, foot/eye coordination. Movement patterns that they've worked on to make really special, but already were pretty much there on some level—they just had to build on them. So on those fronts, to get to the levels of being professional dancers and baseball players, there is an aspect of just being somewhat gifted. Your body picks up skill well and it coordinates it altogether with all of the different systems that are required—the eyes, the brain, the quick reaction time. When you start talking about these high, professional levels, I think that there is enough evidence that shows that there is a correlation between these things and the actual practitioners—to the point where even people who may not have the perfect body types both in dance and in baseball can use those skill sets to be excellent.

Now, I think the difference in baseball is that you can have variations in skill sets that can make you excellent. Many pitchers, for example, cannot become fielders and many fielders cannot become pitchers. There's a reason for that. But, with dance, I think that, on the whole, you need to have a kind of baseline component of things that are similar for each person, because everyone is going to be doing similar movements.

I think that where you get the biggest correlations are in the psychological areas. The drive. The goal-oriented nature. The understanding of and need for repetition to achieve skill. The incredible focus and the ability to mentally block out distraction. The ability to categorize and compartmentalize. The ability to live with and continue to perform with constant pain or discomfort. With the kind of grind that they go through, dancers and baseball players are most likely living day in and day out with something not really feeling good and they're able to find a way to just stick it in a place. I hate using these categories, but, overall, I would classify them as "high pain threshold" people. They're generally not the people who wind up having chronic pain diagnoses. They have things that might hurt them over their entire life spans, but you hardly ever hear them complaining about them. They just keep motoring on. And, in most cases, they're overachievers. In general, those are the ways I would categorize people I've worked with. They have these kind of components that make them driven enough to practice enough to be able to be at that level and stay at that level. Otherwise, they're not going to make it and they give up, because it's a lot of work.

As clients, have you found that dancers and ballplayers are easy to work with?

On the whole, yes. Because of the fact that they're motivated and goal-oriented. The big piece of the puzzle is just making sure that you understand their goals. You have to make a point of understanding what their goals are and what they're really trying to achieve. If you haven't done that, you're going to struggle with it because they're not going to feel like you are giving them what they need. If they feel that you understand their goals and that what you are trying to drive them to and help them with is to get to that goal, they're great. You can tell them, "I want you to do this because I need you to get this for you to get to that goal" and they'll be, like, "Great!" The biggest problem or issue with them is making sure that they don't do too much. They're the people who you really have to rein in. You have to really give them good, solid boundaries of how much you want them to do because, otherwise, they'll go do more. Again, that's their lifestyle. More is not necessarily better, but, in their mindset, it is. "If I do this a hundred times and Dean tells me that it's going to get this good, then if I do it two hundred times, it's got to be better!" No—not necessarily. So, yeah, they're motivated, they're goal-oriented, you give them tasks, you tell them why, you give them the amounts, they come back and they've done it and generally they're better and you can move them on to the next stage. They have that discipline. It's just another thing that falls into their repertoire of "pattern."

You have to explain to them *why*. They want to know *why*. They don't want to just be told, "Do this," which I think is pretty normal for all people, but, in their case, even more so. They really want to know that it's about what they're trying to drive themselves back to. "I need to get back on the stage" or "I have to be able to perform this movement and this movement hurts right now." And I will say, "Okay, because of this, this, and this, we need to strengthen this, we need to give you better stability to balance in this position, we need to be able to get you to land and control this without doing this motion so that you don't strain that, so I want you to 'uptrain' this because of this…." And they say, "Great!" So you have to be specific with them and you have to be confident enough to be specific with them. That's intimidating for some people when it comes to training these people because they want to know the "why" and you have to be able to explain to them "why" and, if not, then get ready, because they'll put you on the spot. And that's as it should be—you *should* be able to tell them why.

Joan Quatrano, Volunteer Coordinator, New York City Ballet[2]

About when and how did you become interested in both baseball and dance?

JQ: Well, my father was a Yankees fan, so games were always on. I grew up with them in the background and it was the thing that I did more than anything else with my father. When I think about my father, the association is always baseball. And at that time they still had doubleheaders on Sunday and we would sit and literally watch all day long. And dance—I was taken by my mother to, actually, New York City Ballet, to *The Nutcracker*, when I was very, very young. And that also was just this transforming experience. I just fell in love with it and bugged her until I took dance lessons as well. So I grew up with both as a child.

We would go to Yankee Stadium all the time. And my whole family went to the Stadium—that was something that everybody did together. We would drive up to Yankee Stadium and go to games. And I would always listen. I remember walking back and forth to school, listening on the radio. This was always part of what I did. I grew up during that wonderful period when Mickey Mantle and Roger Maris were having their great run of records and, in ballet, I became a devoted fan of Rudolf Nureyev. So, as a late teenager, I actually started traveling all over the world—I would buy a ballet ticket and then I would buy a plane ticket to get myself to the performance! It was an incredible time. I mean, I would never do that now—you know, you'd never be sure that anybody would be on the stage! It was an amazing time. They were these very charismatic superstars who drew you in because you cared about them. In ballet, you had this incredibly, blindingly beautiful man who had this passionate partnership with this equally beautiful but older woman. It was an incredible love story. And, in baseball, you had this blazingly brilliant baseball player who was also adorable. Mickey was just an incredibly handsome man, but troubled because this great talent that he had was tempered by severe injury. So you pulled for him. You knew about his family, you knew about his wife, you knew about his children, you knew about his struggles.

Also, everything about the Yankees…. I don't know whether it's partly also because I was part of a generation that was "striving." You know, I was the first person in my family to get a college education, I was the first person in my family to get an advanced degree. And I saw the excellence that was promoted by the Yankees and the excellence on the stage in this art form that I loved. And I somehow just applied it to me and said, "Look, I'm not going to do 'Giselle' and I'm not going to play baseball, but I can be good at something also." It just taught me things about myself. Even to this day when … and you hear this all the time—people will say, "Oh, the Yankees are so boring, I hate the corporate image, I hate the…." All of that I *love* because all of that to me stands for proper presentation, proper preparation, excellence, carrying yourself in a certain way, having pride, knowing how good you are. I mean, I think all of those things are incredibly admirable and that's one of the reasons I love that whole organization—even though, you know, some of the management can drive you crazy.

And, in fact, in discussions here, especially now, we talk about brand management and what does it mean and how you promote a ballet company when the old-time audience members are dying off and the young ones aren't coming in. They focus an awful lot on branding. And nothing is more iconic or no one is better at branding than the Yankees. The staff here, when I go into meetings with the company director and the higher level management, they roll their eyes whenever I start talking about the Yankees. But I *do*—because it's *true*! I mean, I get an email from the Yankees saying, "Glad you bought your tickets. How did you enjoy your experience?" They just—they know how to make you feel. Even though it's ridiculous, they make you feel like you know them and they know you. And that's incredible for such a large organization.

And it teaches you a lot about how to run an organization and how to maintain a fan base.

Yes, it does, it really does. And just when they opened the new stadium, I mean, the "How may I help you?" people walking around—they greet you when you come in, they say "Good night" when you leave, they're always looking to assist you if they can. It really is an amazing operation. And, for their season ticket holders, you have a personal contact. You can place a phone call and they'll call you back. That's amazing to me—when you place a phone call to the Yankees and they call you back! Money is always the end-goal for this team—I mean, I'm not naïve that way. I understand their motivation and their goal. It's not just championships, it's also money. But that's okay and, for both the Yankees and the New York City Ballet, there is that same concern for putting out a really quality product.

In ballet, what we're trying to do now more than anything is to get the audience to understand who the dancers are as people. And that is very, very important. I don't know whether you've noticed some of our photographic campaigns, what the brochures look like. There are very personal pictures of dancers. They try to get you into their personalities. One of the reasons why you become a devoted follower or fan of either the sport or the art form is not only because you love the thing itself, but also because you become attached to the individuals: the stars, the players, or the performers. That personal connection is very important. They become much more human to you.

Do you recall feeling, when you were growing up and enjoying both baseball and dance, that there were connections and similarities?

I don't know that I made them so literally. But I am always aware—and *was* always aware—of the physical skills that are involved in both. Either the way a step is executed, or how graceful somebody looks, or how well somebody can run. I was always aware of that pull. In the same way for tennis—because I started going to Forest Hills very early on. I had seen Ken Rosewall and was a great fan of Bjorn Borg. Just the way that they moved—the skill, their ability to do something on a dime, to stop on a dime. Or to hit a ball that would hit the back of the court or throw somebody out at the plate from center field. Those are amazing skills that I was always interested in and I always admired people who could do that kind of thing. And it was the same thing for dancers.

On the other hand, although I enjoy that kind of physicality, I also was always aware that it was not just that. In ballet, if somebody can turn fifteen times, well, great, but it has to be *artistic* in some way. Or if somebody has a great jump, that's good, too, but it has to *mean* something. So, for me, it's not just the physical ability of someone, but something more, above and beyond that, that counts for something. So I admired players who played that way, with great finesse and intelligence, and then dancers who danced that way. I was always aware of these connections, although I don't know that I specifically thought about it. In some ways, this association was much more apparent for me in tennis. If you go to tennis matches, an awful lot of ballet fans are there. I guess the similarities are very, very much there, with that sport.

I remember when I first went to London to see Fonteyn and Nureyev at Covent Garden, it was heaven. I would go to Wimbledon during the day and then I would go and see performances at Covent Garden at night. That was just *the best*. I remember it was when Bjorn Borg was still playing and I had gone to see matches with him at Wimbledon. And then you'd see other fans who you saw at the Opera House at the tennis stadium. It's interesting—the players that I always seem to gravitate towards are the ones that look conditioned, that have that aesthetic appeal. The players who do not look like conditioned athletes drive me nuts. I think that's one of the things that I've always found so interesting about the Yankees. Usually you don't find out-of-shape players playing for the Yankees. Look at the big deal they made out of Sabathia when he showed up looking unconditioned. That's not a good thing if you're a Yankee—they like you to look a certain way.

Look at Mariano Rivera. I mean, what a great example of someone who just is a great fielder, a great athlete. He looks the part. And I know that I have great prejudice here because I adore Derek Jeter, but this happened all the time at Yankee Stadium when you would hear someone comment who was seeing Derek Jeter in person for the first time. Shortstops are not supposed to be big and he was one of the first really tall ones. When people saw him in person for the first time, they would say, "Oh, my God, look how tall he is! Look at his legs!" They were amazed at the way that he looked, in particular, because he is tall and he is lean and he has this certain look. All of that is such a plus to me and I know it appealed to me— that was the similarity that also appealed to me.

What are other thoughts that you have about the connections at this point?

Well, you have to have this incredible devotion. And one of the things that amazes me and that I'm always in awe of when I work with dancers is that they have decided that this is what they're going to do at a very young age. When most people are playing with dolls or just interested in frivolous things … you're a child … and when you're six or seven or eight and you decide, "I want to study ballet and I'm going to go to class often and I'm going to suffer through pointe shoes because I enjoy this physical activity and then I want to be this." Because you have to make this decision early on. I think it's very similar with baseball players—in a lot of little boys, especially, and little girls playing in Little League. But you do have to make this decision early—that you want to pursue this.

Of course, in baseball, teams can take such a long time to cultivate their young players, and I think that the Yankees tend to take a particularly long time. They season their young stars—you hear about "phenoms" when they're twenty and twenty-one, but usually you don't get a chance to see them until they're maybe twenty-five or twenty-six. I wish you could get them when they're a little younger than that. But I think it's that very early identification of what they want to be that is unusual and is rather remarkable.

And I think it also takes—and you heard Jorge Posada say this when he announced his retirement—it probably also takes family support. You have to bring a kid to a game, you have to bring a kid to lessons—and so many of them talk about that, that their families helped them, that their families supported them, that their fathers played with them or threw a ball to them or taught them how to hit in many cases. There's often that kind of connection, I think, too.

You had mentioned that you do some lecture demonstrations and workshops for kids and teachers where you incorporate baseball movements and ideas. Can you talk about this?

Every once in a while we bring in student groups and, you know, when you have these little boys, you want to … these stereotypes still exist, that dancing is just for sissies or dancing is just for girls. Or sometimes if you want to get the attention of a high schooler, what I do is say, "Who's your favorite ballplayer? Well, you know what? They couldn't get through a ballet class!" And then they look at you like you're crazy. You want to relate to a child in terms of the heroes whom they may have and often those are sports heroes. So if you talk about the kinds of strenuous preparations and activities that are involved in this art form, which looks so effortless, and you tell them that it's so specific and it's so difficult in terms of physical training, then you get their attention and they understand and they appreciate it a little bit more. And the thing I was referring to specifically is that we do show some photographs of baseball players to some of the young children who come in here regularly. We bring in nursery school kids. Again, to get mostly the little boys aware that this is a hard physical thing to do and the way you get them to understand that is to first show them their sports heroes and then they can make the association. One of the other things that we show them when they come into the lobby—we often show them a little videotape that features Balanchine's "Western Symphony." You know, you have the cowboys dancing and that's one of the ways we get the attention of the children. They see the cowboys dancing—men with cowboy hats on and cowboy boots and they're dancing! Then the children can relate to it a little bit more.

It makes me think of the similarities between a company like the New York City Ballet and a team like the New York Yankees—where dedication and commitment are so important for the company and for the team and creating that solid unit is so important, with everyone pulling for one another. Do you see that kind of similarity between a ballet company and a baseball team?

It's totally similar. In this company in particular, the people who want to put themselves forward and who want to be recognized as stars are the ones who don't usually work out. And, with the Yankees, the whole thing about the philosophy of that team and what I think George Steinbrenner really put forth so well is that it is the winning and it is the team that are the most important things. Individual achievements are fine, but, in the end, if you get sixty home runs and the team doesn't win, it doesn't matter. And I think that is what I admire so much, also, about the Yankees and the players who play that way.

And it's absolutely the same in terms of this company. I know the company director always looks askance at people whom he senses are really just out for themselves, who don't understand the "whole." And, in fact, one of the most thrilling things you can see, especially in this company, is when you see, like, the final movement of "Symphony in C" and everybody is on that stage—all ranks, all levels, and they're in those gorgeous black-and-white costumes, and they're all dancing together. It's stunning, it's absolutely stunning. So, yes, those moments are very important and it is very much part of the philosophy of the company, as well. Not one person is above the art.

That makes me think about the whole concept of "breaking out of the corps" in ballet and breaking out of the "utility" role or advancing from the minors in baseball. The whole idea of "getting a shot." In baseball, a player may perform really well whenever he has a chance to play or may be fabulous in the minors and, in dance, a dancer can do really beautifully when he or she is given an opportunity, but it seems that, in many cases, these players and dancers are never able to get ample playing or dancing time—they are never able to "advance," in spite of their excellence and potential for greatness.

I think there are similarities. You sometimes have to bring certain people up—and I think there is definitely a parallel between the development of a baseball player and the development of a dancer. Some are ready very early on and can take the pressure and can live up to the expectations. And then there are other people who take years and years and years to develop their talent. I think Merrill Ashley was in the corps for nine years before she really started to come into her own. So you do have to know how to develop certain people and how to nurture them.

And this is something, in sports, that I think isn't always done well. Especially in New York, where you have the media that gets involved and I think that the Yankee machine gets involved in a lot of that, too. I think you can hurt somebody's development, too, if you don't just leave them alone and let them develop in a certain way. I know Joe Torre always talked about that—in terms of Derek Jeter, in particular. The first year he came up, he mostly sat on the bench towards the end of the season, during a series. And then the next year he got to play, but he saw what it was about first. I think they knew what they had in this player, but you give them a little exposure. You do have to nurture and develop talent very individually and I think in both areas that's true.

Sometimes it seems like you run into a situation where a specific manager or dance company director has a certain perspective or a certain point of view and that can affect a player or dancer's development.

That's exactly the other point. In dance, you may have people in the corps who are brilliant dancers, but if they don't fit into the director's vision or, for some reason, if their aesthetic doesn't match his, they may not ever get a leading role even though they could be leading dancers elsewhere. But, in the case of New York City Ballet, they choose to be here because of the nature of the company, its history, its aesthetic, the choreography—this is the only place they want to dance. And I think it's probably true in sports and in baseball, as well.

Yes, there are frequently players who sit around for a long time and get no real opportunities on a team and then, ultimately, the players get moved or traded and they wind up flourishing elsewhere.

The whole psychological aspect is important—where you play and where you dance. There are dancers who have been stars here and then chose to leave. Miranda Weese, for example. She went to the Pacific Northwest Ballet because she wanted to have a life. She didn't want to dance every single night. Some people here thought she was nuts. She was a brilliant dancer, but she likes to live in the woods, she likes music, she wanted to do other things and they couldn't understand it. And look at how many people get chewed up by the New York media who are talents but they can't take the pressure of the media in New York—certainly playing for the Yankees. They just can't take it—yet, when they go somewhere else, they thrive. So all of that—there are psychological aspects that are very important also. As we all know, the psychology of how you're feeling affects how you perform, whether it's mentally or physically. That's true for anybody and it's very true when you're in a high-profile sport or if you're an artist in a high-profile company. I think those are similarities, too.

What about similarities when it comes to fans of baseball and fans of dance?

I think the people who become rabid fans are the ones who are interested in the details, who know the names of pitchers and so on. I have a lovely seat at Yankee Stadium now from my season tickets. I call it my "subscription." And I have a single ticket and I go on my own on Sunday afternoons. I sit in an area with a group of men who have been coming for years and years and years. These are men who were moved from those seats I was talking about before, those seats in back of home plate—they had these wonderful seats for all these years and then they were bumped to this area. When I started sitting there, they were very nice and very friendly and they talked to me right away and it was nice. Gradually, like when there was a moment in the game when a reliever had to come in, they would say to each other, "I can't see who it is—who's that warming up in the bullpen?" And then I would tell them. They'd look at me and say, "Oh, you know who that is?" And I'd say, "Yes, I know who it is." Or I'd hear them talking about something and one of them would ask, "What was the name of that player?" And I would tell them the name of the player they were talking about. You know, so, gradually, they thought, "Oh, she knows this stuff." That's how you develop this camaraderie between each other, because it *is* more than just, "Oh, isn't that beautiful" at the ballet, or "Oh, look at that home run" in baseball. You know the game, you know the sport, you take the time to find out the nuances.

And the same thing is true in dance. You know what the story of the ballet is. It's like when somebody, for example, comes in and says to me, "Oh, I know all about New York City Ballet and I know all about Balanchine." Sometimes I give them a little test, especially if they tell me they want to be a docent. People do this all the time—they walk in and they say, "Oh, I want to give talks to other people." And I'll say, "Oh, okay. So tell me, what are the two oldest ballets that exist in our repertoire and what years were they done and what company were they done for?" Then this blank look comes on their face—they have no idea. And I'll tell them, "You don't have to answer me, I'm not trying to embarrass you, but *can* you answer that?" And when I know that they can't, I'll say, "Well, it's *Apollo* and *Prodigal Son* and they were done for Diaghilev." But then I know that they *don't* know what they're talking about and those are the differences—when people do learn what it's about and the details and the history and they understand all the components that go into something. And I think those are a lot of the similarities.

As I said, I'm a fan of a lot of other sports. There was a volunteer who died recently who was really not terribly old. We were sports fans as well as ballet fans and she could talk about the skills of Roger Federer versus [Rafael] Nadal and she could talk about the ice skaters that are the top ice skaters in the world and what their qualities are. She knew the nuances and she could talk about them and she knew the history. And that's what distinguishes the people who become the really devoted followers, I think.

Of course, you can carry this to an extreme. But also—it's also like knowing when you have to be there, having to witness something, knowing something is going to be historic. Those things are very important. I mean, when a milestone…. I was at the game when Derek Jeter broke Lou Gehrig's record, even though I sat for an hour and a half in freezing rain, I just wasn't going to leave. And then, of course, I bought tickets for five games in a row because I was damned if I wasn't going to be there for Derek's three-thousandth hit! And it was the most extraordinary experience. It was the most wonderful, communal experience to be in that stadium for those five hits. It was fantastic. And I remember that when I went back for my subscription seat, my seat area mates said to me, "Were you there?" I said, "Sure I was there." They said, "What are you talking about—how did you know when he was going to do it?" I said, "Because I got tickets for five straight games!" They looked at me like I was crazy! But I said, "Well, what else are you going to do?!" So it was funny—only one of the men had done the same thing, so we were identified as the "true fans." It was really funny.

But you have to be. I mean, I could talk about seeing Nureyev do this or that or the other thing. I went to Switzerland once to see Nureyev's production of *Raymonda*. Nobody was doing *Raymonda* at the time. When Rudi first came, he was the one who was putting on a lot of the Russian productions that were never done here. I mean, he did the "Corsaire Pas de Deux" for Fonteyn at the Royal before it had ever really been seen and he did the "Shade" scene in *Bayadere*—he mounted it at the Royal. No one had ever seen the full *Bayadere*. And I traveled to see these things, because if you're a devoted fan and you know something is unique…. I mean, I'm sure it's the same as when an opera singer does something for the first time. That's not my area, I've never been interested in that, but if you are that passionate about something then you feel like you want to be a witness to it.

In terms of the movements in baseball, what do you see that is particularly "dance-like"? Do you see similarities in the movements?

I think there are similarities in the stopping and starting. The acceleration and then deceleration. And also just the sharpness of things and the accuracy—you know, being able to hit things on a dime. I don't mean literally "hitting," but being able to hit a mark, to do something very quickly and maybe unexpectedly. Those are great similarities, I think.

In our workshops, it's literally Jeter's jump throw that we do show people when we're talking about a *jeté*. That's what we do show—we show that picture. I sent a letter about this to the Yankees and they published it in their magazine…. And I love seeing that—I love seeing other players now when they do that. It's a thrill. Someone's whole momentum is going in one direction and then they turn around and throw the ball the other way. Sometimes they don't even have a really good look at what they're doing. Certainly when Derek Jeter does it, he all of a sudden jumps and turns his body and throws the ball and you think, How in the world did that happen? It's amazing, it's a thrilling thing to see.

I'm also wondering if you could talk about your famous desk display—what you actually have collected on your desk and in your work area.

Yes, yes. Well, I'm looking at Jeter's #2 Movado watch right now. I have a lot of his dugout pictures. I have Fonteyn and Nureyev in *Giselle*, Fonteyn and Nureyev with Frederick Ashton, Rudi and Margot at the end of *Romeo and Juliet*. I have a picture of Nureyev's grave. I have a picture of Andre Agassi, who is the other inspiration that I have. *Newsday*—this double-page picture of Jeter in *Newsday* when he got his three-thousandth hit when he has this smile on his face, coming around the bases. Those are things that are inspirational to me and that's what I have. I have a lot of other pictures of Fonteyn and Nureyev. This is a funny aside: A board member came into my office one day—this is years ago—and they looked around and said, "Who is that on the wall?" They were looking at Fonteyn and Nureyev. It was as if because I worked at the New York City Ballet I shouldn't have that on the wall. I looked at them and said, "You know, great is great and inspiration is inspiration and that's it and they're staying there because that's what sustains me." They looked at me and that was it. What a stupid thing to say. Oh, I also have a picture of Mr. Balanchine's headstone.

Have you run into dancers at the New York City Ballet who are baseball fans?

Totally—oh, all the time! We talk about games and they ask me if I'm going and they tell me when they went. Oh, yes. Tremendous. Most of them are Yankees fans! It's a nice bridge in terms of a relationship between me and them, too.

Lynn Parkerson, Artistic Director, Brooklyn Ballet[3]

How did the idea to collaborate with a baseball team originate? What was the inspiration and vision for this project?

LP: I've been to some games in Coney Island and I love the park and the location of the park. It's a beautiful ballpark. And Brooklyn Ballet has always made a strong connection between ballet and sports in our education programs. When we teach in public schools and do residencies, particularly with regard to boys doing ballet, we've talked about Michael

Jordan and Herschel Walker and Lynn Swann doing ballet—different sports figures who, at one point in their careers, have either done ballet or supported the idea of ballet and know how difficult it is and what an athletic endeavor ballet is. So that's always been a piece of our programming and we do have a lot of boys in our programs and many of them have persevered and several are now on their way to becoming professional dancers. So this connection always has been something we know. The Brooklyn Nets recently started and we were just thinking about reaching out to sports institutions. I think one of our staff members reached out to Steve Cohen of the Brooklyn Cyclones and just put forth the idea of having Brooklyn Ballet perform at the baseball stadium during a baseball game. I'm not quite sure *exactly* how it came about, but I believe it was one of the ideas that we were pursuing as part of our outreach efforts and connecting with communities. And Steve Cohen was just gung-ho about it—he just loved the idea.

So Steve came to our studio and we met and we all agreed that we had to do this. Then we started thinking about *how* we could do this, given the structure of the baseball game, which is sacred. It wasn't necessarily about doing a full ballet performance—yet, it was. What would the timing be for this kind of program? Thinking about the Cyclones, they do so many things at the games and this was another thing to try. The idea of kids coming to a baseball game and maybe attracting more girls to the park, knowing that they were going to get to see ballet as part of the evening. And a program like this would be a great vehicle for outreach to schools. It was kind of a way of bringing more people to a baseball game and certainly to expose more people to ballet. There are generally more spectators at a baseball game than at your average ballet performance (unless you're doing some huge ballet event). So we just thought it was a great way to bring the communities together.

Once we decided to do it, that's when the fun really started. We began considering the nine innings and structure of a baseball game, the history of both baseball and ballet. We do a lot of historical work at Brooklyn Ballet, so we felt that this aspect would be very important to explore. We decided to perform five or six times between innings during the course of the game and then do the seventh-inning stretch. We figured that we would perform as people were coming into the stadium, then perform during the national anthem, and then do a pre-game performance. We were doing a summer intensive program at the time, so we also brought all the kids involved in the summer intensive to perform during the pre-game and the seventh-inning stretch. The kids got to demonstrate a ballet class—as the baseball players were warming up, we were warming up, too! So the crowd got to see how physical ballet really is and how important warming up is for both baseball players and dancers. It was really fun to see the two from the purely physical standpoint—the different ways that you warm up the body and how impor-

Artistic director of the Brooklyn Ballet, Lynn Parkerson (photograph by David Becker).

tant that component is to any kind of sincere or high-level athleticism. And dance, certainly, would go into that category.

As far as history and historical connections are concerned, we decided it would be great to show five transformative historical moments in the evolution of both ballet and baseball. And we wanted to make sure that there was a local flavor. For example, the Brooklyn Dodgers beat the Yankees in the World Series in 1955, and that was just a year after George Balanchine premiered *The Nutcracker* at the New York City Ballet. And, of course, if anyone has heard of anything about the ballet, it would be *The Nutcracker* and, since 1955, it has been performed *every year* by the New York City Ballet. So these were great coinciding events in the history of baseball and ballet and we arranged for that information to be projected on the Jumbotron at the ballpark and the announcers announced it, too, and then we would show a two- or three-minute piece from *The Nutcracker*. Then we'd be done and the next inning would begin. So we kind of wove this story throughout the game. Obviously, it was hard to choose just five events from each to highlight, especially when it came to baseball, which has so much history and so many highlights! The last one was that Brooklyn Ballet was founded in 2002 and the Brooklyn Cyclones baseball team was founded in 2001, so we kept that local thread. But we started with the Baroque period for ballet—with Louis XIV—and the beginning, the emergence of baseball. In that case, the dates didn't coincide, although we were talking about the origins of both. With everything else, though, we were able to stick with that one- or two-year difference in major historical moments.

How much time passed between the point when the idea was raised and the date of the actual performance? And what was the process like?

I think that we decided sometime early in 2012—when the teams were just beginning to get ready for the season. The Cyclones knew their schedule and they were starting to slot in their special events. Things like "Medieval Night"—you know, the million events that minor league teams arrange for their home games. So the timing was very good. We had our initial meeting sometime in February or March and we decided on a date in July—a date that worked well for us, during the last week of our summer intensive, which would make it possible to involve the kids in the program. The Cyclones were very interested in generating a lot of publicity about this event and they were also interested in attracting more people to the ballpark in Coney Island from the Downtown Brooklyn area—they have a lot of fans already, particularly from South Brooklyn, but, like us, they are always looking to expand their fan base. And, since we do street performances and events, the Cyclones worked with us in the weeks leading up to the show to spread the word about our collaboration. They have a couple of great mascots and they were able to arrange to have these mascots appear at some of our performances. For instance, we had Sandy the Seagull and Pee Wee appear in tutus and do ballet steps and gestures that were very much in keeping with their mascot personalities. I've always thought mascots were funny, but this whole experience made me appreciate mascots even more! And, really, all of the people in the organization who were involved in the program were such great people—and such characters. There is one guy there named King Henry who is a big part of the Cyclones organization and who was incredibly enthusiastic about the idea. I think he even might have done some ballet in college. He gets dressed up in a special outfit for Cyclones games and does all sorts of things at the ballpark. He's very well known to fans and to everyone on the team and he even has an office in the stadium.

Well, King Henry was definitely interested in being a part of the action and he wanted to wear a tutu for the ballpark show. [As he is] a big guy, though, we wound up needing to construct a special tutu for him, which was actually made out of two tutus, sewn together. At the ballpark, we opened with a Baroque piece that was about King Louis XIV, of France, and the beginnings of ballet. We have a beautiful ballerina who danced the part of Madame Pompadour in the piece and we had King Henry dance with her. He did some steps and a bit of improvising and then the two of them went off together. It was very sweet. Everyone was just so open and wanted to have so much fun with the ballpark show.

We really tried to give as much as we could in every area to integrate both of the organizations and, if we do this again in the future, we'll work on even more integration, such as working the Cyclones' cheerleading squad, the Beach Bums, into the performance a little more. I should add that none of the instances which involved the mascots or any representatives from the Cyclones were meant as a gag. We tried to involve them when it seemed right, when it made sense—like pairing King Henry with Madame Pompadour. And a lot of what wound up happening turned out to be very "off the cuff" and we realized quickly that, in the setting of a ballpark, with so much going on (like advertisements and player introductions) and with no set timing for each inning, we had to be ready for anything, especially considering that we only really had about a minute or a minute and a half to do our pieces throughout the game. One time, the music started a little early, so the dancers just dashed out onto the field and started doing their material, which turned out to be fine. But there wasn't the usual "theatrical protocol," which we knew would be the case. It meant we really had to be "on our toes"! We got there and figured out where everyone would need to be for that big moment! We were never completely sure whether the advertisement would get played before the music for the dance—and sometimes even the announcer didn't know in advance! We might be ready to go out onto the field when, suddenly, it was "Okay, it's time to do the March of Dimes thing!" or "We need to do the Floating Hot Dog!" and then we would need to brace ourselves for the moment when the activity was done and we could start our next piece. It was something! And we had twenty kids from the school that we had to manage and a bunch of board members sitting in a VIP box, so it was really like "All systems go!"

How did you prepare for the event and how did you work with the Cyclones along the way?

Where we danced on the field was limited because we were mostly dancing between innings and, while the dances were taking place, the players in the field were warming up— throwing balls around and getting ready for the inning to start. So our stage turned out to be the foul territory areas between home plate and first base, and home plate and third base. And these were actually huge spaces, so there was plenty of room for the dancing to take place. We rehearsed here in our studios. We created all of the different little segments and the pre-game show right here, mostly by excerpting works that we have done already and putting them together to form a kind of "history" of ballet. I was calling them "dance bites." And we did put together a ten-minute mixed-movement piece, using the hip-hop dancers and the ballet dancers and the Baroque dancers. That was what we wound up doing as part of the pre-game show, as people were coming into the ballpark. That pre-game show was where we had more extended time and where we could do a bit more. We did a photo shoot with the Cyclones players and it was arranged for one of our ballerinas to pose with a player who also was wearing a tutu over his uniform.

It was important for the game to be kept quite separate from what we were doing. Of course, the players, you could see, were peeking from the dugout and watching everything we were doing. You could see that they were really enjoying it. I remember one very nice photo that was taken of one of the players admiring a ballerina as she was in mid-air on the field, in the middle of a leap. We were in a separate space as the players were warming up and we didn't actually dance with them, but, who knows, it is certainly possible that next time there may be a little of that. This first time was such an "unknown" that, in some ways, just having us there was unique and provocative enough! But people really did seem to enjoy us being there.

Did you have time to be on the field before the performance to get a sense of the space and do some on-field rehearsing or was the performance itself the first time that the dancers had a chance to experience the sensation of being out on the baseball field?

We had a little bit of time in the late afternoon and early evening, in between the player warm-ups. And that's when we were able to figure out where on the field we could perform. I would just say, "You're going to do this section here—you just run on and run off!" Some of that didn't even get figured out until right before it happened during the game. And when we did the pre-game show, we got a better sense of where and how the performing would take place. At rehearsals, I had a picture of the baseball diamond in the studio and we knew the sequence of dances in advance and had an idea of when during the game each piece was scheduled to be staged. For instance, between the first and second innings, we knew we were going to do a certain piece and so on. We had everything mapped out and everyone understood what was scheduled to happen, so if we had to change anything, we would be ready and could be more flexible. Early on, for example, we realized that spectators sitting in a certain area of the park were having some trouble seeing things, so we made a decision to alternate where we performed on the field to accommodate all seating areas. So there were things we noticed as they were happening that caused us to make some adjustments.

Fortunately, the material in general was not new for the dancers, so that reduced stress a great deal. They weren't doing anything brand new and didn't have to remember new choreography. You don't want to premiere something in a space that is a bit of a mystery—where you don't even know which direction you will be facing.

Was the music being played over the loudspeaker?

Yes. We were asked to provide the announcer with a CD of all the music, with the tracks in order. The exception was when I wanted to use the same piece of music at different points. I asked if I should just put that same musical selection on the CD again, in order of appearance, and was advised to just note for the announcer to go back to a specific earlier track at that point and he would make sure that the same track was replayed. The spoken sections, though, were live. And, of course, the national anthem was live, so, for our rehearsals, I downloaded about seven different versions of the national anthem that ranged in speed from thirty seconds to two and a half minutes and we created choreography—very simple, very reverent—that you could do fast or slow. We even had nine-year-olds involved and the major lesson to learn was: "We don't know how fast it's going to be, but we can do it in all of these tempos." We based everything on the *words*: "On this word, you're here. On that word, you're there. And how long it takes you to get there depends on what the singer is doing." So the whole thing, really, was working with the unknown.

Even the weather was a factor. Just as the seventh-inning stretch was about to take place, it started to rain—and we were scheduled to do our closing number at that point! So all kinds of things were happening. It definitely teaches you to be adaptable!

Did you incorporate any actual baseball movements into the dance pieces?

The hip-hop dancers did. We did some stuff together, but also gave the hip-hop dancers their own segment, which turned out to be a joint 1980s tribute to the "Golden Age" of hip-hop and the World Series victory by the Mets in 1986. The music was early hip-hop and they used a lot of the "pop and lock" movements from the time. They created a little scenario of someone hitting a baseball, someone catching a baseball. The audience was able to see all of that very clearly.

Now that we're on this subject, I recall that many years ago, sometime in the early 1980s, when I was a solo performer in Germany, I did a dance that incorporated the motions of a baseball pitcher—the way the leg goes up and the spiraling back. I don't remember whether it was all choreographed or if it was improvisation.

But, getting back to the ballpark show, it was all repertoire, so I didn't create anything new that involved baseball. But the guy who directs the hip-hop dancers—a guy who collaborates with me all the time—took the opportunity to connect to baseball. The hip-hop dancers are actually part of Brooklyn Ballet, another part of our company. We started working together sometime around 2004 or 2005. The gentleman who leads the hip-hop troupe is named Michael Fields, but his hip-hop name is Mike Supreme. He's a big guy and, in very much the same way as baseball, our company is made up of people of all shapes and sizes and ethnicities and styles. That is very much another connection. Brooklyn Ballet is a very diverse company. It's very interesting. If you think of countries such as Cuba and the Dominican Republic and Japan—each has a huge ballet tradition and each also has a huge baseball tradition. I am not sure what this implies exactly, but it certainly is a coincidence and is very interesting!

Did you find that the dancers in the company were familiar or comfortable with baseball from the outset, or was baseball something that most company members were not too familiar with?

We have a company member who is from Georgia—not the state, but the country—and I think that this was probably something that was very new for him. But I think that everyone else was *very* familiar with baseball and was just super excited to dance on a baseball field. In some ways, it felt like a sacred space. The diamond and the green grass and the smooth, dark brown dirt. And when you shine the lights on that field, it's such a beautiful, very special atmosphere. You've been watching baseball on television and with your family forever and to bring ballet into that space was really exciting and remarkable. And it somehow "legitimized" some connection that maybe people might not think of and I think, in some ways, it gave the ballet some "weight."

Along these lines, what kind of response did you get, not only from the spectators, but also from performers and players?

We got great feedback. It's funny—I went to a game about two weeks before our performance, just to kind of check out the ballpark and get a better sense of where I was going to put people and all that. Well, as the national anthem was playing before the start of the game, some guy in the stands suddenly yelled out as loud as he could to someone on the field, "Get your fucking hat off!" And, right away, I started thinking, Oh, boy, if this guy sees a tutu on the field, we could be in big trouble! So, I definitely made sure that none of our dancers had a hat on during the national anthem. But I did have choreography planned for the national anthem and I didn't want to change that, so I just kept my fingers crossed! I wasn't trying to be provocative in any way—I just wanted to revere the tradition and have everyone enjoy this experience in a different way. And it turned out that everyone was completely fine with it! There was a ballerina in *arabesque* being lifted with one hand above the head of one of our male dancers when "O'er the land of the free" was being sung and then he dropped her into a fish dive when the song came to its climax and no one seemed to have any problem with it in any way.

I saw the players smiling a lot throughout the game and the fans seemed to be very involved in the whole event. Part of the promotion was that everyone who wore a tutu to the game got a free hot dog, I believe, and had a chance to run the bases after the seventh-inning stretch. So there were a lot of people who showed up wearing tutus—everything from little girls wearing full ballet costumes to older men wearing tutus on their heads! Unfortunately, the weather was not kind to us and it began raining after the seventh inning, so the running of the bases—which our dancers also were going to do—could not happen. But we were able to do everything else that we had planned to do and people seemed genuinely pleased and excited. I wish I would have had a chance to talk a bit more with the players, but things got a bit crazy once the weather turned bad. The end of the game finally did get played, but I think there was a delay of about two hours, so it was a long, long night for the team and they were pretty exhausted.

It got some very good press as well. The *New York Times* was there and, in their story of the event, they featured a really nice photo of one of our ballerinas on the field with a Cyclones player nearby, watching her perform. It was also publicized by the *New York Post* and in various other places. So we did generate a good amount of attention and interest.

Do you have any additional thoughts about how dance and baseball connect?

First of all, the training and the athleticism. Also, both have really rich histories. Ballet isn't necessarily talked about in the same way as baseball, but, if you look at the history of both disciplines, you will find that both have some very colorful characters. There is also that sense of dancers and baseball players knowing where they are in their respective spaces and the incredible timing that is required. In some other sports the action is more "flowing," but baseball, like dance, exhibits a lot of *stillness*. Being where you are for a certain amount of time and not moving, but always being ready to move or even explode when necessary. There is more of a "dynamic timing," as opposed to everyone going at the same speed the whole time. The idea of time and space is very similar.

You also can point to the movements of specific players. The pitcher, for example, can have those super high kicks, the catcher squats down in what we would call a *plié* position, and so forth. A great deal of flexibility is very important in both dance and baseball. And both have very specific movement "vocabularies," although, of course, the vocabulary in ballet has existed for a much longer time!

I also think about the "sacred" traditions that exist in both ballet and baseball and the fear of change that can exist for many fans and followers. In both ballet and baseball, there are strong contingents of folks who are very conservative or "traditionalist" and do not want to see any changes occur at all, while, at the same time, there are others who seem to enjoy some experimentation and updating and adaptation. Of course, I do think that there are probably certain things that you just don't touch. You can refresh things in a certain way and there can be an evolution, but you probably don't want to mess too much with some of the great foundations of either. For instance, you probably don't want to do too much altering to the score of *Swan Lake*, although people *do*—and, at first, that will generally be met with a lot of resistance and negativity. Sometimes things will be able to move through and be accepted, but it seems as though the "classical canon" is something that wants to be preserved. So I think there is flexibility as long as you don't fiddle too much with what would be considered to be the "bedrock" of either ballet or baseball.

And this brings to mind the "color lines" that existed for so many years in both ballet and baseball and how both were kind of broken in the United States at about the same time. There was an unwritten rule or code in both and you simply did not see any black ballet dancers, nor did you see any black baseball players in the major leagues. Actually, we thought about adding this parallel to the show that we did at the Cyclones game. I'm not sure why we didn't, but I definitely would like to see this element added to a future show. The connection between Jackie Robinson and Arthur Mitchell and the integration of Major League Baseball and professional ballet.

That's so true. It is difficult to fathom how difficult it had to have been for both Jackie Robinson and Arthur Mitchell and how strong both had to be to endure the resistance that they were faced with. It also makes you think about similarities that may have existed between Branch Rickey and George Balanchine and how determined both were to see this change take place.

I think in Balanchine's original descriptive writing about what he envisioned for New York City Ballet he made it clear that he was hoping to feature, I believe, eight "Nubian" dancers and eight "Caucasian" dancers. His original idea was to have a black and white company. In ballet, of course, things are still not yet there, but it's almost there and it's now a question of finishing the job. Without a doubt, the situation continues to evolve. And, in terms of "tradition," ballet companies do need to challenge tradition when it comes to casting and the specific roles that dancers are given. Demographics change and cultures come together and we have to get used to it by actually having it *be*, by *doing it*—not by *waiting* for the "right moment," waiting for it to happen. We're not going to get used to it until it happens. There is sometimes an emphasis on having the same types of people doing the same types of steps and I think it's just more interesting when you have *different* kinds of people doing the same steps.

I remember seeing the Stuttgart Ballet many, many years ago and, while they may not have had a very diverse company in terms of race and ethnicity, the dancers in the company were all different shapes and sizes. Before that, I had seen mostly "cookie cutter" kinds of companies, but the Stuttgart was made up of all different physical types and it turned out that the dancing was all completely harmonious. The corps work was completely together— it was as if they were all *breathing* together. So, at that point, even seeing a ballet company made up of dancers who were all different *heights* was something that really seemed different and unusual and interesting and exciting. And, at Brooklyn Ballet, we are certainly striving for diversity. We're very much like a 21st century baseball team in that way!

Steve Cohen, Vice President and Former General Manager, Brooklyn Cyclones[4]

In terms of the partnership with Brooklyn Ballet, can you recall how the Cyclones became involved and how the idea to do a program with the ballet came about?

   SC: I think we had an introduction through the borough president's office and I seem to recall that I proposed the concept of doing a baseball and ballet program to the ballet. I remember that I was looking at doing a "Broadway Night" on a Monday when Broadway is dark and I was trying to connect the dots on how to do something like that. And then when the introduction to the Brooklyn Ballet was made, I started thinking that maybe we could put together a ballet program around a baseball game.

What kind of program were you envisioning at that point?

   Fortunately, it was sort of what actually wound up happening! I was seeing it as being an opportunity for people to watch a game but see an actual ballet performed around it. So I wanted it to be from the time the fans walked through the main gates until the time they left, and I think that the Brooklyn Ballet did a really good job of putting that together. I don't necessarily think that we were trying to tie it into baseball at that point, but that's what ended up coming out of it. The Brooklyn Ballet was able to correlate the performance to important time points in baseball history and, more specifically, Brooklyn baseball history.

What was the experience like for the players individually and the team as a whole?

   Overall, I think it was a great experience for everyone. Of course, once the game was going on, it was hard to know how much the players were taking in, but I know that they thought it was fun and unique—especially when the dancers were coming directly onto the playing field and doing their performances. Our players are somewhat used to some out-of-the-ordinary things happening during our games. I remember that some of our players posed for pictures with members of the ballet—Phillip Evans, for example, did some really cool photos for the media prior to the game with one of the dancers. So I think that the players thought it was an interesting and fun idea and connection.

Vice President and former General Manager of the Brooklyn Cyclones, Steve Cohen (photograph by Marc Levine; courtesy Steve Cohen).

Did you get a sense that the event attracted some new people to the ballpark?

   Yes, definitely. Of course, it's hard to say for sure how many people were coming to a game for the first time, but it felt as though the event gave many new people who might not be big baseball fans a chance to enjoy the experience of being at a game. In terms of families, there might be kids or parents who might not be as interested in baseball as other family members, but this program might have helped those family members enjoy the action a little more and have as much fun at the ballpark as the baseball fans in the family. One family member, for example, might be a big baseball fan and play in the Little League and this would give that young person an opportunity to experience the dance while enjoying the baseball, while another family member might not be a baseball fan but now there's something going on at the game for that family member as well.

Could you see repeating this event in the future?

Oh, definitely, the Cyclones would like to see it happen again. Quite frankly, after the first meeting with the Brooklyn Ballet and once the planning began, the ballet people were probably the ones who had the most work to do to prepare for the event. They were orchestrating—or, I guess I should say, "choreographing"—it, for the most part. I think a lot of it will probably depend upon their interest in doing it again, but I've talked with them and I think that they got a lot out of it, as well. So I am pretty confident that we will make it happen again in the future.

In general, do you see a connection between dance and baseball—or, more specifically, ballet and baseball?

Yes, I think so. We all know that athletes have taken ballet or dance classes throughout the history of sports to help them with their performance on the field. I can't say that every baseball player dances, but we're watching *Dancing with the Stars* and it seems as though the athletes are always contending for the championships. So, yes, I do think that there's that connection.

I should mention that my original concept, when we talked to the ballet…. I don't know if you remember a pitcher who used to be on the Mets named Craig Swan. Well, my original idea for this program was to call the event "Craig Swan Lake" and actually do the ballet *Swan Lake*, and bring in Craig Swan. But we weren't going to wind up doing *Swan Lake*, so it didn't make a ton of sense—and, at the time, I wasn't able to reach out to Craig Swan anyway, so it didn't happen. But, if we did it again, that might be something fun to try. I thought that that would be a really great tie-in between baseball and dance.

5

In Front of the Camera

Film, Television and Video

The urge to capture on film the movements and stories associated with both baseball and dance—and the desire to record the extraordinary images of dancers and ballplayers in action—developed among filmmakers almost immediately following the invention of the motion picture camera. Indeed, prior to the turn of the 20th century, when the art of filmmaking was still in swaddling clothes, some of the medium's greatest innovators, including Thomas Edison, the Lumiére Brothers, and Paul Nadar, were positioning their lenses in front of ballerinas, visual movement artists, and men sporting mustaches, knickerbockers, catcher's mitts, and baseball bats. In 1896, for example, modern dance pioneer Loie Fuller attracted the attention of both Nadar and the Lumiéres, and each produced short silent films featuring Fuller performing her incredible, mesmerizing compositions (which continue to astound viewers).[1] Then, just two years later, in 1898, Edison, according to Robert Cantwell (in a 1969 issue of *Sports Illustrated*), was "able to persuade a Newark amateur baseball team to play before the camera in the backyard of his home."[2] This was followed by Edison's production, in 1899, of what is likely the first visual recording of a version of "Casey at the Bat" (subtitled, "The Fate of a Rotten Umpire").[3]

Since these earliest days, when baseball and dance in the United States each—at the very same time—were experiencing profound structural and philosophic transformations (and as film technology, too, was advancing at breathtaking speed), this "urge" to project images of dancers and baseball players has only grown stronger, resulting in frequent intersections. Thanks to film technology, in fact, the ability to demonstrate the connections that exist between baseball and dance has become a fairly simple task—and, as we shall see in this chapter, this endeavor has become relatively commonplace. It is even possible to suggest that the medium of film—along with its close relations, television and video—provides us with a near-perfect tool for exhibiting the baseball and dance partnership. Consider, after all, the effective use of slow-motion, split screen, and visual juxtaposition, as well as the impact of music on the filmed image (a shortstop leaping for a line drive in slow-motion, for example, as an ethereal and majestic melody by Schubert or Tchaikovsky or Gershwin soars in the background). Consider, too, that it was television that made it possible for millions of viewers to witness, in both movement and words, one of the most unambiguous references to this age-old "partnership." In 2007, the Disney Channel aired the sequel to its highly successful 2006 made-for-TV movie "High School Musical," and included a song-and-dance sequence that took place on a baseball field. The number was called, "I Don't Dance," and, as viewers of "High School Musical 2" observed the familiar actions of baseball blend seamlessly into dynamic dance steps (choreographed by Charles Klapow), the words of the accompanying song, sung by actors Lucas Grabeel and Corbin Bleu, made it very clear just how interconnected these two great art forms happen to be.[4]

In this chapter, we will explore the many ways that filmmakers, television producers, video creators, news reporting services, and even animators have captured and shared images that highlight, intentionally or by happy accident, the baseball-dance link. Well over 100 years of such moving images will be identified and described. The chapter is divided into two larger sections ("Film" and "Television and Video") and these two large sections are subdivided into categories that provide more specificity. In the "Film" section, there are categories for "Feature Films," "Cartoons," and "Shorts and Newsreels," while the "Television and Video" section includes the categories "Musicals, Teleplays, and Made-for-Television Movies," "Variety Shows, Reality Shows, Talk Shows, and Competition Shows," "Comedy and Drama Series Episodes," "Television Specials, Documentaries, and Reports," and "Commercials, Promotions, and Videos." The number of examples for each category will vary; however, the examples that *are* cited will be described in as much detail as possible. Some of the pieces in this chapter will be at least partially familiar from references found in earlier chapters, but most are mentioned in this chapter for the very first time. In all cases, though, examples have been selected because of the clear and unmistakable manner in which the baseball and dance connection is expressed—again, either consciously or serendipitously. It is also important to note, once more, that this is merely a *sampling*, albeit a relatively copious one.

Film

Feature Films

The vast majority of "baseball films"—motion pictures that tell comic or dramatic baseball stories—are decidedly devoid of dance. Yet, even in those movies without a single dance number or musical interlude or scene in which dance is discussed or depicted in some rudimentary fashion, the manner in which baseball activity is presented may be interpreted, in many instances, as "balletic" in nature. Again, as mentioned above, this is due, for the most part, to the employment of such cinematic devices as slow-motion, manipulated lighting, and/or mood-affecting music. Cinematic touches such as these can induce the viewer to experience a pitch or swing or fielding play or even a simple gesture or step by a player, manager, umpire, announcer, fan, or food vendor as *dance*. In a sense, an action that might otherwise be considered commonplace or insignificant is cinematically *elevated* or *enhanced* and what the director presents us with is a beautifully framed vision of what so many writers, broadcasters, social historians, and objective admirers (including Jimmy Cannon, David Falkner, Howard Good, Murray Goodman, Ernie Harwell, Madora Kibbe, Christopher Lehman-Haupt, and Harold Peterson, to name just a few) have referred to as the "ballet of baseball." Howard Good, in *Diamonds in the Dark*, expresses this popular observation with eloquence:

> To watch a double play being completed—the shortstop grabbing the ball and flipping it to the second baseman, the second baseman leaping out of the way of the base runner while pivoting and throwing, the first baseman stretching to pick the throw from the dirt—is to watch something beautiful unfold. If football is a kind of war, with a military vocabulary ("march," "bomb," "blitz," "sack") to designate its characteristic plays, then baseball is a kind of ballet.[5]

Among the numerous examples of "dance-less" baseball films that make painstaking efforts to reveal the balletic or choreographic nature of the game are such emotion-packed works as *42, Bang the Drum Slowly, Eight Men Out, Field of Dreams, Pride of the Yankees,* and what may be characterized as the apex of the dance-less, balletic baseball movie, *The Natural* (which features an epic, climactic, slow-motion home run hit by the hero of the story, Roy Hobbs, that evokes opera as well as ballet). In these films (and in the many more that are not named), the viewer cannot help but feel—thanks to the deliberate storytelling choices of the director and/or cinematographer—that baseball movement is a form of dance.

Of course, when it comes to making the connection between baseball and dance, it is possible to identify an ample number of feature films, both baseball-focused and otherwise, that take a wide range of alternate approaches. In most cases, the connection between dance and baseball is still expressed in visual terms (e.g., a baseball-focused film depicting actual dancing baseball players, a non-baseball-oriented film offering a scene with choreographed baseball activity, a character in a film donning a piece of baseball wardrobe while dancing, the juxtaposition in a feature film of a main character who dances with one who plays ball, etc.). However, from time to time, a film may include a moment of verbal recognition (i.e., some kind of statement about the baseball-dance connection that is made by one or more characters), as well as a visual or physical representation.

It is also important to be reminded of the fact that many early 20th-century baseball stars who performed in vaudeville also were tapped by film producers to appear in movies as lead or special guest actors. Although none of these ball-playing vaudevillians seem to have been asked to dance in their film roles, many did plenty of hoofing on the live stage (as we discussed in chapter 1). Mike Donlin and Rube Marquard, for example, performed no dance routines whatsoever in their respective, pre–1920 feature films, *Right Off the Bat* (1915) and *Rube Marquard Wins* (1912), but both had been watched by thousands of spectators on the vaudeville circuit as they danced up a storm with their glamorous dance partners, Mabel Hite (Donlin) and Blossom Seeley (Marquard). It can be argued that this reality points to another example of the connection between baseball and dance within the context of film. In this case, though, the connection is indirect and, as such, will not be the subject of further discussion in this section or chapter.

Please note that feature films cited are presented in chronological order. Please also note that three motion pictures that contain storylines or scenes that appear to articulate a relationship between baseball and dance—*Lovable Trouble* (1941), *Moonlight in Havana* (1942), and *I Wonder Who's Kissing Her Now* (1947)—could not be accessed prior to the completion of this book and, therefore, are not discussed.

They Learned About Women
(1930, directed by Jack Conway and Sam Wood)

The subject of baseball-playing vaudevillians is the focal point of this early movie musical, which stars well-known stage comics Gus Van and Joe Schenck as two talented members of the successful Blue Sox baseball club who divide their time between the ballpark and the music hall stage (where they perform as the song-and-dance team Burke and Glennon). Probably remembered best as the film that inspired the 1949 Gene Kelly-Frank Sinatra cinema hit *Take Me Out to the Ball Game, They Learned about Women* features dances staged by former

Ziegfeld Follies choreographer Sammy Lee, and eleven musical numbers, including nine original tunes composed by Milton Ager and Jack Yellen (with lyrical assistance in two instances from Gus Van). The theme of dancing-and-singing baseball players is introduced to viewers at the very start, when a headline referring to the vaudeville accomplishments of Burke and Glennon is flashed on the screen in close-up. The film shifts quickly from the vaudeville stage to the spring-training home of the Blue Sox and then to the Blue Sox locker room during mid-season, where a rousing, post-game song-and-dance number, "Ten Sweet Mamas," is performed by the victorious, celebratory players (complete with rhythmic rub-downs and syncopated shoe shines).

More Burke and Glennon routines pop up throughout the remainder of the film, including a few song-and-dance numbers that take place in a vaudeville theater, with Blue Sox teammates in the audience. Additionally, two other members of the team, Tim O'Connor and Sam Goldberg (played, respectively, by Tom Dugan and Benny Rubin), get a chance to do a routine of their own, "When You Were Sweet Sixteen," that comes to a close with a pleasant soft-shoe sequence.

Meet John Doe (1941, directed by Frank Capra)

The cleverly choreographed baseball section in this American cinema classic is easy to overlook. It occurs only briefly and, amid the film's robust sea of social commentary and brilliant dialogue, the scene may be perceived as an evanescent ripple. Still, in much the same way as Fred Astaire's elegant dice-throwing demonstration in *Swing Time* (1936), what the viewer witnesses when Gary Cooper and Walter Brennan begin miming the actions of a pitcher and catcher inside a Washington, D.C., hotel room is, without question, delightfully executed *dance*. And what better sport to spotlight in a Frank Capra film that has so much to say about American values and traditions?

Take Me Out to the Ball Game (1949, directed by Busby Berkeley)

With the possible exception of *Damn Yankees*, there is no other film that illustrates and celebrates the baseball and dance connection more effectively or boisterously than *Take Me Out to the Ball Game*. Based on the 1930 feature film *They Learned about Women* and featuring a cast and crew consisting of current and future movie legends (including the aforementioned Gene Kelly and Stanley Donen), *Take Me Out to the Ball Game* blends baseball and dance from start to finish. The story harkens back to the days of Germany Schaefer, Charley O'Leary, and Nick Altrock—days of ball-playing vaudevillians and ballpark clowns. Gene Kelly, whose true-life boyhood dream was to be a Pittsburgh Pirate,[6] and Hoboken, New Jersey, native Frank Sinatra, appear as turn-of-the-century baseball stars who perform in the off-season as the vaudeville song-and-dance team O'Brien and Ryan. Accordingly, there are numerous instances of dances performed by baseball players and, on more than one occasion, a performance is carried out by players who are outfitted from cap to spikes in baseball garb. In fact, the very first dance routine in the film, executed on a vaudeville stage by O'Brien and Ryan (wearing red and white, baseball-inspired pinstripe suits), is to the tune of the title song and this number is followed in short order by a spring-training song-and-dance routine ("Yes,

Indeedy") performed by O'Brien and Ryan inside their Florida ballpark, with their uniformed Wolves teammates acting as the chorus.

Baseball and dance movements are combined in the film continuously. One particularly notable example is "O'Brien to Ryan to Goldberg," a comic number that features musical star Jules Munshin (who also teamed up with Kelly and Sinatra in the 1949 film *On the Town*). Munshin plays first baseman Nat Goldberg (reminiscent of Benny Rubin's Sam Goldberg in *They Learned about Women*), the third member of the Wolves' great double-play tandem that gives the song its name. The dance performed by the three players is peppered with batting, pitching, and sliding movements and, in a somewhat subtle but poignant touch, both the musical arrangement and choreography manage to celebrate, at one point, the ethnic heritage of each dancing and singing ballplayer by the inclusion of strains and steps that are, unmistakably, Irish and Jewish. Along these lines, it is also important to observe that, later on in the film, Kelly unleashes a phenomenal, muscular tap routine ("The Hat My Dear Old Father Wore upon St. Patrick's Day") that brilliantly blends Irish and American themes and steps. Taken together, these musical numbers seem to reveal a strong interest not only in connecting baseball and dance, but also in expressing and confirming the vital roles played by immigrants and their respective cultures in the overall culture of America—an interest that one would imagine people like Kelly, Sinatra, and Munshin (sons and/or grandsons of immigrants themselves) would almost certainly possess and wish to promote.

Finally, it is worthwhile to mention that, at one point, Kelly, Sinatra, and Munshin offer an on-field, pre-game baseball clowning exhibition. The routine recalls such exhibitions of the distant and more recent past, performed by players and teams at all levels of professional and semi-professional baseball (and perhaps associated most closely with teams in the Negro Leagues). There is a strong degree of historical accuracy in the clowning performed by O'Brien, Ryan, and Goldberg, and, owing to its depiction in this specific medium, a Hollywood musical, the understanding that such a routine, in essence, is yet another form of dance is quite easy to reach by just about anyone sitting in a movie theater.

An American in Paris
(1951, directed by Vincente Minnelli)

Just two years after *Take Me Out to the Ball Game*, Gene Kelly was once again dancing in a baseball cap on the big screen, although, in this instance, the actual subject of the film was not baseball. Instead, Kelly's character, Jerry Mulligan, is an American painter who travels to Paris in search of inspiration, education, and adventure, all of which (and more) he succeeds in attaining. The screenplay, inspired by George Gershwin's glorious 1928 tone poem for orchestra, was written by Alan Jay Lerner, while Kelly himself created the film's exquisite choreography. Kelly, as Mulligan, represents the exuberant spirit and dynamism of the United States and, at an early point in the movie, this "American-ness" is put on full display when the indefatigable Mulligan, with assistance from a legion of excited local school children, performs a charming and thoroughly uplifting version of Gershwin's "I Got Rhythm" on the streets of Paris. What is especially important to note is that sitting atop Kelly's head throughout this number is not the standard beret of a French artist, but, rather, the great example of American millinery excellence, the baseball cap. Much like the choice of choreographer Ruth Page to include a character dressed in a stylized New York Yankees uniform in "Americans in

Paris" (her 1936 concert dance version of Gershwin's musical composition), Kelly seems to have reached for a baseball image to represent the United States in its entirety.

Damn Yankees
(1958, directed by George Abbott and Stanley Donen)

It is quite probable that, for most people, any discussion of a connection between baseball and dance will begin (and sometimes end) with *Damn Yankees*. Produced originally as a Broadway musical comedy in 1955, with outstanding choreography by Bob Fosse, the show and its songs became so popular that, in 1958, Warner Bros. decided to seize the moment and produce a film version, with the bulk of the original Broadway cast (including writer/director George Abbott, and, of course, Fosse) in tow. What resulted was an even bigger hit, which helped to ensure that this baseball-centered musical, based on Douglass Wallop's 1954 book, *The Year the Yankees Lost the Pennant*, would forever be considered a "classic."

Because the original stage version has been discussed so extensively in chapter 1, it is not necessary to reiterate many of the points and descriptions that already have been offered. Still, a few observations about the film are worth sharing. Early on, for example, two neighbors stop on the street to talk with the main character, Joe Boyd (soon to be Joe Hardy), and remark that they have just come from a ballet, although they assure Joe that they also attended a baseball game on the previous day. An interesting coincidence, to be sure! Additionally, the shift from theater stage to motion picture studio provided the production team with many

"Shoeless Joe from Hannibal, Mo." number, choreographed by Bob Fosse, from the 1958 film *Damn Yankees*.

more scenery and setting options. Indeed, as noted by Howard Good (who cites Joseph Andrew Casper's eponymous 1983 biography of director/choreographer, Stanley Donen), much of the baseball field filming was done on "real grass and real dirt at Wrigley Stadium, a minor league park in Los Angeles."[7] This "on location" shooting allowed the number "Shoeless Joe from Hannibal, Mo.," to truly come alive. Howard Good describes the on-field dancing, as choreographed by Fosse, very well:

> Fosse, a baseball fan, drew on the body language of the game for the choreography. The player-dancers flash signs, pound their mitts, and pantomime spearing line drives and stabbing grounders. They conclude by sliding en masse toward the camera in a cloud of dust.[8]

It should be added that, following this culminating slide (which must have induced cheers in movie theaters), the "player-dancers" also uniformly tip their caps to the camera—a typical baseball gesture that also may be a nod to the film's theatrical roots.

In 1967, George Abbott produced an all-new, made-for-TV film treatment of *Damn Yankees*, with Ernie Flatt contributing choreography, while, in 2010, the television dance show *So You Think You Can Dance* featured a rousing rendition of "Shoeless Joe from Hannibal, Mo.," choreographed for two athletic male dancers by Tyce Diorio (to be discussed later in this chapter). As mentioned earlier, the show has been revived countless times on stages throughout the world—once (in 1981) with football star Joe Namath playing the role of Joe Hardy. There are even rumors of a new film version in the works as these words are being written. What is abundantly clear is that anyone who may have some questions about the claim that an intimate relationship exists between baseball and dance need only watch Rae Allen, as newspaper reporter Gloria Tharpe, dancing the steps of Bob Fosse on a baseball field with the entire Washington Senators team in the original, 1958 film adaptation of *Damn Yankees*.

The Bingo Long Traveling All-Stars and Motor Kings (1976, directed by John Badham)

As expressed in the chapter on theater in the late 20th and early 21st centuries, William Brashler's 1973 novel about a barnstorming Negro Leagues baseball team, *The Bingo Long Traveling All-Stars and Motor Kings*, was guided by interviews conducted with one of the greatest players ever to wear a Negro Leagues uniform, James Thomas "Cool Papa" Bell (whose playing career spanned three decades and who was elected to the National Baseball Hall of Fame in 1974). These interviews provided Brashler with a wealth of details about day-to-day life in the Negro Leagues, both on and off the baseball diamond, and, drawing from Bell's vivid accounts, much of the novel exhibited a fair share of historical accuracy. In his 1976 screen adaptation of Brashler's book, director John Badham was able to maintain this attention to detail and this strong interest in historical accuracy.

With an equally "all-star" cast (including James Earl Jones, Billy Dee Williams, and Richard Pryor), the film depicts on-field clowning and shadow ball demonstrations, cakewalking alongside marching bands en route to local baseball parks, and late-night dancing by players at jazz clubs and speakeasies. One exchange between the African American owner of a general store and Bingo Long (Billy Dee Williams), which takes place in the midst of a lukewarm procession by the baseball team to the ballpark, is especially revealing in terms of the relevance and prominence of dance in Negro Leagues baseball, particularly in its waning days:

> General Store Owner: You're barnstorming, you're in show biz! Let me see you kick that mule.
> Bingo Long: You mean like this?
> General Store Owner: No, no! You gotta *cakewalk*! It goes like this…

Choreographer Bernard Johnson, whose own career included a stint with the New York Negro Ballet and a number of tours with the legendary performer Josephine Baker,[9] was hired to create movements and dances that were as authentic and well executed as possible. While we do not get a complete picture of life in the Negro Leagues (the film actually takes place in the period just before integration, when the Negro Leagues were on the cusp of extinction), Badham and his team do offer viewers a convincing account of the pleasures and joys, as well as the frustrations and dangers, of being a black professional baseball player in pre–Jackie Robinson America.

Billy Dee Williams, as Bingo Long, leads his team in a cakewalk to the ballpark in the 1976 film *The Bingo Long Traveling All-Stars and Motor Kings.*

In 1985, Brashler's book was adapted yet again, this time as a musical play, written and produced by Ossie Davis, with songs by George Fischoff and Hy Gilbert, and choreography by tap dance master Henry Le Tang. Although the musical, which is discussed at length in chapter 2, did not succeed in attracting a Broadway producer at the time, it did succeed in further advancing a growing interest in the Negro Leagues in the United States and shedding even more light on the influential presence of music and dance in black baseball culture prior to the breaking of the color barrier in the major leagues in 1947.

A League of Their Own
(1992, directed by Penny Marshall)

Inspired by the story of the short-lived but pioneering All-American Girls Professional Baseball League (AAGPBL) of the 1940s, which was discussed briefly in the previous chapter (in relation to Christopher Fleming's concert dance work of 2000, "Playball!"), Penny Marshall's *A League of Their Own* devotes minimal screen time to the subject of dance. However, the two instances where the baseball and dance connection is made are significant. The first takes place when the members of the Rockford Peaches, the team that is the focal point of the movie, are introduced to their new uniforms, which consist of startlingly short skirts in place of standard flannel baseball pants. At the sight of these skimpy outfits, the players are somewhat aghast. How, after all, are they supposed to bend to field ground balls without giving the fans a "free show" of their undergarments and how can they slide without wreaking havoc on their legs? One player, Doris Murphy (Rosie O'Donnell), exclaims with unfiltered exasperation, "What do you think we are, ballplayers or ballerinas?" In some ways, the officials of the new league and the management of the Peaches likely believed that members of the AAGPBL, in truth, were *both*. Players like Murphy would not have been given contracts without a high skill level. Yet, to a certain degree, the organizers of the league also hoped that the women on each team would display a kind of grace and style that would set them even further apart from their male counterparts on the diamond.

This objective is illustrated in another early sequence in the film, which occurs just after the scene mentioned above. As part of their training, the Peaches are required to receive etiquette lessons. Not surprisingly, these include formal dance instruction, an element that would have been offered to provide assistance both on and off the field.

It is also important to mention the fact that one of the most famous lines in *A League of Their Own*, "There's no crying in baseball" (uttered by Tom Hanks, in the role of Jimmy Dugan, manager of the Peaches), was borrowed twenty years later by the television series *Bunheads* and used in connection with dance. Sutton Foster, playing the former dancer/showgirl-turned-reluctant-ballet-instructor Michelle Simms, reminds a weeping dance student, "There's no crying in baseball—or ballet!"

Stompin' (2007, directed by Nate Thomas)

Baseball and dance come into conflict but ultimately coalesce in this tale of sibling rivalry involving two brothers who attend an historically black college in the United States. Jason Jackson (Christopher Facey) is a star college baseball player who has a promising future as a professional athlete. Jason's brother, Ryan (Shedrack Anderson), on the other hand, is a talented but emotionally troubled member of his fraternity's Step Dance team. Both brothers are gearing up for important competitions in their respective pastimes as the film begins. Ryan, however, is resentful of the lack of support shown by his father, a failed former athlete (Sinbad), and seems to direct the bulk of his anger towards Jason, whom Ryan believes is his father's favored child. The mother of Jason and Ryan (Vanessa Bell Calloway) understands this complex relationship and, very early on, states forcefully to her husband, "[Ryan] likes to Step, Jason likes baseball—deal with it!" Predictably, the tensions that exist lead to tragedy (Ryan's death), but the tragic incident helps to unite the family and the school—and the worlds of baseball and dance converge in a positive, inspirational manner.

Throughout *Stompin'*, baseball and Stepping are on full display and the similarity between each in terms of both athleticism and artistry is emphasized repeatedly. Stepping demonstrations are followed by baseball practice sessions, and the rigorous hours that each brother devotes to the achievement of perfection are made very clear to all viewers. We recognize quickly that success in both baseball and dance requires skill and sweat, intense training involving constant repetition, extreme discipline, an ability to learn from mistakes, and the capacity to focus on what it takes to meet any challenge that is presented at any given moment. *Stompin'* is all about relationships and connections and the ultimate "convergence" occurs when baseball-playing Jason appears at a Stepping competition (the "Greek Show") following his brother's death. Wearing a sweatshirt with Ryan's name emblazoned on the front, Jason, filled with pride and emotion, introduces Ryan's Stepping team as his own "extended family." Jason, the base-baller, reaffirms his intimate, unbreakable bond with Ryan, the dancer, before the eyes and ears of the entire world.

Twilight
(2008, directed by Catherine Hardwicke)

With the song "Supermassive Black Hole," by the British rock band Muse blasting on the soundtrack, a group of beautiful teen vampires engages in a game of "Thunderball"—the vampire version of baseball. Choreographed by Dee Dee Anderson, the game that we witness in this much-anticipated film, based on the best-selling young adult novel of the same name by Stephenie Meyer, is, in truth, much more of a dance segment than a baseball scene, with superhuman leaps, jumps, throws, stretches, slides, swings, and sprints. It is a type of baseball that can be played only by creatures who possess "powers and abilities far beyond those of mortal men," to borrow a line from the *Superman* television series of the 1950s.

As the rain falls in sheets and the thunder crackles and explodes, the vampire squads also let loose, as if they are participating in a kind of religious ritual, which, of course, is how many humans experience baseball in its traditional form. Baseball, in *Twilight*, is taken to the extreme and there is a genuine sense of *ecstasy* that the players seem to feel as they carry out their game in the middle of the dark, rain-soaked forest. These teen vampires are eternally young, breathtakingly attractive, and in possession of supernatural skills—and it is quite evident that they are taking this opportunity to revel in these realities, to celebrate these "gifts." It can be said that they are filled with "spirit" and, as is often the case when a being (mortal or otherwise) finds himself or herself in such a state, what emerges quite naturally is *the dance*. As the game of Thunderball is played by Edward Cullen and his blood-feasting clan, fueled externally by the driving chords of Muse, dance, quite literally, is everywhere. In this case, baseball and dance are one and the same, echoing a sentiment expressed in words and music in the television film *High School Musical 2*, which, coincidentally, had its own release just a year before that of *Twilight*.

Cartoons

The 1930s through the 1950s could be considered the peak period for baseball-related cartoons. Television at this time was still in its infancy and, like the vast majority of cartoons and feature-length animated films produced during this period, these mid-century, baseball-related cartoons were created for the "big screen" and were intended to be shown, along with newsreels and live action shorts, as "companion pieces" for a cinema's main attractions. In later years, once television had established itself in American society and become a popular entertainment medium, many of these cartoons achieved new life as television fare for animation-loving children. Their origins, however, were theatrical.

What is especially exciting about the nine American cartoons that are described briefly below is the extraordinary talent that gave birth to each of them. All nine were released by major Hollywood studios (MGM, Paramount, RKO, Walt Disney Productions, Universal, and Warner Bros.) and were directed by monumental names in animation history (Tex Avery, Dave Fleischer, John Foster, Friz Freleng, Jack Kinney, Seymour Kneitel, Alex Lovy, and George Rufle). All nine also utilize music quite adeptly, add wonderful, frequently zany elements of humor to the general story, and make highly effective efforts to infuse the action with dance and dance-like movements (particularly when it comes to depicting the motions of human and non-human pitchers).

As a kind of "added bonus," one non-American theatrical cartoon is included in this section. This cartoon, *Kitsune no homerun-o* (produced originally in post–World War II Japan and given the title *Seventh Inning Stretch* for U.S. audiences), is especially noteworthy for the striking balletic nature of the animation and the fact that the cartoon itself, directed by Satoshi Morino and animated by Osamu Satomi, may be viewed as a forerunner of the popular "anime" style that would become a worldwide phenomenon in the years to come.

It should be stated that more examples of the baseball-dance connection expressed through animation may be found later in this chapter, in the section devoted to television (this is where discussions of such characters as Snoopy and Homer Simpson will take place).

Aesop's Fables: The Ball Game
(1932, directed by John Foster and George Rufle)[10]

Created by the pioneering animation studio, Van Beuren Productions, and distributed by RKO Radio Pictures, this entertaining, six-minute cartoon depicts an entomological baseball game, featuring two insect-laden teams, the Big Bugs and Little Bugs. With flying, creeping, and darting "players," it is to be expected that dance will emerge at some point. In this case, the dance happens almost immediately, as the two teams, at the very beginning, are shown marching their way, in the manner of baseball barnstormers, down the main street of the hosting town, towards the site of the big game, the local ballpark. The tune, "I Love a Parade," is performed by an orchestra of insects, gathered on a mobile float, as the ball-playing bugs step in time. More dance moves occur a bit later in the short, when a needle-nosed bug, likely either a wasp or mosquito, tracks down a "fly" ball using tap dance steps. The rhythm of the outfielder in pursuit of the soaring missile—a beautiful sight to behold, even when executed by a cartoon insect.

The directing duo of Foster and Rufle remained major players in Hollywood animation, with Foster writing and directing scores of classic cartoons over three decades (including many in the Mighty Mouse series) and Rufle serving as animator and director for such popular series as *Felix the Cat*, *Popeye the Sailor*, and *The Mighty Hercules*, to name just a few.[11]

The Twisker Pitcher
(1937, directed by Dave Fleischer and Seymour Kneitel)[12]

And, speaking of Popeye, in 1937, the brawling sailor with the gentle soul and graceful gait had a chance to show off both his baseball and dance moves in a predictable, but enjoyable, short directed by the powerhouse team of Dave Fleischer and Seymour Kneitel. *The Twisker Pitcher* pits Popeye's Pirates against Bluto's Bears, with Olive Oyl and Bluto's *zoftig*, unnamed lady friend cheering on their respective beaus (and walloping each other in the process) in the box seats. Popeye is shown strutting and jauntily shuffling at the start, while the climax of the cartoon, after the obligatory ingestion of spinach (in this case, freshly grown on the baseball field), explodes with theatrical movements that can only be described as a type of hyper-aggressive dance, resulting in Popeye's vanquishing of Bluto on the baseball diamond. And, once again, the familiar strains of "Take Me Out to the Ball Game" may be heard drifting in the background as the action transpires.

How to Play Baseball (1942, directed by Jack Kinney)[13]

Produced by Walt Disney Pictures, this "instructional" cartoon features the Disney character Goofy in every role. A narrator, describing the pitcher's windup, exclaims, "To the layman, the colorful actions of the pitcher may appear a trifle overdone," and, in order to illustrate this point, Goofy, as the pitcher, displays a series of exaggerated movements as he prepares to release the ball to home plate. What we witness is undeniably dance. Additionally, the actions of the batters, fielders, and runners (Goofy, in all instances) are no less colorful and, in fact, are as stylish and graceful as a tap or ballroom routine performed by the likes of Fred Astaire, Gene Kelly, or Bill "Bojangles" Robinson.

The Screwball (1943, directed by Alex Lovy)[14]

Walter Lantz and Universal joined the party in 1943, with a bit of baseball-themed, animated nuttiness, featuring the off-kilter agent of chaos Woody Woodpecker. After Woody outwits a rather smug ballpark police officer and gains free access to the game between the Drips and the Droops, he somehow manages to enter the game as well and displays a series of snazzy, dance-like movements as he speedily approaches the pitcher's mound and readies himself for the next batter. Woody, truly, is a jitterbugger with red feathers.

Batty Baseball (1944, directed by Tex Avery)[15]

A thoroughly madcap wartime offering by Avery and his stable of artists and writers, this six-minute spoof takes viewers inside W.C. Field, where a game between the Yankee Doodlers and the Draft Dodgers is taking place. The pitcher for the Draft Dodgers (sporting the number 4F), who, save for the catcher, is alone on the diamond (thanks to all other teammates serving in the armed forces), goes through his windups and hurls his delightfully wacky array of pitches in ways that force his body to twist, contort, stretch, and leap in much the same way as an athletic dancer. In typical Avery fashion, the cartoon works on two levels, for kids and adults.

Baseball Bugs (1946, directed by Friz Freleng)[16]

A Bugs Bunny classic from the 1940s, which has been broadcast countless times on television over the years. As the immense and unkempt Gas-House Gorillas pile up the runs against the Tea Totallers, a team consisting of nonagenarian players, Bugs (who is munching on popcorn and carrots outside his rabbit hole near the outfield stands) attracts the attention (and ire) of the Gorillas as a result of his relentless heckling. When the Gorillas surround and threaten him, Bugs agrees to take over for every player on the Tea Totallers for the remainder of the game. Bugs, of course, winds up using his wits, speed, and surprising baseball abilities to defeat the Gorillas. Along the way, we see some fabulous dance-like movements from Bugs on the pitching mound, at bat, and in the field. Viewers also are treated to two famous segments that truly hammer home the relationship between baseball and dance: a Gorilla pitcher winding up in synch to music and a hitting-and-scoring Gorillas conga line that ceases only when the heckling of Bugs proves to be too distracting to ignore. Those foolish Gas-House Gorillas!

Casey at the Bat (1946, directed by Jack Kinney)[17]

With narration supplied by the great comedian Jerry Colonna, this animated rendition of Thayer's immortal poem feels as though it has been choreographed from beginning to end. All characters give the appearance of being members of a well-rehearsed dance troupe, performing a story ballet, with Casey in particular demonstrating true balletic elegance as he turns out his feet, prances, and presents physical shapes that resemble *pliés* and *arabesques*. These beautifully rendered movements are accentuated by the lyricism, lilt, and flair of Colonna's recitation, which is both spoken and sung. Interestingly, in just a few years (in 1953), the American composer, William Schuman, would create a live opera based on the Casey story (*The Mighty Casey*), which would be followed a year later by a Disney-produced, dance-infused sequel to the 1946 cartoon (once again directed by Kinney), entitled *Casey Bats Again*. As discussed in earlier chapters, the "Americana" movement was in full swing and "Casey at the Bat," clearly, was prime source material for this expansive cultural campaign.

Base Brawl (1948, directed by Seymour Kneitel)[18]

Kneitel, part of the creative team responsible for 1937's *The Twisker Pitcher*, was back in 1948 to direct another dance-laced baseball cartoon, this time involving a game between two teams of animals, the Forest All-Stars and the Jungle Jumbos. Chock-full of moan-worthy sight gags (a high ball depicted as a cocktail glass hurtling towards the batter; actual goose eggs, laid by a nesting goose, taking the place of zeros on the scoreboard when the ballpark announcer describes another scoreless inning; etc.), this cartoon's primary showcase of baseball's connection to dance occurs in the final segment, when the turtle umpire initiates a follow-the-bouncing-ball rendition of "Take Me Out to the Ball Game." After completing the first two verses, the bouncing ball, rather mysteriously, is replaced by what appears to be a dancing chipmunk. Then, in the end, the baseball conga line that was used so brilliantly just two years before, in *Baseball Bugs*, is reprised, this time with mice. These mice, who are members of the Forest All-Stars, have such a small strike zone that the pitcher for the Jumbos simply cannot avoid walking one after another. Whether or not this scene in *Base Brawl* inspired Bill Veeck of the St. Louis Browns to send the diminutive base-baller Eddie Gaedel up to the plate to pinch hit on August 19, 1951—in a regulation game against the Detroit Tigers—is difficult to determine (Gaedel, too, achieved a base-on-balls after four consecutive pitches). However, what the borrowing of Friz Freleng's conga line most certainly *did* inspire was the recognition that the game of baseball and the world of dance have much in common.

Casey Bats Again (1954, directed by Jack Kinney)[19]

Disney and Kinney, as mentioned above, were back again in 1954 with a charming sequel to their 1946, Jerry Colonna-narrated cartoon version of Ernest Thayer's "Casey at the Bat." In this second installment, Casey, who has retired from baseball, is the father of nine daughters. Perhaps taking a cue from the All-American Girls Professional Baseball League (AAGPBL), which was in its final year of existence in 1954, Casey's nine daughters are portrayed as talented baseball players—so talented, in fact, that they form a successful professional baseball team (fittingly called the "Caseyettes"). In a humorous, somewhat outlandish scene (which takes place at a crucial moment at the end of the game that will determine the winner of the so-called "Female Championship"), Casey actually does get an opportunity to redeem himself at the plate. His daughters, though, prove to be the true heroes of the story and, throughout the cartoon, viewers are treated to depictions of the Caseyettes in action, demonstrating the athletic grace of the young women. The nine lithe members of the Caseyettes likely would be as aesthetically pleasing in tutus as they are in baseball uniforms.

Kitsune no homerun-o (*Seventh Inning Stretch*) (1949, re-released in 1957, directed by Satoshi Morino)[20]

Just after World War II, the Japanese animation director Satoshi Morino worked on a number of shorts with animator Osamu Satomi, which featured foxes as main characters (the "*Kitsune* Series").[21] One of these shorts, created in 1949 and released in the United States in 1957, told the story of a baseball game between the Foxes and the Rabbits and contained an extraordinary number of images that are strikingly balletic in nature. Indeed, *Kitsune no homerun-o* (changed to *Seventh Inning Stretch* for its U.S. release), begins with a march onto the baseball field by both teams that reminds one immediately of two pieces choreographed in later years for the New York City Ballet, "Stars and Stripes" (1958) and "Union Jack" (1976), by the man who is considered by many to be the greatest dance-maker of the 20th century, George Balanchine. It is probable that Balanchine never saw the 1949 cartoon; however, there is no denying the fact that the creators of *Kitsune no homerun-o*, like Balanchine, understood the choreographic qualities of a procession and, when it comes to Japanese baseball, this belief in the necessity of a spectacular and highly choreographed opening parade or procession prior to the commencement of an important baseball game is still quite strong. During the opening ceremonies for the annual National High School Baseball Summer Championship Tournament, carried out by tradition in Japan's historic Koshien Stadium, the young "shaven-headed" tournament players "march lockstep into the stadium" following a "rousing spectacle of sound and color that is worthy of the Olympics."[22]

More evocations of dance occur when the star of the Foxes, Homer Fox, is shown warming up. As the English-speaking narrator of the translated version of the cartoon says of Homer, "He takes his warmups seriously," the animators present him doing his stretches as though he is standing at the ballet barre. Moreover, both the Foxes and the Rabbits are rendered with exquisite postures and move to and from the batter's box, pitcher's mound, infield, and outfield with the strides and motions of well-trained dancers. If the game stopped suddenly and a short ballet segment from *The Nutcracker* or *Carnival of the Animals* broke out, there would be no feeling at all of incongruity.

Shorts and Newsreels

The theatrically released film shorts and newsreels that are discussed below express the so-called "ballet of baseball" through the application of physical comedy or acrobatics. Similar to the cartoon section, examples are drawn exclusively from the mid-20th century, when the vast majority of baseball-related film shorts and newsreels were created. Among the popular physical comedians featured in these short films and newsreels were such bona fide stars as

Joe E. Brown, Ray Bolger, and, from the Three Stooges, Shemp Howard, while former professional baseball player, Jackie Price, demonstrated his remarkable acrobatic skills in two nine-minute productions, *Diamond Demon* and *Baseball's Acrobatic Ace*. In each instance, the primary figures are able to transform the common actions and oft-observed rituals of baseball into pure entertainment, infused heavily with the stylings of dance.

Dizzy and Daffy (1934, directed by Lloyd French)[23]

Aside from making it possible for the viewer to experience the thrill of watching the actual pitching motions of Dizzy and Daffy Dean, this madcap, eighteen-minute short allows audience members to observe the comic skills of Shemp Howard—minus the accompaniment of his (more well-known) comedy partners, Moe and Larry (together, of course, known as the Three Stooges). Shemp, here, is a "sight-challenged," right-handed pitcher, whose nickname just happens to be Lefty. Lefty Howard pitches for the semi-pro team, the Shanty Town No Sox—a team that also includes both of the Dean brothers (referred to initially by their proper, real-life given names, Jerome and Paul). During the game that takes place in the first half of the film, Lefty is the starting pitcher against the Farmer White Sox and his pitching motions consist of eccentric dance movements and familiar baseball clowning gestures. Sadly, Lefty's vision problems, ultimately, cause the No Sox manager to remove him from the game, replacing him with the very "raw" Jerome (soon to be re-christened by Lefty as "Dizzy"). Dizzy, as one might anticipate, is phenomenal and it is not long before he and his brother—and, rather incomprehensibly, Lefty—are signed by the St. Louis Cardinals, a circumstance that provides the director, Lloyd French, with another opportunity to highlight Lefty (a.k.a. Shemp) Howard's physical clowning prowess on the baseball field.

Diamond Demon (1947, directed by Dave O'Brien) and *Baseball's Acrobatic Ace* (1955, directed by Jack Eaton)[24]

These two nine-minute films feature the astounding ex-ballplayer, Jackie Price, who performed eye-popping baseball stunts and acrobatics before, during, and after baseball games worldwide in the 1940s and 50s. In his autobiography, *Veeck—As in Wreck*, maverick baseball team owner Bill Veeck referred to Price as an "artist" rather than a clown and described at length some of his outlandish feats:

> Jackie Price was playing shortstop for Milwaukee when I came out of the service. I would get to the park early in the morning, look out the window and there would be Jackie practicing the most phenomenal kind of tricks. Not tricks really, either; feats of skill. Jackie would be playing catch—catching and throwing—while standing on his head. He would install a portable trapeze set in a batter's box, hang down by his knees and hit a pitched ball. He could place two catchers side by side and, in one motion, throw a fast ball to one of them and a curve to the other. He could stand at home plate and, again in the same motion, throw one ball to the pitcher's mound and the other to second base. He could stagger three fellows a few feet apart and, in that one motion, throw a different ball to each of them. Sometimes he would be bouncing over the outfield in a Jeep. Jackie would shoot a baseball out of a pneumatic tube, go diving after it and with split-second timing, reach out and catch it backhanded while the Jeep was somehow looking out for itself.[25]

Many of Price's jaw-dropping, seemingly impossible routines are captured in all their wondrous glory in *Diamond Demon* and *Baseball's Acrobatic Ace*—two shorts that prove the incredible claims of Bill Veeck to be irrefutable. It becomes immediately obvious to the viewer that the relationship between what Price does on a baseball field and what is done by a well-trained, highly skilled, confident, and fearless dancer on a concert stage is extraordinarily close, to be sure.

As an addendum, it is worth noting that Jackie Price's occasional performing partner was the magnificent Max Patkin, the renowned baseball clown whose performing career spanned six decades and whose wild ballpark exhibitions were often referred to as examples of "eccentric dance." Both Patkin and Price, by the way, were employed by the Cleveland Indians simultaneously for a time and their boss was none other than the aforementioned baseball front-office madman Bill Veeck.[26]

Newsreels of the 1930s and 1940s

Throughout the 1930s and '40s, American film stars and celebrities were captured repeatedly in theatrical newsreels as they played baseball in so-called "charity games" and at special promotional events. Inevitably, the newsreel footage included displays of clowning and physical comedy, all of which bore a striking resemblance to on-field dancing. Most notably, the annual "Leading Men vs. Comedians" charity game, which was played in Hollywood, provided ballpark spectators, as well as hundreds of thousands of moviegoers, an opportunity to observe famous entertainers—including Mischa Auer, Milton Berle, Joe E. Brown, Buddy Ebsen, Danny Kaye, Edgar Kennedy, Harpo Marx, and the Ritz Brothers—performing their unique brand of comic theatrical baseball.[27]

On a related note, the nine-minute, 1939 film short *Hollywood Hobbies* (directed by George Sidney and produced by MGM), contained a closing, three-minute segment filmed at that year's Leading Men vs. Comedians game.[28] With such Hollywood stars as Virginia Bruce, James Cagney, George Murphy, Mary Pickford, Tyrone Power, Cesar Romero, James Stewart, Spencer Tracy, and Jane Withers cheering them on from the grandstands, numerous screen stars engage in pitching, hitting, fielding, running the bases—and *dancing* on the diamond. Milton Berle, for one, is seen skipping gracefully to his shortstop position, while the Ritz Brothers (wearing what appears to be striped long johns) actually break out into a beautiful, elegant waltz near home plate.

Television and Video

"With the advent of television, a new outlet is open to dance and a new field of exploration is open to the dancer…. Television is in an early formative stage, with every opportunity for experiment and it extends an invitation to the dancer, choreographer and composer to try this new, exciting medium."[29] These words were written by Edward Padula of the National Broadcasting Company's Department of Television for a 1939 *Dance Magazine* article, entitled, "The Dance in Television." Padula proceeds to describe a number of recently broadcast dance pieces and lauds the fact that "[t]elevision has been eclectic in its taste" when it comes to performers and styles selected for such screenings (which, at this "formative" stage, were rather difficult to access by the general public).[30] Among the pieces singled out by Padula was one the author characterized as "probably the most ambitious undertaking" to date: Hanya Holm's "Metropolitan Daily."[31]

"Metropolitan Daily," in essence, was a choreographed portrait, as envisioned by Holm, of a city newspaper (from front page to back) and a shining example of Americana. Holm and her all-female company were invited by NBC to perform the fourteen-minute piece live, in front of a television camera, in NBC's New York television studio. The performance would then be broadcast in "real time" on a public television set that was exhibited at the 1939 New York World's Fair.[32] The production would become the first work of modern dance to be aired on the exciting new medium of television and, by coincidence, this landmark performance just happened to contain a segment devoted to baseball. In other words, from the earliest days of televised dance, the baseball and dance connection has been a prime point of reference.

Indeed, in the years that followed the NBC broadcast of "Metropolitan Daily," there have been surprisingly frequent occurrences on television (and, more recently, in video) of baseball themes and movements incorporated into multiple dance forms. Moreover, dance has been known to pop up on television and in video with great regularity in baseball settings and it has become apparent that many television production and/or creative teams have made a conscious effort to acknowledge, spotlight, and even promote the similarities that exist between ballplayers and dancers. Needless to say, there are abundant examples that can be cited. Some of the more noteworthy or representative ones are included in the six categories below.

Musicals, Teleplays, and Made-for-Television Movies

"High Pitch" (CBS; *Chrysler Shower of Stars*; May 12, 1955)[33]

William Frawley and Vivian Vance, who were household names in 1955 as a result of their roles as Fred and Ethel Mertz on the popular television comedy series *I Love Lucy*, starred in this baseball-themed, made-for-television musical. At the center of the story is singing sensation Tony Martin, who plays Ted Warren, a former member of the Brooklyn Hooligans baseball team who, after being traded to the rival Spartans, becomes one of baseball's top sluggers. The Hooligans find themselves in last place (again) at the start of "High Pitch," while the Spartans are able to clinch the pennant, thanks to a game-ending blast by Warren (whose enmity for the Hooligans is shared with the world when he is interviewed in the celebratory Spartans' clubhouse by legendary baseball announcer Mel Allen (playing himself). To make matters even sadder, it is revealed that the Hooligans are in jeopardy of folding due to decreased revenue. Frawley, as Hooligans' manager Gabby Mullins, prays for a miracle and his prayer is answered when the team is bought by Dorothy Meadows, a world-famous opera singer (portrayed by real-life professional soprano Marguerite Piazza), who happens to be a lifelong fan of the Hooligans. In order to put the Hooligans back into contention and attract fans to the ballpark, Meadows has a plan: bring Warren back to Brooklyn.

The songs that are sung and danced to in "High Pitch" are a mix of old and new. The opening number, performed in the clubhouse of the Spartans (just after the conclusion of the pennant-winning game), is the familiar 1935 Fields/Oppenheimer/McHugh tune, "I Feel a Song Coming On" (sung here by Martin), and there is plenty of victory dancing that is carried out by the players. Later in the show, a group of opera singers, which includes another popular vocalist, Yma Sumac, presents an explosive rendition of "Take Me Out to the Ball Game." This is followed by a Vivian Vance-led song-and-dance number performed by the wives of Hooligan players, "What a Life (Is the Life of a Ballplayer's Wife)." After Warren (Martin) and Meadows (Piazza) declare their love for each other in a lovely, but dance-free, interpretation of Harold Arlen and Ted Koehler's "Let's Fall in Love," a cocktail party is thrown for the surging Hooligans and Meadows, thrilled with her team and her newfound love, leads the nattily dressed Hooligans in a jaunty version of the contemporary rock 'n' roll/R & B sizzler "Dance with Me, Henry" (a chart-topper for Georgia Gibbs in 1955). Finally, after approximately fifteen ensuing minutes of anguish, the show's climax arrives, highlighted by a stirring reprise of "Take Me Out to the Ball Game," this time sung as a duet—with dance steps added—by Martin and Piazza.

The dances in "High Pitch" were created by the dancer/choreographer James Starbuck, whose résumé includes stints at the San Francisco Opera Ballet and the Ballet Russe de Monte Carlo, as well as steady work on television, on stage, and in film.

"A Man's Game"
(NBC; *Kaiser Aluminum Hour*; April 23, 1957)[34]

Lew Daniels, big league manager of the New York Titans, hears that a great catching prospect named Chub Evans is playing amateur baseball while working on a farm in rural Alabama. Hungry for a new secret weapon to help spark the Titans, Daniels telephones Evans and lets Chub's sister, Josephine, know that he is on his way to Alabama to watch her brother play. Josephine, who goes by the name of Jo, immediately calculates that Tom, her beau, might "be elevated from hired hand to partner on her father's farm"[35] if Chub gets a contract from the Titans, which would permit the wedding plans of Jo and Tom to be accelerated. Jo, whose own skills as a pitcher are rather formidable, proceeds to prepare Chub for the tryout. Daniels makes it to Alabama, travels to the Evans family farm, and, after watching Chub work out with Jo, realizes that a star prospect is in his sights. The potential star, though, is not Chub—it is Jo. Daniels manages to convince the owner of the team, Mr. Rockman, that signing Jo will be great for the Titans and for Major League Baseball in general. Approval is granted, Jo ultimately accepts the offer, and, $40,000 later, Jo and Tom, now married, are off to the spring-training home of the Titans in Florida.

Predictably, the vast majority of the current Titans are somewhat resistant to the idea of a player from the opposite sex joining the team. Daniels, however, is confident, and the wives of Titan players are nearly ecstatic. In the Titans' locker room, in fact, the wives confront their doubting husbands, who are rebelliously singing "It's a Man's Game in a Man's World." The wives, like an invading and conquering army, pick up the team's arsenal of Louisville Sluggers and use them as dancing canes, proclaiming boldly as they dance, and sing in response.

Jo, now nicknamed "Mighty Jo," begins to dazzle the Titans with her extraordinary pitching abilities and her astounding assortment of pitches (including the "double doodle" fastball and a curve ball that breaks both inside and outside). In song, the male players and Jo conduct a lively conversation that reveals the conflicting viewpoints concerning a woman's "place" when it comes to baseball and society as a whole. The men throw everything they can muster at Jo in order to discourage her efforts. But Jo, with a wise and wily grin, tosses back lines that are clever and funny, making it very clear that she is fully capable of performing at a level that is equal to and possibly beyond that to which the male Titans already have ascended.

We watch the Titans play spring-training games, as pitching and batting movements are carried out to music. Jo is superb and it is not long before the male players begin to accept her as a fellow Titan. Daniels and Rockman are overjoyed and cannot wait for the season to start, predicting, in the song, "Lament for the Whole Baseball World" (with a few dance moves tossed in for good measure), that the Titans will devour all opponents. Unfortunately, in spite of the excitement and the claim made by Daniels to Jo just before she signed the contract that Jo and the Titans would break new ground, Jo is never able to pitch a regular season game. As it turns out, her opening-day jitters are actually a symptom of pregnancy and, to avoid any complications, she decides to quit and devote herself to motherhood. It is still 1957, after all.

Nannette Fabray plays Jo in "A Man's Game," while Daniels is portrayed by Lew Parker (best known as Lou Marie, Ann Marie's father on Marlo Thomas's 1966-71 television situation comedy, *That Girl*). Veteran actor/dancer Gene Nelson is cast as Jo's husband, Tom. Dancing occurs with great frequency and, remarkably, the choreographer responsible for these on-field and locker room moves is Robert Joffrey, who would go on to form the Joffrey Ballet, one of the most successful and highly acclaimed dance companies in the United States. There are clear reference points in "A Man's Game" to Jackie Robinson and to the All-American Girls Professional Baseball League. Even more so, perhaps, are the connections to 1955's *Damn Yankees* and to the similarly named television special that would air just one year later, in 1958: Gene Kelly's "Dancing—A Man's Game." Though the show, in the end, reveals a sensibility that is very much in tune with that of the 1950s in terms of sexuality and the role of women, there is a bit of mild subversion that filters through. Jo, very clearly, *does* have the ability to compete with—and surpass—her male counterparts. She simply needs to be given the opportunity. And this is expressed quite beautifully through dance. The closing segment, in truth, says it all. As the locker room door opens, the players exit, still singing and dancing to "It's a Man's Game in a Man's World." Last to depart are Jo and Tom. Immediately before the shot ends and the commercial break begins, Jo faces the camera, executes a pitching windup, hugs Tom, and, with a great big smile, releases a magnificent leg kick straight at the camera lens, demonstrating the incredible relationship between the dancer and the athlete and letting all of us know that she is a force to be reckoned with.

You're a Good Man, Charlie Brown (NBC; *Hallmark Hall of Fame*; February 9, 1973)[36]

In 1965, CBS became the first television network to produce and air a special based on Charles Schulz's popular syndicated comic strip, "Peanuts." The special was *A Charlie Brown Christmas*, and, beginning with that broadcast, "Peanuts" and CBS developed what seemed like an unbreakable partnership. Indeed, between 1965 and 1972, no less than seven animated "Peanuts" specials and two "Peanuts" documentaries were produced by CBS. On February 9, 1973, however, a surprise was in store for all "Peanuts" fans when the Broadway and Off

Broadway musical theater sensation, *You're a Good Man, Charlie Brown*, was filmed for television and shown not on CBS, but on the Tiffany Network's rival NBC.

Whatever legal maneuvers may have been at play behind the scenes in Hollywood, NBC's decision to purchase the television rights to the stage show meant that Snoopy's glorious suppertime sonata, complete with blissful gyrations and gesticulations, was made available to television watchers everywhere. Additionally, of course, the stirring baseball-based harmonies and gestures of "T.E.A.M. (The Baseball Game)" were now on display for all—even non-theatergoers—to behold, providing the homes of America with a close-up look at the dance of the diamond.

For a lengthier discussion of *You're a Good Man, Charlie Brown*, please refer to Chapter 2, which presents details about the Off Broadway and Broadway versions of the musical.

Bleacher Bums (WTTW/PBS; May 15, 1979)[37]

On May 15, 1979, the Chicago affiliate of the Public Broadcasting System, WTTW, aired a live performance of the Organic Theater Company's experimental stage production *Bleacher Bums*, which premiered in Chicago in 1977. Much of the original cast, led by actors Joe Mantegna and Dennis Franz, was kept intact, as was the overall spirit of the show. For ninety minutes—over the course of nine innings—television viewers had a chance to look more closely at the boisterous denizens of Wrigley Field's "cheap seats." From the game's beginning to end, and despite the fact that no formal choreographer was hired for the production, the movements of these "bleacher bums" took on the appearance, as stated in Chapter 2, of "one long dance."

This 1979 television special was re-broadcast by WTTW in 1984.

You're a Good Man, Charlie Brown (CBS; November 6, 1985)

CBS, in 1985, responded to NBC by presenting its own, all-animated production of Clark Gesner's musical *You're a Good Man, Charlie Brown*. The storyline and songs from the original stage show were fully retained and, once again, Linus, Lucy, Sally, Schroeder, and (most importantly) Snoopy were out there on the baseball field, singing and dancing the spirited song of unity, "T.E.A.M. (The Baseball Game)."

It's Spring Training, Charlie Brown (CBS; Produced in 1992; Released on video in January 1996)[38]

The blending of baseball and dance may be witnessed with some frequency in the vast catalog of "Peanuts" animated specials. To Snoopy, Charlie Brown's wily, multi-talented pup (and, perhaps, the most skilled member of Charlie Brown's generally hapless baseball team), the baseball field really is a stage and, on numerous occasions (e.g., CBS's 1966 baseball-themed "Peanuts" offering, *Charlie Brown's All-Stars*), Snoopy may be seen dancing in the outfield and on the base paths. The joy Snoopy feels while playing baseball is expressed through dance and, when baseball is depicted in a "Peanuts" special, one can be relatively certain that Snoopy, at some point, will strut his stuff.

What makes *It's Spring Training, Charlie Brown* so unique is that a full-fledged, professionally choreographed baseball dance number is featured. The number is led by Franklin, the first African American character to appear in any of the "Peanuts" comic strips or animated movies, and the music that drives the dance is hip-hop. As Franklin performs a baseball "rap," baseball activities and baseball-inspired dance moves are carried out by the "Peanuts" gang to the rhythm of the beat, and Snoopy, once again, takes center stage for a well-choreographed, painstakingly animated solo dance sequence. The show's production credits inform us that this hip-hop choreography was crafted by Kimberly Bowie, who, quite obviously, realized that contemporary sounds and styles suited baseball rather perfectly. (Fifteen years later, in 2007, Matthew Gerrard and Robbie Nevil would reach this same conclusion, as they devised and developed their choreography for *High School Musical 2*, to be discussed in greater detail shortly.)

One added note: *It's Spring Training, Charlie Brown* was scheduled to be aired by CBS in 1992, but, for an unknown reason, the broadcast never took place. Instead, in 1996, the half-hour special was released on video by Paramount, meaning that the show was not seen by the general public until four years after the full production was completed.

Bleacher Bums (Showtime; April 7, 2002)

In 2001, a new film version of *Bleacher Bums* was developed for television by Paramount and Showtime. Although the premiere screening of the film took place at the Chicago International Film Festival, the film's "official" television debut, on the Showtime Network, occurred on April 7, 2002. The new treatment boasted a veteran director, Saul Rubinek, and an impressive cast of TV and stage actors, as well as luminaries from the world of live improvisational comedy, including Charles Durning, Brad Garrett, Wayne Knight, Peter Riegert, and Mary Walsh. Some critics did not take kindly to this slightly modified rendering, which changed the name of the centerpiece team from the Chicago Cubs to the fictitious Chicago Bruins and the name of the primary venue from Wrigley Field to Lakeview Park (*Chicago Tribune* writer Steve Johnson, for example, recommended that the movie, like an unsuccessful pitcher, be sent "to the showers"[39]); however, the focus on the fans was, by and large, retained and the moments celebrating the "ballet of baseball" were present once more. Of course, many still were not satisfied. Said Johnson, "[T]his movie version only makes you yearn for another revival of the play or, better yet, a visit to the Wrigley bleachers themselves."[40]

High School Musical 2
(Disney Channel; August 17, 2007)

The Disney Channel released the made-for-television film *High School Musical* in January 2006, and the reception was enormous. Almost eight million Americans tuned in and Disney understood that it had a major "money maker" in its hands.[41] Sequels were planned and, in less than two years, the Disney Channel broadcast the second installment in the series, *High School Musical 2*, resulting in an even larger viewership—this time, more than seventeen million in the United States alone.[42]

What was especially exciting about the follow-up film, at least in the context of this study, was the fact that one featured number took place on a baseball field, with characters

Corbin Bleu and Lucas Grabeel perform "I Don't Dance," in the made-for-television movie *High School Musical 2* **(2007).**

in uniform, dancing and singing as they played their game. As mentioned in the opening segment of this chapter, the song being sung by the players (led by Corbin Bleu as Chad Danforth, and Lucas Grabeel as Ryan Evans) was entitled, "I Don't Dance," and, contrary to the song's title, plenty of dancing, as well as ball playing, occurred between the song's opening and closing notes. Moreover, it is possible to make a claim that this single song, in both movement and lyric, managed to convey the message in a manner that was more convincing and clear than almost any other example cited in this chapter that the bond between the disciplines of dance and baseball is natural and unbreakable. Indeed, the song, composed by Matthew Gerrard and Robbie Nevil, reminds us that, by simple observation, the idea that a powerful connection exists between baseball and dance can be said to be, in truth, *self-evident*.

The choreography for "I Don't Dance," supplied by Charles Klapow, is guided entirely by the "ballet of baseball." Pitching, batting, fielding, running, and idiosyncratic preparatory ball field gestures are sprinkled throughout the number, as performers prove they cannot help but dance as they go about the ordinary business of playing the game. The information transmitted by these movements is then bolstered by the lyrics of the song.

The appeal and importance of the song was not lost on the baseball establishment. The Little League, for example, selected "I Don't Dance" as the official song of its own World Series.[43] And, as far as Major League Baseball was concerned, its full blessing was granted to Disney when approached about the creation of a promotional video that would incorporate segments from baseball "highlight reels" and feature actual major league players, dressed in the uniforms of their respective teams, singing (or, more accurately, reciting) lines from the song.[44] Thus, prior to the August 17 television premiere of *High School Musical 2*, viewers and Internet users had a chance to see an "I Don't Dance" video, containing the musical sequence from the film edited with authentic Major League game footage and recordings of more than a dozen players standing on various baseball fields and declaring for the camera, "I don't dance!" Participants included such familiar names and faces as Bronson Arroyo, Ryan Howard, Jake Peavy, Jimmy Rollins, C. C. Sabathia, Nick Swisher, and Justin Verlander. Even Japanese transplant, pitcher Takashi Saito, joined the party, delivering his "I don't dance" line in Japanese rather than English. The video was able to magnify the ideas about the relationship between dance and baseball that were illustrated in the made-for-television movie by adding more shots of players executing real plays and carrying out a wide range of common ballpark movements that display dance-like qualities. The video even offered entertaining shots of players intentionally performing—or, in some cases, *attempting* to perform—various dance steps, both on the field and in the dugout. To anyone watching this promotional video and, ultimately, the made-for-television musical, there was no mistaking the genuine connection, the reality that baseball and dancing, at the core, were the "same game."

Variety Shows, Reality Shows, Talk Shows, and Competition Shows

Admiral Broadway Revue (NBC; April 22, 1949)[45]

In 1950, NBC premiered a comedy variety series that not only wound up being a tremendous hit in its time, but also turned out to be one of the most influential television programs in history.[46] The program was called *Your Show of Shows* and among its stunning stable of writers and performers were Sid Caesar, Imogene Coca, Carl Reiner, Max Liebman, Mel Brooks, and Neil Simon. In its five-year run (1950–54), the show also showcased a galaxy of extraordinary guest stars, such as Pearl Bailey, Constance Bennett, Douglas Fairbanks, Jr., Jose Greco, Rex Harrison, Veronica Lake, Alicia Markova, Maria Tallchief, and Rudy Vallee, to name just a few. The program's blend of frequently brilliant, generally madcap sketch comedy and live performances by some of the era's most outstanding dancers, singers, and actors, combined with its relatively lengthy broadcast lifespan, served to create a lasting impression among viewers and television observers. In this early stage of television history, *Your Show of Shows* was a remarkable "bridge" for members of the American public who were transitioning to the new medium of television from the world of motion pictures (as well as from the world of radio). If the program was—and is considered to be—an entertainment landmark and a launching pad for some of the country's most talented writers and performers, there is ample support for this claim.

Still, it is fascinating to learn that *Your Show of Shows*, in truth, rose from the ashes of another, quite similar, television comedy variety series which featured many, if not most of the members of the cast and crew of *Your Show of Shows* and which lasted a mere nineteen episodes prior to its June 1949 cancellation. The show, also broadcast by NBC, was called *Admiral Broadway Revue*. Like *Your Show of Shows*, Sid Caesar and Imogene Coca shared the spotlight and the all-star writing team included Mel Brooks and Max Liebman. Outlandish comedy routines and live performances by top entertainers of the day were interspersed and music for the incredible array of acts and sketches was provided by the Charles Sanford Orchestra. Legendary dance partners Marge and Gower Champion were mainstays, and some of the show's individual episodes were designed around a specific theme, such as contemporary newspaper headlines and international travel.

One such theme was chosen for the thirteenth episode of the series. The title of the episode was "County Fair" and, as one may surmise, the focal point of the show was the experience of attending such a typical American event. Caesar and Coca, for example, offered a comic sketch involving a straight-laced father and his demanding daughter in search of their favorite fair foods, while the Champions performed a dance that illustrated some typical fair activities, such as riding a merry-go-round and playing midway games. Some off-topic segments, such as a Katherine Dunham–like dance called "After the Mardi Gras" performed by Janet Collins, and a comic spoof of the wrestler Gorgeous George, by Sid Caesar, were also included in the episode. However, the "county fair" theme reappeared consistently and the show concluded with a lengthy mini-musical connected intimately to the central theme. The musical was described as a "baseball ballet."[47]

Essentially, the number was a variation on "Casey at the Bat," with Caesar playing the role of Lucky, a handsome slugger for the Tenderville team who possesses a monumental weakness for the ladies—a weakness that causes him to strike out at a crucial moment of the game (being played at the fair) against the East Side Tigers. There is musical narration from beginning to end ("the story of Tenderville's disaster") and, rather predictably (considering the fact that this segment is described as a "ballet"), there also is plenty of dancing, complete with movements based on pitching, catching, swinging, and umpiring. Ballplayers are in uniform and, in terms of dance, opportunities are created for solos, duets, and larger ensembles. In the end, as is the case with most dance and theatrical interpretations of "Casey at the Bat" (including those by Lisa de Ribere and William Schuman), the humiliated baseball hero succeeds in uniting with his true love and walking off the field and away from the ballpark with dignity and a new understanding of life.

The choreographer for this episode was James Starbuck, whose work was described by *New York Times* dance critic Jennifer Dunning as "pioneering"[48] and who performed, as stated previously, with such companies as the San Francisco Opera Ballet and the Ballet Russe de Monte Carlo prior to becoming a dance-maker for television, as well as Broadway and Hollywood. In the 1950s, one of Starbuck's prime gigs was *Your Show of Shows*.

Chrysler Shower of Stars (CBS; February 17, 1955)[49]

Just three months before the *Chrysler Shower of Stars* television series aired the created-for-television musical "High Pitch" (discussed in the previous section), the same CBS television series presented a variety show episode which provided viewers with another example of baseball "theatrics." In this episode, broadcast on February 17, 1955, the comedian and actor Larry Storch (whose comic skills would become much more widely known in the 1960s, when he landed the role of Corporal Randolph Agarn on the television series *F Troop*), appeared in a short, wordless solo sketch about the ups and downs of a baseball umpire. Dancing, per se, was not part of this sketch, but Storch's marvelous, exaggerated mime actions could be classified quite easily as performance art, with intense "flavors" drawn from the world of dance.

The Danny Kaye Show (CBS; September 25, 1963)[50]

Danny Kaye, the "triple threat" star of such motion pictures as *Hans Christian Andersen*, *The Secret Life of Walter Mitty*, and *The Court Jester*, was rewarded, in 1963, with his own CBS variety show, which provided him with the opportunity to exercise his substantial talents as a singer, dancer, actor, comedian, and artistic collaborator. A weekly television series also enabled Kaye to incorporate his passion for baseball into some of his skits and routines. On September 25, 1963, while the Los Angeles Dodgers, the team that Kaye, a Brooklyn boy, still rooted for, were finishing up a superb regular season and getting ready for their World Series run, Kaye's variety show premiered. Fittingly, Kaye took advantage of this historic "opening night" to introduce a comedy segment that paid tribute, simultaneously, to two of his greatest loves: Broadway and baseball.

The segment was based on Kaye's imagining how three popular Broadway musicals might sound if they had baseball as a central theme. *My Fair Lady* became *My Fair Umpire*, while *West Side Story* turned into *Horsehide Story*, and *Music Man* was transformed into *Baseball Man*. Choreography, of course, was included (with some assistance from dance creator Tony Charmoli) and what Kaye gave his audience was a baseball music-and-dance extravaganza. Clearly, Kaye was able to recognize the close connections that exist between the balletic game of baseball and the athleticism of choreography. Considering that Kaye's own abilities spanned all of the arts (including painting and writing), this recognition is not at all hard to understand and it is little wonder that the transition between stage movement and ball field movement was, for Kaye, so seamless.

Also worthy of note is the fact that exactly one year before Danny Kaye's CBS series was launched, Reprise Records released a 45-rpm recording by Kaye called "The D-O-D-G-E-R-S Song (Oh Really? No, O'Malley!)."[51] The A-side tribute to the National League pennant contenders, composed by Kaye, Herbert Baker, and Kaye's wife, Sylvia Fine, was backed by another baseball song, "Myti Kaysi at the Bat," a humorous interpretation of "Casey at the Bat," adapted by Fine and Baker. Additionally, Kaye's love of baseball led him, in 1976, to become one of the original investors in the new Major League Baseball franchise, the Seattle Mariners, and he remained a part-owner of the team until 1981.

"Bob Hope Variety Special" (NBC; October 25, 1963)[52]

Like Danny Kaye, Bob Hope was a dedicated and passionate baseball fan whose love of the sport drove him to invest a hefty slice of his ample earnings as an entertainer into partial ownership of a Major League Baseball team. In Hope's case, the team was the Cleveland Indians (the team he had rooted for as a child) and his role as partial owner began in 1946.[53] Ten years later, in 1956, Hope reinforced his fondness for baseball when he appeared on the *I Love Lucy* show and participated in a baseball-themed song-and-dance routine with Lucille Ball and Desi Arnaz that will be discussed below in greater detail. This 1956 showcase of baseball and dance was not the last time Hope would facilitate the merger of these two disciplines via television. Indeed, on October 25, 1963, NBC aired the "Bob Hope Variety Special" (the fourth installment of *Bob Hope Presents the Chrysler Theatre*) and, in between comedy skits and songs performed by Hope and his glittering gallery of Hollywood guests (including Andy Griffith, Martha Raye, and Jane Russell), a delightful top-hat-white-tie-and-tails rendition of "We're in the Money" was shared with the world by the three most prominent members of the World Series-winning Los Angeles Dodgers: Tommy Davis, Don Drysdale, and Sandy Koufax. *Jet Magazine*, in its October 31, 1963, issue, described the trio as "dapper" and one look at the photograph that appeared in the magazine confirms this assessment.[54] Davis, Drysdale, and Koufax, each in the prime of his respective career, look positively Broadway-ready.

Bob Hope's Salute to the 75th Anniversary of the World Series (NBC; October 15, 1978)[55]

The 75th anniversary of Major League Baseball's World Series provided baseball fan (and executive) Bob Hope with a wonderful theme for yet another NBC television special. Coincidentally (and, in terms of this study, quite happily), Hope's grand celebration also turned out to be a magnificent showcase for dance, driven by the movements and culture of the game. Making a relatively rare television appearance on the show (motivated, undoubtedly, by his love of baseball and his friendship with fellow Major League Baseball team owner Hope), Danny Kaye contributed two song-and-dance numbers that brought the audience to its feet. Kaye's first routine was a reprise of "Baseball Man," his comic baseball-infused spoof of Meredith Wilson's *Music Man* (performed originally on his own 1963 television variety special). Then, at the conclusion of the show, Kaye, with great fanfare, performed an uplifting version of "Take Me Out to the Ball Game," accompanied by a chorus of singing-and-dancing Little League-aged boys in baseball uniforms. Following the final note, wild cheers from the spectators were quite audible.

The show also included a remarkable rendition of the *Damn Yankees* song, "Whatever Lola Wants (Lola Gets)," complete with provocative dancing, performed by the popular Latin American entertainer (and ex-wife of bandleader Xavier Cugat), Charo. Finally, as an added treat, Hope chose to re-broadcast the clip, from his October 31, 1963, television special, featuring Tommy Davis, Don Drysdale, and Sandy Koufax singing and dancing the song, "We're in the Money," dressed not in their Los Angeles Dodgers' flannels, but, instead, in "dapper" formal attire.

Eye on Dance (WNYC/PBS)[56]

In 1981, choreographer and former dancer Celia Ipiotis teamed up with video artist Jeff Bush to launch the dance-focused Public Broadcasting System television program *Eye on Dance*. Their goal was "to propel dance literacy"[57] and, in order to advance this ideal, Ipiotis, who hosted the show, and Bush brought in special guests from every corner of the dance universe, as well as a multitude of individuals who worked in related fields outside of this diverse but relatively finite universe, for compelling interviews supplemented with rare film clips and photographs. The show lasted until 1992 and, according to the official *Eye on Dance* website, more than 325 episodes were aired, many featuring individuals who rarely consented to be interviewed.[58] *Eye on Dance* also presented inventive and sometimes surprising interviewee pairings and panels, often constructed around a fascinating topic in dance history, dance theory, and/or dance culture.

Along these lines, it is possible to identify at least six *Eye on Dance* episodes that touched upon the subject of "sports and dance"—how the two areas intersect, how they differ, and how each is perceived in different segments of society. Three of these six shows will be discussed in this section.

Episode 136; November 25, 1984[59]

Featured in this episode, which boasted the no-nonsense title, "Athleticism in Dance," were Olympic gold medal figure skater Robin Cousins, and Toby Towson, an NCAA champion gymnast who was instrumental in developing "gymnastic dance," a performing art that fuses gymnastics, modern dance, and ballet. At the time of the interview, Towson was the director of the New York City-based American Acrobatic Dance Theatre, a company that he co-founded as the Musawwir Gymnastic Dance Company in the mid–1970s.

Cousins and Towson discuss the similarities between athletics and dance in terms of training and performance and the ways in which dance and sports complement and aid one another when it comes to developing both body and mind. There is also discussion of the prevailing cultural association, particularly in the United States, and particularly among men, of dance and femininity, especially in the case of ballet, and, by contrast, how physically prepared and "athletic" dancers must be in order to carry out movements successfully, making something that is technically difficult look effortless—a point that is uttered repeatedly by dancers and choreographers (George Balanchine, Alicia Graf Mack, Gene Kelly, Nick Ross, and Edward Villella, among others) when speaking of dance "artistry."

The episode also includes a conversation with another athletic-minded dance-maker, Elizabeth Streb, a childhood softball player whose dynamic company of dancers, in 1987, would perform at the Metrodome in Minneapolis, during a doubleheader between the hometown Minnesota Twins and the visiting New York Yankees.[60]

Episode 208; January 16, 1987[61]

As described in the opening chapter of this book, the January 16, 1987, installment of *Eye on Dance* was devoted to a comparison of "attitudes" of dancers and athletes, particularly in terms of training, injuries, and competition. Four distinguished guests were presented in this eye-opening episode, including Kirk Peterson and Ian (Ernie) Horvath from the world of professional dance; Dr. Joel Solomon, a sports physician whose patients included many professional athletes; and Ron Darling, one of the star pitchers of the 1986 World Champion New York Mets. The lively discussion between Ipiotis and her four guests revealed, almost immediately, the striking similarities in attitude that exist between athletes (and, specifically, baseball players) and dancers. As stated earlier, Peterson (a dancer-choreographer who had worked with such companies as the American Ballet Theatre and the San Francisco Ballet), Horvath (the founder of Cleveland Ballet and a former member of the American Ballet Theatre and the Joffrey Ballet), Solomon, and Darling expressed in vivid detail the fears that exist in both players and dancers in relation to injuries and the reasons professional performers will often get back on the field or stage while they are in extreme pain. A genuine sense of connectedness and a clear mutual understanding quickly developed among the guests. There is no question that the episode's goals were accomplished. Viewers could not help but recognize that the work of the dancer and the baseball player is fraught with pursuits, pleasures, and pitfalls that are extremely close, and often identical in nature.

Episode 249; March 17, 1988[62]

Baseball player-turned-boxer-turned-ballet star Edward Villella was the centerpiece of this episode, which was titled, appropriately enough, "The Male Dancer as Athlete."[63] Villella describes his introduction to ballet, which resulted from a baseball-related accident, and talks about his life before New York City Ballet, which included college letters in both boxing and baseball. Villella also explains the similarities and differences between dance and athletics and talks about his efforts to introduce dance exercises and training to kids in high school and college, including those involved in sports.

So You Think You Can Dance
(FOX; Season 7, Episode 14; July 14, 2010)[64]

For this episode of the popular dance competition show *So You Think You Can Dance*, Broadway-style choreographer Tyce Diorio staged his own version of "Shoeless Joe from Hannibal, Mo.," the show-stopping baseball number from *Damn Yankees* (which, as we discussed earlier in the book, was choreographed for the original Broadway production and subsequent film by Bob Fosse). Two male dancers (Kent Boyd and Neil Haskell), fully outfitted in baseball garb, performed Diorio's breakneck, baseball-driven steps with vigor and skill, resulting in a rousing ovation. Undoubtedly, many viewers, both in the studio and at home, had never witnessed Fosse's ballpark choreography, but they clearly enjoyed Diorio's energetic interpretation, perhaps leading at least a few to seek out the 1958 film.

So You Think You Can Dance
(FOX; Season 9, Episode 6; June 27, 2012)[65]

In honor of the forthcoming Major League Baseball All-Star Game, to be aired in July on the FOX Television Network, *So You Think You Can Dance* returned to a baseball theme for one number on the June 27, 2012, show. This time, the choreographer was Christopher Scott and, instead of reaching back into the Broadway catalog, Scott selected a contemporary song, "Resolve" by Nathan Lanier, upon which to construct his movements. Once again, though, the steps were inspired by those actions, such as hitting and pitching and catching and running, that are part and parcel of the baseball movement vocabulary. Three dancers—Cole Horibe, Brandon Mitchell, and Cyrus "Glitch" Spencer—were employed by Scott and each was dressed in a unique baseball uniform, emblazoned with the letters "SYTYCD" (an acronym of the show's title). Dancers also carried baseball bats, which, as expected, were used repeatedly as props throughout the brief routine. Like the previous, 2010 baseball-inspired dance piece choreographed by Tyce Diorio, this high-intensity offering was a "show-stopper," prompting one of the regular series judges, Mary Murphy, to exclaim, "You hit that out of the ballpark!"

Oh Sit! (CW Television Network;
Season 1, Episode 10; October 3, 2012)[66]

Kat Graham, a pop singer and one of the young stars of the teen-oriented television series *The Vampire Diaries*, appeared as a musical guest on this youth-targeted "high-stakes, high-octane musical chairs competition" show on October 3, 2012. Graham and her record company, A&M/Octone, had recently released an album entitled, *Against the Wall*, which contained four songs, including one called "Heartkiller." This song was sung by Graham on the show and a corresponding dance routine was created for her and two male accomplices. Rather mysteriously, Graham and her small entourage were outfitted in baseball costumes and the bulk of the energetic choreography was based on movements commonly associated with baseball. The two male backing dancers also toted baseball bats, which served as handy props throughout the three-minute piece. It is, of course, rather difficult to determine whether or not this dance routine was inspired in any way by the baseball numbers that achieved so much acclaim in 2010 and 2012 on *So You Think You Can Dance*. What is perhaps even more intriguing to ponder, though, is the fact that baseball-themed choreography would be so appealing to two 21st-century television shows with such clear intentions to attract young viewers. Baseball, it seems, was once again "hip."

Dancing with the Stars (ABC; Season 17, Week 2; September 23, 2013)[67]

The "hipness" continued in 2013, when a baseball-focused routine was created for the popular television dance competition series *Dancing with the Stars*. One of Season 17's most talented celebrity contestants turned out to be Corbin Bleu, who, in 2007, earned a permanent and prominent place in our imaginary "Baseball and Dance Hall of Fame" when he performed the song, "I Don't Dance," in *High School Musical 2*. In the second week of Season 17, Bleu and his partner, Karina Smirnoff (whose place in the "Baseball and Dance Hall of Fame" also was cemented when she became engaged to major league pitcher Brad Penny in 2010),[68] were given the daunting task of creating and delivering a jive routine. In order to carry out this task in show-stopping fashion, Smirnoff and Bleu devised a "can't miss" plan: look to *High School Musical 2* for inspiration and take advantage of Bleu's "youth appeal." And so, a song ("Kiss You") by the teen idol band One Direction was chosen as the engine of the routine and the choreography incorporated the baseball-centric dynamism and exuberance of "I Don't Dance," casting Bleu, familiarly, as the star high school baseball player and Smirnoff as the athletic and enthusiastic cheerleader who leaves the sidelines in order to engage in a personal jive with her hero. As the lights came on, Smirnoff, in her cheerleader outfit, and Bleu, in his baseball uniform, stood, in tableau, in the team locker room. In a flash, as the music pumped, Bleu disposed of the baseball bat that he had been holding behind his head and executed an infield slide. The remainder was all energy, all jive, all coated generously with the seasoning of baseball, leading to massive applause and pushing Bleu and Smirnoff closer to the second place finish to which they ascended in the season finale.

Comedy and Drama Series Episodes

I Love Lucy (CBS; Season 6, Episode 1; October 1, 1956)[69]

Bob Hope was the special guest star in this episode, which features the famous rendition of the song "Nobody Loves the Ump" (music by Eliot Daniel, and lyrics by Larry Orenstein), sung and danced by Hope and his two performing partners, Desi Arnaz and Lucille Ball, while wearing full baseball umpire regalia. The fact that reruns of *I Love Lucy* continue to be shown and continue to be both in demand and beloved translates into generation upon generation of new viewers being exposed to the simple but effective baseball choreography created by film and television veteran Jack Baker for this 1956 episode.

The Odd Couple (ABC; Season 4, Episode 2; September 21, 1973)

The oft-mentioned Edward Villella, former *premier danseur* of the New York City Ballet and former baseball standout in high school and college, guest starred in this episode of the television series based on playwright Neil Simon's Tony Award-winning comedy about fastidious, arts-loving photographer Felix Unger (Tony Randall) who separates from his wife and moves in with his polar-opposite friend Oscar Madison (Jack Klugman), a divorced sports writer who lives in a messy New York City apartment. References to the baseball and dance connection occur throughout the episode, beginning with one of the earliest scenes, when Oscar, sporting his ubiquitous New York Mets baseball cap, arrives at the ballet studio where Villella is rehearsing with a group of young ballerinas-in-training and mentions to Villella that he (Oscar) has just injured his shoulder (in this case, while playing football). Villella takes the opportunity to describe his own sports background and proceeds to teach Oscar how to do a *port de bras*, which, Villella reveals, will give Oscar added strength and help him heal—a ballet exercise that can be used to aid a sports-related injury. Felix, who is a member of Villella's ballet-appreciation society, also is at the studio and is bothered by Oscar's lack of enthusiasm for the arts. He complains to Villella, "The only thing he's interested in in life is sports. Culturally, he's a helpless case." Villella, though, is sympathetic: "Hey, listen, ballet and sports are compatible." Later on, Villella gives Oscar more ballet exercises to help with his recovery.

At the conclusion of the episode, a student performance, which is scheduled to include guest appearances by Villella (as well as Oscar and Felix), takes place in Newark, New Jersey. Prior to this performance, however, is a scene involving Oscar and Felix and two other "Odd Couple" regulars, Murray the Cop (Al Molinaro), and Felix's girlfriend, Miriam (Elinor Donahue). Murray has been enlisted by Felix to pick up Edward Villella from Lincoln Center and take him to the theater in Newark. Problems arise, and Murray is forced to explain. The scene, it turns out, is peppered with baseball allusions:

> *Murray:* They switched the lineup of the dance numbers over there and he told me to tell you he's going to be late.
> *Miriam:* How late, Murray?
> *Murray:* I don't know. He was supposed to dance lead-off, but they put him in the clean-up spot.
> *Felix:* What does that mean?
> *Oscar:* It's baseball. He was supposed to go first, but now he's going to go fourth.
> *Felix:* That means he's going to be a half hour late, at least.
> *Oscar:* Murray, go back and be ready to pick him up right away.
> *Murray:* I'll cover the bases, Oscar.

The fact that baseball was given such prominence in this episode makes perfect sense considering that Edward Villella was involved. Not only was he a sports-minded person in his own right, but, even more so, he was passionately interested in attracting young, sports-minded boys to dance and demonstrating to individuals everywhere the intimate connections between sports and dance—passions that he exercised over and over again in his school residencies, his lecture demonstrations, and his television specials. Indeed, it is worth remembering that just three years after the filming and airing of this *Odd Couple* episode (entitled "Last Tango in Newark"), Edward Villella created "Dance of the Athletes" for the CBS series *Festival of Lively Arts for Young People*. This special television event, featuring professional dancers and athletes (including pitcher Tom Seaver and catcher Jerry Grote of the New York Mets), is discussed in the next section.

The Simpsons (FOX; Season 2, Episode 5; November 8, 1990)

This episode from the second season of the long-running, astoundingly successful animated television series *The Simpsons* is entitled, "Dancin' Homer," which pretty much says it all. Homer Simpson, the bumbling but lovable Simpson family patriarch, becomes the official, on-field mascot for the local minor league baseball team, the Springfield Isotopes, and, as one may guess, shows off his very own brand of highly "animated" dance moves, providing the lackluster Isotopes with some much-needed "spark."

Princess Nine (NHK in Japan, ADV Films in North America; 1998)[70]

Originally produced in 1998 as a television *anime* series in Japan and then released with English language translation in North America on DVD and VHS in the same year by ADV Films, *Princess Nine* is the story, in animation, of an all-girls baseball team, from the Kisaragi School for Girls, that strives to attain a berth at Japan's National High School Baseball Championship, played annually in legendary Koshien Stadium. Music is pervasive in the series, and one of the girls, right fielder Yoko Tokashiki, is known to have a dream of becoming "a baseball star who can also sing and dance."[71] In the musical soundtrack to the show, a wordless song that is associated with Tokashiki, composed by Masamichi Amano, is given the title, "The Singing and Dancing Baseball Player." The show lasted one season, consisting of twenty-six episodes, and two recordings of the show's music were released in CD format in 2003.

7th Heaven (WB Television Network; Season 9, Episode 15; February 14, 2005)[72]

At the core of this long-lasting, "family-friendly" television series was Reverend Eric Camden (Stephen Collins), his large and loyal family, and his frequently troubled stable of parishioners and neighbors. In most episodes, a moral dilemma was faced and conquered by the show's conclusion, with much drama and wholesome comedy tossed in along the way. In the ninth season of "7th Heaven," with regular characters advancing in age, some slightly "racier" storylines began to appear and even a bit of creative experimentation could be noticed. Episode 15 (formally titled "Red Socks") was one such example. Constructed as a musical, complete with singing and dancing, "Red Socks" took advantage of its Valentine's Day broadcast date and presented viewers with a melancholy study of the many facets of love. Included in this musical rumination was a song-and-dance segment that took place on a high school baseball field. Meant to serve as a support device for Rev. Camden's lovelorn teen daughter, Ruthie, the song, "Accentuate the Positive," was performed by Ruthie's heartthrob (and Kennedy High School baseball team member), Vincent, along with a chorus line of uniformed baseball buddies, employing baseball bats as props and executing unmistakably baseball-inspired dance moves. "Shoeless Joe from Hannibal, Mo." it most certainly was *not*; however, thanks to the "Red Socks" episode of *"7th Heaven,"* baseball's relationship to dance was made clear to a new generation of viewers very likely unfamiliar with such shows and films as *Damn Yankees* and *Take Me Out to the Ball Game.*

Bunheads (ABC Family Channel; Season 1, Episode 2; June 18, 2012)

In the second episode of this inventive, quirky, and much too short-lived television series, the main character, Michelle Simms (played by Broadway star, Sutton Foster), connects ballet and baseball when, facing a room full of emotionally charged teen and pre-teen dance students, she puts a special spin on a line from the film, *A League of Their Own.* Paraphrasing Tom Hanks (in the role of Jimmy Dugan), Michelle emphatically reminds her pupils that "there's no crying in baseball—or ballet!" Also worth noting is the fact that, in a much later episode, a guest appearance was made by Kent Boyd, who, as described in the previous section, had performed a baseball-themed dance number on *So You Think You Can Dance* in 2010.

Bunheads, despite ample praise from an army of high-powered television critics, lasted only two seasons; however, in those two seasons, the show's choreographer, Marguerite Derricks, succeeded in creating an impressive catalog of dance pieces that utilized wonderfully unconventional movements, songs, and sources of inspiration. Had the show survived a bit longer, it seems more than likely that Derricks would have reached into her magic choreographic bag and pulled out a crazy little baseball routine to go along with her ruminations on paper versus plastic, coal mining, and rats.

Smash (NBC; Season 1, Episode 1; February 6, 2012)[73]

The intention of this lavishly produced, "musical drama" series—which, like *Bunheads,* lived a mere two seasons before being canceled—was to give viewers a window into the creation of a Broadway show. The show at the center of the story, of course, was a fictional one, and the "window" also permitted views of personal lives and the interactions, sometimes savory and frequently scandalous, taking place between characters both on and off the stage. Tears, joy, sweat, deceit, ambition, competition, love, rage, and triumph all figured prominently in the twenty-six episodes, and a litany of real-life royalty from Broadway and television drifted in and out of the action, both on camera and behind the scenes.

One such luminary was dancer-choreographer Joshua Bergasse, and, in the show's inaugural ("pilot") episode (aired on February 6, 2012), he was given an opportunity to contribute a pivotal baseball-inspired dance number. *Bombshell* was the title of the fictional musical being developed in the story and this fictional show was based on the life and death of Marilyn

Monroe. Because Monroe was married for a time to baseball great Joe DiMaggio, it was decided that an elaborate song-and-dance routine reflecting this baseball/Hollywood connection. This routine, choreographed by Bergasse, was given the title, "The National Pastime," and, in the show's first episode, the routine was featured, with Megan Hilty (as auditioning actress Ivy Lynn) performing the role of Monroe. Dancers clad in baseball uniforms, executing baseball movements, acted as the chorus for Monroe and, once again, the spirit of *Damn Yankees* was revived in living rooms across North America and the world.

An exciting postscript to this discussion of *Smash* is the news that Bergasse was selected as choreographer for a new stage musical version of the iconic 1988 baseball film *Bull Durham*.[74] At the time of this writing, the musical-to-be is still in production; however, there is no doubt that any revised edition of this book will devote ample space to this much-anticipated stage adaptation.

Television Specials, Documentaries and Reports

"Metropolitan Daily" (W2XBS/NBC; June 1, 1939)

As Jennifer Dunning of the *New York Times* points out in her 1992 obituary of the choreographer Hanya Holm: "In 1939, she became the first concert dancer to present her work on television in the United States."[75] In 1939, television was a brand new medium, and, since very few people owned a television set and because the broadcast range for those few programs that did get aired was so limited, members of the public often had their fledgling experiences with television in a public sphere. One such public showcase existed, in 1939, at the New York World's Fair and, on June 1 of that year, Holm and her all-female dance company were invited to the new NBC television studio in New York City to perform a piece while being filmed. To mark this special occasion, Holm chose a relatively new piece that was truly "all-American"—a delightful study in dance of a typical American newspaper, with a score by an American composer (Gregory Tucker), danced by a troupe of American women. The piece, "Metropolitan Daily," was, of course, choreographed by an artist whose original home was in Europe; however, Holm, since arriving in America, had embraced the country and the "Americana" movement of the country's artists with great passion.[76] What better way of celebrating her newfound passion than by presenting this celebration of America in dance at an international festival being held in America's greatest, most progressive and diverse city?

As mentioned previously, "Metropolitan Daily" contained a closing section which highlighted a newspaper's sports pages. Near the finale, the sport of baseball was featured and, as the dancers Louise Kloeper and Harriet Roeder performed Holm's carefully choreographed baseball movements, the piece advanced to its climax, leaving images of the National Pastime in dance lodged comfortably and joyfully in the minds of early television viewers. Much more televised dance was to come in the weeks and months (and years) that followed the broadcast of "Metropolitan Daily" in 1939. But it was the spectacle of baseball choreography that appeared at television's dawning—baseball's dynamism, baseball's grace, baseball's drama, baseball's moments of calm and its explosions of energy, baseball's fairness and sense of democracy, baseball's blend of teamwork and individuality, and, always, baseball's simultaneous pursuit of perfection and acceptance and embrace of (and delight for) the imperfect, the unusual, and the "different." Holm understood that these qualities, approaches, and sensibilities were linked intimately with those of American dance and with the essential spirit of America. In a very real way, the dance of baseball *was* the dance of the entire country and it belonged not only inside the ballparks but also on the concert dance stage—and both kinds of performances could be captured by a television camera and shared with the people of the nation and beyond.

"The Mighty Casey" (CBS; *Omnibus*; March 6, 1955)

In March of 1955, two years after its rather "quiet" stage premiere in Hartford, Connecticut, and just two months before the Broadway opening of *Damn Yankees*, William Schuman's operatic interpretation of Ernest Thayer's "Casey at the Bat," dubbed "The Mighty Casey," made its appearance for the first time on television. The presentation took place on the Ford Foundation-supported *Omnibus* series, broadcast on the CBS network, with virtually all of the original 1953 production, including song arrangement and staging, as well as dancing, kept intact, albeit with a different cast and conductor. In 1953, only a smattering of spectators made the trip to Hartford's Burns School Auditorium to see the performance, with its libretto by Jeremy Gury, firsthand. Now, thanks to the extensive "reach" of television, opera buffs, baseball fans, and other curious members of the public were finally given an opportunity to experience what could be characterized as a major new work by a major American composer—and a work that was steeped in "Americana," to boot.

Critical reaction to Schuman's work turned out to be mixed. Many such critics, including Jay S. Harrison of the *New York Herald Tribune*, and Donald Kirkley of the *Baltimore Sun*, heaped praise on the choral and ensemble sections, the approach to the subject matter, and even the baseball movements,[77] while some others, particularly Harold C. Schonberg of the *New York Times*, ranted at length about Schuman's "quasi-modern" score, the acting skills of the performers ("Who taught them [the members of the Mudville team] how to hold a bat?"), and even the work's very title (said Schonberg with exasperation, "Why on earth wasn't it called 'Casey at the Bat'?").[78] Still, even detractors (and, in truth, most negative reviews came from critics whose musical style preferences did not include composers such as Schuman) agreed in general that the effort was quite valiant. And, as Jeffrey S. Stern points out in his University of Miami doctoral dissertation about *The Mighty Casey*, Schuman's "decision to depict the drama" through "dance and pantomime" was a clear indication that *The Mighty Casey* was "closely connected to Schuman's musical theatre predecessors," such as Rodgers and Hammerstein, Rodgers and Hart, etc.[79] This was opera infused with Broadway blood and at the core was America's National Pastime, complete with choreography inspired by the actions associated with the game itself, both on and off the field (concessionaires, groundskeepers, ticket sellers, and local fans were major players).

As mentioned in Chapter 2, Schuman and Gury's work has been revived for the stage a number of times in subsequent years; however, no other production seems to have been created for television since the 1955 *Omnibus* special. As an aside, it is interesting to note that, when it was aired on March 6, 1955, Schuman, obviously excited by the prospect of a recent work being broadcast live for a national audience, organized a viewing party at his home.[80] At this party, Schuman and his wife distributed "questionnaires" to all guests, which contained humorous but hopeful questions, such as "I believe that *The Mighty Casey* will do more for baseball than: (a) Abner Doubleday, (b) Casey Stengel, (c) Radio and television, (d) Ballantine Ale." Clearly, this questionnaire was meant to amuse; however, it is also fairly evident that Schuman had some grand aspirations for his baseball opera. With the Broadway arrival of *Damn Yankees* on the horizon, it is not at all outlandish to speculate that Schuman, who "considered seriously a career as a professional ballplayer" in his youth,[81] had his own dreams of seeing such dance segments from *The Mighty Casey* as "Twilight of the Big Game," "Dance of the Hawkers," and "The Rhubarb Dance" performed with a full orchestra on the stages of theaters like the Adelphi and the 46th Street, both of which would showcase, in the coming spring, the splendid choreography created by Bob Fosse for the *Damn Yankees* musical numbers, "Shoeless Joe from Hannibal, Mo.," "The Game," and "(You Gotta Have) Heart."

"Dancing—A Man's Game"
(NBC; *Omnibus*; December 21, 1958)[82]

Film legend, master dancer, and childhood baseball hopeful Gene Kelly produced and hosted this groundbreaking exploration of the similarities and relationships that exist between athletics and dance. Kelly invited an All-Star roster of professional male athletes to the television studio to demonstrate the primary movements of each respective sport and followed up each demonstration by having a professional (American) dancer re-create these movements in the context of ballet or modern dance. Kelly then discussed the similarities and relationships of movement, in an attempt to reinforce the idea that dancing is, indeed, "a man's game" and the fact that dance and sports spring from the same point of origin. Such outstanding—and famous—sports figures as Dick Button (ice skating), Bob Cousy (basketball), Sugar Ray Robinson (boxing), and Johnny Unitas (football) are highlighted, as is Mickey Mantle, who was, perhaps, the most popular—and most "masculine"—professional baseball player in the world in 1958. Mantle's form as a ballplayer—on the base paths, in the field, and at the plate—is characterized by Kelly as "dancing ... a beautiful, rhythmic thing to watch." And, as Mantle demonstrates his method of chasing down a fly ball and his approach to stealing second base, Kelly has a dancer perform similar movements. The commonalities are impossible to miss.

Kelly's own style of dancing was referred to quite often as "athletic" or "muscular," and he was determined, as was Ted Shawn thirty years before and as would be Edward Villella in the proceeding thirty years, to make dance more attractive to boys and men. With American dance becoming more and more distinct in terms of style and with the relative spate of recent stage and screen productions blending baseball and dance, "Dancing—A Man's Game" was broadcast at an ideal time. And there is no doubt that Kelly's production helped to inspire Edward Villella's subsequent exploration of dance and sports, "Dance of the Athletes" (produced in 1976 and discussed below). Villella, in fact, was one of the four male dancers who appeared on "Dancing—A Man's Game" (the others being stage and screen dancers Patrick Adiarte and Lou Wills, Jr., as well as Kelly himself). The one questionable element contained in the show was its emphasis on the difference between dance that is "appropriately" masculine and that which is, to borrow a word from the program, more "effeminate" in nature (and, thus, "inappropriate" for male dancers). Kelly, though, is quick to point out that there is a difference between "grace of movement" and "effeminacy of movement" and he states that "it is wrong to mistake one with the other." It is important to remember, of course, that this was still the 1950s. Important to remember, too, is that, even with the reinforcement of some stereotypes, Gene Kelly's "Dancing—A Man's Game" advanced in a big way the idea that fathers could give their blessings to sons who may be more interested in weekend dance lessons than Little League.

"Edward Villella: Man Who Dances" (NBC; *Bell Telephone Hour*; March 8, 1968)[83]

This extraordinary portrait of Edward Villella's awe-inspiring abilities as both a dancer and an educator begins with the following statement by the narrator:

> He was a welterweight boxing champion of the New York Maritime Academy. Now he is a star of the new generation of male dancers that is exciting the world of ballet with breathtaking speed, power, and manly art.

The documentary then shifts to an exemplary day in 1967, when Villella was scheduled to dance "an exhausting succession of three major roles" for the New York City Ballet, which led, ultimately, to brilliant achievement, but which also came close to causing physical calamity. Villella is filmed literally collapsing off stage after a performance of "Tarantella," plagued by severe muscle spasms and a leg that was thoroughly locked and throbbing with pain.

We next see Villella, with dance partner Patricia McBride, delivering a lecture demonstration to an auditorium filled with tough-looking male high school students. The narrator remarks, "The less likely his [Villella's] audiences may be, the more Villella is challenged to put across his view of ballet." Students are shown laughing and groaning, looking bored and contemptuous when Villella and McBride are introduced. Yet, almost immediately, Villella is able to captivate and engage his spectators. Villella describes his own baseball background and uses his knowledge of baseball to enlighten students about the "manly art" of ballet. At one point, for example, Villella explains the similarities and differences between baseball and ballet movement:

> Now, when an outfielder is chasing a fly ball, that's movement. He's running, he has a technique, but he runs the fastest way he can to the point where he has to get the ball and, if he jumps, he jumps the best way he can. Fine. And he makes the catch. Spectacular, looks great, and so on. Now, if I were to do the same thing—let's eliminate catching the ball, let's say running and jumping. It's not the fastest way I can move; it's not the way that's easiest for me to move. I have to move within the rules and regulations. I have to hold my shoulders down; I have to hold my arms in a certain position. My legs have to be in a certain way. My feet have to be pointed, my legs have to be turned out. I have all of these things going on when I'm doing that simple run and jump.

Incredibly, by the end of Villella's lengthy introduction, the students are completely spellbound. When McBride is brought into the action, the entire auditorium is paying careful attention and, by the end, the students are cheering loudly.

Finally, we hear about Villella's past and the feelings that he has while he is dancing. His words are astoundingly reminiscent of those uttered by countless baseball players:

> You get this feeling of exhilaration. You also get, in a strange way, *involved* with that exhilaration, to the point where nothing else is happening in the world.... When you're having a great performance, you're aware only that it's *so easy*. It's so smooth. And when you're finished, you always say, "I could have done much better than that. Why didn't I do *that*?" And then it all sinks in and you say, "Wow, that was something. That was extra special."

In both ballet and baseball, nothing can compare with the mystical, magical phenomenon of being "in the zone." What a player like Hideki Matsui of the New York Yankees experienced in the final game of the 2009 World Series, when he had three pivotal hits, including a home run, and recorded six runs-batted-in, is connected intrinsically to the feelings expressed by Villella in "Man Who Dances."

"Dance of the Athletes" (CBS; *Festival of Lively Arts for Young People*; September 26, 1976)

Drawing inspiration from his earlier experience as a featured performer in Gene Kelly's 1958 television special, "Dancing—A Man's Game," as well as his work as a dance educator and "ambassador" and his passion for involving boys and men in dance, Edward Villella developed a television special in 1976 that sought to "demonstrate the similarities in the disciplines, thought processes, and problems" of dancers and athletes.[84] The show was called "Dance of the Athletes" and it was broadcast on the CBS television network, as part of the network's *Festival of Lively Arts for Young People* series. Villella recruited twelve professional dancers and six sports professionals to participate and highlighted three major elements of connection: "the body, the space, [and] the mental preparation."[85]

The program was divided into two distinct segments, the first of which featured the actions and words of the professional athletes, juxtaposed with parallel dance movements and expressions—an approach that bore some resemblance to the one employed by Gene Kelly in "Dancing—A Man's Game." Among the sports pros were two members of the New York Mets baseball club: pitcher Tom Seaver, and catcher Jerry Grote. Villella allows Seaver and Grote, along with his other sports guests, to demonstrate and comment on each of the three aforementioned "elements of connection." We learn, for example, not only about the similarities in training that exist between that of a baseball player and that of a dancer ("The body," says Seaver, "is the instrument"),[86] but also about the intricate "partnering" that is carried out by the pitcher and the catcher, so reminiscent of the partnering that must be mastered by male and female dancers. Norma McLain Stoop, in her 1976 review of "Dance of the Athletes" in *Dance Magazine*, writes the following:

> Villella explains that the secret of partnering is instinctive rapport between two people. Seaver and Grote insist that they are always "in the middle of each other's minds" and that "a pitcher and a catcher who work together make a winning ballclub."[87]

Stoop adds that a clip of Seaver's pitching wind-up and follow-through "seems the most beautiful of movements."[88]

What viewers get in the second half of "Dance of the Athletes," appropriately enough, is a dance piece, choreographed by Edward Villella and performed by the show's ensemble of professional dancers, which showcases the athleticism of dance and the essential "naturalistic" quality inherent in both disciplines. "Dance of the Athletes" picked up the torch passed along twenty years before by Gene Kelly in "Dancing—A Man's Game" and carried it a few laps further. Villella's roster of sports stars included two female champions—U.S. Open tennis winner Virginia Wade, and Olympic gymnast Muriel Grossfield—and a dance troupe made up of both men and women. The message was clear: all dancers are athletic, and all athletes display qualities of the dance in their performance. Villella, in many ways, was attempting to open up not one door, but *two*. Men can dance, and women can play. The fact that the "Battle of the Sexes" tennis match between Billie Jean King and Bobby Riggs occurred only three years prior to the broadcast of "Dance of the Athletes" is no mere coincidence. American attitudes were shifting and Villella recognized this as the perfect time for a program that explored gender roles and invited a new examination of the so-called "appropriateness" of activities and occupations that had been associated hitherto with masculinity and femininity. Creating such a program for a series aimed at young people was perfectly in keeping with Villella's own pursuits as an emissary of dance: let kids know that the worlds of dance and sports are equally relevant, equally exciting, equally beautiful, equally physical, equally acceptable as pastimes and professions, and very much alike in character. And, of course, make it clear that while differences do exist, these differences serve to make the relationships that exist between disciplines such as ballet and baseball even stronger and more vital. "Dance of the Athletes" was an educational tool, but quite a lovely and enjoyable one to experience.

Monday Morning (CBS; April 23, 1979)

Edward Villella was profiled once again in the April 23, 1979, installment of this weekday morning television news magazine. Recently named chairman of National Dance Week, Villella, in addition to discussing his current projects, his aspirations, and his past work, spends time talking about the evolution of dance in the United States and describes the so-called "American style" of dance and what makes it so distinct. Villella also devotes a good portion of the interview to comparing athletics (and, in particular, baseball) and dance and expresses his admiration for the 1978 World Champion New York Yankees. Notably, Villella marvels at the 1978 World Series exploits of New York Yankees' third baseman Graig Nettles. As Villella reviews the "Nettles catalog" of spectacular leaps and dives, he remarks in awe, "I think he was as graceful and as lovely as the best of classical dance."

Billy Sunday: Baseball, the Bible, and Ballet (WCET-TV/PBS; 1983)

In 1948, the pioneer of "Americana" in dance, Ruth Page, brought an experimental new work to the concert dance stage, following nearly five years of preparation, that was based on the life of the baseball-player-turned-fire-and-brimstone-evangelist, Billy Sunday. The work, entitled "Billy Sunday, or Giving the Devil His Due," was created for the Ballet Russe de Monte Carlo (with text contributed by J. Ray Hunt) and its premiere took place at the City Center in New York City on March 2. Basing the piece on Sunday's famously ferocious and rousing sermons, Page blended dialogue and movement and sprinkled throughout the work many of the baseball metaphors ("I know the fast pitches of the Devil!") and baseball-inspired movements that were used by Sunday in his preaching. "Billy Sunday," however, was retired by Page after a rocky European tour, due primarily to the less-than-favorable reviews that were generated, both in the United States and abroad, regarding the piece's musical score.[89] The work remained unperformed for the next thirty-five years.

Then, in 1983, the former Ballet Russe principal dancer who was cast in the original role of Billy Sunday, Frederic Franklin, realized that the time had come for Ruth Page's "Billy Sunday" to be re-introduced to the people of America and the world.[90] Franklin, a universally respected figure in the world of dance, approached the director of the Cincinnati Ballet, David McLain, about a possible revival of the work, and a plan was developed. McLain arranged for a new score to be composed by the company's musical director, Carmen DeLeone, and Franklin agreed to stage the work. Simultaneously, the Cincinnati Ballet itself was undergoing a substantial change as an economically motivated decision was made to merge the company with the New Orleans City Ballet, resulting in the amalgamated Cincinnati Ballet/New Orleans City Ballet. The revived and revised production of Ruth Page's "Billy Sunday" would be the newly fused company's inaugural offering.

Of course, such a major revival could not help but spark the interest of the media, and the Public Broadcasting System's Cincinnati affiliate, WCET-TV, decided to become involved in this exciting event, which was historic on a local, regional (Page, after all, was a Chicago-based artist), and national scale. What better way to celebrate this landmark occasion than with a television special that not only presented the performance of "Billy Sunday," but also the history of the work? And, given the work's subject matter, who possibly could be more appropriate to serve as narrator than local, regional, and national baseball hero, Johnny Bench, the perennial All-Star catcher of the Cincinnati Reds?

WCET-TV's 1983 production was given the title, *Billy Sunday: Baseball, the Bible, and Ballet*, and Bench's narration proved to be chock-full of observations concerning the links between baseball and dance.[91] Describing the feeling that arises in a baseball player after hitting a home run, for example, Bench remarks, "Dancers, certainly athletes of an artistic bent, must feel something similar when they master a difficult step or succeed in a challenging role." Later on, as he discusses the extended period of time it took Ruth Page to bring "Billy Sunday" to fruition, Bench, whose narration was composed by dance historian Andrew M. Wentink, makes the following comment:

> It took Ruth Page five years to get "Billy Sunday" even close to what she wanted. Like putting together a winning baseball club, the success of a ballet depends on its collaborators, choreographer, composer, designer, dancers working together as a team. And Ruth Page had a hard time just finding the right team.[92]

Even the opening segment of the WCET program highlights the baseball and dance connection, as we see a clip of Bench hitting a massive home run against the Pittsburgh Pirates in game 5 of the 1972 National League playoffs before the attention shifts to the creation of the dance piece.

The final portion of the special brings us the dance itself, which, as discussed earlier in this book, contains a substantial dose of baseball-inspired choreography, as well as sermons overflowing with baseball-laden oration. PBS opted to broadcast this locally produced performance documentary on various stations throughout the country, thereby bringing the creative integration of baseball and dance, expressed and delivered by the surprising messenger team of Johnny Bench and Ruth Page, to viewers from coast to coast. And this time, thanks in large part to new music that proved to be much more suitable to Page's choreography, reviews of the ballet were overwhelmingly positive. To quote *New York Times* critic Jack Anderson, the 1983 production was "a beautiful revival" and "a real hoot."[93]

Sunday Morning (CBS; May 5, 1991)

Reporter Bill Geist traveled to Pittsburgh for a special feature on the process of preparing for the performance of Lisa de Ribere's baseball ballet *The Mighty Casey*, by the Pittsburgh

Ballet Theatre. Geist opened his eight-minute segment by remarking, "There's been kind of a curious coming together in recent days of baseball and ballet," observing further, "They're not doing 'the Wave' yet at the ballet, but just about." Geist's report included interviews with de Ribere and various dancers, as well as clips of Tommy Sandt, a Pittsburgh Pirates coach and former Major League Baseball player, offering baseball pointers to male and female members of the ballet company. At one point, after being asked by Geist about the subject matter of the ballet, de Ribere commented, "To me, it was a natural," and explained that baseball players and ballet dancers use "a lot of similar movements."

Billy Sunday, or Give the Devil His Due
(WTTW-TV/PBS; September 16, 2007)

After Ruth Page's *Billy Sunday, or Give the Devil His Due* was brought back from thirty-five years of obscurity by the Cincinnati Ballet in 1983 (and filmed for television by WCET-TV in Cincinnati), another two decades passed before the 1948 work returned to the concert dance stage. In 2007, the Ruth Page Center for the Arts in Chicago commissioned its own performance group, Concert Dance, Inc., or CDI, to once again revive Page's synthesis of dance and spoken word, which was then approaching its sixtieth anniversary.[94] In conjunction with the CDI venture, the Chicago-area film production company HMS Media was brought on board to document the revival and arrangements were made with Chicago's PBS affiliate, WTTW-TV (Channel 11), to air the taped performance.

The actual show was staged for the camera at Northeastern Illinois University and, for the WTTW broadcast, HMS Media was able to include a wealth of archival footage from the 1930s and '40s, as well as contemporary interviews and footage from CDI rehearsals, thus transforming the television special into a full-fledged documentary. On September 16, 2007, Ruth Page's remarkable fusion of baseball and dance returned to the households of Chicago, setting the stage for the live performances of "Billy Sunday" that would follow in late September, also at Northeastern Illinois University.[95]

Yankees on Deck (YES Network; July 8, 2012)[96]

In order to be proficient as a catcher in baseball, a player must be able to squat for extended periods of time, spring up from this squatting position in a split second in order to chase a bunt or pop-up or drill a laser-like throw of 90–120 feet to one of the infield bases, and remain in frighteningly close proximity to solid wooden bats being swung by other players of all sizes while maintaining a steady eye on balls being hurled in his or her direction at speeds of up to 105 miles per hour. It is, therefore, safe to say that baseball catchers may have the toughest, most physically challenging job on the baseball diamond.

So what can catchers do to stay fit and prolong their careers? In the case of Russell Martin, who acted as the starting catcher for the New York Yankees in 2011 and 2012 (after five years with the Los Angeles Dodgers and before he assumed the role of starting catcher for the Pittsburgh Pirates in 2013), the ability to avoid long-term injuries and keep in shape is "all about balance." This is precisely why Martin, in 2012, decided to receive training in the Brazilian martial art of *capoeira*, a fighting technique that utilizes all parts of the body, but especially the legs, and, in practice, bears an uncanny resemblance to *dance*.

Martin's experimentation with *capoeira* was documented in the July 8, 2012, episode of the program, *Yankees on Deck*, a team news series broadcast on the YES Network, a Yankees-owned cable television station. In this series segment, Martin trained with the professional *capoeira* group, Tampa Maculele, and had a chance to demonstrate his newly learned skills in front of the camera as Tampa Maculele performed stunning excerpts from their own *capoeira* repertoire. Martin declared, "I believe in being a complete athlete and being balanced," and described how such training and skills contributed to the fulfillment of this belief. By hitting the "mute" button on the television remote control, it was possible to feel as though dance was the focal point of the show and that Russell Martin and Tampa Maculele were not exhibiting fighting forms, but, instead, performing beautifully choreographed dance steps.

60 Minutes (CBS; November 25, 2012)[97]

Lesley Stahl, a member of the on-camera reporting squad for the much-decorated television news magazine *60 Minutes*, hosted a special profile of the New York City Ballet during the show's November 25, 2012, installment. At an early point in Stahl's segment, she compared the world-renowned ballet troupe to a baseball team. Said Stahl, "The dancers are like the New York Yankees—except in tutus and tights." Stahl's characterization, of course, related not only to the fact that, like the New York Yankees in the world of professional baseball, the New York City Ballet could be considered to be the most storied "franchise" in the realm of professional ballet, but also to the fact that the performers on both teams are similarly athletic and well-trained and only differ, really, in terms of costume (and, in certain cases, gender).

This kind of comparison, as it turns out, was made numerous times by members of the media in the early 21st century. For example, Gia Kourlas, dance critic for the *New York Times* and *Time Out New York*, stated, in a 2009 review of the Martha Graham Dance Company, that "a Martha Graham dancer is like a baseball player at bat: taut with nerves, a seemingly still form quivers on the brink of something momentous."[98] Reporter Marcie Sillman of the Seattle-based radio station, KUOW, also referenced baseball in a 2011 story about the labors and dreams of the young dancers in the school of the Pacific Northwest Ballet (PNB). Expressing the struggles and fears of the talented teens who toil each day in the school as they strive to gain admittance into the professional company, Sillman had this to say:

> Becoming a "PD" [a member of the school's Professional Division] is kind of like getting drafted for a baseball farm team. They spend a couple of years training and waiting for that call up to the majors. But PDs have no guarantee they'll be hired by PNB, or any other ballet company.[99]

Ignoring the specific discipline, the difference between the baseball player and the dancer, once again, lies, essentially, in the costume.

Hot Stove (MLB Network; January 10, 2013)

Josh Rutledge, a young outfielder for the Colorado Rockies, was a guest on the Thursday, January 10, 2013, edition of this off-season baseball talk show. The hosts of the show, former All-Star second baseman Harold Reynolds, and long-time sports commentator Matt Vasgersian, had plenty of baseball-related questions for Rutledge; however, the subject that seemed to excite both Reynolds and Vasgersian most of all was the identity and occupation of the woman whom Rutledge was presently dating, Laura McKeeman. It was widely known that McKeeman was scheduled to be a contestant in the upcoming Miss America pageant, representing the state of Florida, and, in response to a question from Reynolds and Vasgersian, Rutledge revealed that he would be present in the auditorium on the night of the pageant to lend his support. The two *Hot Stove* hosts then mused about the "talent" component of the Miss America pageant and asked Rutledge what kind of presentation McKeeman was preparing if she had to perform. Rutledge replied that McKeeman, who covered the Tampa Bay Rays for FOX Sports before taking a job with the San Diego Padres,[100] would be doing a *dance routine.* According to Rutledge, McKeeman "does ballet *en pointe.*" Indeed, prior to becoming Miss Florida and before turning her occupational attention to baseball, McKeeman danced with the Orlando (Florida) Ballet and was given offers to join both the Nashville and Sarasota ballet companies, both of which she turned down in order to devote her time to sports reporting and broadcasting.

This discussion revived memories of the announcement, in 2010, of the (short-lived) engagement of Karina Smirnoff, professional ballroom dancer and regular cast member on the ABC television series *Dancing with the Stars,* to major league pitcher Brad Penny. The connection between baseball and dance, clearly, can manifest itself in a myriad of ways!

Commercials, Promotions and Videos

As noted earlier, the advent of the Internet and the emergence of cable television have led to a monumental increase in the accessibility of baseball images and footage. Accordingly, thanks to the proliferation of portable video cameras and hand-held computers that are capable of recording moving images, the amount of footage that is being created by both professional and amateur filmmakers is astronomical. What all of this means is that now, in this second decade of the 21st century, it has become almost commonplace for human beings with access to a television and/or computer to be introduced to filmed baseball plays that closely resemble dance movements, dance routines inspired by baseball, and actual dancing baseball players. The ability to understand the powerful relationship that exists between dance and baseball has never been so easy to acquire.

Sports networks, such as ESPN and Major League Baseball's very own MLB, display images of dancing fans, mascots, groundskeepers, players, managers, coaches, and cheerleading squads, particularly when it comes to promoting the network or producing highlight segments, reels, and shows. On the 2011 MLB show, *Intentional Talk*, for example, hosts Chris Rose and (former player) Kevin Millar developed a reputation not only for broadcasting humorously embarrassing baseball moments, but also for sharing entertaining clips of on-field and off-field dancing engaged in by baseball personnel and baseball-related non-personnel alike. When Seattle Mariners' infielder Munenori (Munie) Kawasaki was filmed dancing in the dugout prior to the start of Mariners games in 2012, these images "went viral" on the Internet, as did images of Boston Red Sox players—such as Hideki Okajima, Dustin Pedroia, Jason Varitek, Kevin Youkilis, and, of course, the "Lord of the Dance," Jonathan Papelbon—jigging at the 2007 World Series victory parade in Boston. And when Cuban-born Cervilio Miguel Amador, a principal dancer with the Cincinnati Ballet, was invited to throw out the first pitch before a Reds-Brewers game in August 2013, the double pirouette that he executed in advance of his near-perfect toss to home plate was immortalized on film and shown repeatedly on newscasts and sports shows, finally becoming a "must-see" video on YouTube. Furthermore, many stories also remarked on the fact that Amador, a baseball fan, was throwing his pitch to another Cuban émigré, All-Star closer Aroldis Chapman, while yet another Cuban defector, Reds' starting pitcher Johnny Cueto, looked on in astonishment. "Baseball and Ballet Collide on First Pitch," read the headline of Joe Kay's August 25, 2013, Associated Press story.[101]

YouTube and other video-sharing websites, including those designed by the respective video creators, also have facilitated access to music videos which promote specific artists and recordings of amateur and professional dance shows and recitals. Many of these videos feature baseball-inspired choreography, and quick, simple "keyword" searches connect seekers with a vast collection of examples. Music videos containing images of baseball-inspired dance span genres, including rock 'n' roll (John Fogerty's "Centerfield," Bruce Springsteen's "Glory Days," and Wrong Side of Dawn's "Baseball," which contains an abbreviated recitation of "Casey at the Bat"), "metalcore" (A Day to Remember's "I'm Made of Wax, Larry, What are You Made of?"), country ("The Greatest," by Kenny Rogers), and hip-hop (Macklemore and Ryan Lewis's "My Oh My," a tribute to Seattle Mariners' Hall of Fame announcer Dave Niehaus, and two completely different songs with the title, "Batter Up"—one by Nelly and St. Lunatics, as well as one by Class A, featuring Lil Chuckee).

In terms of recordings made of baseball-themed dance performances, many that have been mentioned in the present and previous chapters may be accessed easily with just a few computer keystrokes. At the same time, video recordings of on-field dance exhibitions, filmed inside a baseball stadium or on a practice field, are abundant on YouTube and elsewhere. In an instant, one may be able to choose between the wild action of a "rain delay dance-off" involving members of the University of Nebraska and California State University at Bakersfield 2012 baseball teams; the glorious spectacle of an in-game performance by the Manatees, the all-male cheerleading squad employed from 2008–2011 by the Miami (formerly Florida) Marlins; and the homespun joy of a "modern" square dance demonstration, held in 2013 at Hadlock Field, home of the AAA Portland (Maine) Sea Dogs. And if online searchers happen to get a hankering to watch a baseball manager instruct his team's fans in the fine art of cha-cha and other ballroom standards, they may view a sampling of video clips taken while ex-major leaguer Bobby Valentine was managing the Chiba Lotte Marines of Japan's Pacific League.[102] Valentine, a one-time ballroom dance champion, took it upon himself, during the years 2004–09, to encourage more women to attend Marines' games by providing on-field dance lessons, many of which were filmed and shared via the Internet.

Also plentiful on YouTube and other video-sharing sites are images, often recorded and released by online news outlets, of baseball players, coaches, and managers participating in dance shows. Around the winter holidays, for example, a great many members of the baseball community provide support to local arts organizations and dance schools by making guest appearances in special holiday productions, such as *The Nutcracker*. Likewise, in order to attract new audiences to dance, numerous ballet companies invite current and retired baseball players to perform a featured role, at various points throughout the year, in a traditional or more contemporary "story ballet." Many of these appearances, of course, are filmed, and it is relatively common for these videotaped recordings to make their way to the Internet. Clips of Don Mattingly, as Mother Ginger in *The Nutcracker* (2011), and Mike Piazza, as the Gangster in *Slaughter on Tenth Avenue* (2013), performing on stage, respectively, with the Evansville

Ballet and the Miami City Ballet, are popular online fare, as are videotaped shots, from 2007, of Alex Cora, Mike Lowell, Jonathan Papelbon, and Dustin Pedroia, then members of the Red Sox, performing ballroom dance routines at the Boston charity event, "Dancing with the All-Stars," which was organized by Lowell to aid victims of cancer.

Two particularly representative video creations turn out to be promotions, not for a network or for the game as a whole, but for a product and a player in pursuit of a berth at the Major League All-Star game. The product is one that has been long associated with the game of baseball: Bazooka Bubble Gum. For decades, the rock-hard pink rectangle of gum inserted into packages of baseball cards—the gum that millions and millions of Americans recall chewing as children—was manufactured by Bazooka, the brand of bubble gum that also was famous, since the end of World War II, for its penny price and for the small, folded comics found inside its wrappers (starring the feisty, eye-patched character, Bazooka Joe, and his odd gallery of friends). Bazooka, in 2006, released a series of commercials meant to enliven the brand's image and, simultaneously, reinforce its status as an American "classic." What better way to do this than by injecting baseball into the mix, along with sounds and movements that reflected contemporary tastes? As a result, one commercial set on a baseball field was created, complete with rhythmic, "boy band" music and dance steps that would feel right at home in an MTV music video.[103] All performers were dressed in baseball costumes, and even an umpire was included. The effect was similar to the baseball dance sequence that would appear in *High School Musical 2* just one year later: baseball and dance are the same game—and bubble gum (especially Bazooka) makes this natural combination even more perfect.

The player promotion happened in 2009, when fans were being called upon by Major League Baseball to participate, for the first time, in the selection of the "final" player for each league's All-Star team. In the National League, one of these players was Pablo "Panda" Sandoval, the talented and good-natured third baseman for the San Francisco Giants. As the All-Star break approached, Sandoval was playing exceptionally well. His very good statistics, combined with his status as a genuine "fan favorite," made him a strong choice for the National League (NL) All-Star team roster. Still, the four other NL players who were being considered for the final, thirty-third spot by fans in 2009—Christian Guzman of the Nationals, Matt Kemp of the Dodgers, Mark Reynolds of the Diamondbacks, and Shane Victorino of the Phillies—were all playing well and each certainly had his own group of rooters. What effort could be made, therefore, by Sandoval devotees to help "push" Panda "over the top"? A music video, of course—and one that included copious amounts of infectious dancing, to boot!

The video—"Vote for Pablo!"—was produced by the Giants and, in addition to dynamic clips of Sandoval at bat and in the field, as well as endearing shots of Panda flashing his popular smile, the video featured the actor Jon Heder re-creating the dance moves that turned his 2004 film character, Napoleon Dynamite, into a worldwide cult superstar.[104] The entire project was an astounding conglomeration of popular culture, meant to capture the hearts, minds, and funny bones of the general public. Baseball and dance, sports and the performing arts, spectators and professional practitioners—all elements working together, making complete sense, understanding and respecting one another, and enjoying the ride. Pablo Sandoval, in the end, failed to garner enough fan votes to advance to the All-Star game (the laurels, instead, were placed on the head of Shane Victorino); however, the campaign to elect him raised fan awareness and helped to turn the process of voting, as pointed out by *New York Times* writer

Lynn Zinser, into "something fun."[105] Fans could relate to the equation of dance and baseball. Way back in 1946, Murray Goodman wrote, "Athletics and dancing—particularly the ballet—have a startling kinship."[106] This deep-rooted kinship, subconsciously or otherwise, was not at all difficult for fans to recall when viewing the exuberant "Vote for Pablo!" promotional video.

The ballet of baseball, the athleticism of the dance. Meditating on this relationship, cultural historian Richard Geer has said the following:

> All of the barriers erected between dance and sport are, in the final analysis, insignificant compared to the similarities of these forms which depend on the energized movement of the human body in space and time. We will never be able to totally detach one from the other. What links them together at their deepest level is that both forms challenge gravity and endurance, both stretch the envelope of fundamental human aptitude in ways that facilitate the growth and development of this complex animal over millions of years. Sport and dance are both ritual, both play…. At their deepest level, a level that most likely can never be laid bare, dance and sport are wonderfully interwoven.[107]

In his study of baseball's great defensive players, *Nine Sides of the Diamond*, David Falkner expresses the sentiments of Geer in a slightly different, more baseball-centric fashion:

> Think of these leaping, diving, acrobatic, behind-the-back, tumbling, upside-down, hair-flying, gravity-defying disappearing and appearing acts, where you are faced with arms stronger than javelin throwers', legs and feet trickier than tap dancers', hands as fast as three-card-monte dealers'. If you are an impartial witness, you may share with sportswriter Jimmy Cannon the sense that baseball is a higher art than ballet because the artistry of baseball is not aided by choreography.[108]

To make his point, Cannon, of course, exaggerates. His—and Geer's and Falkner's—essential idea, though, is unmistakable: baseball and dance are joined at the hip. Sometimes this hip must undergo a bit of repair—and baseball players and ballet dancers frequently suffer the same kinds of injuries to their very own hips in the course of their careers (and often find themselves being operated on by the same surgeons); however, in spite of the bumps, the bruises, and the unavoidable setbacks, the connection remains inseparable, the bond solid. Same game.

The fictionalized picture-book version of Babe Ruth conversing with a herd of sports reporters in Tim Shortt's *Babe Ruth Ballet School* offers this noteworthy comment:

> The sports reporters asked why his hitting was unstoppable. "Fellas," said Babe Ruth, "you might think me funny, but I credit my dance lessons. The dance you see, helps my balance and my movement." "But, Babe, dancing's so girlish," said the sports reporters.
>   "Fellas," said Babe Ruth, "I'm an athlete and dancing is athletic."[109]

The Babe's own daughter, Julia, reminds us in the memoir that she published about her illustrious father, *Major League Dad*, that the "real life" Ruth shared this outlook:

> Of all the dances that were popular in the 1920s and '30s, Daddy loved the fox-trot most of all. I delighted in gliding around our living room with him while a record—one of the old, big, round ones—played on our phonograph machine. I had very few dates that I enjoyed dancing with as much as I did with Daddy. He had a superb sense of timing on the dance floor, maybe the same timing that made him such a great pitcher and hitter. I just loved to dance with him.[110]

If the man who is considered by many fans to be the greatest baseball player in the history of the game can recognize the connection between baseball and dance to be so intimate, so powerful, and so clear, then the rest of us, surely, must acknowledge that this belief possesses a tremendous amount of legitimacy. Indeed, baseball historian Harold Peterson has attempted to excavate even more ancient roots in his investigation of the relationship between baseball and the performing arts. Peterson, in *The Man Who Invented Baseball*, writes:

> And have you ever wondered why a dance should be called a "ball" or a "ballet" and a song a "ballad"? This will drive balletomanes mad, but it is true: Ballet derives from some of the same early ball games we have been discussing…. And you thought calling baseball a "ballet" was a phony affectation?[111]

For Peterson, baseball and dance are limbs that spring from a single, primal tree—a contention that is supported by dance historians who have pointed out that "the ancients" took it for granted that "dancers were athletes and athletes, dancers."[112] Says Celia Ipiotis, "[I]n Ancient Greece, it was part of the natural training of an athlete to dance."[113] North American Indian groups, including the Cherokee, the Choctaw, and the Sioux, also developed, in centuries past, ritual "ball play dances" that were carried out before, during, and after the playing of their sacred ball games—ball games, mind you, that took place, in general, from summer to fall (i.e., "baseball season").[114]

In complete honesty, therefore, it is not really surprising to discover that dance has been associated with baseball for nearly as long as baseball itself has existed in the United States. Nor is it a shock to observe the many occasions where baseball and dance converge, particularly on the stage and screen. It is, however, a great source of pleasure and even awe to note the incredible diversity and sheer multitude of examples that have amassed since the 19th century. It is also fascinating to be reminded of the fact, as Stephen Manes expresses in his book, *Where Snowflakes Dance and Swear* (and as we discussed at length in this book's initial chapters on theater and concert dance), that the histories of dance and baseball in America are remarkably parallel, with the so-called "modern era" for both commencing at around the very same time, in the early 20th century.[115]

Finally, too, it is both interesting and worthwhile to recall this book's opening passage, wherein the overwhelming success of the New York Mets in 1986 was attributed in large part to the ballet regimen introduced that year by team physician, Dr. James Parkes, and dance instructor, Steve Cedros. Keeping this in mind, we may turn once again to prima ballerina and baseball fan Marianna Tcherkassky, who, in a 1983 *Daily News* interview, observed that her habit of arriving early to New York Yankee games alerted her to the woeful insufficiency of the pregame exercises engaged in currently by Yankee players. According to Tcherkassky, "I would love to give the Yankees a ballet class, because I think they could warm up better and help prevent injuries. In baseball, players go out and do some stretches and run a couple of times up and down the field, and they think they're ready. That's just not enough."[116] Although it is likely that the Yankees, who reached the postseason a grand total of zero times between 1981 and 1995, turned a deaf ear to Tcherkassky's wise and carefully considered advice, it is all too probable that a *Daily News* reader from the New York Mets organization was paying very close attention. Quite clearly, a recognition of the true connections that exist between baseball and dance will not merely set you free—it may even help you win the World Series.

Final Thoughts
Interviews with Moses Pendleton and Edward Villella

Moses Pendleton, Choreographer: "Baseball" (Date of Interview: May 4, 2011)

Moses Pendleton: When you take on any new project, you have to approach it with a passion. At one time, I was pretty insanely passionate about baseball—every detail of that game and how it could be translated into some viable entertainment or dance theater form. So there was a lot of research and study.

The idea of gardening—I'm coming back to baseball. As I'm looking out over the field, I'm reminded of Bart Giamatti's *Take Time for Paradise*. It was a very inspiring book for me. Of course, what we're talking about is bringing nature into the cities in the form of parks. It was a baseball field, but it was also a park. It was a place to recreate—to re-create your energy. And I always thought that that was an interesting idea—that it was very connected, actually, to nature and to green grass. The first impression that you might have when you walk into a stadium is that essence of green. And we start "Baseball" with the "Green Monster"—it's called "The Spirit of Green." The first piece is just the light coming over a green field and then out of that the mound comes and things start developing. "The Spirit of Green." So the very first thought about it was the color green. And of course there's Giamatti, the park, nature, spring, new beginnings—everything that baseball kind of signifies. When you hear the crack of the bat and the smell of the glove. Spring training.

I got excited about it—not only to make a piece on baseball, but to be invited by the San Francisco Giants to help commemorate the opening of their new spring-training stadium in Scottsdale, Arizona. And the fact that we were invited as a dance company to share a dressing room with Roger Craig, the man who invented the split-fingered fastball, was absolutely hallucinatory for me. And there was a lot of enthusiasm in the company to be out on the field with the Giants, working and doing calisthenics with them—doing stretches and running wind sprints with Willie McGee and Will Clark and Dusty Baker and the whole Giants team.

Now that I'm getting back into baseball, I'm thinking that it's criminal that we don't continue to perform this—at least in America and Cuba and the Dominican Republic. They took baseball out of the Olympics, I believe. I even have a baseball signed by the Dusseldorf Bears—a German team. And the Parma Hams, an Italian baseball team, gave me a bat.

Back to the initial impulse. The company went down to Scottsdale and everyone loved being there, in the desert. The idea of seeing how physical it was and, being an athlete myself, having played the game, and considering that part of my aesthetic with Momix is how do you put an aesthetic on the athletics—this all seemed like such a natural way to go. Seeing people running, throwing, sliding, jawing, doing all of this stuff was something that I was very used to seeing—but seeing it on a professional level was all very interesting. And to see their interest in us! The exchange was truly inspiring. I think that they were all just thrilled to see the dancers—they couldn't believe the flexibility and power of Momix. And these were professional ballplayers. So there was a mutual respect that jump-started the program.

And, of course, you can't talk about this production without talking about "Diamonds Are Forever." The other reason that we were there was to do some kind of live theater addition to what Tom Seaver was chairing, which was the Smithsonian exhibit of personal impressions of the game of baseball in American art and literature and photography and much more. It was an exhibition that was touring the country and it came to Scottsdale. So, in conjunction with our training with the Giants, we were also trying to put together a little number that would be a live theater equivalent to a Rauschenberg painting and a Calder sculpture and all of this going on in the gallery. The audience would just come into the auditorium and see a short piece, which, initially, was called "Bat Habits" and not "Baseball." That was a number that lasted approximately twelve minutes and, ultimately, that evolved into "Baseball" in a couple of years.

But "Bat Habits" was the live theater addition to the art event. I was very influenced and inspired not only by the game, which I loved and suffered over (being a Red Sox fan), but also by how many liberties other respected artists took with the idea of the game. And this freed me up to think that I could interpret baseball in a wild and interesting and funny way— and maybe a poetic way. What is the mythology of baseball? What is the essence of turning or spinning or what is called "winding up" and other things? And where did it begin? There were some discrepancies as to how to do this piece. You might start with the essence or the spirit of the green that became a volcanic mountain in the pitcher's mound. And the Green Monster was made with dancers under this fabric that rose up and I used projections of the stadiums to have this kind of spirit, this essence of what almost looked like a giant katydid coming up out of the field. So there was that idea. And then we were thinking, in the early days, what were the origins of baseball? You go back to cricket and you go back to rounders and we go back to Neanderthal times, when the essence of baseball really was these two primitives who were interested in the same space or the same woman and they had to decide this—one with a rock and one with a club and they went after each other. And then they realized, as they were trying to club each other and stone each other with this boulder—the one primitive throws the boulder and the other primitive whacks it with the log and that might have been the first bat-and-ball exchange. It's really funny, and the girls all come out and egg them on—they're kind of cheerleading them on—and then it gets more formalized. That was the first game of baseball and those were the origins and beginnings of our National Pastime.

We had a lot of fun with it, going back and just

Choreographer of "Baseball," Moses Pendleton (photograph by Edward Webb; used with permission from Moses Pendleton and MOMIX).

imagining. And, of course, you can imagine anything and that was what this exhibition, "Diamonds Are Forever," did do for me. It freed me up to think that we can take liberties with the game. Liberties *artistically* with the game. And, as I said, the game is more than just the game—it's the fans, it's the stadium, it's the experience of going out and recreating in a park in the middle of an urban center. Many things. It was something to root for. A love of going out and encountering the unknown. In sports, you see, you don't know the outcome, so you get excited. And I suppose you don't know the outcome of a dance. But there is an entertainment and a theater that was created. My other discussion about this, in terms of origins, was that, in the early days, I think it was the Busch family that needed to find a way to sell beer on a mass level, so they organized this little entertainment, this sport, but really it was about selling beer to tens of thousands who would come out for this kind of ridiculous activity. But at least they got to sell a lot of beer. So it was the beer companies that really made baseball. Beer and baseball. And if you see the piece, we do a Bud commercial, with oversized barrels dancing to James Brown's "I Feel Good." That's lots of fun to watch. We also do a Wheaties commercial. So we do a couple of them, mixed right in with the flow of the dance.

In typical fashion, I was trying to find some logic. In the evolution of baseball, we started in the beginning, then moved up through various elements in the game. The poignancy of the process was that I was planning to follow the 1994 season from spring training through the World Series and then, on August 14, 1994, baseball went on strike. So, as I was following the game, right in the middle of our making this full evening piece, suddenly there was no baseball. The company and I were terrifically shocked. The headlines were extraordinary— you know, in the *New York Post*: "Baseball Dead!" and so many others and it was about the strike. But that gave me a potential to not only entertain and fascinate people with the physical abilities of Momix and weave the company's dance abilities into the fabric of baseball, but also I had an idea that now we had a point of pathos, some sadness in terms of, suddenly, the great celebration of this game and "We Are the Champions" and the World Series and everything else was just stopped dead in its tracks. So I began to put together a series of headlines saying this and then playing very, almost funereal Arvo Part music to these slow-moving, waxed, nude female forms and kind of doing the "baseball wake" at the end. So it gave me a little curve to the evening, because of the strike. It was the end of baseball and, yet, out of the ashes, it should be resurrected. So I have an epilogue done to Lorene McKennitt's "Prospero's Speech," which seemed appropriate. It featured a guy in a ski boot singing "Prospero" from Shakespeare in a ski boot. He does a slow-motion version of letting this helium ball release and he goes off the vertical line like a sculpture from Roman times and releases the ball and slowly floats up into the heavens and then there's that image from Michelangelo of Adam touching God, but there was a baseball in between them. Some painter took that and put a ball there. It was also about just taking a classic piece of art and putting a baseball somewhere. So it gave a very poignant and interesting poetic curve to the evening.

However, later on, as we continued to perform the piece, the strike ended, baseball came back, so to keep talking about the strike didn't seem so relevant. But, a few years later, I thought that, by then, the strike was very passé, so I took out those projections of the headlines about the demise and death of baseball and replaced them with headlines about the death of Mickey Mantle. Mickey Mantle had just died and that was big news in the baseball world. So I thought that in the middle of the height and the glory of playing Queen's "We Will Rock You" and "We Are the Champions," all of a sudden, we would shift to Mickey Mantle's death.

Instead of a passage about the death of baseball, it would be about the passing of baseball heroes. I used the same music and the same choreography, but the point of it was really the passing of baseball heroes rather than the stopping of the game.

Part of the information that I give in Momix is very multi-media, with front projections. So you see movements of eight or ten dancers dressed in stripes with bats, swinging. But they would be seen in superimposition to a series of either a baseball field or some other textures that would be seen through a scrim upon which images were being projected. So it gave a kind of three-dimensional, painterly feeling to the visual, physical theater, which was the show. I also think that this got a lot of the visual art world interested—to see how visual, sculptural this piece was. So it did actually become quite connected to "Diamonds Are Forever" in terms of the artists and painters of America who were impressed enough by baseball to make some of their art on the subject.

It all fits together really beautifully. Can you talk about the circumstances that led to Momix being invited to do a piece in conjunction with "Diamonds Are Forever"? How did that come about?

MP: Momix had been performing at the Scottsdale Center for the Arts in Arizona for many years. This particular season there was this exhibition, chaired by Tom Seaver, called "Diamonds Are Forever." The exhibition included paintings and writings and pictures and then Tom Seaver would go along with it and he would make a speech about baseball and talk and come chair the art event. Since we had this relationship with the Scottsdale Center for the Performing Arts, we were asked if we would be interested in having them commission, in conjunction with the San Francisco Giants, a piece that would help to celebrate the exhibition and the new stadium in Scottsdale. I don't know what the Giants actually put into it financially, other than allowing us free reign to train with them and do all that. It was really, I think, a commission from the Scottsdale Center for the Performing Arts. But it all happened so that we went down there and had this experience with the team to help bring some more interest and energy to the opening of their brand-spanking-new spring-training stadium, which was great. This was the Cactus League.

So that's how we did it. The first piece, as I said, was called "Bat Habits," and that was received very favorably. It was 1994, and then the Scottsdale Center said that if we came back in 1996 they would like to give us a further commission or at least give us a week of performances if we could take "Bat Habits" and extend it into a full-evening work. So it was done in stages and then we came back and did the full-evening work called "Baseball." It was really "Momix's Baseball." There were many names that we tossed around, such as "It Takes Four Balls to Walk" and "Balls," which may have sold more tickets.

It sounds as though you were really trying to attract new audiences to dance.

Yeah, I think we were trying to cross over into the sports world. People who go to see baseball—a lot of them aren't very interested in modern dance. But throughout the years, the piece was successful. Wherever we would go when we were touring with the show, such as St. Louis and San Francisco, the sponsors would let the local professional teams know that the show was happening and invite them to the show. And in several places—which was a lot of fun—a baseball player would come out in front of the curtain and throw out the first pitch and I would catch it. We did this with a St. Louis Cardinal pitcher and when we were up in Pittsfield, Massachusetts, we went to MASS MoCA and there we had Jim Bouton throw out the first pitch and introduce Momix. In my research, I also enjoyed very much several meetings I had with Tim McCarver. I knew his daughter, Kathy, and she thought, if we were doing something about baseball, that I should talk with the person who probably knows more about baseball than just about anyone on the planet—her dad. So she made arrangements for me to go and have lunch with him at the St. Regis in New York. He and I had a very interesting talk about some of the fine points of baseball, from a catcher's point of view. Anyone who was able, over the years, to successfully catch Bob Gibson, you really ought to be in awe of. Even when he's on your team, you don't really trust him, I think—imagine how he intimidated the opposition!

Another high point of all this is when we were premiering "Baseball" in Canada, in Toronto. We did choreography to the American national anthem, so the big question in Canada was, "Do we also need to choreograph the Canadian national anthem?" Well, probably the most famous rock band in Canada at the time was Rush and it turns out that one of the members of Rush, Geddy Lee, is a huge baseball fan—he has collections of baseballs in his house. Geddy and I became friends and he agreed to record Rush's version of "O, Canada" for our Canadian premiere of "Baseball." And to make it even more thrilling, the Toronto Blue Jays agreed to have Moses Pendleton throw out the first pitch in the SkyDome, when the Cleveland Indians—with Albert Belle—were in town. And, of course, when Cleveland plays in Toronto, there are fifty thousand fans in the stadium and half of them are Indians fans who drive up from Cleveland. I didn't think I was too nervous until they actually handed me the ball. Momix was going to do a little pre-game performance, as well. We actually performed a bit of "Bat Habits" or "Baseball" right out on the third-base line, in front of fifty thousand fans.

So I go to throw out the first pitch and, just as I stare down to look for the signs (and it wasn't the Blue Jays' catcher—I think it was the left fielder, a pretty agile guy, fortunately), I looked up at the Jumbotron and saw myself fifty feet high and then I started to sweat a bit. I shook off the sign and the crowd was starting to get uneasy, saying things like, "Throw the ball, you idiot!" Finally, I reared back—and I was on the rubber, I did it all correctly—and I fired some "high heat" that was more than high. It was wide by about twelve feet, heading towards the Indians' dugout. It actually looked like I was trying to bean Albert Belle, who was standing near the dugout. The guy who was catching ran and made a diving catch and he got a big cheer out of that. So that was a thrill, anyway, for me.

It sounds as though you did a great job of marketing the show and connecting with baseball fans.
Yes. A lot of people who like baseball came to see this and they really enjoyed it. It's fun, it's entertaining, and it's probably our funniest piece.

I also remember you mentioning in our last discussion that some of the San Francisco Giants came to see the show in Scottsdale.
They did. We went out with Dusty Baker. He was the third-base coach at the time, since Roger Craig was the manager, but soon afterwards, he did become the manager. He and other members of the Giants really liked the show and we went out and had drinks with Dusty after the show. They were really excited. And in Philadelphia, we had our "Baseball" man running around at a dinner with the Philadelphia Phillies and the Phillie Phanatic was chasing him. It was a bit ridiculous, but that kind of thing goes on. As I said, I'm most proud to have gotten a baseball signed by the Parma Hams team. I did a number for another event in New

York, which was in conjunction with the opening of a different baseball exhibition at the American Folk Art Museum. I got to meet Yogi Berra and Phil Rizzuto and had some pictures taken with them and got to talk with them throughout the evening. That was also quite a thrill. We did a twenty-minute piece from "Baseball" for this kind of black-tie gala to raise money for the museum. A lot of events like that happened because we had this piece, "Baseball."

How did you prepare and train your dancers for both "Bat Habits" and "Baseball"?

Many of them had athletic skills and had played some baseball previously and they were a lot easier to deal with. I have to say that one of the most difficult things to do with both men and women who have never thrown a baseball is to get them to look like they *could*. That was difficult. So we really had to go through some very detailed positions, in terms of swinging the bat and throwing the ball, so that one wouldn't look like an idiot—so that they really looked like ballplayers out there and not dancers. They had to be able to do the moves and play the characters—they had to be able to throw the ball and swing the bat. That took a lot more doing than I had anticipated—as I said, not so much with people who had done this before, but if they never had, it could look very awkward, almost like the right-handed members of the company were throwing with their left hands, which would look ridiculous. That was a challenge. And there was definitely a lot of aerobic activity and lots of physical challenges, but that's typical of Momix shows.

They are a professional athletic team in that way. We have an injured reserve, just like any other team. People are going to the doctors every day to get therapy and massage. There are pulled muscles and broken bones. It comes with the territory—very similar to ballplayers. In fact, we just had two people who were rehearsing a piece today who go and see Dr. Bazos, who is the head of the Yankees physical-training component. He goes down to Yankee Stadium to work with the Yankees and is a big sports fan. He also works with the Knicks. Here, he has a facility called New Milford Orthopedics and we actually send our dancers over to see him after he's just seen professional ballplayers. So we do see the same medical people as ballplayers. We just had a boy who tore his meniscus and his surgery was expedited as a result of our friendship with Justin Tuck of the New York Giants. Justin was able to get immediate surgery for the dancer. So there is also that kind of connection and identification between sports and dance. We have sports-medicine people come over and talk to the dance company about how to warm up, how to stretch, and how to avoid injuries. They have the same talk with ballplayers. I mean, you think of a guy who's a $20 million ballplayer and he goes out and pulls his hamstring, what good is he to the team, to the franchise? So the injuries in sports are really costly and really important to take care of—and they are with Momix, as well.

When you were working out with the Giants in Scottsdale, did you assist at all with their training?

We did some stretches with them. We did wind sprints with Willie McGee and tried to keep up with them and, in exchange, we did some easy, kind of yogic-type stretches. They didn't do much of that back in the 1950s or so—they had their scotch and their cigarettes and whatever it was. Now it's much more technical—there is a lot more attention paid to really being in incredible shape in order to make your game better. The same thing happened with Tiger Woods and golf. They suddenly are getting really scientifically trained and they do cross-training and they do diet and they have all of these people around them to try to help them, too.

Did you take the dancers out to play baseball and did you and the dancers go to any baseball games as you were rehearsing "Baseball"?

Yeah, we went to a few games. We also watched games on television, just to get them familiar with the sport. We used to talk baseball as well. I would insist upon it, every time I would go into warmups and rehearsal. There were several of us who would sit around and talk about what happened in the games the night before. "Did you see this?" or "Did you hear that?" Baseball talk—talkin' ball. Get everybody revved up. I used to go into the studio before the warmups and we would talk ball. That was the energizer. Talk ball and then start doing your ballet barre. And then talk ball while you're doing your ballet barre. And then go out and shag some flies—we'd be shagging flies and having batting practice. Sometimes for hours we'd play with these Styrofoam balls in the studio, which is a cool effect. At the very end of "Baseball," the focus of the whole game and the whole theater was just this object—the ball— and two people playing catch. Just this fascination with playing a game of catch. It was done to Erik Satie's "Gymnopédies"—very emotional, very sad music. If you take that ball into the studio, which is not a very big space, you can fire the ball really rapidly and, of course, it's Styrofoam, so it becomes this very cinematic experience. As you release the ball at full velocity, it breaks into "half-time" about halfway across the studio space, as if it were a cinematic, slow-motion version of a baseball being thrown. We would never get tired of playing this and we would sometimes spend hours just firing these Styroballs at each other. And you can make them curve and dip and do all kinds of strange action. We actually got very good at pitching this—it was like a Wiffle ball. We had a lot of fun. We would spend hours after rehearsal just playing, tossing this ball, and, as I said, you can do it in a fairly tight space because it doesn't go very fast after you throw it. It has hang time.

So we got everybody involved in that and that is kind of the essence of the game. The fascination of having an object—whatever it is that you energize and you throw—sent through space and it's caught by someone else and sent back. It's very profound. Something in our genes enjoys it.

It sounds like a great effect and a wonderful way to end the show.

We ended it with—we had the curtain calls and everything and everybody comes out on the diamond and takes their bows. Then, as everyone is trotting off after taking their bows, one dancer stops and looks down and sees a ball. He picks it up and he looks and sees that there is someone on the other side of the stage who didn't quite leave the stage. That dancer on the other side of the stage then looks up and sees the dancer with the ball. Then they start to throw the Styrofoam ball to each other and, as they are doing so, the curtain starts closing. So what you see is them throwing the ball and then, eventually, you see just the ball going back and forth, but almost in that cinematic slow-motion way. It has that kind of "flotation" and the Erik Satie music is playing as this is taking place. It's really a beautiful ending. All you see is that white ball at the end and then, finally, the curtain closes.

Was the approach to this piece very collaborative? It seems as though that is the general Momix philosophy. Was that the case with this piece, as well?

Oh, yes. I never have a total idea of what I want to do. I like to be a catalyst—to come in and set up situations and then we collaborate, work together. We develop material and videotape each day. I try to set it up so that there is an atmosphere of play. Speaking of games!

It *is* a game, as Giamatti says, and that's very important. I put that kind of game philosophy into making new work. We work very hard at our play. You know, did Shakespeare write plays or did he write works? I like to keep it more in the play world. When it's fun, you don't look at the clock and you're not thinking about choreographing—you're just playing, like children at recess. I like to be someone who can set up some of the rules of the game that we play, which might be just improvising on swinging bats, putting in some music that can act as a stimulator to break people down. Every time you go into making a new experience, you need to kind of break down those blocks and release the body, so that they can react and act spontaneously and improvise. It takes some doing to do that—you have to be free enough to do that and to be good actors, you see. With Momix it isn't just how you move, but what kind of character is moving. How can you project being a primitive? If we have a human baseball, what does he look like and how does he act? His only plight in the show is to try to avoid getting pummeled by "bat people." Poor thing—he gets beaten to a pulp. But, of course, we're all rooting for him to be beaten. It's a comedy of errors—it's slapstick or "slapbat." More "slapbat" comedy. There is a lot of fun when you put one of the dancers on rollerblades and have him flying around the studio and then have other people with pretty solid wooden dowels covered with a little Styrofoam clobbering the hell out of him. That's great fun, but you have to be in the mind for that *Commedia dell'arte, Pulcinella* kind of thing.

The method for me is sometimes putting quadrophonic sound, setting up a situation— in this case, some baseball idea—and then playing with it. Let the company riff on it a bit, videotape it, and then shape it. Then, under the next morning's sobriety, we see shards of new information that will further the piece. But the key idea is to have fun. You know, Knute Rockne had everybody dancing in football. He played music because the bodies have to be rhythmical and they have to be able to be loose. Any top athlete has got to get in that zone and do things without even thinking. It's motor memory that has to be in gear. It's similar to dance. You have to be able to be that way and relax and, as I say, have fun with it.

I was a long-distance runner and a cross-country skier and there was a lot of discipline in both activities. A lot of the most inspiring people in my creative life were actually my ski coaches. They were the ones who really taught me about training and how to get second and third winds, and you need to know this when you're choreographing. Sometimes when you're working over material, you might have to repeat something twenty-five times, but if you're so out of shape that you can only repeat it five times, the choreography can't get realized. So you need people to be in really good shape so that you can realize the choreography. That's an important part of it. And just to put out this idea that the life of the body is something heroic and necessary and, actually, if you can get through your time here on this earth with a lot more energy and more fun and all that—I mean, what's the mind without the body? It's a Greek ideal. I try to get people to read *Sun and Steel*, by Mishima. It's his autobiography and it's an inspirational book. Antonin Artaud's *The Theater and Its Double*, his famous book that formed much of physical theater in this country, is a bible. Artaud's *Affective Athleticism*—this is interesting to see about taking the body to another level and reveling in it and using it as a way to move beyond the body.

These kinds of things my coaches taught me somewhat and I teach Momix people this and, when something is done very well, I say, "That was a great move, a great dance, a great show tonight everybody, and, therefore, it merits further rehearsal." Like any good coach. Like Phil Jackson, for example. He's a master of the Zen mind, of bringing out the best in his players. Bringing out the best in your dancers is very similar. You work on their psychology and their will. In baseball, there are 162 games a year and it's hard to keep that up. With Momix, we perform throughout the year and some people have been doing the same dance, the same piece for three years and, like doing the same sport, it's very tiring. Fortunately, they have an audience that gives them a standing ovation and then they need me to proudly sing their praises and put them in the heroic mode—make them feel as though they are Knights of the Round Table. Bring in the mythologies. There's a reason for it. Elevate the day-to-day affairs and all the drudgery. Turn it into gold. It's very alchemical, ultimately. You spin all of these elements in your life and your creative life and then, hopefully, you put them in that retort and it comes out something golden. Golden piece of choreography, golden ideas, a golden state of mind.

It's very inspiring.

Yes, well I was known as The Motivator—The MO-tivator. You have to be this way. I learned this from my Austrian ski coaches. Every summer, I didn't go to ballet camp, I went to Mount Hood in Oregon and skied with the Austrian ski team. These guys were mad and enthusiastic and they really were another level of energy and so incredibly competent physically. It's the same with basketball, baseball, and other sports. Some of the great coaches—they're *motivators*, they can make their team work. And there are always human-resource problems with a company or a team. We now have thirty-five dancers in the company—it's a big team. Imagine all of the personal issues and just the nuts and bolts of running an international dance company with three different shows working around the globe simultaneously. We have one company that just finished doing a premiere in Guangzhou, China, another one out in St. Louis, and another one in Spain—all at the same time. We'll be going to Russia and we were actually on our way to Cairo, Egypt, last week but it got canceled because things were just too tricky. So there is all that need to keep in tune with your personnel and to try to motivate and inspire them. That's part of the job.

This seems like something that would be useful in just about every job that you can think of.

That's true, and I think that a lot of ex-ballplayers go into business and politics and so on because they have incredible discipline. The key word is discipline. Many people have talent, many people have visions, but it's whether or not you have the discipline to realize those visions, those artistic notions—that's the hard work. The discipline—not to get distracted. Follow-through—that's a baseball term. It's amazing how that ball will end up in a catcher's mitt by how you follow through—where your weight goes after you throw it. It's really interesting.

Everything has to be working together.

Like Zen Archery. It's a similar principle of how to place that ball. The athlete has that ability to "visualize." You see it in high-jumpers. They go over the high jump before they do it. Once you see yourself there—once you see the ball in the strike zone before it's there. So you're almost ahead of yourself in time. This visualization. You do that in dance all the time. I use those techniques as well. There's a lot of stuff that I've learned over the years, beginning way before I became involved in dance. I went out to the Esalen Institute and worked with psychologists and group dynamics and encounters. And I'm answering that question about collaborations because I started as co-founder of Pilobolus. I worked in groups and that was a very '60s kind of thing. The collective. That idea was coming out of anti-establishment people, students around the country who were moving to other ways of communicating. And it became something that business uses today—think tanks. Collaborative work was what I was interested in—group dynamics and being aware of that. The commune, back in those days. Pilobolus was a collective and so you have to understand the shortcomings and, of course, compromising. We're not collective enough in this country—we're in gridlock. But this is something that is very important in a team. A team has to have an identity and leaders who will keep everybody in line and keep them inspired. I would imagine that is the same with some of these poor, less-financed teams that have to struggle. They have to stay motivated somehow—to play well even though they're losing every other game or even more than that.

You inspire your players or your dancers by respecting them and you respect them by telling them what you really feel that they can do to make themselves better and make the team better or make the show better. The young people in Momix, they're just out of school, out of college, and some of them didn't even go to college. They're young and being formed and we want to feel, when they go through the Momix "Institution" here, the Institute of the Momix Experience, that they go away better people and more mature and enlightened and it's not just doing moves but how they approach themselves and how they react and relate to other people. That's important and it's personal and, hopefully, it's educative and we do something positive in the world here. And we let them know, as hard as it is and full of drudgery and all that kind of stuff that you put up with, that the work itself actually inspires so many thousands of people in so many different cultures, and they should be proud of it. This is an important aspect of it. As I said, there is that parallel between successful teams and successful dance companies.

And, obviously, you have people who work with you who are trusted and respected.

Yes, we have our dance captains and our senior members and our lieutenants. Fortunately, I have a good support group. My principal job is to be a wandering head into the back oakwoods with my headphones on and daydreaming of at least the beginning structures of the next Momix creation. As we have several shows running and they have to be maintained, we have someone who is running day-to-day affairs here—all the nuts and bolts and human resources and the logistics and you can't imagine how many details have to be worked out to get the company to the Cairo Opera House and back safely. That kind of thing.

But I'm still out in the woods. You know, Mr. Pendleton is always unavailable but he's wired in the wilderness and hopefully coming up with a few shards and fragments of ideas that ultimately will get distilled and boiled into the next dance theater piece. Sometimes that can happen by reading a poem, or you might see it in the garden. As John Lennon would say, "Life happens to you when you're busy doing other things." And that's the life you want to capture because that's very close to your heart.

I just got my honorary doctorate from the University of the Arts in Philadelphia last year. And not only am I a doctor, but what nearly took the skin off my bones was the fact that I was asked to do the commencement speech. So I had to wear my cap and gown and come out at the Academy of Music, in front of three thousand people and fully videotaped on the Jumbotron. Talk about throwing out the first pitch! But I had to come out and give a twenty-five-minute commencement address and that was very challenging for me. There's so much information out in the world and the essence of my speech was to talk about how important it is to disconnect for a while—how important it is for people to not stay wired all the time. Get out and get away from the computers and try something a little different. Go into nature, into the wilderness. Garden. There's a lot of information out there. I never thought that we really would say how the world is, but, instead, how it might be in a fantasy and how much fantasy and imagination are an integral part of our reality. They always say "American ingenuity," imagination, invention, fixing the world, making it better. Maybe you make it better by going back to some very elemental, basic things like not losing contact with light and water and trees and the forms and energies that are not human but actually create our humanity if you can identify with them. I've always felt like that was something I was searching to do. Maybe I'm just an old goat getting older. I don't know if I'm getting wiser, but I'm on to something, for sure. And I spend a great deal of time, not with humans, but with trees and plants.

Part of what we're doing here is brain training. Training the mind to control the body. Sometimes the mind says feed the body correctly so that the body can play a better game of baseball or dance better, or whatever. And if I were running a team, I would offer select reading lists. I remember my coaches would have us read the writings of the great Czech long-distance runner Emil Zatopek. He wrote about that sublime moment when you're kicking into your third wind, when everybody else has given up, exhausted. They're just not running hard enough. Just that glory. It bridges on masochism, I guess, and martyrdom. But athletes really know that and I'm coming back to this idea that that kind of training is missing in some of the dance world, and that's what I offer. Ballet-trained people like to come up here and get this immersion in nature and another way of dealing with the body and disciplining it to make them better dancers. And a lot of it is allowing them to find their own movements. I never say just how to move so much as I try to allow them to find their own movement and I'll put it in the right context and they will look good. That's what a good director should be doing—directing them into the right places to make it look natural. For example, if somebody is three hundred pounds, you're not going to stick him in at shortstop right away. You've got to understand that there are different positions to play, even in the dance world. Every new piece you make, you've to see what you have before you can establish what you think you're going to do movement-wise. You've got to see how they move.

I build it out that way. I build it out in a very natural process. I let the games be played. I videotape for six months and, sure enough, to everyone's shock and surprise and, hopefully, pleasure, you see something borne out of this collective effort and out of this direction in terms of "collectifying" the energies and the capabilities of a certain group. I am also a bit like a talent scout. Just like any ball team. Like the U–Conn Huskies. They've got their suits running all over the high schools looking for the next freshman who's going to be the next Maya Moore. They already have her, I think. They're out there—talent scouts. The same with baseball. Imagine how many Little League games and Pony League games are being watched by somebody who's connected to the Phillies or the Cardinals or whatever. They're watching them—and we should do the same. So much talent. You're looking for potential. That's what I'm beginning to realize. The Moses Pendleton Momix Farm Team is what we should be developing. Triple-A in Momix. It's a great idea. They learn the rep in half the time, just as a financial decision. You put the out the word that Moses Pendleton is going to be directing a summer colony for dance and there are some parents who've just spent forty thousand dollars a year on Juilliard. Maybe they'd like their son or daughter who just graduated from Juilliard to have this experience. It may be a cost-effective way to develop new material and I stay with young, excited people, because I do like that, as well.

Some people are just frightened to death about being creative. They just want to be told what to do—just how to move, what's the choreography. It's hard. It's hit or miss—hit or mix. You have to keep mixing, keep mixing. You have to have faith. But the process itself is trying, it's challenging, and, as the director of it, I like to keep it fun so that we get more done.

I see Momix as a kind of visual, physical theater. Sometimes I start with a vision—the sculpture, the painting, the picture first. Sometimes we use props to extend the body, to create new means of locomotion and new emotions from that. Extensions of the body. Sometimes it's a costume. Where does a costume stop and when does it become a prop? If you have an arm elongated through fabric and then into a stick with a hand on it, is that a prop or is that a costume? But I think we start visually. Sometimes we just go down to Kmart or the hardware store and find some sewer pipe—it's all grist for the creative mill. We just did that for our piece, "Botanica." We don't have a big budget, so we just got some corrugated sewer pipe and we turned it into night crawlers! It was very trippy and very cool. You just bring stuff into the studio. There's another piece that we call "Solar Flares." We just happened to be noodling around with those colorful, Styrofoam swimming pool "noodles" that are used to teach kids to swim. We started playing with them and then got a whole bunch of orange ones and sharpened the tips so that they looked more dendroid-like and made a sun dance out of them. It was a wonderful effect and it was created simply from these cheap, little things that you can buy in Walmart. You bring stuff into the studio and start playing with it and that's how it develops.

Jean Erdman, the wife of Joseph Campbell, ran a company that I believe was called "Theater of the Open Eye." When she passed away, somebody who worked with or managed the company was going through all of her stuff, which was stored in a warehouse. There were two white sculptures of youths in the warehouse and they were going to be dumped. Someone who was going to be taking them to the dump looked at them and thought, You know, this is something that Moses ought to look at before they get thrown away. And he brought them over to the studio and I said, "God, this is a cool thing," and we started playing with them. Eventually, those two sculptures became part of "Baseball." But that's how it happens, you see—just by accident.

There were so many other interesting items in "Baseball." We made a giant glove out of foam and inside each finger was a dancer. That was just something we thought of doing. Sometimes it's just a question of scale. Large, oversize baseballs that float around, and the Styroballs. In "Baseball" we had bats and balls and gloves—the three primary icons—to play with. We are very much like painters or sculptors—we create the look and then find a way to move it with bodies through time and space and make it dance. Many times we're not humans dancing, we're marigolds or centaurs. We're very prop-minded, we're a "prop-er" company, we're "propping ourselves up." Many times I would use bodies in a Pilobolus sense—you combine several bodies to form an organism or some kind of contraption or sculpture that you couldn't do with a single body. That was kind of the essence of Pilobolus. The use of multiple bodies to create other sculptures. It was a painterly, sculptural approach to movement—create the picture first, whatever you could do to design the visual, and then apply it to music and time and space and then choreograph. The choreography comes at the end—the picture is first.

I'm wondering if you could talk a little about your childhood and those early experiences with base-ball and dance.

I used to spend hours with a tennis ball and drew out a strike zone on the side of my father's dairy barn in Vermont and I'd mound up a bit of sand and make a mound and I would play Curt Gowdy and the Boston Red Sox on the radio—I had an extension cord coming out of the barn. I remember in the afternoons I would just be firing along and pitching along with the game for hours. Firing a tennis ball at the barn. My lived baseball experience was doing that. I did play Little League and Pony League for a while—I was a catcher and a pitcher. That's kind of the way it is when you're that young—you move around. But my upbringing, really, was that I was born and raised on a dairy farm in Northern Vermont, and my father's dream, which was also my dream, was to create the perfect Holstein-Friesian cow, and Momix was like an artificial milk supplement for veal calves. That's where the name comes from. So it's all very agri-based. That's what it is—Momix. It's like Meow Mix. I used to feed it to my calves. Purina, I think, put it out. So that was my upbringing. If my father had a sick cow, he deemed it more important to get me out of school to come to the vet to see how to deal with that cow. That was my education. As I'm speaking to you now, I'm looking at the very same bowl and cow over my desk, which were over my father's desk in Vermont.

My father passed away, sadly, when I was twelve and so that whole dream of raising those cows and being a breeder of Holsteins kind of went down the drain, so to speak. I kind of escaped from that tragedy by having my summers spent with surrogate fathers in Mt. Hood, Oregon—the Austrian ski team. So I went from a farm boy—turning from a boy and his calf to a boy and his mountain, whose dream was to be a downhill racer. I was quite a good skier, and I still am. Then I came back and I enrolled in Dartmouth College, to be with Al Merrill, who was the U.S. Nordic ski coach. He was very interested in my going there—I got their early decision and never applied anywhere else. I had broken my leg before and I started taking some cross-country and got good at that and then I went to Dartmouth. Well, on the second day of ski practice at Dartmouth, I broke my leg a second time and then I took a dance class to recuperate and get myself back in shape for the ski team. I ran twenty miles a day and I was in top shape. What the skiers did back then, which was dangerous, was they played soccer in the fall to train for skiing. Of course, the problem was that half of the skiers didn't know how to play soccer, so they ended up kicking each other instead of the ball—and that's what happened to me. It shattered my tibia and I spent the first three months in a cast up to my thigh and then began to take the dance class and met Alison Chase, the dance instructor at Dartmouth. I did this initially to get back in shape for skiing and then I started getting very interested in dance and music. I got involved with a different crowd of people. I might have been a real jock and gone to SAE fraternity and been straight as an arrow and been a great skier. But I ended up kind of strung out on morphine and getting involved in theater and meeting a different crowd of people up there. It's interesting. Those were the breaks.

Soon after taking the first dance class—a *month* after taking the first dance class—we were performing the first piece we had ever made, which was called "Pilobolus." I remember, just by an accident, being invited early on to open up for a Frank Zappa concert at John Green Hall at Smith College. Someone who was the manager of the Living Theater and who was also booking Frank Zappa happened to see the piece performed at Goddard College or some-place and he liked it. So he talked to Frank Zappa and said that he thought it would work better than some crappy opening band, and Zappa agreed to give it a try. And we had three thousand screaming Smith girls at the end of our piece, "Pilobolus," which lasted about ten minutes. Then Zappa came out with Flo and Eddie of the Turtles and went on to perform this amazing rock symphony. We were "charged," to say the least. I will always remember, at the end of the concert, Zappa coming up to us and referring to us as "Theater of the Very Far Out." It wasn't dance, it was "Theater of the Very Far Out"—he coined that phrase. He asked us if we could come to Iowa City the next day—they had another gig to do the very same thing. We said, "We'd love to, Mr. Zappa, but we have a math exam tomorrow and we have to get back to school." But the seed was sown and I remember meeting in the Dartmouth Cemetery, having lunch over the graves and surrounded by the spirits of the old Dartmouth people, and saying to my colleagues who performed "Pilobolus" with me, "Maybe we've got something going here." That was the kind of "formative moment."

So there was a series of accidents, from the death of my father when I was twelve, to having the dairy career shattered, to the breaking of the leg and having the ski career shattered—but it created the dance career. You just have to go with the flow. Life is a great instructor if you allow it to be. It does instruct, it doesn't destruct. And we had people encouraging us and it was very successful and we were doing all kinds of things at a very early age, especially compared to how long we were involved in the business. So Pilobolus was very formative and, as you know, I've continued on. I did Pilobolus for a while and that collective kind of lost its steam and I wanted to form my own company, Momix. I was asked to do the closing ceremonies for the Winter Olympics in 1980 in Lake Placid and started doing some other kinds of movement and work and formed Momix in 1980. So it's over thirty years old now. It's moved from a duet show that was a little offshoot from Pilobolus to a company that has three shows working around the globe simultaneously. But it's still a mom-and-pop organization that I do with my mate, Cynthia Quinn—she and I and an office of one in this old Victorian house in Litchfield County in New England. It's still part of the farm, it's still rural, but we have a converted horse barn as a dance studio. Everyone goes out behind the tree—there's no plumbing. It's not like the Ailey Studio in New York or anything like that. But we have gardens and lakes and a busy schedule. This has been an interesting life and I've moved up. So you've taken Moses off the farm, but you haven't really taken the farm out of him.

Many of the pieces do reflect the athletic from the skiing and the organic and the natural and the world of nature, whether it's "Opus Cactus," which was all about the desert world, or "LunarSea," which was all about moonlight and black light and otherworldly behavior, or "Baseball," or "Passion," or "Botanica." So I have moved around a bit, but not really that much. I always half-jokingly say that I'm from "NoNew"—North of New England—but I ended up in "SoNew"—Southern New England. I am the "New English Patient," ultimately. That might be a subtitle for the movie that I'm trying to do.

It's interesting, when you've had enough time that elapses, to go back to the early '80s. I wish I had recorded certain things back in the '60s when I was out as a new dancer and a member of the San Francisco Sexual Freedom League. I got my first performing experience dancing out in Golden Gate Park for Quicksilver Messenger Service. I did a lot of that. I also wanted to say that even before Pilobolus, we had a theater—all of us escapists, when it was the Vietnam War and nobody wanted to go to business school. This was the Flower Generation—the Beatles, the alternative methods of being. We all headed to my family farm, where my father had his Holsteins, and we formed the Vermont Natural Theater. And I must tell you that one of the more formative events was my putting a white sheet over my head and offering to an audience of forty or fifty people, including the head of the Vermont Council on the Arts, to sit on an adjacent hillside as I created a little ghostlike figure with myself in the sheet, in front of fifty head of milking Holsteins. And as I moved in a zigzag pattern down this green hillside, they would follow me, being very curious. And, as I progressed and the cows and I moved faster, they would follow me and they would begin to stampede and run, chasing me. Hopefully, the experience for the audience was that it was perhaps the first time that they had ever experienced stampede. And by milking Holsteins, mind you—with udders slushing left and right. And coming directly at them. This was the point in the theater. And just before reaching the object of the pursuit, I would dive into a ditch and disappear and the cows would immediately stop and someone would ring a little bell and the cows would start grazing again. Then the audience was encouraged to move off into the spruce woods, where someone was doing a one-legged solo on a spruce log. This was a tour, a four-mile tour throughout my family farm called the Vermont Natural Theater.

I've always loved being outside and I've always loved the theater and this was a way to try to incorporate these passions: being outside and just loving to perform and being theatrical. And this was pre–Pilobolus, to create the Vermont Natural Theater, using natural light, hillsides, great scale, choreographing for Holsteins. This was in 1968 and 1969. And this is something that I still have today.

To get back to baseball for a moment, can you talk about your experience as a Red Sox fan during that incredible 1986 World Series against the Mets?

Well, being a Red Sox fan or, I suppose, being a die-hard baseball fan of any team, there is a certain amount of superstition. I had a close friend who was a doctor and who was a Mets fan. We wouldn't watch the games together, but we'd be on the phone and we would always talk about who would draw "first blood." The Series was mythical and, of course, in game 6, the Red Sox were one strike away from winning something that they hadn't won for decades and decades. I never watched the game sitting down, because I was too nervous. But I remember pacing in the room and I wore knee-high red socks while I watched every game on television—by myself, because no one would want to be around me. I was too fidgety and too nervous. I would yell and scream and stomp. When that ball went through Bill Buckner's legs, I remember just slamming my foot into the floor and drove a three-inch splinter of wood almost up into my ankle, right through my foot. I was just skewered there. And all during the mayhem that ensued after the ball went through Buckner's legs, I was limping and spurting blood out of my foot. Coming out of my red sock, like the Red Sea. Moses bleeding and skewered like he'd been spiked by this. And then, of course, my doctor friend called me up on the phone and heckled me as I was spurting blood out of my red sock. Of course, years later, when Curt Schilling was pitching with a bloody sock the year the Red Sox finally did win the World Series, I was reminded of my own experience. Well, I had a bloody sock in 1986. I was a fan who literally bled for that team. Crucified by them! But it was painful, both physically and mentally. I don't think anybody from "Red Sox Nation" really got over that. When the Red Sox did finally win the World Series, it was like finally getting Bin Laden after ten years. There was some closure when the Red Sox finally won the World Series—and in most dramatic fashion, mind you, after being down three games to none. That was truly amazing. And, I think, after that, it will never be the same, because the Red Sox did finally win. They were always going to set you up and then destroy you. And, finally, when they did win, I don't want to say that the Red Sox Nation softened, but it received some kind of closure over that 1986 moment.

Bill Buckner, of course, never really seemed to recover psychologically. I have since then gone over and analyzed that play and, although he did deserve goat horns, he certainly wasn't the only one. There were many other people who screwed up.

Are there any ballplayers whom you consider to be especially "dancer-like"?

Jacoby Ellsbury would be one in the modern day. There are smooth cats like Frank Robinson. Lou Brock was incredible—he was a dancer on the bases. Rickey Henderson, in his prime, was also great to watch, just in terms of that. I love watching Omar Vizquel. I love watching the "Web Gems"—some of them are extraordinary and mind-boggling. There was one I saw involving a pitcher who did a whole 360, rolled on the ground, and fired the ball to first to get the guy out. They had to play this over and over again. It was the most remarkable play. I think it was a bunt or something and he dove to the left and then he had to slide in to get to the ball quickly because it just kind of squibbled into "No Man's Land"—and as he slid by the ball, he grabbed it and threw it as he was sliding by it. It was amazing. Of course, with the technology today, you can see the poetry of motion in slo-mo. It could be scored to music very easily—you know, with some Wagnerian overture. Poetry in motion.

Most of my favorite players, of course, are from the Red Sox. There are no Yankees I really like, although, since the Red Sox won the World Series, I've softened up a bit. Also, with free agency, things are a little disheartening. Players are moving around so much—you wonder, are you just rooting for individuals or teams? I think that's one of the downsides of free agency. They've lost all allegiance. Once you're a Red Sox player, it would be nice if you were always there, but one day you are and then you're not and then you're back again.

Edward Villella, Dancer, Choreographer, Teacher, Company Director (Date of Interview: April 25, 2011)

Edward Villella: I grew up in Bayside, Queens. I was the only Italian in an all-Irish neighborhood, so I learned how to fight very quickly. It was a typical blue-collar neighborhood. My father ran a truck in the Garment Center and I had some pals on the street who also had truck-driver fathers. That sets the scene for how I grew up. In a neighborhood like that, you play a lot of stickball in the streets, bicycle tag, sandlot baseball, and softball up in the schoolyard. I loved baseball and I had a certain natural ability. I could catch, throw, and hit. I also ran very fast. I was pretty strong for a small kid and I was the feistiest of all the kids.

Was there any particular position that you liked to play?

EV: I played infield and outfield on our neighborhood ball teams. When I went to high school I won my letters in baseball. I played shortstop, left field, and pitched. Then when I got to college, I played the outfield. I had a very strong arm.

Did you have a favorite team when you were growing up?

The Brooklyn Dodgers, of course, were my favorite team. My favorite players were Duke Snider, a wonderful outfielder who could hit, and Carl Furillo, who made spectacular catches and had a great arm. And in the infield there was Pee Wee Reese, Billy Cox, and Gil Hodges. I had a real love and passion for "them there bums."

Did you have any aspirations of your own to pursue baseball as a career?

No aspirations. I was just not big enough to think about it professionally. I did, however, pursue baseball in high school and college, where I also boxed.

So at this point, I believe, you had some kind of baseball injury that led to the opening up of the world of dance to you. Could you talk a bit about this?

In the streets, we also played something called "running bases," which was a game where you got in a rundown between sewers. I was trying to get back to one of the sewers when I got hit in the back of the head with a hardball and was knocked unconscious. I got dragged home by my pals and was deposited on the steps of the stoop of my house. My mother and sister were away at that time at my sister's local ballet school. When my mother and sister returned home, a neighbor informed them of what had happened and my mother got very upset. She said, "We can't trust you on the streets anymore." Being very feisty and physical, I had lots of cuts, bruises, and stitches. So she said, "You are now coming to your sister's ballet class!" I got dragged there and I had to watch forty giggling girls and their mothers. I was going crazy, sitting there and bored to death, and then they started to jump. I then went to the back of the room and started flying around, imitating them. The teacher took one look at me and went to my mother and said, "Get him out of here or put him in tights at the barre."

That's how I started. I was humiliated. I used to wear my baseball uniform over my tights and I had my cap, glove, and bat. I would walk up two flights to the school backwards. My rationale was that if any of my friends saw me, I hoped that they would think I was going out to play baseball, not inside to point my toes.

How old were you at this point?

I was about seven or eight at this point. A year or two later, my mother heard about the School of American Ballet, which was the New York City Ballet's school, directed by the great choreographer George Balanchine. My sister auditioned there and was given a scholarship and then, as they were leaving, my mother offhandedly said, "Oh, you know I have a son at home who also dances, but he's not very interested." They replied, "A son? A boy? Can he *walk*?!" My mother then dragged me in to audition and, bingo, I was at one of the most prestigious and elegant ballet schools in the world and offered a scholarship. I was ten at the time.

That was the turning point of my life. I was exposed to some of the greatest and most won-

Dancer, choreographer, teacher, and company director, Edward Villella (photograph courtesy Edward Villella).

derful professional dancers and artists of the day. I was very impressed with the demeanor of these dancers. They had such a wonderful sense of their physicality. I began to understand that you could speak with your body with a very special physical language. I knew that this was what I wanted to do.

For the next six years, I became passionate, but my sister was not. She declared, "I don't want to do this anymore. I have had enough." My mother was devastated and she said, "I don't want to hear the word 'ballet' in this house ever again." I immediately said, "Wait a minute—I like this stuff and I'm getting good at it." My dad said, "No more for you, either— you are going to college." So at the end of my sixteenth year (I made high school in three years), I was sent to the New York State Maritime College at Fort Schuyler in the Bronx. They didn't offer ballet there as an elective, so I stopped dancing for four years. I desperately missed the physical activity, so I turned to baseball and boxing while, deep inside, I always knew I wanted to be a dancer.

During my third year, I started to sneak off the base and take classes in Manhattan and finally presented myself to George Balanchine. He remembered me and offered me a job. When my father learned that I was going back to dancing he was so upset that he stopped talking to me. When I became a professional dancer, I sent my parents two tickets to my second opening night. My dad said, "Okay, we'll come, but we probably won't be able to find you in the back row." I responded, "Come and, if you like it, I'll leave word with the stage doorman to come backstage. If you don't, I'll understand." There were four ballets on that evening and I had three principal roles. At the end of the evening, the curtain came down and I was standing on stage, pouring sweat. Balanchine came on the stage and started giving me my corrections in the physical language that we spoke. The curtain then goes up on a dark house, the stagehand comes out and places the night light center stage and departs. Mr. Balanchine and I finish our conversation, shake hands, and he goes off stage right. I go off stage left and then hear and see something in the wing. There are my mother and father in the wing in tears. The three of us just laughed, hugged, and cried. And my father became a balletomane and started handing out my pictures and reviews in the Garment Center. It was such a relief to finally have parental approval about something that I wanted to make my life.

When you were just starting out and as you continued to take classes, did you see the connection between the sports that you were playing and the dance that you were doing?

There are many similarities and parallels to all of the agilities to sophisticated movements. Bending, stretching, jumping, running, moving forward, backward, and side to side. The major difference can be traced to training. Generally, baseball has less formalized approaches, whereas ballet is much more of a completely formalized investigation of all of our physicality. For instance, we train both right and left. We lift our arms not far from the shoulders, but from the back to involve our whole body. The most obvious difference is the way we train our legs and feet. We do a complete articulation of our technique for an hour and a half to warm up. We begin the warmup focusing on our legs and feet for thirty-five to forty minutes on that alone every morning. When I began ballet training, my legs were gradually becoming stronger and stronger and actually powerful. While I was playing sandlot baseball, I realized that the dance part of it was supporting the athletic part of it. When I was boxing in college, the strength in my legs continued throughout a match. By the third round, my legs were still fresh, whereas my opponent's leg support was diminishing. I also became more aware of an increase in quickness and the development of more accurate timing. So, yes, it was early on that I understood those connections.

And did you feel that your background in sports ever helped and possibly hurt your dance training?

I did not feel any negative side effects because I understood the ballet challenges and how both could be compatible. Condition reflexes are obvious in both areas. When on stage, partnering and supporting a woman, the timing is so refined it's like splitting a note in order to anticipate her moving off balance. The strength to lift is one thing, but if your timings are not together, it will not go well, as well as the timings to gently put her down. Weightlifters, for instance, have the responsibility of getting the weights over their heads, but bringing the weights down is not their responsibility.

Can you talk about the training that you need to go through as a male dancer to be able to do lifts—the lifting of a human body above your head and often holding it there for an extended period?

When you learn to partner, you do not start with lifts. You start with supporting a woman on her balance with your hands and arms. This begins to develop a conditioning in your upper body. When you are ready to lift, you have to place your hands accurately. When you lift and move a woman, you have to be aware of a push hand and a guiding hand and, as you bring her down, you bring your elbows into your body for additional support to put her down with care and sometimes to place her on her delicate pointe shoe. That commonality and timing are critical. It's like watching a second baseman feeding a ball to a shortstop and making a double play. It's like a little dance around second base. They are partners, just as we are partners. The idea of teamwork on the field is similar to that in ballet. It's like speaking a physical language.

I'm also wondering about the feelings you have when you're dancing and when you're playing ball. The exhilaration, and so on. Can you talk about this?

"Exhilaration" is a very good description of the feeling that you get when you do either of these forms of physical accomplishment to the best of your ability and your endorphins start flowing. This "high" stayed with me for about two hours after I left the field or the stage. I guess the difference might be that when you are on stage the intensity does not stop, whereas in athletics it's more intermittent.

I remember an interview that you did many years ago where you said that you were always striving for that feeling where everything just felt right, where everything seems to "click."

In sports, they call it "being in the zone." As a dancer, you've got to be in your "zone" in company class, throughout your six hours of rehearsal each day, and, of course, when the curtain goes up for a performance.

You've already talked a little about what you feel is dance-like about baseball. Is there anything else you might like to add?

We are all physical and about movement. I once did a television special called "Dance of the Athletes" and I took a number of athletic disciplines and compared them to dance. I used Tom Seaver, the baseball pitcher; Virginia Wade, the tennis champion; and Bob Griese, the great quarterback. I interviewed these incredible athletes and then shot them on their fields of play. I intercut their athletic gestures with ballet gestures, which thereby illustrated the similarities. This took place in the first half of the show. In the second half, I choreographed an abstract ballet that was based on their gestures. It was very well received.

That reminds me of the Gene Kelly TV special that you did in the late 1950s, "Dancing—A Man's Game." Do you have any recollections of that show, especially working with Gene Kelly and Mickey Mantle?

It was my first television show. It was very interesting. The producers compared figure skating and other sports to ballet. I remember that, at one point, they had Dick Button on ice in one studio and they intercut that with me doing similar balletic turns and jumps in a second studio.

How did you get involved in the show?

I had just recently joined the New York City Ballet and whenever a new male dancer arrives, there is always a buzz—and especially with me, because I had been a baseball player and a boxer and I just came out of a military school. Here was this young male dancer who could jump and leap and turn in America's greatest company, so I would imagine that it was obvious to the producers that I might be able to contribute to the premise of the show.

Did you have a chance to speak with any of the athletes on the show?

I didn't have much of a chance to speak with the athletes, but I do have a related story to tell. After I stopped dancing, I was invited to be a judge for a beauty pageant. One of the other judges turned out to be Earl "the Pearl" Monroe, the great Knicks basketball star. Earl the Pearl! We got to talking and I told him that I had received a call from Madison Square Garden, asking me to come and work with both the Knicks and the New York Rangers. Earl looked at me and said, "Ballet? Man, we can't even get everybody to look in the same direction for the team picture!"

That's so funny! Did you actually wind up giving ballet lessons to the Knicks and Rangers?

No, unfortunately, I didn't have enough time at that point to work with the Knicks and Rangers. Several years later, though, I did get an invitation from West Point to be Artist in Residence and work with their football, baseball, and lacrosse teams. I used to refer to them as "the herd." The floor of the gymnasium would vibrate as these huge guys would come lumbering in. It was obvious that they did not want to be there and listen to a ballet dancer. I approached it from the angle that we were both physical and there were many similarities. I asked how they warmed up—what they did when they hit the field. I finally got one of them to say, "We stretch." So I asked him to demonstrate. He crossed his legs and bent over to stretch his hamstrings. I showed him a very similar stretch that we did. I finally got them up on their feet and asked them to show me their jumping exercises. They demonstrated their jumping jacks and I then showed them a similar jump, but took my arms up in a circle over my head and then down to my side. Then I reversed it. Just the changing of the arms added a dimension that their warmups did not include and added another dimension related to mind coordination.

Do you think that if there were training regimens similar to the ones you worked on with the West Point athletes there would be more agile athletes and fewer injuries in sports?

I think so. The regimen that I was working with on the West Point athletes has further possibilities. Just a further focus on the turning of the feet in a very concentrated manner could be helpful. We seek full flexibility from our feet, including full extension and pointing of the toes. We have a knee bend which is called a *plié*. It is critical in both the landing of a jump and pushing off. We are trained so that we view the landing not as the end of the jump; it is the beginning of the next gesture. It provides continuity of gesture. Our principle of turnout of the entire body incorporates the entire body simultaneously. We are constantly prepared. It is something inherent in us that is relentless. With us it's important to carry out these approaches under our ideal circumstances.

My situation, however, was very different. I grew up in the early days on very hard stages. On TV, in fact, there were cement stages. This resulted in my receiving nine broken toes, stress fractures in both legs, an inoperable knee, three hip replacements, a serious bad back, and arthritis. None of that came from my early athletics.

I remember that television special, "Man Who Dances," that showed you dancing three principal roles in one evening—you had to fill in for another dancer who was injured. You got injured in the first piece and then still went out and did the next two pieces with your injury and still somehow got through it! It was pretty painful to watch.

It's still painful to experience, actually! In the matinee, I had my own very demanding piece and had to dance another demanding piece for an injured colleague. This extra work caused me to collapse on stage while I had a major piece to dance in the evening program, the "Rubies" section from Balanchine's "Jewels."

In terms of education, I'm wondering if you could talk about the educational work that you did with kids. Again, I remember the scene in "Man Who Dances" that showed you going into a high school—maybe it was your old high school—and doing a lecture demonstration for a group of very tough boys.

They certainly didn't want to come and watch ballet! When the principal told them that the lecture was going to be ballet, it was received with lots of groans and rolling of the eyes. You should have seen the expressions! I finally got them interested when I told them I had been a welterweight boxing champion in college. At the beginning, they were skeptical and bored. Then I told them how I arrived at the position of the hands, which is a tight fist that opens into a circular form of the position of the hands. I knew that I had their attention when I looked down and saw all of the tough guys in the front row looking down at their own hands and opening their fists. At the end, they were standing and clapping and cheering.

What are your feelings about getting boys to dance? Do you feel like things have changed at all?

Things *have* changed, but not totally. There is a prevailing opinion that what classical ballet dancers do seems "overly poetic." However, I have found that there are some young men who, when exposed to sophisticated dance, get intrigued and would like to be involved. Over the years I have received dozens of letters from young men who did take up dance. These young men tell me that their fathers allowed this because they had seen me on TV. Of course, I relate to them because of my own experience with my father.

What made your mom interested in having your sister dance and take ballet lessons?

My mom was an orphan and wanted her daughter to have all of the things she never had.

Are there any baseball players whom you consider to be particularly balletic?

The great star Joe DiMaggio had the most beautiful line and form and moved with extraordinary grace. A modern-day athlete would be former Yankee second baseman Robinson Cano. He has the beauty and grace in his performance of a superb dancer. He has an almost effortless swing and, with the timing and speed of his bat, it is beautiful to watch. In the same manner of a great dancer, he shows no effort. Ichiro Suzuki, too, is just amazing.

In New York City Ballet or with any other company, did you ever dance anything with a sports theme or something that might have had a sports orientation?

The one ballet that pops into my mind is "Apollo," with choreography by Balanchine and music by Stravinsky. Balanchine portrayed this Greek god with underlying elements of soccer players, bicycle riders, a bull fighter, chariot drivers, and masculine images based on athletic ideas.

Were Balanchine or Robbins fans of baseball or any sports?

Not that I know of. I do remember one phrase from Mr. Balanchine when I joined New York City Ballet in 1957: "In politics, it is Eisenhower; in sports, it is Mickey Mantle; in ballet, it is woman."

Do you have any final thoughts that you might like to share?

The only thing I would say is that I was a far better baseball player for having taken ballet as a kid.

Appendix: Baseball and Dance in Youth Literature

Stories that contain references to the intersection of baseball and dance, as well as those featuring entire plots devoted to the relationship, are not uncommon in literature created for and/or geared towards young people (children, tweens, and teens). Below are some examples, along with some lines from each book to demonstrate the manner in which the intersection or relationship is represented.

The Babe Ruth Ballet School by Tim Shortt (Buffalo, NY: Firefly Books, 1996)
- "Issy had a secret that she couldn't tell Babe. The thing she loved most, even better than baseball, was dancing" [p. 8].
- "Babe met Issy as she was leaving. 'I've been talking to some guys about doing a vaudeville show in the off-season,' he said. 'And this big Hollywood producer might want to do a moving picture with me. So I'm thinking if I can come to your classes, dancing would be good training. You know, for the stage and all'" [p. 16].
- "Babe Ruth quickly became one of Miss Ilona's favorite students. Teacher's pet, the other dancers called him. At the ballpark, Babe was slugging more home runs than ever. When he didn't hit a homer, he hit a double or a triple. The sports reporters asked why his hitting was unstoppable. 'Fellas,' said Babe Ruth, 'you might think me funny, but I credit my dance lessons. The dance, see, helps my balance and my movement.' 'But, Babe, dancing's so girlish,' said the sports reporters. 'Fellas,' said Babe Ruth, 'I'm an athlete and dancing is athletic'" [p. 16].

Baseball Ballerina by Kathryn Cristaldi; illustrated by Abby Carter (New York: Random House, 1992)
- "Mom thinks baseball is for boys. She wants me to do girl things. That is how I got stuck taking ballet lessons" [p. 6–7].
- "Every class is the same. First we line up at the barre. Then we practice the five positions. First position. Second position. Third position. I make a face. There is only one position for me. Shortstop" [p. 16].
- "Sometimes I pretend I am up at bat. 'Heels on the floor! Shoulders back! Point the toes!' she shouts. Who knows? Maybe pointy toes will help my swing" [p. 18].
- "Afterward, the Sharks give me high fives. 'You were great!' they say. I feel like a just hit a home run. Maybe ballet isn't so bad after all. But I still like baseball best!" [p. 48].

Baseball Ballerina Strikes Out! by Kathryn Cristaldi; illustrated by Abby Carter (New York: Random House, 2000)
- "I love baseball. I am on a team called the Sharks. My coach calls me a baseball ballerina. That is because I play baseball. And I take ballet lessons" [p. 5].
- "Mr. Lee says that ballet has helped my game. 'In ballet you have to keep on your toes,' he tells me. 'The same goes for baseball.' Good thing I do not have to wear a tutu on the baseball field!" [p. 10–11].

Baseball Fever by Johanna Hurwitz (New York: Avon Books, 2000; originally published in 1981 by William Morrow and Company)
- "Ezra loved the ease with which the players moved. His mother had once taken him to see the ballet, and he thought the dancers leaped into the air just like baseball players jumping for high fly balls" [p. 53].

Baseball Joe Around the World by Lester Chadwick (New York: Cupples & Leon Company, 1918)
- "There were three or four sketches and vaudeville turns before Altman, who, of course, was the chief attraction as far as Joe and his folks were concerned, came on stage. He had a clever skit in which baseball 'gags' and 'patter' were the chief ingredients, and as he was a natural humorist his act went 'big' in the phrase of the profession" [p. 9–10].

Christy's Magic Glove by Gibbs Davis; illustrated by George Ulrich (New York: Bantam Skylark, 1992)
- "Christy Chung stood up. 'If Walter had been paying attention we would have won.' She pointed at Walter. '*You* threw to the wrong base.' Walter's ears burned. 'How would you know? You were doing ballet in the outfield!'" [p. 2].
- "'I'm in training already,' said Christy. '*Ballet* training. It's great for baseball.' Walter rolled his eyes. 'Ballet classes help me to concentrate,' said Christy. She twirled in a straight line across the Pizza Palace" [p. 5].
- "Walter marched up to Otis. 'What're you doing here?' Otis turned pink. 'Christy said ballet would help me lose weight.' 'That's right,' said Christy, 'Otis has a lot of potential. With a little practice he could be a good dancer. Show them your plié, Otis.' Otis smiled and walked to the center of the room. He placed his heels together and bent his knees about twelve inches apart. His arms formed a perfect circle in front of him. The class clapped. Otis smiled from ear to ear" [p. 22].
- "Christy started running across the grass. As the ball started falling Christy pushed off. She sprang through the air like a rocket, like a bird, like a ballerina! Her arms reached out and *smack!* the ball plopped into the pocket of her glove. Christy covered the ball with her free hand and landed in a graceful plie. She smoothed down her tutu and smiled" [p. 63].
- "Johnny Crandall flapped his cape like bat wings. 'Here's a cheer for the Never Sink Nine!' he yelled back. 'You catch our fly balls every time! We're the bats but you can fly! Your ballerina jumps so high!'" [p. 65].

Emily's Eighteen Aunts by Curtis Parkinson; illustrated by Andrea Wayne von Koniglsow (Toronto: Stoddart Kids, 2002)

- "Sarah had an aunt who took her to the ballet. Chris had grandparents who cheered at her baseball games. James had an uncle who treated him to banana splits" [p. 1].
- "Afterward, Aunt Roxie said, 'Sorry, Emily, I guess ballet isn't for me. I love baseball, though'" [p. 15].

Lucky Summer by Laura McGee Kvasnosky (New York: Dutton Children's Books, 2002)

- "'I'm going out for Summer League baseball here,' I say. She looks uninterested. 'Before we moved, I played for the Santa Cruz Giants. I hit four home runs last year.' That should impress her. 'Baseball is okay,' says Lucinda. 'But what I like is dance.' She lifts her chin. 'Ballet mostly, but tap and modern, too. I'm taking Spanish dancing this summer.' She throws one arm above her head and sits up straight as a queen" [p. 8].
- "When I get back to the cabin, Lucinda has finished her braiding marathon. I ask her to play catch with me. 'I don't play baseball, remember?' she says. 'I dance.' She throws her arms out and twirls across the screen porch, landing on her bed. 'Well, I don't usually dance,' I tell her, 'but last night I tried—and it wasn't as bad as I thought it would be.' Lucinda reluctantly agrees to give baseball a try. We play catch, starting about ten feet apart and taking a step back after every throw. She's a right hander, not much of a throw but a pretty good catch, even using my mom's mitt, which is too big for her" [p. 84].

Max by Rachel Isadora (New York: Macmillan, 1976)

- "Max is a great baseball player. He can run fast, jump high, and hardly ever misses the ball. Every Saturday he plays with his team in the park. On Saturday mornings he walks with his sister Lisa to her dancing school. The school is on the way to the park. One Saturday when they reach the school, Max still has lots of time before the game is to start. Lisa asks him if he wants to come inside for a while…. Now Max has a new way to warm up for the game on Saturdays. He goes to dancing class" [p. 1–3, 26].

The Short-Stop by Zane Grey (New York: Grosset & Dunlap, 1909)

- "Then this master of ceremonies ordered the Jacktown team into the field, tripped like a ballet-dancer to his position behind the catcher, and sang out in a veritable clarion blast: 'P-l-a-e-y B-a-w-l!'" [p. 37].

Slide, Katie, Slide! by Joe E. Palmer (Los Angeles: Remlap Publishing, 1994)

- "'Now, I see these très marvelous Baseball people performing. Oh, how they return the performances of le grande ballet, with their impossible moves of grace made time after time. Once again, I am in fascination of my days of being young and overjoyed.' 'I never thought of Baseball in that way. But I surely see what you mean. Those men capable of making it to the Big Leagues, or near to that, must have, as you say, "très marvelous" coordination of mind and body.' 'My dear friend, Blanche, you and I must attend more Baseball games together … ballet performances too whenever possible'" [p. 263–4].

Tomboy Row by Ruth Langland Holberg; illustrated by Grace Paull (Eau Claire, WI: E. M. Hale and Co., 1952)

- "It was only a few minutes' ride to the depot. Row pointed to the ball field where she had spent many hours playing baseball. Kiki cried out, 'Oh, I'm a fan and I listen to games on the radio and I play too when I visit my grandmother in Connecticut.' Rowena wished with all her heart that Kiki was not leaving. They would have fun together playing ball if it was summer. They stood on the platform and Kiki read her composition: 'I love dancing. I love the graceful movements that take you places. Dancing is something only the people who love it can do. I take ballet lessons, but I love all kinds of dancing. When I go to a ballet I come out of the playhouse with a feeling of awe that cannot be compared. A person cannot be a ballet dancer without years of hard working. If I am ever a ballet dancer I will always remember when I was a small girl taking ballet lessons and looking with awe at the stage where I so wished I would dance. The End'" [p. 59].
- "'I wish Kiki was with us today,' Doody said. 'Remember what fun we had with her? She plays baseball, and maybe Hibbie would let her play. She is a wonderful dancer, too.' Then, seeing Row's wistful expression and knowing how Row felt about dancing, Doody added, 'But best of all she's a tomboy just like you.' Rowena smiled happily and echoed Doody's wish'" [p. 193].

Tuesday's Child by Nancy Baron (New York: Athenaeum, 1984)

- "That last statement hurt. What did she mean, I wasn't graceful? She had obviously never seen me gliding over toward right field for a high fly ball, or sliding into second base, or swinging a bat. My swings were beautiful, even when I struck out, and I had spent hours practicing my slides with the cushions on the TV room floor to make sure I looked right" [p. 24].
- "There was one thing, though, that I had to make sure my mother never found out, and that was how the dancing seemed to be helping me with, of all things, my baseball" [p. 72].
- "It was when I was sliding into 'third base' feet first for the second time that I noticed it was easier than it had ever been before. My legs felt stronger and my body seemed lighter. I did it again just to make sure, and, yes, it was easier. Then I remembered that my legs hadn't been as cramped and achy after a ballet class the last few times. Maybe the dancing was doing some good, after all. I wasn't getting graceful, but I was getting stronger. It was an exciting thought at first. I could continue doing the leg exercises, even after I was no longer taking dancing, just to keep my legs in shape" [p. 73].
- "'What I am saying,' he explained slowly, 'is that ballet is obviously not for you. We have decided that if you are still interested, you could take tap dancing lessons next year. Any kind of dancing can make a person graceful, and you once mentioned that you might be willing to try tap.' ... I imagined myself wearing a top hat and carrying a cane, tapping to a complicated rhythm, my feet going so fast they were a blur, the people around me clapping wildly with the beat. I was willing to give it a chance" [p. 109].

Chapter Notes

Introduction

1. Maury Allen, "Ballet Helps Mets Pass 'Barre' Exam," *New York Post*, October 24, 1986.

2. Moses Pendleton, interview by the author, March 11, 2009.

3. For an interesting discussion, see Murray Goodman, "Sports and the Dance," *Dance Magazine*, September 1946, 24-25.

4. Ken Burns and Lynn Novick, "About the Film: Where Memory Gathers," Introduction to *Baseball: A Film by Ken Burns*: www.pbs.org/kenburns/baseball/about/ (accessed March 22, 2015).

5. "Dancing—A Man's Game," produced by Robert Sandek Associates for WNBC-TV *Omnibus* series, directed by Gene Kelly and William A. Graham; written by Gene Kelly; narrated by Gene Kelly and Alistair Cooke. Originally telecast on December 21, 1958. Available in Jerome Robbins Dance Division, New York Public Library for the Performing Arts.

6. Edward Villella, interview by Bob Schieffer, *Monday Morning*, CBS-TV, April 23, 1979.

7. A. Bartlett Giamatti, *Take Time for Paradise: Americans and Their Games* (New York: Summit, 1989), 42.

8. Bill Althaus, "Zoned In: Truman's Barker Starts Senior Year on a Torrid Pace," *The Examiner* (Independence, MO), April 3, 2009: http://www.theexaminer.net/homepage/x180623743/Zoned-in-Truman-s-Barker-Starts-senior-year-on-a-torrid-pace (accessed April 10, 2009).

9. "Man Who Dances: Edward Villella," VHS, produced by Robert Drew and Mike Jackson for NBC-TV *Bell Telephone Hour*; directed by Nathan Kroll and Donald Voorhees; narrated by Don Morrow. Originally telecast on March 8, 1968. Available in Jerome Robbins Dance Division, New York Public Library for the Performing Arts.

10. Ron Darling, Ian "Ernie" Horvath, Kirk Peterson, and Dr. Joel Solomon, interview by Celia Ipiotis, *Eye on Dance*, WNYC-TV, January 16, 1987.

11. Giamatti, *Take Time for Paradise*, 40.

12. Sheryl Flatow, "The Ballet of Baseball: More Than a Game, It's Art to This Dancer," *Daily News* (New York, NY), April 23, 1983.

13. Tom Rawe, interview by Jeff Friedman, August 27, 2001, transcript, Jerome Robbins Dance Division, New York Public Library for the Performing Arts.

14. "Man Who Dances: Edward Villella."

15. Villella, Schieffer interview.

Chapter 1

1. Noel Hynd, *Marquard and Seeley* (Hyannis, MA: Parnassus Imprints, 1996), 43.

2. Quotes from the *New York World* and the *New York Globe*, cited in Hynd's *Marquard and Seeley*, 43.

3. Hynd, 39.

4. Ibid., 5.

5. Joe Laurie, Jr., *Vaudeville: From the Honky-Tonks to the Palace* (New York: Henry Holt, 1953), 124.

6. Cited in Dan Epstein, *Big Hair and Plastic Grass: A Funky Ride through Baseball and America in the Swinging '70s* (New York: St. Martin's Press, 2010), 240.

7. Patrick Jones, *Connecting Young Adults and Libraries, Second Edition* (New York: Neal-Schuman, 1998), 38.

8. George B. Kirsch, *The Creation of American Team Sports: Baseball and Cricket, 1838–72* (Urbana and Chicago: University of Illinois Press, 1989), 188.

9. Ibid.

10. Edward J. Rielly, *Baseball: An Encyclopedia of Popular Culture* (Santa Barbara, CA: ABC-CLIO, 2000), 210.

11. Ibid.

12. Information about these (and other) songs may be found in *Baseball in Music and Song: A Series in Facsimile of Scarce Sheet Music*, compiled by Harry Dichter (Philadelphia, PA: Musical Americana, 1954. Also see George B. Kirsch's *Baseball in Blue and Gray: The National Pastime During the Civil War* (Princeton and Oxford: Princeton University Press, 2003), 18-23.

13. Agnes deMille, *America Dances* (New York: Macmillan, 1980), 36.

14. Additional information about ballet in 19th-century America may be found in a variety of sources, including Walter Terry's *The Dance in America* (New York: Harper and Row, 1956). Two articles that provide good information about popular pre–1900 American ballet stars are: "The Wild Doe: Augusta Maywood in Philadelphia and Paris, 1837-1840," by Maureen Needham Costonis (*Dance Chronicle*, vol. 17, no. 2, 1994, 123-48), and Mariella Trevino's entry, "Mary Ann Lee and Augusta Maywood," in *Celebrating Women in American History* (New York: Facts on File, 2011).

15. Terry, *The Dance in America*, 32.

16. This is brought out very clearly by Hynd and Laurie, Jr., in addition to such baseball and vaudeville historians as John DiMeglio, Michael E. Lomax, and Jules Tygiel in their respective books, *Vaudeville U.S.A.* (Bowling Green, OH: Bowling Green University Popular Press, 1973), *Black Baseball Entrepreneurs, 1860-1901*

(Syracuse, NY: Syracuse University Press, 2003), and *Past Time: Baseball as History* (New York: Oxford University Press, 2000).

17. Cited in Harold Seymour and Dorothy Seymour Mills, *Baseball: The Early Years* (New York: Oxford University Press, 1960), 345.

18. Hynd, 39.

19. "Helen Dauvray's Choice: To Be Married This Morning to John M. Ward," *New York Times*, October 12, 1887.

20. Ibid.

21. Howard W. Rosenberg, *Cap Anson 2: The Theatrical and Kingly Mike Kelly: U.S. Team Sport's First Media Sensation and Baseball's Original Casey at the Bat* (Arlington, VA: Tile Books, 2004), 73.

22. Ibid.

23. Ibid.

24. Ibid.

25. Rosenberg, 76.

26. Ibid.

27. Hynd, 39.

28. Rosenberg, 74.

29. Ibid.

30. Frederick G. Lieb, *The Baseball Story* (New York: G. B. Putnam's Sons, 1950), 79.

31. Program notes for presentation of "The Baseball Music Project," held at Krannert Center for the Performing Arts, University of Illinois, Champaign-Urbana, on November 12, 2010. Program notes by Rob Hudson, Assistant Archivist, Carnegie Hall. Citation may be found on p. 14.

32. Steve Henson, "King's Ransom: Autograph of 19th-Century Baseball Icon 'King' Kelly Could Fetch 200K," *The Postgame*, November 18, 2011: www.thepostgame.com/blog/throwback/201111/kings-ransom-auotgraph-19th-century-baseball-icon-king-kelly-could-fetch-200k (accessed August 21, 2012).

33. Lieb, 79.

34. Henson, "King's Ransom."

35. Hudson, "The Baseball Music Project," 14.

36. Henson, "King's Ransom."

37. Ibid.

38. References in this paragraph are drawn from Rosenberg and Hudson.

39. Advertisement in the *Poughkeepsie Daily Eagle*, December 25, 1893, 5.

40. Rosenberg, 56.

41. Ibid.

42. Peter M. Gordon, "King Kelly," Society for American Baseball Research: sabr.org/bioproj/person/ffc40dac (accessed January 17, 2015).

43. Ibid.

44. *Poughkeepsie Daily Eagle*, December 25, 1893, 5.

45. Hudson, "The Baseball Music Project," 15.

46. See Rosenberg, 58, and H. Allen Smith, Ira Smith, and Leo Herschfield, *Low and Inside: A Book of Baseball Anecdotes, Oddities, and Curiosities* (Halcottsville, NY: Breakaway Books, 2000), 29.

47. Cited in Cliff and Linda Hoyt, "Charles Hoyt, Popular Playwright of the Gay Nineties," December 23, 2009: choyt48.home.comcast.net/-choyt48/choyt_run.htm (accessed August 30, 2012). Review appeared in *New York Times*, February 19, 1884.

48. *The Spokesman-Review*, January 14, 1899,10; and the *Daily Alta Californian*, May 15, 1888, 8.

49. Rosenberg, 57.

50. Ibid., 58.

51. David Fleitz, "Cap Anson on Broadway," www.cnet.org/~dlfleitz/cap2.htm (accessed August 30, 2012).

52. David L. Fleitz, *Cap Anson: The Grand Old Man of Baseball* (Jefferson, NC: McFarland, 2005), 239.

53. Image of the original playbill was accessed on January 18, 2015 through the following public auction website: www.liveauctioneers.com/item/4965510. It also was accessed on August 30, 2012 by using the following URL: www.pbagalleries.com/view-auctions/catalog/id/168/?page=4.

54. Peter Golenbock, *Wrigleyville: A Magical History Tour of the Chicago Cubs* (New York: St. Martin's Press, 1999), 86.

55. Rielly, *Baseball: An Encyclopedia of Popular Culture*, 210.

56. Lomax, *Black Baseball Entrepreneurs, 1860–1901*, 77.

57. Tygiel, *Past Time: Baseball as History*, 122.

58. Donn Rogosin, *Invisible Men: Life in Baseball's Negro Leagues* (New York: Atheneum, 1983),102.

59. Lomax, 77, and James Weldon Johnson, *Black Manhattan* (New York: Atheneum, 1968; originally published in 1930), 64.

60. Lomax, 77.

61. Ibid., 76.

62. John J. Evers and Hugh S. Fullerton, *Touching Second: The Science of Baseball* (Chicago: Reilly & Britton, 1910), 24.

63. Seymour and Mills, *Baseball: The Early Years*, 345.

64. Hynd, 5.

65. DiMeglio, *Vaudeville U.S.A.*, 4.

66. Terry, 32.

67. Rielly, *Baseball: An Encyclopedia of Popular Culture*, 297.

68. Cited in Stephen A. Riess, *Touching Base: Professional Baseball in American Culture in the Progressive Era* (Westport, CT: Greenwood, 1980), 21-22.

69. Ibid., 13-14, 22.

70. Ibid., 22-23.

71. Terry, 215.

72. Ibid., 216.

73. Hynd, 43.

74. Wes. D. Gehring, *Joe E. Brown: Film Comedian and Baseball Buffoon* (Jefferson, NC: McFarland, 2006), 14.

75. Ibid.,10-11.

76. Ibid., 30.

77. Ibid., 30-31, 56.

78. Ibid.,11.

79. Ibid.,12.

80. Paul E. Bierley, *The Incredible Band of John Philip Sousa* (Champaign, IL: University of Illinois Press, 2006), 51.

81. Ibid. (Also see Hudson, "The Baseball Music Project," 14.)

82. Hudson, 14.

83. Stage Attracts Baseball Stars," *New York Times*, October 22, 1911, 33; and "Noted Ball Players Who Will Be Stars of the Stage," *San Francisco Call-Bulletin*, November 8, 1911, 11.

84. Lester Chadwick, *Baseball Joe around the World* (New York: Cupples & Leon, 1918), 9-10.

85. See the following sources: Hynd, 43; Laurie, Jr., 124-25; Al Stump, *Cobb: A Biography* (Chapel Hill, NC: Algonquin Books, 1994), 149; Richard Bak, "Profile: Detroit Tigers' Prankster Herman 'Germany' Schaefer," *Hour Detroit*, March 29, 2012: www.hourdetroit.com/Hour-Detroit/April-2012/Playing-for-Laughs/ (accessed September 5, 2012); Richard Bak, "The Madcap Life of Germany Schaefer, Baseball's Clown Prince," *Detroit Athletic Co.*, August 23, 2012: blog.detroitathletic.com/2012/08/23/the-madcap-life-of-germany-schaefer-baseballs-clown-prince (accessed September 5, 2012); and Michael Betzold, "Mike Donlin," Society for American Baseball Research: sabr.org/bioproj/person/3b51e847 (accessed September 5, 2012).

86. Hynd, 43.

87. Ibid.

88. Ibid.

89. Betzold, "Mike Donlin."

90. Hynd, 43-44; and Betzold.

91. Laurie, Jr.,125.

92. Hynd, 44.

93. Laurie, Jr.,125.

94. See Bak, "The Madcap Life of Germany Schaefer, Baseball's Clown Prince," and "Stage Attracts Baseball Stars," *New York Times*, October 22, 1911, 33.

95. "Stage Attracts Baseball Stars," *New York Times*, 33.

96. Numerous sources describe this connection, including James E. Elfers, *The Tour to End All Tours: The Story of Major League Baseball's 1913-1914 World Tour* (Lincoln, NE: University of Nebraska Press, 2003), 23; and Frank Russo, *The Cooperstown Chronicles: Baseball's Colorful Characters, Unusual Lives, and Strange Demises* (London: Rowan and Littlefield, 2014), 111.

97. "Rube Marquard," National Baseball Hall of Fame, "Hall of Famers": baseballhall.org/hof/marquard-rube (accessed January 19, 2015).

98. Hynd,113-14.

99. Ibid.,114-15.

100. Ibid.,138.

101. Ibid.,138-39.

102. Ibid., 142-46; Laurie, Jr., 125.

103. Hynd, 146.

104. Lyrics cited in Hynd, 143.

105. Hynd recounts the full story in his richly detailed book.

106. Anthony Slide, *The Encyclopedia of Vaudeville* (Westport, CT: Greenwood, 1994), 461.

107. Hynd, 200.

108. Rob Neyer and Eddie Epstein, *Baseball Dynasties: The Greatest Teams of All Time* (New York: Norton & Co., 2000), 77.

109. Laurie, Jr., 125.

110. Neyer and Epstein, *Baseball Dynasties*, 77.

111. Riess, *Touching Base*, 23.

112. Ibid.

113. Hynd, 55, and Laurie, Jr., 125.

114. "Stage Attracts Baseball Stars," *New York Times*.

115. "Noted Ball Players Who Will Be Stars of the Stage," *San Francisco Call-Bulletin*.

116. Hynd, 137, and Laurie, Jr., 125.

117. Hynd, 137.

118. "Police Probing Slavin Beating," *The New York Clipper*, August 11, 1920, 31.

119. "Noted Ball Players Who Will Be Stars of the Stage," *San Francisco Call-Bulletin*.

120. Laurie, Jr., 126–127; "Noted Ball Players Who Will Be Stars of the Stage," *San Francisco Call-Bulletin*; and "Stage Attracts Baseball Stars," *New York Times*.

121. "Stage Attracts Baseball Stars."

122. References are taken from the following five sources: Hynd, 55-56, 133-34; Laurie, Jr., 125-27; "Noted Ball Players Who Will Be Stars of the Stage"; Harold Seymour and Dorothy Seymour Mills, *Baseball: The Golden Age* (New York: Oxford University Press, 1971), 116-18; and "Stage Attracts Baseball Stars."

123. Seymour and Mills, *Baseball: The Golden Age*, 118.

124. Don Carson, "Baseball Funnyman Dies: Long Illness is Finally Fatal to Nick Altrock," *Hopkinsville New Era* (Hopkinsville, KY), January 21, 1965, 16.

125. John Kelly, "Nick Altrock: A Life Rich in the Stuff of D.C. Baseball Lore," *Washington Post*, September 20, 2011: www.washingtonpost.com/local/nick-altrock-a-life-rich-in-the-stuff-of-baseball-lore/2011/09/20/gIQAv1fOik_story.html (accessed September 5, 2012).

126. Paul Votano, *Stand and Deliver: A History of Pinch-Hitting* (Jefferson, NC: McFarland, 2003), 41.

127. Information regarding the Altrock-Schacht partnership comes from the articles by Carson and Kelly, as well as Laurie, Jr., 127–128; Jimmy Powers, *Baseball Personalities: The Most Colorful Figures of All Time* (New York: Rudolph Field, 1949), 37; and Peter M. Gordon, "Nick Altrock," Society for American Baseball Research: sabr.org/bioproj/person/aea7c461 (accessed September 5, 2012).

128. References and quotes in this paragraph are taken from the following sources: Tom Wilson, "Cap Makes Popular Showing in Galesburg," *The Galesburg Register-Mail* (Galesburg, IL), November 13, 2007: www.galesburg.com/columnists/x9496129 (accessed September 13, 2012); Howard W. Rosenberg, "Recapping a Bit of Toledo's History," *Toledo Blade*, November 8, 2006: www.toledoblade.com/Mud-Hens/2006/11/08/Recapping-a-bit-of-Toledo-s-history.html (accessed September 13, 2012); "At the Theaters: Cap Anson a Hit," *Cedar Rapids Evening Gazette*, September 16, 1913, 7; "Old Cap Anson Before Footlights: Will Sing, Dance and Recite—Other Diamond Stars on Bill," *Syracuse Daily Journal*, 1913; "Anson's Attitude," *Sporting Life*, March 22, 1913, 10; and "'Pop' Anson Becomes Buck and Wing Dancer," *San Francisco Call-Bulletin*, March 21, 1911, 23.

129. Fleitz, *Cap Anson: The Grand Old Man of Baseball*, 304-05.

130. Ibid., 305.

131. Laurie, Jr.,126.

132. See, for example, Laurie, Jr.,126, and Slide, 195.

133. Julia Ruth Stevens with Bill Gilbert, *Major League Dad* (Chicago: Triumph Books, 2001), 12.

134. Ibid., 66.

135. Tim Shortt, *The Babe Ruth Ballet School* (Buffalo, NY: Firefly Books, 1996), 16.

136. See, for example, Laurie, Jr., 126-27.

137. For more information about the show, please see the following three sources: "New Show for the Whitney," *Billboard*, March 16, 1910, 32; Otis L. Colburn, "Summer Events in Chicago," *The New York Dramatic Mirror*, July 23, 1910, 14; and Mark Aubrey's May 7, 2013, blog post for *Baseball Nuggets*, featuring images of original photographs and reviews, including a full review of the show from the February 19, 1911, edition of *The Spartanburg Herald*: baseballnuggets.blogspot.com/2013/05/my-cinderella-girl.html (accessed March 7, 2014). Additionally, a digital image of the program from the original Chicago production is made available by the Chicago Public Library: digital.chicagopublib.org/cdm/ref/collection/CPB01/id/4940 (accessed March 22, 2015).

138. Quote from Peck's work may be found in *Early Innings: A Documentary History of Baseball, 1825-1908*, compiled and edited by Dean A. Sullivan (Lincoln, NE: University of Nebraska Press, 1995),155.

139. Gerald Bordman and Thomas S. Hischak, *The Oxford Companion to American Theatre, Third Edition* (New York: Oxford University Press, 2004), 631. See also Gerald Bordman and Richard Norton, *American Musical Theatre: A Chronicle, Fourth Edition* (New York: Oxford University Press, 2010), 253.

140. W.L. Hubbard, "News of the Theaters: The Umpire," *Chicago Daily Tribune*, December 4, 1905, 9.

141. Ibid.

142. See Kathleen Riley, *The Astaires: Fred and Adele* (New York: Oxford University Press, 2012), 35; and Peter Levinson, *Puttin' on the Ritz: Fred Astaire and the Fine Art of Panache* (New York: St. Martin's Press, 2009), 15.

143. Levinson, 15, and Barbara Stratyner, "Ned Wayburn and the Dance Routine: From Vaudeville to the Ziegfeld Follies," Society of Dance History Scholars: https://sdhs.org/index.php?option=com_content&view=article&id=39&Itemid=1 (accessed September 27, 2012).

144. Levinson, 15.

145. Riley, 35.

146. See Fred Astaire, *Steps in Time: An Autobiography* (New York: Harper Collins, 2008, 32–35; originally published by Harper and Brothers, 1959).

147. Riley, 35.

148. Ibid.

149. Ibid., 35-36.

150. Ibid., 36-37.

151. Levinson, 17.

152. New York Public Library for the Performing Arts, *The Great American Revue: How Florenz Ziegfeld, George White and Their Rivals Remade Broadway* (exhibition program, April 19–July 27, 2012), 3.

153. Ibid., 6.

154. For more information about Kosloff and Mason, see the Internet Broadway Database (IBDb), maintained by The Broadway League: ibdb.com/production.php?id=7043 (accessed January 25, 2015).

155. Winter Garden Company, *The Passing Show of 1915* (New York: G, Schirmer, 1915), 94-97.

156. "Show Reviews: Passing Show of 1915," *Variety*, June 4, 1915, 14. See also "Plays and Players," *Brooklyn Life*, June 5, 1915, 20.

157. This poster was featured in the exhibition, "The Great American Revue," held at the New York Public Library for the Performing Arts, April 19-July 27, 2012.

158. Rogosin, *Invisible Men*, 102.

159. Ibid., 102-03.

160. Ibid., 119.

161. Rielly, 210.

162. Cheryl Hogan, "The Boys of Summer: African Americans and Baseball in Plaquemines Parish": www.louisianafolklife.org/LT/Articles_Essays/lfmboys.html (accessed September 10, 2012).

163. Tygiel, *Past Time: Baseball as History*, 122-23.

164. Rogosin, 145-47.

Interlude: Choreographers on Dance and Baseball

1. Chris Black, interview by the author, December 15, 2011.

2. Gail Conrad, interview by the author, March 18, 2011.

3. Ana Maria Tekina-eirú Maynard, interview by the author, April 27, 2011.

Chapter 2

1. References are drawn from the following three sources: Bob Francis, "Collegiate Review: Here's the Pitch," *Billboard*, December 27, 1947, 44; "Hasty Pudding Show Tonight," *New York Times*, December 19, 1947, 34; and "Pudding Show Opens Tonight," *The Harvard Crimson*, December 10, 1947: www.thecrimson.com/article/1947/12/10/pudding-show-opens-tonight-pa-months/ (accessed October 11, 2012).

2. Virginia Clark, "Schuman's First Opera, 'The Mighty Casey,' Expression of Interest in Music, Baseball," *The Standard-Star* (New Rochelle, NY), January 22, 1952.

3. *EAV Music Appreciation Series: Schuman, Casey at the Bat*, notes by Walter Simmons, 1980. Publication may be found in the Joseph W. Polisi: William Schuman Research Papers, Juilliard School Archives, New York, NY.

4. Ibid.

5. "Gregg Smith Directs 'The Mighty Casey' in Catchy and Vivacious Performance," *New York Times*, May 17, 1976, 41.

6. Jeffrey Sandell Stern, *The Mighty Casey: A Study of the Performances and Editions of William Schuman's One-Act Opera*, Doctoral Dissertation (Coral Gables, FL: University of Miami, 2012), 36-37: scholarlyrepository.miami.edu/cgi/viewcontent.cgi?article=1724&context=oa_dissertations (accessed January 27, 2015).

7. Ibid., 42-48.

8. Harold C. Schonberg, "Casey Bats Again with Same Result," *New York Times*, May 5, 1953, 34.

9. Cited in Simmons, *EAV Music Appreciation Series: Schuman*, Casey at the Bat.

10. Jay S. Harrison, "'Casey at the Bat' Opera Presented," *New York Herald Tribune*, March 7, 1955.

11. Allen Hughes, "Opera: 'Mighty Casey,'" *New York Times*, August 31, 1967, 28.

12. Ethan Mordden, *Coming Up Roses: The Broadway Musical in the 1950s* (New York: Oxford University Press, 1998),104.

13. Ibid.,103.

14. Ibid.

15. *The Golden Apple: A Musical in Two Acts*, written by John Latouche, music composed by Jerome Moross (New York: Random House, 1954), 55.

16. Mordden, *Coming Up Roses*, 86.

17. Lewis Funke, "Theatre: The Devil Tempts a Slugger," *New York Times*, May 6, 1955, 17.

18. Mordden, 101.

19. "Damn Yankees," *New York Times*, April 17, 1955, SM67.

20. Funke, "Theatre: The Devil Tempts a Slugger," 17.

21. Ibid.

22. Mordden, 101.

23. Ann Barzel, "Dance and Physical Education for Boys: Dancing is a Man's Game," prepared for Illinois Arts Council. Found in Ann Barzel Papers, 1912-2005, Series 3, Box 58, Folder 1931, housed in the Newbery Library, Chicago.

24. Mordden, 101.

25. Louis Calta, "'Damn Yankees' at Bat Tonight: Baseball Musical Starring Gwen Verdon at Stephen Douglass is at 46th St.," *New York Times*, May 5, 1955, 40.

26. Ethan Mordden, *Open a New Window: The Broadway Musical in the 1960s* (New York: Palgrave Macmillan, 2001), 250-51.

27. Ibid., 250.

28. Vincent Canby, "Charlie Brown to Stay Awhile: 'Peanuts' Show is a Hit—Schulz May See It in April," *New York Times*, March 9, 1967, 44.

29. Mel Gussow, "Theater: 'Charlie Brown': Characters of 'Peanuts' Move to Broadway," *New York Times*, June 2, 1971, 33.

30. Walter Kerr, "Theater: Charlie Brown and Combo: Musical Adapted from Comic Strip 'Peanuts,'" *New York Times*, March 8, 1967, 51.

31. Ibid.

32. See Canby, 44, as well as Andrew S. Hughes, "'Peanuts,' and Cracker Jack, Too," *South Bend Tribune*, December 23, 2007: articles.southbendtribune.com/2007-12-23/news/26767075_1_charles-m-schulz-museum-peanuts-charlie-brown (accessed January 27, 2015) and John Updike, "Sparky from St. Paul," *The New Yorker*, October 27, 2007: www.newyorker.com/magazine/2007/10/22/sparky-from-st-paul (accessed January 27, 2015).

33. Canby, 44.

34. See, for example, Gussow, 33.

35. See the following five sources for additional information: Marcia Froelke Coburn, "The Audacity of Hope," *Chicago Magazine*, September 22, 2008: www.chicagomag.com/Chicago-Magazine/September-2008/The-Audacity-of-Hope/ (accessed January 25, 2015; Giovanna Breu, "Chicago's Stubborn Bleacher Bums and the Cubs Have Waited for 'Next Year' Since 1945," *People*, October 1, 1979: www.people.com/people/archive/article/0,,20074720,00.html (accessed January 27, 2015); Richard Christiansen, *A Theater of Our Own: A History and a Memoir of 1,001 Nights in Chicago*

(Evanston, IL: Northwestern University Press, 2004); Kathi Scrizzi Driscoll, "'Bleacher Bums': A Baseball Fan Dance," *Cape Cod Times*, June 10, 2010: www.capecod times.com/article/20100610/ENTERTAIN/6110303/-1/rss10?template=printart (accessed August 2, 2010); and the Organic Theater Company website: www.organ ictheater.com/organic/news/history/index.shtml (accessed January 27, 2015).

36. Melanie Lauwers, "Take a Seat with These 'Bleacher Bums,'" *Cape Cod Times*, June 12, 2010.

37. Ibid.

38. Christiansen quote cited on Organic Theater Company website.

39. Joe Hughes, "Kritics Korner: 'Bleacher Bums' a Hit," *Technology News* (Illinois Institute of Technology, Chicago), August 29, 1977, 6.

40. Steve Dale, "Ex-Cubs are in Starting Lineup for 'Bleacher Bums' Benefit," *Chicago Tribune*, June 9, 1989, Section 7, J.

41. Driscoll, "'Bleacher Bums': A Baseball Fan Dance."

42. Ibid.

43. Robert W. Creamer, "It's So, Joe: The Black Sox Scandal Has Come Out Swinging as an Opera," *Sports Illustrated*, August 3, 1981, 6.

44. Ibid.

45. Ibid.

46. Ibid.

47. Sid Smith, "Jackie Robinson and the Great American Pastime: But Will His Life Make a Good Musical?" *Chicago Tribune*, April 11, 1993: articles.chicagotribune.com/1993-04-11/entertainment/9304110151_1_jackie-robinson-great-american-pastime-first-black-player (accessed January 30, 2015).

48. Fred Ferretti, "A Musical Celebrates an Athlete," *New York Times*, November 8, 1981, D4.

49. Eleanor Blau, "'The First' Delays Opening to Nov. 17," *New York Times*, November 4, 1981, C26.

50. Sid Smith, "Jackie Robinson and the Great American Pastime."

51. Frank Rich, "Stage: 'First,' Baseball Musical: Back in Ebbets Field," *New York Times*, November 18, 1981, C25.

52. Robert W. Creamer, "Jackie is the 'First' Again," *Sports Illustrated*, November 30, 1981: www.si.com/vault/1981/11/30/826178/jackie-is-the-first-again-baseball-is-back-on-broadway-with-a-lively-musical-about-jackie-robinson (accessed January 30, 2015).

53. Rich, C25.

54. Ferretti, D1 & D4.

55. Ibid., D4.

56. Sid Smith, "Jackie Robinson and the Great American Pastime."

57. Frank Rich, "Theater: 'Diamonds,' A Revue about Baseball," *New York Times*, December 17, 1984: www.nytimes.com/1984/12/17/arts/theater-diamonds-a-revue-about-baseball.html (accessed October 19, 2012).

58. See Rich, "Theater: 'Diamonds,' A Revue about Baseball," and John Beaufort, "This Good-Natured Celebration of Baseball is a Hit But Not a Homer; 'Diamonds' Musical Revue," *Christian Science Monitor*, December 28, 1984: www.csmonitor.com/1984/1228/1228/122842.html (accessed October 19, 2012).

59. Beaufort, "This Good-Natured Celebration..."

60. Ibid.

61. Rich, "Theater: 'Diamonds,' A Revue about Baseball."

62. Beaufort, "This Good-Natured Celebration..."

63. Ibid.

64. The following three sources were consulted for this section: Dan Sullivan, "Stage Review: Marcel Marceau: The World Behind the Mask," *Los Angeles Times*, March 29, 1984, M7; Janice Arkatov, "Nine Slices of the Sporting Life," *Los Angeles Times*, June 29, 1984, G2; and Dan Sullivan, "Stage Review: 'Sporting Goods' Has Short Sizes," *Los Angeles Times*, July 2, 1984, H1, 4–5.

65. Arkatov, "Nine Slices of the Sporting Life," G2.

66. Ibid.

67. Sullivan, "Stage Review: 'Sporting Goods' Has Short Sizes," H5.

68. James Mote, *Everything Baseball* (New York: Prentice Hall Press, 1989), 129.

69. "Season Tickets to Goodspeed at Last Year's Rates," *The Day* (New London, CT), March 14, 1985, 47.

70. Ibid.

71. Mel Gussow, "Stage: A Baseball Musical, 'Bingo!'" *New York Times*, November 7, 1985, C36.

72. Richard F. Shepard, "Going Out Guide: At Bat," *New York Times*, October 24, 1985, C22.

73. Gussow, "Stage: A Baseball Musical, 'Bingo!'" C36.

74. Glenn Collins, "Men of 'Falsettoland' As Their Old Selves But with New Fears," *New York Times*, July 23, 1990, C11.

75. Frank Rich, "The 'Falsetto' Musicals United at Hartford Stage," *New York Times*, October 15, 1991, C16.

76. Ibid.

77. ibid, C13.

78. Ibid.

79. Ann Spiselman, "Options: Summer Events Worth Staying in Town For," *Crain's Chicago Business*, August 5, 1995: www.chicagobusiness.com/article/19950805/ISSUE01/10009142/options-summer-events-worth-staying-in-town-for (accessed January 30, 2015). See also Richard Christiansen, "'The Golden Apple' is Ripe for Picking," *Chicago Tribune*, July 30, 1995: articles.chicagotribune.com/1995-07-30/entertainment/9507300004_1_off-broadway-golden-apple-lyrics (accessed January 30, 2015).

80. Christiansen, "'The Golden Apple' is Ripe for Picking."

81. See Puckett Publishing website: pucketpublishing.com/batterup/index.html (accessed January 4, 2012).

82. Ibid.

83. John Busdeker, "'Casey at the Bat' Inspired Show 'Batter Up' Opens This Weekend at Renaissance Theatre," *The Huntsville Times* (Huntsville, AL), May 14, 2009: blog.al.com/thebus/2009/05/casey_at_the_bat_inspired_show.html (accessed January 4, 2012).

84. Puckett Publishing website.

85. See Suzanne Bixby, "Talkin' Broadway: Boston: The Curse of the Bambino," *Talkin' Broadway*: www.talkinbroadway.com/regional/boston/boston9.html (accessed August 31, 2012); and Jenna Russell, "Having a

Ball on Stage: New Musical Traces the Bambino's Curse," *Boston Globe*, April 19. 2001, 6.

86. See Bixby, "Talkin' Broadway: Boston: The Curse of the Bambino"; and G. L. Horton, "'Curse of the Bambino,'" *Theater Mirror: New England's LIVE Theater Guide*: www.theatermirror.com/cotblsobglh.htm (accessed August 31, 2012).

87. Roger Bentley, "'Bambino' in Stoneham Scores Big," *Theater Mirror: New England's LIVE Theater Guide*: www.theatermirror.com/RBcobttg.htm (accessed August 31, 2012).

88. Beverly Creasey, "Play Ball!" *Theater Mirror: New England's LIVE Theater Guide*: www.theatermirror.com/BEVtcirhovey.htm (accessed November 21, 2012).

89. Heidi Waleson, "Street Scenes: Opera on a Brooklyn Sidewalk," *Wall Street Journal*, September 5, 2007: online.wsj.com/article_email/SB118894606447517416 (accessed November 23, 2012).

90. "Dan Sonenberg's Opera, 'The Summer King,' Selected for 2013 Preview by Fort Worth Opera," Press Release, University of Southern Maine, School of Music, issued October 10, 2012: usm.main.edu/music/dan-sonenbergs-opera-%E2%80%8B-summer-king-%E2%80%8Bselected-2013-debut-fort-worth-opera (accessed November 23, 2012).

91. Ibid.

92. Waleson, "Street Scenes: Opera on a Brooklyn Sidewalk."

93. Ben Meiklejohn, "In the Right Field," *The Phoenix*, March 12, 2007: thephoenix.com/boston/music/35089-in-the-right-field/ (accessed November 23, 2012).

94. Video excerpts of Manhattan School of Music production can be found online at www.danielsonenberg.org/tsk-look-and-listen (accessed November 23, 2012).

95. See Waleson, as well as Lauren Dula, "Triple Play," *The Brooklyn Paper*, August 18, 2007: www.brooklynpaper.com/stories/30/32/30_32tripleplay.html (accessed November 23, 2012).

96. Ibid.

97. Ibid.

98. Christopher Hyde, "Review: 'The Summer King' Arias a Moving Performance," *Portland Press Herald* (Portland, ME), April 15, 2012: www.pressherald.com/2012/04/15/the-summer-king-arias-a-moving-performance_2012-04-16/ (accessed November 23, 2012).

99. University of Southern Main press release, October 10, 2012.

100. Ibid.

101. Kathi Scrizzi Driscoll, "'Bleacher Bums': A Baseball Fan Dance."

102. Melanie Lauwers, "Take a Seat with These 'Bleacher Bums.'"

103. John Anderman, "Red Sox Musical Comes to ART: The Red Sox, Race, and Show Tunes? They're All in 'Johnny Baseball,'" *Boston Globe*, May 9, 2010: www.boston.com/ae/theater_arts/articles/2010/05/09/behind_the_creation_of_johnny_baseball_a_musical_drama_about_boston_red_sox_history/ (accessed January 4, 2012).

104. Frank Rizzo, "Legit Reviews: Johnny Baseball,"

Variety, June 3, 2010: www.variety.com/review/VE11 17942916 (accessed November 12, 2012).

105. Anderman, "Red Sox Musical Comes to ART."

106. Cited in Adam Hetrick, "*Johnny Baseball* Musical Gets Extra Innings at American Repertory Theatre," *Playbill*, June 11, 2010: www.playbill.com/news/article/johnny-baseball-musical-gets-extra-innings-at-american-repertory-theatre-169173 (accessed November 12, 2012).

107. Robert Nesti, *Johnny Baseball*," Edge Media Network, June 6, 2010: www.edgeboston.com/index.php?ch=entertainment&sc3=performance&id=106575 (accessed November 12, 2012).

108. Peter Pucci, interview by the author, April 21, 2011.

109. Ibid.

110. Rizzo, "Legit Reviews: Johnny Baseball."

111. Nancy Grossman, "'Johnny Baseball,' American Repertory Theatre," *Talkin' Broadway*: talkinbroadway.com/regional/boston/boston165.html (accessed November 12, 2012).

112. Anderman.

113. Rizzo.

114. Fern Siegel, "Stage Door: *National Pastime*," *Huffington Post*, August 16, 2012: huffingtonpost.com/fern-siegel/stage-door-pasti_b_1784343.html (accessed November 11, 2012).

115. Frank Scheck, "Tapping into Baseball & Broadway Lore," *New York Post*, August 15, 2012: nypost.com/2012/08/16/tapping-into-baseball-bway-lore (accessed November 11, 2012).

116. Ibid.

117. See the official website for the musical: nationalpastimethemusical.com.

118. Siegel, "Stage Door: *National Pastime*."

119. Ibid.

120. Brian Scott Lipton, "Theater Continues Its Love Affair with Our National Pastime," TheaterMania.com, August 12, 2012: theatermania.com/new-york-city-theater/news/08-2012/theater-continues-its-love-affair-w_60409.html (accessed August 12, 2012).

121. Siegel.

122. Thomas Peter, "Broadway-Aimed *National Pastime* Musical Will Play Baseball Hall of Fame," *Playbill*, February 25, 2010: www.playbill.com/news/article/broadway-aimed-national-pastime-musical-will-play-baseball-hall-of-fame-166226 (accessed November 27, 2012).

123. Juan-Jose Gonzalez, "Luis Salgado Choreographs New Musical about Baseball Legend Roberto Clemente," BroadwayWorld.com: broadwayworld.com/article/Luis-Salgado-choreographs-New-Musical-about-Baseball-Legend-Roberto-Clemente-20111101-page2 (accessed January 4, 2012).

124. Ibid.

125. Julian Garcia, "Baseball Legend Clemente's a Hit, Again," *Daily News* (New York, NY), November 19, 2011: articles.nydailynews.com/2011-11-19/news/30420775_1_celia-cruz-willie-nelson-baseball-legend (accessed November 11, 2012).

126. Gonzalez, "Luis Salgado Choreographs New Musical about Baseball Legend Roberto Clemente."

127. Marc Miller, "NY Review: 'DC-7: The Roberto Clemente Story,'" *Backstage*, February 17, 2012: www.backstage.com/review/ny-theater/off-broadway/ny-review-dc-7-the-roberto-clemente-story/ (accessed November 11, 2012).

128. Brian Scott Lipton, "Patrick Ryan Sullivan to Star in Engeman Theatre's *Broadway, Baseball and Beer*," TheaterMania.com, June 7, 2012: www.theatermania.com/long-island-theater/news/06-2012/patrick-ryan-sullivan-to-star-in-engeman-theatres-_57986.html (accessed November 28, 2012).

129. See www.patrickryansullivan.net/bio.htm.

130. Neil McKim, "*Shadowball*—A Jazz Opera": *Classical-music.com*: The Official Website of *BBC Music Magazine*, July 2, 2010: www.classical-music.com/blog/shadowball-jazz-opera (accessed November 27, 2012).

131. See McKim, as well as John Fordham, "*Shadowball*, Mermaid, London," *The Guardian*, July 1, 2010: www.theguardian.com/music/2010/jul/01/shadowball-review (accessed November 27, 2012).

132. McKim.

133. Ibid.

134. Hackney Music Development Trust, official website: www.hmdt.org.uk/community_shadowball_1.html (accessed November 27, 2012).

135. McKim.

136. Ibid.

137. "An Opera in a League of Its Own!" Sheffield Theatres, Crucible Lyceum Studio website, June 14, 2012: www.sheffieldtheatres.co.uk/about/news/press-releases/an-opera-in-a-league-of-its-own/ (accessed November 27, 2012).

138. McKim.

139. Quotes taken from two sources: "An Opera in a League of Its Own!" Sheffield Theatres, Crucible Lyceum website, and "Shadowball Jazz Opera Awarded Olympic Games 'Inspire Mark,'" *YES: Yamaha Education Supplement*, Spring 2010, 5.

140. Fordham, "*Shadowball*, Mermaid, London."

141. "The Post Game Show—The Story of Shadowball," *HMDT Music's Channel*, uploaded February 6, 2012: https://www.youtube.com/watch?v=eVYy65y7qcc (accessed February 15, 2015).

142. "An Opera in a League of Its Own!"

143. "Shadowball Jazz Opera Awarded Olympic Games 'Inspire Mark,'" *YES: Yamaha Education Supplement*.

144. Lowell Ullrich, "Forgotten Frasers New Fiction P," *The rovince* (Vancouver, BC, Canada), June 5, 2011: www2.canada.com/theprovince/news/sports/story.html?id=242f5126-8aad-4acb-a1ce-4066199160ba&p=1 (accessed October 16, 2012).

145. Ibid.

146. "Presentation Explores Adapting a Book to the Stage," *New Westminster News Leader* (New Westminster, BC, Canada), March 22, 2011: www.newwesttnewsleader.com/entertainment/118460604 (accessed February 15, 2015).

147. Ullrich, "Forgotten Frasers New Fiction."

148. Renee Bucciarelli, correspondence with author, October 19, 2012.

149. Ibid.

150. Ibid.

151. Ibid.

152. Lisa Leff, "'Take Me Out to the Opera': SF Opera Hopes to Hit High Note with Ballpark Show," *USA Today*, September 28, 2007: usatoday30.usatoday.com/sports/baseball/2007–09-28–3713913626_x.htm (accessed August 11, 2012).

153. Ibid.

154. Ibid.

155. Erin Fitzgerald, "Opera in the Outfield to Be Held Sept. 22 at Nationals Park," *The Southwester*, September 8, 2011: thesouthwester.com/2011/09/08/opera-in-the-outfield-to-be-held-sept-22-at-nationals-park/ (accessed February 15, 2015).

156. Lavanya Ramanathan, "Opera in the Outfield at Nats Park: What to Know before Saturday's 'Don Giovanni' Show," *The Washington Post* "GOG Blog," September 26, 2012: www.washingtonpost.com/blogs/going-out-guide/post/opera-in-the-outfield-at-nats-park-what-to-know-before-saturdays-don-giovanni-show/2012/09/26/932f3d80-0753-11e2-a10c-fa5a255a9258_blog.html (accessed February 15, 2015)

157. "If You HD Stream It, They Will Come! WNO's Barbiere Grand Slam," *Opera Chic*, September 11, 2009: operachic.typepad.com/opera_chic/2009/09/wno-barbiere.html (accessed February 15, 2015).

158. Steve Cohen, interview by the author, October 24, 2012.

159. "Broadway Musical MVPs: 1960-2010: The Most Valuable Players of the Past 50 Seasons," Press Release, November 2, 2011: www.prlog.org/11716103-broadway-musical-mvps-1960-2010-the-most-valuable-players-of-the-past-50-seasons.html (accessed January 4, 2012).

160. "Joe's View: 'Musical MVPs': 50 Years of Broadway as a Sport," Hearst Connecticut Media Group, February 18, 2013: blog.ctnews.com/meyers/2013/02/18/'musical-mvps'-50-years-of-broadway-as-a-sport (accessed February 15, 2015).

161. Ibid.

Interlude: Choreographers and Dancers on Dance and Baseball

1. Louis Kavouras, interview by the author, March 15, 2011.

2. Peter Pucci, interview by the author, April 21, 2011.

3. Nick Ross, interview by the author, August 16, 2011.

Chapter 3

1. Harold Seymour and Dorothy Seymour Mills, *Baseball: The Early Years* (New York: Oxford University Press, 1960), 345.

2. Ibid.

3. Steven A Riess, *Touching Base: Professional Baseball and American Culture in the Progressive Era* (Urbana and Chicago, IL: University of Illinois Press, 1983), 19.

4. *American Patterns: Three Decades of Dance*, VHS, produced and directed by David W. Hahn, researched and written by Andrew M. Wentink, narration written by Melanie Ray, narrated by Studs Terkel (Chicago: De-
lores Kohl Educational Foundation, 1982). Available in Jerome Robbins Dance Division, New York Public Library for the Performing Arts.

5. Isadora Bennett, "The Oldest-Youngest Art," *Winslow-Fitz-Simmons*, promotional brochure (New York: Strand Press, 1939), 4. Digital copy of the publication is made available by University of Iowa Libraries: digital.lib.uiowa.edu/cdm/ref/collection/tc/id/55823 (accessed February 15, 2015).

6. Ruth Page, *Page by Page* (New York: Dance Horizons, 1978), 123.

7. Ruth Page, interview by Studs Terkel, in *American Patterns: Three Decades of Dance*.

8. Walter Sorell, *Hanya Holm: The Biography of an Artist* (Middletown, CT: Wesleyan University Press, 1969), 54.

9. John Briggs, "Ballet Goes American," *Dance Magazine*, December 1946, 49.

10. Walter Terry, *The Dance in America* (New York: Harper & Brothers, 1956),123; John Martin, *America Dancing: The Background and Personalities of Modern Dance* (New York: Dodge, 1936; New York: Dance Horizons, 1968), 245-46. Citations refer to the Dance Horizons edition.

11. Terry, *The Dance in America*, 68.

12. Material relating to "Americans in Paris" may be found in the Ruth Page Collection, 1918-1970, housed in the Jerome Robbins Dance Division of the New York Public Library for the Performing Arts.

13. Material relating to "Metropolitan Daily" may be found in the Hanya Holm Collection, housed in the Jerome Robbins Dance Division of the New York Public Library for the Performing Arts.

14. Ruth Franck, "Holm Dance Group Delights Audience: Originality of Program Inspires Awe at First But Proves Exciting," review of "Metropolitan Daily," Swarthmore College, Swarthmore, PA, *Swarthmore Phoenix*, November 14, 1939.

15. For more information, see the articles "Dance for Television" and "The Dance in Television," the latter written by Edward Padula, which appeared in the October 1939 issue of *Dance Magazine* (pages 10-11). Photographs from the television production of "Metropolitan Daily" are presented on page 11. Also see Jennifer Dunning's obituary of Hanya Holm, *New York Times*, November 4, 1992, as well as "Television Shows Include Comedians," *New York Sun*, May 27, 1939.

16. Material relating to "Casey at the Bat" may be found in the following Newbery Library (Chicago) collections: The Ann Barzel Dance Research Collection, 1830-2010; the Ann Barzel Papers, 1912-2005; and the Stone-Camryn Studio Records, 1922-1984. Additional material may be found in the Ann Barzel Dance Film Archive, housed in the Harold Washington Library Center, Chicago Public Library.

17. Walter Camryn, "Performing in Chicago: During the Depression Years," *Upstairs Bulletin*, November 15, 1979, 4.

18. Review of "Casey at the Bat," performed by Walter Camryn & Group, Goodman Theatre, Chicago, February 5, 1939, *Dance Magazine*, April 1939.

19. "Dance Council Recital Shows Novel Themes," *Chicago Daily Tribune*, May 3, 1940, 21.

20. Ann Barzel, "Bentley Stone," in *American National Biography*, Volume 20 (New York: Oxford University Press, 1999), 842.

21. Frank Cullen, Florence Hackman, and Donald McNeilly, *Vaudeville Old & New: An Encyclopedia of Variety Performers in America*, Volume One (New York: Routledge, 2006), 734-735.

22. Sarah Magee, "Dance Artists Thrill Yates Concert Audience," *Geneva Daily Times* (Geneva, NY), January-March 1952: fultonhistory.com/Newspaper11/Gen evaNYDailyTimes/GenevaNYDailyTimes1952Jan-Mar1952Grayscale/GenevaNYDailyTimes1952Jan-MarGrayscale-0936.pdf (accessed February 15, 2015); "Mata and Hari to Perform Here in Washington Hall," *The Notre Dame Scholastic*, March 11, 1960, 9.

23. See also Mabel Watrous, "Dance Troupe Highly Praised: Mata and Hari Enliven Community Series," *The Spokesman-Review* (Spokane, WA), January 26, 1950, 9.

24. "Night Clubs—Vaude: Empire Room, Palmer House, Chicago: Thursday, June 26," *Billboard*, July 5, 1952, 18.

25. Watrous, "Dance Troupe Highly Praised."

26. Material relating to "Billy Sunday" may be found in the Ruth Page Collection, 1918-1970, housed in the Jerome Robbins Dance Division, New York Public Library for the Performing Arts. Additional material may be found in the Ruth Page Papers, 1900–1991, housed in the Newbery Library, Chicago, as well as the Ann Barzel Dance Film Archive, Chicago Public Library. Also used for this section: *Billy Sunday: Baseball, the Bible, and Ballet*, VHS, 1983.

27. Ruth Page, "Lecture on Billy Sunday Ballet," found in Ruth Page Papers: Works: Articles and Essays (Box 2, Folder 55), Newbery Library, Chicago.

28. Ibid.

29. Ibid.

30. Ibid.

31. See Abstract in entry for New Dance Group Collection, Library of Congress: lcweb2.loc.gov/digilib/ihas/loc.natlib.scdb.200033868/default.html (accessed February 2, 2013).

32. See Joanna G. Harris, "Anna Sokolow, 1910–2000," *Jewish Women's Archive*: jwa.org/encyclopedia/article/sokolow-anna (accessed February 2, 2013); Robin Wander, "Stanford Dance Reconstructs Anna Sokolow's Signature Work *Rooms*," *Stanford News*, February 9, 2012: news.stanford.edu/news/2012/February/dance-rooms-020912.html (accessed February 15, 2015).

33. *The Feld Ballet*, VHS, produced by Judy Kinberg for WNET-TV "Dance in America" series, directed by Emile Ardolino, narrated by John Lithgow. Originally telecast on May 16, 1979. Available in Jerome Robbins Dance Division, New York Public Library for the Performing Arts."

34. *Womensports and In Between*, VHS, videotaped by Eva Maier and Kate Parker at Jim May Studio, New York, May 17, 1976. Available in Jerome Robbins Dance Division, New York Public Library for the Performing Arts.

35. Much information in this section comes from an interview conducted by the author with Gail Heilbron Steinitz on January 7, 2013.

36. *In the Beginning...*, VHS, produced by Patricia Hruby in 1976. Available in Jerome Robbins Dance Division, New York Public Library for the Performing Arts.

37. Edition used for this study: Theresa Purcell Cone and Stephen L. Cone, *Teaching Children Dance, 2nd Edition* (Champaign, IL: Human Kinetics, 2005), 140-41.

38. *Chris Chadman Workshop*, VHS, videotaped in performance on September 4, 1980. Available in Jerome Robbins Dance Division, New York Public Library for the Performing Arts.

39. *Mime Choreo Showcase III*, VHS, videotaped in performance at the Theater of the Riverside Church, New York, on October 28, 1984, during the Riverside Dance Festival, by Lee A. Goldman. Available in Jerome Robbins Dance Division, New York Public Library for the Performing Arts.

40. Anna Kisselgoff, "Dance: Mimes at Riverside Festival," *New York Times*, October 30, 1984: www.nytimes.com/1984/10/30/arts/dance-mimes-at-riverside-festival.html (accessed December 21, 2012).

41. Much information in this section comes from an interview conducted by the author with Gail Conrad on March 18, 2011.

42. Jennifer Dunning, "The Dance: Gail Conrad," *New York Times*, January 13, 1985: www.nytimes.com/1985/01/13/arts/the-dance-gail-conrad.html (accessed February 16, 2015).

43. Ibid.

44. Much information in this section comes from an interview conducted by the author with Louis Kavouras on March 15, 2011.

45. Barbara Cloud, "Artistic Feat," *UNLV Magazine* (Las Vegas, NV), Spring 2000: www.joesuniverse.org/unlvmagazinearticle.html (accessed December 10, 2012).

46. Ibid.

47. *Clarence Teeters: American Dance Festival*, VHS, videotaped in performance at the American Dance Festival, Duke University, Durham, NC, 1986. Available in Jerome Robbins Dance Division, New York Public Library for the Performing Arts.

48. *Heavenly Earth*, VHS, Henry Yu Dance Company videotaped in performance at the National Theatre, Taipan, Taiwan, on December 12, 1989. Available in Jerome Robbins Dance Division, New York Public Library for the Performing Arts.

49. Amber Wu, "Nation's Trailblazing Giants of Dance Honored with Retrospective," *Taiwan Today*, December 12, 2008: taiwantoday.tw/ct.asp?xItem=468 31&CtNode=450 (accessed December 6, 2012).

50. Jennifer Dunning, "Review/Dance: Henry Yu Returns with a Style of His Own," *New York Times*, July 29, 1991: www.nytimes.com/1991/07/29/arts/07/29/arts/review-dance-henry-yu-returns-with-a-style-of-his-own (accessed December 6, 2012).

51. Much information in this section comes from an interview conducted by the author with Lisa de Ribere on March 21, 2011.

52. Lisa de Ribere, interview by Bill Geist, *Sunday Morning*, CBS-TV, May 5, 1991.

53. Daphne Hurford, "Ballet Takes a Swing at Baseball: 'The Mighty Casey' Pairs the National Pastime with Dance in a New Sporting Ballet," *Sports Illustrated*, December 3, 1990, 19-20.

54. Lisa de Ribere, interview by Bill Geist.

55. Much information in this section comes from two interviews conducted by the author with Moses Pendleton, one on March 11, 2009 and one on May 4, 2011.

56. See also George Vecsey, "Dance: 'Baseball,' Unlike Anything the Babe Knew," *New York Times*, December 11, 1994: www.nytimes.com/1994/12/11/arts/dance-baseball-unlike-anything-the-babe-knew.html (accessed January 4, 2013).

57. Ibid.

58. Robin Rauzi, "Theater: Pitching a Concept," *Los Angeles Times*, March 26, 1998: articles.latimes.com/1998/mar/26/entertainment/ca-32741 (accessed January 4, 2013).

59. *David Dorfman Dance*, VHS, videotaped in performance at The Kitchen, New York, NY, May 19-22, 1994. Available in Jerome Robbins Dance Division, New York Public Library for the Performing Arts.

60. Catherine Barnett, "Athletes' Suites: David Dorfman Turns Jocks into Performing Dancers," *Sports Illustrated*, November 1, 1993: www.si.com/vault/1993/11/01/129690/athletes-suites-david-dorfman-turns-jocks-into-performing-dancers (accessed February 16, 2015).

61. Ibid.

62. See Suzanne Carbonneau, "David Dorfman," on the official David Dorfman Dance website: www.daviddorfmandance.org/view_press.php?id=7 (accessed February 16, 2015). Also see William Harris, "An Eccentric Who Likes to Make Things Accessible," *New York Times*, February 16, 1997: www.nytimes.com/1997/02/16/arts/an-eccentric-who-likes-to-make-things-accessible.html (accessed February 16, 2015).

63. Carbonneau, "David Dorfman."

64. Ibid.

65. Lewis Segal, "Dance Review: Saxes, Music and Monologues at Santa Monica's Highways," *Los Angeles Times*, February 2, 1993: articles.latimes.com/1993-02-02/entertainment/ca-838_1_dan-froot (accessed February 16, 2015).

66. Miriam Seidel, "Joining Messages with Movement," *Philadelphia Inquirer*, October 1, 1994: articles.philly.com/1994-10-01/entertainment/25870259_1_david-dorfman-dance-lisa-race-work-shapes (accessed February 16, 2015).

67. Barnett, "Athletes' Suites: David Dorfman Dance Turns Jocks into Dancers."

68. "David Dorfman Dance Returns to Bates Dance Festival," *Bates News* (Lewiston, ME), July 16, 1997: www.bates.edu/news/1997/07/16/david-dorfman-returns (accessed February 16, 2015).

69. Barnett, "Athletes' Suites."

70. Elizabeth Zimmer, quoted on official David Dorfman Dance website: www.daviddorfmandance.org/repertory.php (accessed February 16, 2015).

71. Barnett, "Athletes' Suites."

72. Carbonneau, "David Dorfman."

73. Barnett.

74. Ibid.

75. Ibid.

76. Frank Rizzo, "Trading Places: Athletes Turn to Dance at Jacob's Pillow for Artistic and Physical Edification," *Hartford Courant*, June 8, 1997: articles.courant.com/1997-06-08/entertainment/9706060045_1_

dance-team-dance-workshop-choreographer-david-dorfman (accessed February 16, 2015).

77. Ibid.

78. Sadie Feddoes, "Gala Marks Anniversary of Jackie Joining Dodgers," *New York Amsterdam News*, May 31, 1997, 9.

79. Ibid.

80. Much information in this section comes from an interview conducted by the author with Peter Pucci on April 21, 2011.

81. See, for example, Jack Anderson, "Dance Review: Hoop Schemes, Dreams and Happy Feet," *New York Times*, May 6, 1998: www.nytimes.com/1998/05/06/arts/dance-review-hoop-schemes-dreams-and-happy-feet.html (accessed February 16, 2015), and Elis Lotozo, "A Dance-Sport Fusion Melds Past and Present," *Philadelphia Inquirer*, March 19, 2002: articles.philly.com/2002-03-19/news/25342763_1_peter-pucci-plus-dancers-dance-and-sports-evening-length-dance (accessed February 16, 2015).

82. Quotation taken from official Peter Pucci Plus website: www.pucciplus.com (accessed December 6, 2012).

83. See www.pucciplus.com/sport.html (accessed December 6, 2012).

84. The Peter Pucci Plus official website provides helpful information—including video clips— about the various venues in which "Pucci: Sport" has been performed.

85. Elizabeth Schwyzer, "Cowboy Hats and Baseball Bats," *Santa Barbara Independent*, September 14, 2006 (updated September 28, 2006): www.independent.com/news/2006/sep/14/cowboy-hats-and-baseball-bats/ (accessed December 6, 2012).

86. Ibid.

Interlude: Choreographers and Dancers on Dance and Baseball

1. Lisa de Ribere, interview by the author, March 21, 2011.

2. Christopher Fleming, interview by the author, March 10, 2011.

3. Marianna Tcherkassky, interview by the author, April 23, 2011.

Chapter 4

1. Much information in this section comes from an interview conducted by the author with Christopher Fleming on March 10, 2011.

2. Christopher Fleming, interview by the author, March 10, 2011.

3. Ibid.

4. Much information in this section comes from an interview conducted by the author with Ana Maria Maynard Tekina-eirú on April 27, 2011. See also "Dance: Arts Listings: Recommended: Puerto Rican Folkloric Dance Company: Celebrando, State Theater, June 24," *The Austin Chronicle* (Austin, TX): www.prfdance.org/publicity/Chronicle.feature.June2001.htm (accessed February 20, 2015).

5. Ana Maria Maynard Tekina-eirú, interview by the author, April 27, 2011.

6. Ibid.

7. Tim Cusack, "Decadance vs. The Firebird—a Hip-Hop Ballet," nytheatre.com: The Digital Magazine of New York Indie Theater, August 15, 2004: www.ny theatre.com/Review/tim-cusack-2004-8-15-decada nce-vs-the-firebird-a-hip-hop-ballet (accessed February 5, 2013).

8. Jennifer Dunning, "Dance Review: New Plumage and Rap Song for a Certain Russian Bird," *New York Times*, August 23, 2004, 4.

9. Cusack, "Decadance vs. The Firebird—a Hip-Hop Ballet."

10. Much information in this section comes from two interviews conducted by the author with Chris Black, one on March 13, 2009 and one on December 15, 2011.

11. Chris Black, interview by the author, December 15, 2011.

12. Ibid.

13. Chris Black, interview by the author, March 13, 2009.

14. "Dancing for a Home Run," *Dance Magazine*, September 2007, 25.

15. Black, interview by the author, December 15, 2011.

16. Black, email message to author, March 12, 2009.

17. Ibid.

18. Black, interview by the author, March 13, 2009.

19. Black, interview by the author, December 15, 2011.

20. Ibid.

21. Information about "Opening Day at Fenway Park" taken from USC School of Theatre "Step into Spring" performance program (April 26 and 27, 2007, at the Bing Theatre): dramaticarts.usc.edu/media/332 51/2007sis.pdf (accessed February 5, 2013). See also: https://www.youtube.com/watch?v=xRmSZvJlv1g (video clip of performance of "Opening Day at Fenway Park," filmed at Bing Theatre, University of Southern California, in 2007).

22. See dancetroupe.mit.edu/shows/S11/ (accessed February 5, 2013).

23. Information about "Baseball Dance" and Cocoon Central Dance Team was taken from the following online sources: cocooncentraldanceteam.tumblr.com (official website, accessed February 10, 2013) and www. youtube.com/watch?v=qPOMetZnpas (clip of "Baseball Dance," filmed at The Moon on July 28, 2009, accessed February 10, 2013).

24. Deborah Jowitt, "Laura Peterson Rides Lumberob's Beats," *Village Voice*, February 18, 2009: www. villagevoice.com/2009-02-18/dance/laura-peterson-rides-lumberob-s-beats-tiffany-mills-stretches-tomo rrow-s-legs (accessed December 23, 2011).

25. Tom Phillips, "Laura Peterson Choreography, 'Forever,'" danceviewtimes: writers on dancing, February 20, 2009: www.danceviewtimes.com/2009/02/forever-.html (accessed February 16, 2015).

26. Jowitt, "Laura Peterson Rides Lumberob's Beats."

27. Phillips, "Laura Peterson Choreography, 'Forever.'"

28. Ibid.

29. For an informative review of "Uptown," see Julie Bloom, "Turn on the Victrola and They'll Dance," *New York Times*, December 8, 2009: www.nytimes.com/2009/12/09/arts/dance/09rushing.html?pagewanted-=all&_r=1& (accessed February 20, 2015).

30. Donn Rogosin, *Invisible Men: Life in Baseball's Negro Leagues* (New York: Atheneum, 1983), 122-23.

31. Much information in this section comes from the author's interview by the Ana Maria Maynard Tekina-eirú, April 27, 2011.

32. "Puerto Rican Folkloric Dance Staging *Boricua Beisbol* on December 4th," *Austin On Stage*, reprinted on official website of the Puerto Rican Folkloric Dance and Cultural Center on November 22, 2011: www.austin onstage.com/prfdancexmas2011news (accessed February 20, 2015).

33. Nancy Flores, "Boricua Beisbol at the Long Center," *Austin American-Statesman*, December 13, 2011: www.prfdance.org/publicity/Statesman.BoricuaBeisbol 2011.LongCenter.pdf (accessed February 20, 2015).

34. Ibid.

35. Provided on the official Puerto Rican Folkloric Dance and Cultural Center website: www.prfdance.org/perform11.htm (accessed February 20, 2015).

36. Much information in this section comes from two interviews conducted by the author, one with Lynn Parkerson on October 19, 2012, and one with Steve Cohen on October 24, 2012.

37. *Streb: Pop Action*, VHS, directed and produced by Michael Blackwood (New York: Michael Blackwood Productions, 2001). Available in Jerome Robbins Dance Division, New York Public Library for the Performing Arts.

38. Daniel Gibson, "Take Us Out to the Ball Game," *Native Peoples*, November/December 2002, 14.

39. "ICON Dance Complex Slides into First: Beth Hubela Choreographs History *Where Dance Meets Baseball*," press release, Elizabeth Barry & Associates (Englishtown, NJ), July 14, 2010: www.ebandassociates.com/enews/ebpr071410.html (accessed December 23, 2011).

40. "Baseball Meets Ballet at the Brooklyn Cyclones," press release, Brooklyn Ballet, March 15, 2012: brook-lynballet.org/press/releases/120315 (accessed October 10, 2012).

41. Lynn Parkerson, interview by the author, October 19, 2012.

42. Eric P. Newcomer, "Between Innings, Ballerinas Take the Field," *New York Times*, July 24, 2012: cityroom. blogs.nytimes.com/2012/07/24/between-innings-ballerinas-take-the-field/ (accessed October 10, 2012).

43. "Baseball Meets Ballet at the Brooklyn Cyclones," press release, Brooklyn Ballet.

44. Ibid.

45. Newcomer, "Between Innings, Ballerinas Take the Field."

46. "North Carolina Dance Theatre: Carmen," Blumenthal Performing Arts, October 17-23, 2013: www. blumenthaarts.org/events/detail/nc-dance-carmen (accessed March 11, 2014).

47. See the following promotional video for more information: "Sasha Janes' Carmen—North Carolina Dance Theatre," October 2, 2013: https://www.youtube.com/watch?v=tBHjX1lXj4E (accessed March 11, 2014).

48. Rebecca Ritzel, "'Carmen' Starts Up North, Then Heads to Charlotte," *Charlotte Observer*, August 19, 2013: www.charlotteobserver.com/2013/08/19/4248050/carmen-starts-up-north-then-heads.html#.Ux8u1M70g4A (accessed March 11, 2014).

49. *In the Beginning…*, VHS, produced by Patricia Hruby in 1976. Available in Jerome Robbins Dance Division, New York Public Library for the Performing Arts.

50. Theresa Purcell Cone and Stephen L. Cone, *Teaching Children Dance, 2nd Edition* (Champaign, IL: Human Kinetics, 2005), 140.

51. See https://www.youtube.com/watch?v=RHiZzFH3ig4 (accessed February 20, 2015).

52. See https://www.youtube.com/watch?v=a97z-SYKCn0 (accessed February 20, 2015).

53. See https://www.youtube.com/watch?v=DR8c_kO35d0 and https://www.youtube.com/watch?v=Ebnrb26jfko (both accessed February 20, 2015).

54. Howard Good, *Diamonds in the Dark: America, Baseball, and the Movies* (Lanham, MD: Scarecrow Press, 1997), 82.

Interlude: Therapist, Coordinator, Director and a Baseball Executive

1. Dean Caswell, interview by the author, April 25, 2011.

2. Joan Quatrano, interview by the author, January 25, 2012.

3. Lynn Parkerson, interview by the author, October 19, 2012.

4. Steve Cohen, interview by the author, October 24, 2012.

Chapter 5

1. See the following online resources (all accessed February 22, 2015): www.moma.org/explore/multimedia/audios/244/2437; www.imdb.com/title/tt1219047; and www.imdb.com/title/tt2008603.

2. Robert Cantwell, "Sport was Box-Office Poison," *Sports Illustrated*, September 15, 1969: www.si.com/vault/1969/09/15/612748/sport-was-box-office-poison (accessed February 22, 2015). Also see www.loc.gov/item/00563587 (accessed February 22, 2015).

3. See the following online resources: Daniel Eagan, "Baseball on the Screen," *Smithsonian Magazine*, April 4, 2012: www.smithsonianmag.com/arts-culture/baseball-on-the-screen-171974554/?no-list&no-ist (accessed February 22, 2015); and John Thorn, "Baseball Film to 1920," *MLBlogs Network*, May 22, 2012: ourgame.mlblogs.com/2012/05/22/ (accessed February 22, 2015).

4. See https://www.youtube.com/watch?v=HDxfwKE8g2E and https://www.youtube.com/watch?v=-adRzZdFEvw (both accessed February 22, 2015).

5. Howard Good, *Diamonds in the Dark: America, Baseball, and the Movies* (Lanham, MD: Scarecrow Press, 1997), 82-83.

6. *Voice of America*, "Gene Kelly, 1912-1996: His Movies Made Dance Popular in America," transcript of radio broadcast by Steve Ember and Shirley Griffith,

May 5, 2007: learningenglish.voanews.com/content/a-23-2007-05-05-voa1-83133837/127573.html (accessed February 22, 2015).

7. Good, *Diamonds in the Dark*, 91.

8. Ibid., 87.

9. For more information about Johnson, see Guide to the Bernard Johnson Papers MS.P.053, published by the University of California at Irvine, Special Collections and Archives: www.oac.cdlib.org/findaid/ark:/13030/kt658038tm/admin/#ref106 (accessed February 22, 2015).

10. To view: https://www.youtube.com/watch?v=2CYGZbx5vag (accessed February 22, 2015).

11. For Foster, see www.imdb.com/name/nm0287888/; for Rufle, see www.imdb.com/name/nm0749354/ (both accessed February 22, 2015).

12. To view: https://www.youtube.com/watch?v=hg3Lu9Y-9-Q (accessed February 22, 2015).

13. To view: https://www.youtube.com/watch?v=gcFvtWpuqpl (accessed February 22, 2015).

14. To view: www.dailymotion.com/video/xmf55u_woody-woodpecker-the-screwball-1943_shortfilms (accessed February 22, 2015).

15. To view: https://archive.org/details/TexAveryMGM19510606SymphonyInSlang (accessed February 22, 2015).

16. To view: www.dailymotion.com/video/x23xecl_bugs-bunny-baseball-bugs-1946_shortfilms (accessed February 22, 2015).

17. To view: https://www.youtube.com/watch?v=2C8aZLNoWro (accessed February 22, 2015).

18. To view: https://www.youtube.com/watch?v=1S-LnYIPJI (accessed February 22, 2015).

19. To view: https://www.youtube.com/watch?v=Aq9ur0VfVn0 (accessed February 22, 2015).

20. To view: https://www.youtube.com/watch?v=uAvE0n9PvHY (accessed February 23, 2015).

21. For additional information about Satoshi Morino and Osamu Satomi, see the following online sources: www.imdb.com/name/nm1703627/ and www.imdb.com/name/nm1704874 (both accessed February 23, 2015).

22. Robert Whiting, *You Gotta Have Wa* (New York: Macmillan, 1989), 241.

23. To view (in two parts): Part One: https://www.youtube.com/watch?v=EfVZgGICh58; and Part Two: https://www.youtube.com/watch?v=ExvXUu1fXTQ (both accessed February 23, 2015).

24. To view *Diamond Demon*: https://www.youtube.com/watch?v=_Jflun5Cylc (accessed February 23, 2015). *Baseball's Acrobatic Ace* is not available presently for free viewing via video-sharing sites.

25. Bill Veeck with Ed Linn, *Veeck—As in Wreck: The Autobiography of Bill Veeck* (New York: G. B. Putnam's Sons, 1962), 107.

26. Ibid., 105-07.

27. For more information about and images of these games, please refer to the following resources: "Movie Stars and Comics at the Bat," *Los Angeles Times*, July 30, 1938: articles.latimes.com/2006/jul/30/local/me-a2anniversary30 (accessed February 23, 2015); Rob Edelman, "Buster Keaton, Baseball Player," *The National Pastime*, 2011, reprinted by the Society for American Base-

ball Research: sabr.org/research/buster-keaton-baseball-player (accessed February 23, 2015); "Hollywood Screen Idols Play 'Greatest Baseball Game,'" *Eugene Register-Guard* (Eugene, OR), July 30, 1938, 1; "Stars Play Baseball in Hollywood," British Pathé, issued November 8, 1938: www.britishpathe.com/video/stars-play-baseball-in-hollywood/query/US+BASEBALL (accessed February 23, 2015).

28. To view: https://www.youtube.com/watch?v=i3Xr5F71O7w (accessed February 23, 2015).

29. Edward Padula, "The Dance in Television," *Dance Magazine*, October 1939, 10.

30. Ibid.

31. Ibid.

32. Jennifer Dunning, "Hanya Holm is Dead at 99; Influential Choreographer," *New York Times*, November 4, 1992: www.nytimes.com/1992/11/04/theater/hanya-holm-is-dead-at-99-influential-choreographer.html (accessed February 23, 2015); "Television Shows Include Comedians," *New York Sun*, May 27, 1939; and "Dance for Television: What the Newest Amusement Medium Means," *Dance Magazine*, October 1939, 10-11.

33. To view: https://www.youtube.com/watch?v=Na9mv42ql5s (accessed February 23, 2015).

34. Available in the Paley Center for Media, New York.

35. From summary for *The Kaiser Aluminum Hour*: "A Man's Game (TV)," created by Paley Center for Media, New York: www.paleycenter.org/collection/item/?q=kaiser+aluminum+hour+man's+game&p=1&item=T:16000 (accessed February 23, 2015).

36. Available in the Paley Center for Media, New York.

37. For additional information, see Richard Christiansen, "A Comedy in Nine Innings," *Chicago Tribune: TV Week*, May 13, 1973, 1, 3.

38. For more information, see www.imdb.com/title/tt0173933/combined (accessed February 28, 2015). To view dance sequence, see https://www.youtube.com/watch?v=z5STH3abklY (accessed February 28, 2015).

39. Steve Johnson, "Send 'Bleacher Bums' Movie to the Showers," *Chicago Tribune*, April 5, 2002: articles.chicagotribune.com/2002-04-05/features/0204050012_1_bleacher-bums-home-team-movie (accessed February 20, 2014).

40. Ibid.

41. Edna Gunderson, "'High School,' the Musical," *USA Today*, February 27, 2006: usatoday30.usatoday.com/life/movies/news/2006-02-27-high-school-musical_x.htm (accessed March 1, 2015).

42. "Premiere of 'High School Musical 2' Breaks Ratings Record," *New York Times*, August 18, 2007: www.nytimes.com/2007/08/18/arts/television/18cnd-disney-html?ref=arts (accessed March 1, 2015).

43. "Who Says Big Leaguers Don't Dance?" MLB.com/Entertainment, August 2, 2007: mlb.mlb.com/news/article_entertainment.jsp?ymd=20070802&content_id=2125248&vkey=entertainment&text=.jsp (accessed March 1, 2015).

44. Ibid.

45. Available in the Paley Center for Media, New York.

46. Much has been written about the widespread in-

fluence of *Your Show of Shows*. For example, see Alex Dobuzinskis and Steve Gorman, "Comic Great Sid Caesar of 'Your Show of Shows' Dies at 91," *Reuters*, February 12, 2014: www.reuters.com/article/2014/02/13/us-sidcaesar-idUSBREA1B20H20140213 (accessed March 1, 2015).

47. From Summary for "Admiral Broadway Revue: County Fair (TV)," created by Paley Center for Media, New York: www.paleycenter.org/collection/item/?q=admiral+revue+county+fair&p=1&item=T:27634 (accessed March 1, 2015).

48. Jennifer Dunning, "James Starbuck, 85, TV Dance Innovator," *New York Times*, August 19, 1997: www.nytimes.com/1997/08/19/arts/james-starbuck-85-tv-dance-innovator.html (accessed March 1, 2015).

49. To view: https://archive.org/details/ShowerOfStars17February1955 (accessed March 1, 2015).

50. For additional information see the following two online resources: ctva.biz/US/MusicVariety/DannyKayeShow_01_(1963–64).htm (accessed January 1, 2014), and www.tv.com/shows/the-danny-kaye-show/september-25–1963–176210 (accessed March 1, 2015).

51. See the following online resources for more information: www.baseball-almanac.com/poetry/dodgers.shtml (accessed March 1, 2015) and www.kcet.org/shows/classic_cool_theater/web-extras/inspector-general-in-classic-cool-context.html (accessed March 1, 2015).

52. For more information, please see the following two sources: Bernie Harrison, "TV Tonight: Bob Hope Special Salutes World Series," *The Times-News* (Hendersonville, NC), October 14, 1978, 16; and "1963 Black History Viewed through Magazines," which contains an image from *Jet Magazine* (October 31, 1963 issue), featuring a photo of Don Drysdale, Tommy Davis, and Sandy Koufax dancing on the "Bob Hope Show" (October 25, 1963): https://www.flickr.com/photos/vielles_annonces/sets/72157636905651664/detail (accessed March 1, 2015).

53. Mark Dawidziak, "For Our Favorite Son Bob Hope, All Roads Lead Back Home to Ohio," *Cleveland Plain Dealer*, May 29, 2003: www.cleveland.com/homegrown/index.ssf?/homegrown/more/hope/allroads.html (accessed March 1, 2015).

54. See image from *Jet Magazine*, reproduced on https://www.flickr.com/photos/vielles_annonces/sets/72157636905651664/detail/ (accessed March 1, 2015).

55. See Harrison, "TV Tonight: Bob Hope Special Salutes World Series."

56. The official *Eye on Dance* website, www.eyeondance.org/danc.cfm, provides much information about the series. Additionally, the Jerome Robbins Dance Division of the New York Public Library for the Performing Arts houses the *Eye on Dance* Records, 1966–1995, as well as videotapes of many episodes of the series.

57. See the official *Eye on Dance* website: www.eyeondance.org/dance.cfm.

58. Ibid.

59. "Athleticism in Dance: Sports Influence on Dance," VHS, available in Jerome Robbins Dance Division, New York Public Library for the Performing Arts.

60. See *Streb: Pop Action*, VHS, directed and pro-

duced by Michael Blackwood (New York: Michael Blackwood Productions, 2001). Available in Jerome Robbins Dance Division, New York Public for the Performing Arts.

61. "Comparing the Attitudes of Dancers and Athletes," VHS, available in Jerome Robbins Dance Division, New York Public Library for the Performing Arts.

62. "Arts Innovators: Dance from George Balanchine," VHS, available in Jerome Robbins Dance Division, New York Public Library for the Performing Arts.

63. Title is provided on the official *Eye on Dance* website: www.eyeondance.org/videotape/educational.cfm (accessed March 1, 2015).

64. To view: https://www.youtube.com/watch?v=guARy6iM-dM (accessed March 5, 2015).

65. To view: https://www.youtube.com/watch?v=JJYFNi1J_xc (accessed March 5, 2015).

66. To view: https://www.youtube.com/watch?v=3df6WzuNpvo&index=50&list=PLoxZEHfwmTn5MveOBTpCi93ZWB8QQdsnl (accessed March 5, 2015).

67. To view: https://www.youtube.com/watch?v=5wJJVIAGu0Y (accessed March 5, 2015).

68. Mark Gray, "Karina Smirnoff is Engaged to Brad Penny," *People*, November 7, 2010: www.people.com/people/article/0,,20440183,00.html (accessed March 5, 2015).

69. To view: https://www.youtube.com/watch?v=gZGx7EKytZc (accessed March 5, 2015). For additional information, please refer to the Internet Movie Database (IMDb): www.imdb.com/title/tt0609285 (accessed March 5, 2015); and James Sheridan and Barry Monush, *Lucille Ball FAQ: Everything Left to Know about America's Favorite Redhead* (Milwaukee, WI: Applause Theatre & Cinema Books, 2011).

70. Some additional information may be found by accessing the Internet Movie Database: www.imdb.com/title/tt0302166/ (accessed March 15, 2015).

71. See www.absoluteanime.com/princess_nine/yoko.htm (accessed December 18, 2013).

72. Clip of the baseball dance segment may be viewed by using the following URL: https://www.youtube.com/watch?v=YSnjAE2LQk0 (accessed March 15, 2015).

73. To view "National Pastime" dance sequence: https://www.youtube.com/watch?v=1RclopMo9Kc (accessed March 15, 2015).

74. Charles Isherwood, "Batter Up, Onstage with Songs," *New York Times*, September 16, 2014: www.nytimes.com/2014/09/17/theater/bull-durham-a-musical-adaptation-of-the-1988-movie.html?emc=eta1&_r=0 (accessed September 17, 2014).

75. Dunning, "Hanya Holm is Dead at 99; Influential Choreographer," *New York Times*, March 4, 1992.

76. Please see the two previously cited articles from the October 1939 issue of *Dance Magazine*: "Dance for Television: What the Newest Amusement Medium Means" (pages 10-11), and Edward Padula, "The Dance in Television" (page 11).

77. See Jay S. Harrison, "'Casey at the Bat' Opera Presented," *New York Herald Tribune*, March 7, 1955; and Jeffrey Sandell Stern, *The Mighty Casey: A Study of the Performances and Editions of William Schuman's One-Act Opera*, Doctoral Dissertation (Coral Gables, FL: University of Miami, 2012), 36-37: scholarlyrepository.mia

mi.edu/cgi/viewcontent.cgi?article=1724&context=oa_dissertations (accessed January 27, 2015).

78. Harold C. Schonberg, "There is No Joy in 'Casey' Opera: TV Setting of Baseball Saga Strikes Out Esthetically—Poem Held More Musical," *New York Times*, March 7, 1955.

79. Stern, 44-45.

80. A copy of the questionnaire and information about the viewing party may be found in the Joseph W. Polisi: William Schuman Research Papers, Juilliard School Archives, New York.

81. *EAV Music Appreciation Series: Schuman, Casey at the Bat*, notes by Walter Simmons, 1980. Publication may be found in the Joseph W. Polisi: William Schuman Research Papers, Juilliard School Archives, New York.

82. "Dancing—A Man's Game," directed by Gene Kelly and William A. Graham, produced by Robert Saudek Associates for WNBC-TV *Omnibus* series and telecast originally on December 21, 1958. Viewed originally in reel format at Jerome Robbins Dance Division, New York Public Library for the Performing Arts. Now available in DVD format, Archive of American Television series, E1 Entertainment.

83. "Man Who Dances: Edward Villella," VHS, produced by Robert Drew and Mike Jackson, narrated by Don Morrow, televised on the *Bell Telephone Hour*, NBC-TV, March 8, 1968. Available in Jerome Robbins Dance Division, New York Public Library for the Performing Arts.

84. Norma McLain Stoop, "Dancevision," *Dance Magazine*, November 1976, 98.

85. Ibid., 99.

86. Ibid.

87. Ibid.

88. Ibid.

89. "HMS Produces Revival of Ruth Page's 1946 'Billy Sunday' Ballet as Ch. 11 Dance Special," *Ruth L. Ratny's Reel Chicago*, September 14, 2007: www.reelchicago.com/article/hms-produces-revival-ruth-pages-1946-brbilly-sunday-ballet-ch-11-dance-special (accessed March 1, 2014).

90. Jack Anderson, "Ballet: The Cincinnati/New Orleans City Troupe," *New York Times*, October 10, 1983: www.nytimes.com/1983/10/10/arts/ballet-the-cincinnati-new-orleans-city-troupe.html (accessed March 2, 2014).

91. "Billy Sunday: Baseball, the Bible, and Ballet," VHS, produced by Greater Cincinnati Television Educational Foundation, directed by Taylor L. Feltner, written by Andrew M. Wentink, narrated by Johnny Bench (Cincinnati: WCET-TV, 1983). Available in Jerome Robbins Dance Division, New York Public Library for the Performing Arts.

92. Ibid.

93. Anderson, "Ballet: The Cincinnati/New Orleans City Troupe."

94. See "HMS Produces Revival of Ruth Page's 1946 'Billy Sunday' Ballet as Ch. 11 Dance Special," and CDI (Concert Dance Inc.) web page: www.ruthpage.org/cdi (accessed March 1, 2014). A WBEZ 91.5 radio segment about the production also may be heard via the following link: www.wbez.org/episode-segments/billy-sunday-celebrated-dance (accessed March 1, 2014).

95. "A Day at the Ballpark," *Newcity Stage*, September 27, 2007: newcitystage.com/2007/09/27/a-day-at-the-ballpark/ (accessed March 1, 2014).

96. To view: https://www.youtube.com/watch?v=5QR0pmogH8 (accessed March 15, 2015).

97. Transcript of the *60 Minutes* segment may be found on the CBS News website: "NYC Ballet Forges the Art Form's Future," November 25, 2012: www.cbsnews.com/news/nyc-ballet-forges-the-art-forms-future (accessed March 15, 2015).

98. Gia Kourlas, "The Spirit May Suffer, Yet Still It Endures," *New York Times*, May 14, 2009: www.nytimes.com/2009/05/15/arts/dance/15grah.html (accessed March 15, 2015).

99. Transcript of radio broadcast may be found on KUOW website: Marcie Sillman, "What It Takes to Become a Ballerina," November 22, 2011: www2.kuow.org/program.php?id=25167 (accessed March 15, 2015).

100. Lane DeGregory, "New Miss Florida Laura McKeeman Hopes to Blaze Trails for Women in Sports Broadcast," *Tampa Bay Times*, July 20, 2012: www.tampabay.com/features/humaninterest/new-miss-florida-laura-mckeeman-hopes-to-blaze-trails-for-women-in-sports/1241327 (accessed February 21, 2014).

101. Joe Kay, "Baseball and Ballet Collide on First Pitch at Reds Game," *KOMO News*, August 25, 2013: www.komonews.com/news/offbeat/Baseball-and-ballet-collide-on-first-pitch-at-Reds-game-221018191.html (accessed March 15, 2015).

102. A particularly entertaining story about Valentine's experience in Japan appeared in *Sports Illustrated* in 2007: Chris Ballard, "Bobby V's Super Terrific Happy Hour, *Sports Illustrated*, April 30, 2007 (posted online on November 6, 2007): www.si.com/more-sports/2007/11/06/valentine0430 (accessed March 8, 2014, originally published in print form in the April 30, 2007 issue of *Sports Illustrated*).

103. To view: https://www.youtube.com/watch?v=IZSXjafXKXc (accessed March 15, 2015).

104. For information about the video, see Lynn Zinser, "Getting Out the Vote for Pablo," *New York Times*, July 10, 2009, 1. To view video: m.mlb.com/video/v5468463/the-giants-urge-fans-to-vote-for-pablo-sandoval (accessed March 15, 2015).

105. Zinser, "Getting Out the Vote for Pablo," 1.

106. Murray Goodman, "Sports and the Dance," *Dance Magazine*, September 1946, 24.

107. Richard Geer, "Linked by Tradition—100,000 Years of Dance and Sport," *JOPERD*, May/June 1992, 40.

108. David Falkner, *Nine Sides of the Diamond: Baseball's Great Glove Men on the Fine Art of Defense* (New York: Times Books/Random House, 1990), 5.

109. Tim Shortt, *The Babe Ruth Ballet School* (Buffalo, NY: Firefly, 1996), 16.

110. Julia Ruth Stevens with Bill Gilbert, *Major League Dad: A Daughter's Cherished Memories* (Chicago: Triumph Books, 2001), 66.

111. Harold Peterson, *The Man Who Invented Baseball* (New York: Charles Scribner's Sons, 1969, 1973), 49–50.

112. Geer, "Linked by Tradition—100,000 Years of Dance and Sport," 39.

113. "Athleticism in Dance: Sports Influence on Dance" (*Eye on Dance*, episode 136), VHS, available in Jerome Robbins Dance Division, New York Public Library for the Performing Arts.

114. "Ball play dances" conducted by the Sioux and Choctaw were identified in the period of 1828-30 by George Catlin. Also see James Mooney, "The Cherokee Ball Play," *The American Anthropologist* (April 1890), 105-32.

115. Stephen Manes, *Where Snowflakes Dance and Swear* (Seattle, WA: Cadwallader & Stern, 2011), 7-11.

116. Sheryl Flatow, "The Ballet of Baseball: More Than a Game, It's Art to This Dancer," *Daily News* (New York, NY), April 23, 1983.

Bibliography

Books

Astaire, Fred. *Steps in Time: An Autobiography*. New York: Harper Collins, 2008, 32-35; originally published by Harper and Brothers, 1959.

Bierley, Paul E. *The Incredible Band of John Philip Sousa*. Champaign, IL: University of Illinois Press, 2006.

Bordman, Gerald, and Richard Norton. *American Musical Theatre: A Chronicle, Fourth Edition*. New York: Oxford University Press, 2010.

Bordman, Gerald, and Thomas S. Hischak. *The Oxford Companion to American Theatre, Third Edition* New York: Oxford University Press, 2004.

Chadwick, Lester. *Baseball Joe Around the World*. New York: Cupples & Leon, 1918.

Christiansen, Richard. *A Theater of Our Own: A History and a Memoir of 1,001 Nights in Chicago*. Evanston, IL: Northwestern University Press, 2004.

Cone, Theresa Purcell, and Stephen L. Cone. *Teaching Children Dance*, 2nd edition. Champaign, IL: Human Kinetics, 2005.

Cullen, Frank, Florence Hackman, and Donald McNeilly. *Vaudeville Old & New: An Encyclopedia of Variety Performers in America*, Volume One. New York: Routledge, 2006.

de Mille, Agnes. *America Dances*. New York: Macmillan, 1980.

Dichter, Harry, Compiler. *Baseball in Music and Song: A Series in Facsimile of Scarce Sheet Music*, Philadelphia: Musical Americana, 1954.

DiMeglio, John. *Vaudeville U.S.A.* Bowling Green, OH: Bowling Green University Popular Press, 1973.

Elfers, James E. *The Tour to End All Tours: The Story of Major League Baseball's 1913-1914 World Tour*. Lincoln: University of Nebraska Press, 2003.

Epstein, Dan. *Big Hair and Plastic Grass: A Funky Ride through Baseball and America in the Swinging '70s*. New York: St. Martin's Press, 2010.

Evers, John J., and Hugh S. Fullerton. *Touching Second: The Science of Baseball*. Chicago: Reilly & Britton, 1910.

Falkner, David. *Nine Sides of the Diamond: Baseball's Great Glove Men on the Fine Art of Defense*. New York: Times Books/Random House, 1990.

Fehler, Gene. *Dancing on the Basepaths: Baseball Poetry and Verse*. Jefferson, NC: McFarland, 2001.

Fleitz, David L. *Cap Anson: The Grand Old Man of Baseball*. Jefferson, NC: McFarland, 2005.

Gehring, Wes. D. *Joe E. Brown: Film Comedian and Baseball Buffoon*. Jefferson, NC: McFarland, 2006.

Giamatti, A. Bartlett. *Take Time for Paradise: Americans and Their Games*. New York: Summit, 1989.

Golenbock, Peter. *Wrigleyville: A Magical History Tour of the Chicago Cubs*. New York: St. Martin's Press, 1999.

Good, Howard. *Diamonds in the Dark: America, Baseball, and the Movies*. Lanham, MD: Scarecrow Press, 1997.

Hynd, Noel. *Marquard and Seeley*. Hyannis, MA: Parnassus Imprints, 1996.

Johnson, James Weldon. *Black Manhattan*. New York: Atheneum, 1968; originally published in 1930.

Jones, Patrick. *Connecting Young Adults and Libraries*, second edition. New York: Neal-Schuman, 1998.

Kirsch, George B. *Baseball in Blue and Gray: The National Pastime during the Civil War*. Princeton and Oxford: Princeton University Press, 2003.

_____. *The Creation of American Team Sports: Baseball and Cricket, 1838–72*. Urbana and Chicago: University of Illinois Press, 1989.

Latouche, John, and Jerome Moross. *The Golden Apple: A Musical in Two Acts*. New York: Random House, 1954.

Laurie, Joe, Jr. *Vaudeville: From the Honky-Tonks to the Palace*. New York: Henry Holt, 1953.

Levinson, Peter. *Puttin' on the Ritz: Fred Astaire and the Fine Art of Panache*. New York: St. Martin's Press, 2009.

Lieb, Frederick G. *The Baseball Story*. New York: G. B. Putnam's Sons, 1950.

Lomax, Michael E. *Black Baseball Entrepreneurs, 1860–1901*. Syracuse, NY: Syracuse University Press, 2003.

Manes, Stephen. *Where Snowflakes Dance and Swear*. Seattle, WA: Cadwallader & Stern, 2011.

Martin, John. *America Dancing: The Background and*

Personalities of Modern Dance. New York: Dodge, 1936; New York: Dance Horzons, 1968.

McGimpsey, David. *Imagining Baseball: America's Pastime and Popular Culture.* Bloomington and Indianapolis: Indiana University Press, 2000.

Mordden, Ethan. *Coming Up Roses: The Broadway Musical in the 1950s.* New York: Oxford University Press, 1998.

_____. *Open a New Window: The Broadway Musical in the 1960s.* New York: Palgrave Macmillan, 2001.

Mote, James. *Everything Baseball.* New York: Prentice Hall Press, 1989.

Neyer, Rob, and Eddie Epstein. *Baseball Dynasties: The Greatest Teams of All Time.* New York: Norton & Co., 2000.

Page, Ruth. *Page by Page.* New York: Dance Horizons, 1978.

Peterson, Harold. *The Man Who Invented Baseball.* New York: Charles Scribner's Sons, 1969, 1973.

Powers, Jimmy. *Baseball Personalities: The Most Colorful Figures of All Time.* New York: Rudolph Field, 1949.

Rielly, Edward J. *Baseball: An Encyclopedia of Popular Culture.* Santa Barbara, CA: ABC-CLIO, 2000.

Riess, Stephen A. *Touching Base: Professional Baseball in American Culture in the Progressive Era.* Westport, CT: Greenwood, 1980.

Riley, Kathleen. *The Astaires: Fred and Adele.* New York: Oxford University Press, 2012.

Rogosin, Donn. *Invisible Men: Life in Baseball's Negro Leagues.* New York: Atheneum, 1983.

Rosenberg, Howard W. *Cap Anson 2: The Theatrical and Kingly Mike Kelly: U.S. Team Sport's First Media Sensation and Baseball's Original Casey at the Bat.* Arlington, VA: Tile Books, 2004.

Russo, Frank. *The Cooperstown Chronicles: Baseball's Colorful Characters, Unusual Lives, and Strange Demises.* Lanham, MD: Rowman & Littlefield, 2014.

Seymour, Harold, and Dorothy Seymour Mills. *Baseball: The Early Years.* New York: Oxford University Press, 1960.

_____ and _____. *Baseball: The Golden Age.* New York: Oxford University Press, 1971.

Sheridan, James, and Barry Monush. *Lucille Ball FAQ: Everything Left to Know about America's Favorite Redhead.* Milwaukee, WI: Applause Theatre & Cinema Books, 2011.

Shortt, Tim. *The Babe Ruth Ballet School.* Buffalo, NY: Firefly Books, 1996.

Slide, Anthony. *The Encyclopedia of Vaudeville.* Westport, CT: Greenwood, 1994.

Smith, H. Allen, Ira Smith, and Leo Herschfield. *Low and Inside: A Book of Baseball Anecdotes, Oddities, and Curiosities.* Halcottsville, NY: Breakaway Books, 2000.

Sorell, Walter. *Hanya Holm: The Biography of an Artist.* Middletown, CT: Wesleyan University Press, 1969.

Stern, Jeffrey Sandell. *The Mighty Casey: A Study of the Performances and Editions of William Schuman's One-Act Opera,* doctoral dissertation. Coral Gables, FL: University of Miami, 2012.

Stevens, Julia Ruth, with Bill Gilbert. *Major League Dad.* Chicago: Triumph Books, 2001.

Stump, Al. *Cobb: A Biography* (Chapel Hill, NC: Algonquin Books, 1994), 1.

Sullivan, Dean A., compiler and editor. *Early Innings: A Documentary History of Baseball, 1825–1908.* Lincoln: University of Nebraska Press, 1995.

Terry, Walter. *The Dance in America.* New York: Harper and Row, 1956.

Tygiel, Jules. *Past Time: Baseball as History.* New York: Oxford University Press, 2000.

Veeck, Bill, with Ed Linn. *Veeck—As in Wreck: The Autobiography of Bill Veeck.* New York: G. B. Putnam's Sons, 1962.

Votano, Paul. *Stand and Deliver: A History of Pinch-Hitting.* Jefferson, NC: McFarland, 2003.

Whiting, Robert. *You Gotta Have Wa.* New York: Macmillan, 1989.

Articles

Allen, Maury. "Ballet Helps Mets Pass 'Barre' Exam." *New York Post,* October 24, 1986.

Althaus, Bill. "Zoned In: Truman's Barker Starts Senior Year on a Torrid Pace." *The Examiner* (Independence, MO), April 3, 2009: www.examiner.net/x180623743/Zoned-in-Truman-s-Barker-starts-senior-year-on-a-torrid-pace (accessed December 4, 2015).

Anderman, John. "Red Sox Musical Comes to ART: The Red Sox, Race, and Show Tunes? They're All in 'Johnny Baseball,'" *Boston Globe,* May 9, 2010: www.boston.com/ae/theater_arts/articles/2010/05/09/behind_the_creation_of_johnny_baseball_a_musical_drama_about_boston_red_sox_history/ (accessed January 4, 2012).

Anderson, Jack. "Ballet: The Cincinnati/New Orleans City Troupe," *New York Times,* October 10, 1983: www.nytimes.com/1983/10/10/arts/ballet-the-cincinnati-new-orleans-city-troupe.html (accessed March 2, 2014).

_____. "Dance Review: Hoop Schemes, Dreams and Happy Feet," *New York Times,* May 6, 1998: www.nytimes.com/1998/05/06/arts/dance-review-hoop-schemes-dreams-and-happy-feet.html (accessed February 16, 2015).

"Anson's Attitude." *Sporting Life,* March 22, 1913, 10.

Arkatov, Janice. "Nine Slices of the Sporting Life," *Los Angeles Times,* June 29, 1984, G2.

"At the Theaters: Cap Anson a Hit." *Cedar Rapids Evening Gazette*, September 16, 1913, 7.

Bak, Richard. "The Madcap Life of Germany Schaefer, Baseball's Clown Prince," *Detroit Athletic Co.*, August 23, 2012: https://www.detroitathletic.com/blog/2012/08/23/the-madcap-life-of-germany-schaefer-baseballs-clown-prince/ (accessed September 5, 2012).

_____. "Profile: Detroit Tigers' Prankster Herman 'Germany' Schaefer," *Hour Detroit*, March 29, 2012: www.hourdetroit.com/Hour-Detroit/April-2012/Playing-for-Laughs/ (accessed September 5, 2012).

Ballard, Chris. "Bobby V's Super Terrific Happy Hour, *Sports Illustrated*, April 30, 2007 (posted online on November 6, 2007): www.si.com/more-sports/2007/11/06/valentine0430 (accessed March 8, 2014, originally published in print form in the April 30, 2007 issue of *Sports Illustrated*).

Barnett, Catherine. "Athletes' Suites: David Dorfman Turns Jocks into Performing Dancers," *Sports Illustrated*, November 1, 1993: www.si.com/vault/1993/11/01/129690/athletes-suites-david-dorfman-turns-jocks-into-performing-dancers (accessed February 16, 2015).

"Baseball Meets Ballet at the Brooklyn Cyclones," press release, Brooklyn Ballet, March 15, 2012: brooklynballet.org/press/releases/120315 (accessed October 10, 2012).

Bentley, Roger. "'Bambino' in Stoneham Scores Big," *Theater Mirror: New England's LIVE Theater Guide*: www.theatermirror.com/RBcobttg.htm (accessed August 31, 2012).

Beaufort, John. "This Good-Natured Celebration of Baseball is a Hit But Not a Homer; 'Diamonds' Musical Revue," *Christian Science Monitor*, December 28, 1984: www.csmonitor.com/1984/1228/1228/122842.html (accessed October 19, 2012).

Betzold, Michael. "Mike Donlin," Society for American Baseball Research: sabr.org/bioproj/person/3b51e847 (accessed September 5, 2012).

Bixby, Suzanne. "Talkin' Broadway: Boston: The Curse of the Bambino," *Talkin' Broadway*: www.talkinbroadway.com/regional/boston/boston9.html (accessed August 31, 2012).

Blau, Eleanor. "'The First' Delays Opening to Nov. 17," *New York Times*, November 4, 1981, C26.

Bloom, Julie. "Turn on the Victrola and They'll Dance," *New York Times*, December 8, 2009: www.nytimes.com/2009/12/09/arts/dance/09rushing.html?pagewanted=all&_r=1& (accessed February 20, 2015).

Breu, Giovanna. "Chicago's Stubborn Bleacher Bums and the Cubs Have Waited for 'Next Year' Since 1945," *People*, October 1, 1979: www.people.com/people/archive/article/0,,20074720,00.html (accessed January 27, 2015).

Briggs, John. "Ballet Goes American," *Dance Magazine*, December 1946, 49.

Busdeker, John. "'Casey at the Bat' Inspired Show 'Batter Up' Opens This Weekend at Renaissance Theatre," *The Huntsville Times* (Huntsville, AL), May 14, 2009: blog.al.com/thebus/2009/05/casey_at_the_bat_inspired_show.html (accessed January 4, 2012).

Calta, Louis. "'Damn Yankees' At Bat Tonight: Baseball Musical Starring Gwen Verdon at Stephen Douglass is at 46th St.," *New York Times*, May 5, 1955, 40.

Camryn, Walter. "Performing in Chicago: During the Depression Years," *Upstairs Bulletin*, November 15, 1979, 4.

Canby, Vincent. "Charlie Brown to Stay Awhile: 'Peanuts' Show is a Hit—Schulz May See It in April," *New York Times*, March 9, 1967, 44.

Carson, Don. "Baseball Funnyman Dies: Long Illness is Finally Fatal to Nick Altrock," *Hopkinsville New Era* (Hopkinsville, KY), January 21, 1965, 16. Review of "Casey at the Bat," performed by Walter Camryn & Group, Goodman Theatre, Chicago, February 5, 1939, *Dance Magazine*, April 1939.

"Casey at the Bat" performed by Walter Camryn & Group, Goodman Theatre, Chicago, February 5, 1939 (Review), *Dance Magazine*, April 1939.

Christiansen, Richard. "A Comedy in Nine Innings," *Chicago Tribune: TV Week*, May 13, 1973, 1, 3.

_____. "'The Golden Apple' is Ripe for Picking," *Chicago Tribune*, July 30, 1995: articles.chicagotribune.com/1995-07-30/entertainment/9507300004_1_off-broadway-golden-apple-lyrics (accessed January 30, 2015).

Clark, Virginia. "Schuman's First Opera, 'The Mighty Casey,' Expression of Interest in Music, Baseball," *The Standard-Star* (New Rochelle, NY), January 22, 1952.

Cloud, Barbara. "Artistic Feat," *UNLV Magazine* (Las Vegas, NV), Spring 2000: www.joesuniverse.org/unlvmagazinearticle.html (accessed December 10, 2012).

Coburn, Marcia Froelke. "The Audacity of Hope," *Chicago Magazine*, September 22, 2008: www.chicagomag.com/Chicago-Magazine/September-2008/The-Audacity-of-Hope/ (accessed January 25, 2015).

Colburn, Otis L. "Summer Events in Chicago," *The New York Dramatic Mirror*, July 23, 1910, 14.

Collins, Glenn. "Men of 'Falsettoland' As Their Old Selves But with New Fears," *New York Times*, July 23, 1990, C11.

Costonis, Maureen Needham. "The Wild Doe: Augusta Maywood in Philadelphia and Paris, 1837–1840." *Dance Chronicle* 17, no. 2 (1994): 123–148.

Creamer, Robert W. "It's So Joe: The Black Sox Scandal Has Come Out Swinging As an Opera," *Sports Illustrated*, August 3, 1981, 6.

_____. "Jackie is the 'First' Again," *Sports Illustrated*, November 30, 1981: www.si.com/vault/1981/11/30/826178/jackie-is-the-first-again-baseball-is-back-on-broadway-with-a-lively-musical-about-jackie-robinson (accessed January 30, 2015).

Creasey, Beverly. "Play Ball!" *Theater Mirror: New England's LIVE Theater Guide*: www.theatermirror.com/BEVtcirhovey.htm (accessed November 21, 2012).

Cusack, Tim. "Decadance vs. The Firebird—A Hip-Hop Ballet," *nytheatre.com: The Digital Magazine of New York Indie Theater*, August 15, 2004: www.nytheatre.com/Review/tim-cusack-2004-8-15-decadance-vs-the-firebird—a-hip-hop-ballet (accessed February 5, 2013).

Dale, Steve. "Ex-Cubs are in Starting Lineup for 'Bleacher Bums' Benefit," *Chicago Tribune*, June 9, 1989, Section 7, J.

"Damn Yankees." *New York Times*, April 17, 1955, SM67.

"Dan Sonenberg's Opera, 'The Summer King,' Selected for 2013 Preview by Fort Worth Opera," Press Release, University of Southern Maine, School of Music, issued October 10, 2012: usm.main.edu/music/dan-sonenbergs-opera-%E2%80%8B-summer-king-%E2%80%8Bselected-2013-debut-fort-worth-opera (accessed November 23, 2012).

"Dance Council Recital Shows Novel Themes," *Chicago Daily Tribune*, May 3, 1940, 21.

"Dance for Television: What the Newest Amusement Medium Means," *Dance Magazine*, October 1939, 10-11.

"Dancing for a Home Run," *Dance Magazine*, September 2007, 25.

"David Dorfman Dance Returns to Bates Dance Festival," *Bates News* (Lewiston, ME), July 16, 1997: www.bates.edu/news/1997/07/16/david-dorfman-returns (accessed Feburary 16, 2015).

Dawidziak, Mark. "For Our Favorite Son Bob Hope, All Roads Lead Back Home to Ohio," *Cleveland Plain Dealer*, May 29, 2003: www.cleveland.com/homegrown/index.ssf?/homegrown/more/hope/allroads.html (accessed March 1, 2015).

"A Day at the Ballpark," *Newcity Stage*, September 27, 2007: newcitystage.com/2007/09/27/a-day-at-the-ballpark/ (accessed March 1, 2014).

DeGregory, Lane. "New Miss Florida Laura McKeeman Hopes to Blaze Trails for Women in Sports Broadcast," *Tampa Bay Times*, July 20, 2012: www.tampabay.com/features/humaninterest/new-miss-florida-laura-mckeeman-hopes-to-blaze-trails-for-women-in-sports/1241327 (accessed February 21, 2014).

Diamond, Jared. "Baseball's Masked Men Show Their Inner Hams on Strike Three," *Wall Street Journal*, August 11, 2011: www.wsj.com/articles/SB10001424053111904006104576500353920412590 (accessed December 6, 2015).

Dobuzinskis, Alex, and Steve Gorman. "Comic Great Sid Caesar of 'Your Show of Shows' Dies at 91," *Reuters*, February 12, 2014: www.reuters.com/article/2014/02/13/us-sidcaesar-idUSBREA1B20H20140213 (accessed March 1, 2015).

Driscoll, Kathi Scrizzi. "'Bleacher Bums': A Baseball Fan Dance," *Cape Cod Times*, June 10, 2010: www.capecodtimes.com/article/20100610/ENTERTAIN/6110303/-1/rss10?template=printart (accessed August 2, 2010).

Dula, Lauren. "Triple Play," *The Brooklyn Paper*, August 18, 2007: www.brooklynpaper.com/stories/30/32/30_32tripleplay.html (accessed November 23, 2012).

Dunning, Jennifer. "The Dance: Gail Conrad," *New York Times*, January 13, 1985: www.nytimes.com/1985/01/13/arts/the-dance-gail-conrad.html (accessed February 16, 2015).

_____. "Dance Review: New Plumage and Rap Song for a Certain Russian Bird," *New York Times*, August 23, 2004, 4.

_____. "Hanya Holm is Dead at 99; Influential Choreographer," *New York Times*, November 4, 1992: www.nytimes.com/1992/11/04/theater/hanya-holm-is-dead-at-99-influential-choreographer.html (accessed February 23, 2015).

_____. "James Starbuck, 85, TV Dance Innovator," *New York Times*, August 19, 1997: www.nytimes.com/1997/08/19/arts/james-starbuck-85-tv-dance-innovator.html (accessed March 1, 2015).

_____. "Review/Dance: Henry Yu Returns with a Style of His Own," *New York Times*, July 29, 1991: www.nytimes.com/1991/07/29/arts/07/29/arts/review-dance-henry-yu-returns-with-a-style-of-his-own (accessed December 6, 2012).

Eagan, Daniel. "Baseball on the Screen," *Smithsonian Magazine*, April 4, 2012: www.smithsonianmag.com/arts-culture/baseball-on-the-screen-171974554/?no-list&no-ist (accessed February 22, 2015).

Edelman, Rob. "Buster Keaton, Baseball Player," *The National Pastime*, 2011, reprinted by the Society for American Baseball Research: sabr.org/research/buster-keaton-baseball-player (accessed February 23, 2015).

Feddoes, Sadie. "Gala Marks Anniversary of Jackie Joining Dodgers," *New York Amsterdam News*, May 31, 1997, 9.

Ferretti, Fred. "A Musical Celebrates an Athlete," *New York Times*, November 8, 1981, D4.

Fitzgerald, Erin. "Opera in the Outfield to Be Held Sept. 22 at Nationals Park," *The Southwester*, September 8, 2011: thesouthwester.com/2011/09/08/opera-in-the-outfield-to-be-held-sept-22-at-nationals-park/ (accessed February 15, 2015).

Flatow Sheryl. "The Ballet of Baseball: More Than a Game, It's Art to This Dancer," *Daily News* (New York, NY), April 23, 1983.

Flores, Nancy. "Boricua Beisbol at the Long Center," *Austin American-Statesman*, December 13, 2011: www.prfdance.org/publicity/Statesman.Boricua Beisbol2011.LongCenter.pdf (accessed February 20, 2015).

Fordham, John. "*Shadowball*, Mermaid, London," *The Guardian*, July 1, 2010: www.theguardian.com/music/2010/jul/01/shadowball-review (accessed November 27, 2012).

Francis, Bob. "Collegiate Review: Here's the Pitch." *Billboard*, December 27, 1947, 44.

Franck, Ruth. "Holm Dance Group Delights Audience: Originality of Program Inspires Awe at First But Proves Exciting," review of "Metropolitan Daily," Swarthmore College, Swarthmore, PA, *Swarthmore Phoenix*, November 14, 1939.

Funke, Lewis. "Theatre: The Devil Tempts a Slugger," *New York Times*, May 6, 1955, 17.

Garcia, Julian. "Baseball Legend Clemente's a Hit, Again," *Daily News* (New York, NY), November 19, 2011: articles.nydailynews.com/2011-11-19/news/30420775_1_celia-cruz-willie-nelson-baseball-legend (accessed November 11, 2012).

Geer, Richard. "Linked by Tradition—100,000 Years of Dance and Sport," *JOPERD*, May/June 1992, 39-41.

Gibson, Daniel. "Take Us Out to the Ball Game," *Native Peoples*, November/December 2002, 14.

Goodman, Murray. "Sports and the Dance." *Dance Magazine*, September 1946, 24-25.

Gonzalez, Juan-Jose. "Luis Salgado Choreographs New Musical about Baseball Legend Roberto Clemente," BroadwayWorld.com: broadwayworld.com/article/Luis-Salgado-choreographs-New-Musical-about-Baseball-Legend-Roberto-Clemente-20111101-page2 (accessed January 4, 2012).

"Gregg Smith Directs 'The Mighty Casey' in Catchy and Vivacious Performance," *New York Times*, May 17, 1976, 41.

Gordon, Peter M. "King Kelly," Society for American Baseball Research: sabr.org/bioproj/person/ffc40dac (accessed January 17, 2015).

_____. "Nick Altrock," Society for American Baseball Research: sabr.org/bioproj/person/aea7c461 (accessed September 5, 2012).

Gray, Mark. "Karina Smirnoff in Engaged to Brad Penny," *People*, November 7, 2010: www.people.com/people/article/0,,20440183,00.html (accessed March 5, 2015).

Grossman, Nancy. "'Johnny Baseball,' American Repertory Theatre," *Talkin' Broadway*: talkinbroadway.com/regional/boston/boston165.html (accessed November 12, 2012).

Gunderson, Edna. "'High School,' the Musical," *USA Today*, February 27, 2006: usatoday30.usatoday.com/life/movies/news/2006-02-27-high-school-musical_x.htm (accessed March 1, 2015).

Gussow, Mel. "Stage: A Baseball Musical, 'Bingo!'" *New York Times*, November 7, 1985, C36.

_____. "Theater: 'Charlie Brown': Characters of 'Peanuts' Move to Broadway," *New York Times*, June 2, 1971, 33.

Harris, William. "An Eccentric Who Likes to Make Things Accessible," *New York Times*, February 16, 1997: www.nytimes.com/1997/02/16/arts/an-eccentric-who-likes-to-make-things-accessible.html (accessed February 16, 2015).

Harrison, Bernie. "TV Tonight: Bob Hope Special Salutes World Series," *The Times-News* (Hendersonville, NC), October 14, 1978, 16.

Harrison, Jay S. "'Casey at the Bat' Opera Presented," *New York Herald Tribune*, March 7, 1955.

"Hasty Pudding Show Tonight," *New York Times*, December 19, 1947, 34.

Henson, Steve. "King's Ransom: Autograph of 19th-Century Baseball Icon 'King' Kelly Could Fetch 200K," *The Postgame*, November 18, 2011: www.thepostgame.com/blog/throwback/201111/kings-ransom-auotgraph-19th-century-baseball-icon-king-kelly-could-fetch-200k (accessed August 21, 2012).

Hetrick, Adam. "*Johnny Baseball* Musical Gets Extra Innings at American Repertory Theatre," *Playbill*, June 11, 2010: www.playbill.com/news/article/johnny-baseball-musical-gets-extra-innings-at-american-repertory-theatre-169173 (accessed November 12, 2012).

"HMS Produces Revival of Ruth Page's 1946 'Billy Sunday' Ballet as Ch. 11 Dance Special," *Ruth L. Ratny's Reel Chicago*, September 14, 2007: www.reelchicago.com/article/hms-produces-revival-ruth-pages-1946-brbilly-sunday-ballet-ch-11-dance-special (accessed March 1, 2014).

Hogan, Cheryl. "The Boys of Summer: African Americans and Baseball in Plaquemines Parish": www.louisianafolklife.org/LT/Articles_Essays/lfmboys.html (accessed September 10, 2012).

"Hollywood Screen Idols Play 'Greatest Baseball Game,'" *Eugene Register-Guard* (Eugene, OR), July 30, 1938, 1.

Horton, G. L. "Curse of the Bambino," *Theater Mirror: *New England's LIVE Theater Guide*: www.the atermirror.com/cotblsobglh.htm (accessed August 31, 2012).

Hubbard, W. L. "News of the Theaters: The Umpire," *Chicago Daily Tribune*, December 4, 1905, 9.

Hughes, Allen. "Opera: 'Mighty Casey,'" *New York Times*, August 31, 1967, 28.

Hughes, Andrew S. "'Peanuts,' and Cracker Jack, Too," *South Bend Tribune*, December 23, 2007: articles.southbendtribune.com/2007-12-23/news/26767075_1_charles-m-schulz-museum-peanuts-charlie-brown (accessed January 27, 2015).

Hughes, Joe. "Kritics Korner: 'Bleacher Bums' a Hit," *Technology News* (Illinois Institute of Technology, Chicago), August 29, 1977, 6.

Hurford, Daphne. "Ballet Takes a Swing at Baseball: 'The Mighty Casey' Pairs the National Pastime with Dance in a New Sporting Ballet," *Sports Illustrated*, December 3, 1990, 19-20.

Hyde, Christopher. "Review: 'The Summer King' Arias a Moving Performance," *Portland Press Herald* (Portland, ME), April 15, 2012: www.pressherald.com/2012/04/15/the-summer-king-arias-a-moving-performance_2012-04-16/ (accessed November 23, 2012).

"ICON Dance Complex Slides into First: Beth Hubela Choreographs History *Where Dance Meets Baseball*," press release, Elizabeth Barry & Associates (Englishtown, NJ), July 14, 2010: www.ebandassociates.com/enews/ebpr071410.html (accessed December 23, 2011).

"If You HD Stream It, They Will Come! WNO's Barbiere Grand Slam," *Opera Chic*, September 11, 2009: operachic.typepad.com/opera_chic/2009/09/wno-barbiere.html (accessed February 15, 2015).

Isherwood, Charles. "Batter Up, Onstage with Songs," *New York Times*, September 16, 2014: www.nytimes.com/2014/09/17/theater/bull-durham-a-musical-adaptation-of-the-1988-movie.html?emc=eta1&_r=0 (accessed September 17, 2014).

Jenkins, Lee. "Infield Frolic: A Pair of Cards on the Mets," *New York Times*, February 24, 2004, D1, D5.

"Joe's View: 'Musical MVPs': 50 Years of Broadway as a Sport," Hearst Connecticut Media Group, February 18, 2013: blog.ctnews.com/meyers/2013/02/18/'musical-mvps'-50-years-of-broadway-as-a-sport (accessed February 15, 2015).

Johnson, Steve. "Send 'Bleacher Bums' Movie to the Showers," *Chicago Tribune*, April 5, 2002: articles.chicagotribune.com/2002-04-05/features/0204050012_1_bleacher-bums-home-team-movie (accessed February 20, 2014).

Jowitt, Deborah. "Laura Peterson Rides Lumberob's Beats," *Village Voice*, February 18, 2009: www.villagevoice.com/2009-02-18/dance/laura-peterson-rides-lumberob-s-beats-tiffany-mills-stretches-tomorrow-s-legs (accessed December 23, 2011).

Katz, Jeff. "Plié Ball! Baseball in American Dance," in *The Cooperstown Symposium on Baseball and American Culture, 2009-2010*, edited by William M. Simons (Jefferson, NC: McFarland, 2011), 27-41.

Kay, Joe. "Baseball and Ballet Collide on First Pitch at Reds Game," *KOMO News*, August 25, 2013: www.komonews.com/news/offbeat/Baseball-and-ballet-collide-on-first-pitch-at-Reds-game-221018191.html (accessed March 15, 2015).

Keefe, Maura. "Is Dance a Man's Sport Too?" in *When Men Dance*, edited by Jennifer Fisher and Anthony Shay (New York: Oxford University Press, 2009), 91-106.

Kelly, John. "Nick Altrock: A Life Rich in the Stuff of D.C. Baseball Lore," *Washington Post*, September 20, 2011: www.washingtonpost.com/local/nick-altrock-a-life-rich-in-the-stuff-of-baseball-lore/2011/09/20/gIQAv1fOik_story.html (accessed September 5, 2012).

Kerr, Walter. "Theater: Charlie Brown and Combo: Musical Adapted from Comic Strip 'Peanuts,'" *New York Times*, March 8, 1967, 51.

Kisselgoff, Anna. "Dance: Mimes at Riverside Festival," *New York Times*, October 30, 1984: www.nytimes.com/1984/10/30/arts/dance-mimes-at-riverside-festival.html (accessed December 21, 2012).

Kleinman, Seymour. "Dance and Sport: The Tie that Binds, or the Bind that Ties?" *JOPERD*, May-June 1992, 42-44.

Koenig, Bill. "BP: A Pregame Symphony," *USA Today Baseball Weekly*, May 24-30, 1995, 8-11.

Kourlas, Gia. "The Spirit May Suffer, Yet Still It Endures," *New York Times*, May 14, 2009: www.nytimes.com/2009/05/15/arts/dance/15grah.html (accessed March 15, 2015).

Lauwers, Melanie. "Take a Seat with These 'Bleacher Bums,'" *Cape Cod Times*, June 12, 2010.

Leff, Lisa. "'Take Me Out to the Opera': SF Opera Hopes to Hit High Note with Ballpark Show," *USA Today*, September 28, 2007: usatoday30.usatoday.com/sports/baseball/2007-09-28-3713913626_x.htm (accessed August 11, 2012).

Lipton, Brian Scott. "Patrick Ryan Sullivan to Star in Engeman Theatre's *Broadway, Baseball and Beer*," TheaterMania.com, June 7, 2012: www.theatermania.com/long-island-theater/news/06-2012/patrick-ryan-sullivan-to-star-in-engeman-theatres-_57986.html (accessed November 28, 2012).

_____. "Theater Continues Its Love Affair with Our National Pastime," TheaterMania.com, August 12, 2012: theatermania.com/new-york-city-theater/news/08-2012/theater-continues-its-love-affair-w_60409.html (accessed August 12, 2012).

Lockwood, Wayne. "Batting Practice: It's More Than Just Hitting a Ball," *Baseball Digest*, October 1998, 44-48.

Lotozo, Elis. "A Dance-Sport Fusion Melds Past and Present," *Philadelphia Inquirer*, March 19, 2002: articles.philly.com/2002-03-19/news/25342 763_1_peter-pucci-plus-dancers-dance-and-sports-evening-length-dance (accessed February 16, 2015).

Magee, Sarah. "Dance Artists Thrill Yates Concert Audience," *Geneva Daily Times* (Geneva, NY), January-March 1952: fultonhistory.com/News paper11/GenevaNYDailyTimes/GenevaNYDaily Times1952Jan-Mar1952Grayscale/GenevaNY DailyTimes1952Jan-MarGrayscale-0936.pdf (accessed February 15, 2015).

"Mata and Hari to Perform Here in Washington Hall," *The Notre Dame Scholastic*, March 11, 1960, 9.

McKim, Neil. "*Shadowball*—A Jazz Opera," *Classical-music.com: The Official Website of BBC Music Magazine*, July 2, 2010: www.classical-music.com/blog/shadowball-â€"-jazz-opera (accessed November 27, 2012).

Meiklejohn, Ben. "In the Right Field," *The Phoenix*, March 12, 2007: thephoenix.com/boston/music/35089-in-the-right-field/ (accessed November 23, 2012).

Miller, Marc. "NY Review: 'DC-7: The Roberto Clemente Story,'" *Backstage*, February 17, 2012: www.backstage.com/review/ny-theater/off-broadway/ny-review-dc-7-the-roberto-cleme nte-story/ (accessed November 11, 2012).

Mooney, James. "The Cherokee Ball Play," *The American Anthropologist*, April 1890, 105-32.

"Movie Stars and Comics at the Bat," *Los Angeles Times*, July 30, 1938: articles.latimes.com/2006/jul/30/local/me-a2anniversary30 (accessed February 23, 2015).

Nesti, Robert. "Johnny Baseball," Edge Media Network, June 6, 2010: www.edgeboston.com/index.php?ch=entertainment&sc3=performance&id=106575 (accessed November 12, 2012).

Newcomer, Eric P. "Between Innings, Ballerinas Take the Field," *New York Times*, July 24, 2012: cityroom.blogs.nytimes.com/2012/07/24/between-innings-ballerinas-take-the-field/ (accessed October 10, 2012).

"New Show for the Whitney," *Billboard*, March 16, 1910, 32.

"Night Clubs-Vaude: Empire Room, Palmer House, Chicago: Thursday, June 26," *Billboard*, July 5, 1952, 18.

"North Carolina Dance Theatre: Carmen," Blumenthal Performing Arts, October 17-23, 2013: www.blumenthaarts.org/events/detail/nc-dance-carmen (accessed March 11, 2014).

"Noted Ball Players Who Will Be Stars of the Stage," *San Francisco Call-Bulletin*, November 8, 1911, 11.

"Old Cap Anson Before Footlights: Will Sing, Dance and Recite—Other Diamond Stars on Bill," *Syracuse Daily Journal*, 1913.

Padula, Edward. "The Dance in Television," *Dance Magazine*, October 1939, 10.

Peter, Thomas. "Broadway-Aimed *National Pastime* Musical Will Play Baseball Hall of Fame," *Playbill*, February 25, 2010: www.playbill.com/news/article/broadway-aimed-national-pastime-musical-will-play-baseball-hall-of-fame-166226 (accessed November 27, 2012).

Phillips, Tom. "Laura Peterson Choreography, 'Forever,'" danceviewtimes: writers on dancing, February 20, 2009: www.danceviewtimes.com/2009/02/forever-.html (accessed February 16, 2015).

"Police Probing Slavin Beating," *The New York Clipper*, August 11, 1920, 31.

"'Pop' Anson Becomes Buck and Wing Dancer," *San Francisco Call-Bulletin*, March 21, 1911, 23.

"Premiere of 'High School Musical 2' Breaks Ratings Record," *New York Times*, August 18, 2007: www.nytimes.com/2007/08/18/arts/television/18cnd-disney-html?ref=arts (accessed March 1, 2015).

"Presentation Explores Adapting a Book to the Stage," *New Westminster News Leader* (New Westminster, BC, Canada), March 22, 2011: www.newwesttnewsleader.com/entertainment/118 460604 (accessed February 15, 2015).

"Pudding Show Opens Tonight," *The Harvard Crimson*, December 10, 1947: www.thecrimson.com/article/1947/12/10/pudding-show-opens-tonig ht-pa-months/.

"Puerto Rican Folkloric Dance Staging *Boricua Beisbol* on December 4th," *Austin On Stage*, reprinted on official website of the Puerto Rican Folkloric Dance and Cultural Center on November 22, 2011: www.austinonstage.com/prfdancexmas20 11news (accessed February 20, 2015).

Ramanathan, Lavanya. "Opera in the Outfield at Nats Park: What to Know before Saturday's 'Don Giovanni' Show," *The Washington Post*, GOG Blog, September 26, 2012: www.washingtonpost.com/blogs/going-out-guide/post/opera-in-the-outfield-at-nats-park-what-to-know-before-sat urdays-don-giovanni-show/2012/09/26/932f3 d80-0753-11e2-a10c-fa5a255a9258_blog.html (accessed February 15, 2015).

Rauzi, Robin. "Theater: Pitching a Concept," *Los Angeles Times*, March 26, 1998: articles.latimes.com/1998/mar/26/entertainment/ca-32741 (accessed January 4, 2013).

Reyneke, Dreas. "Dancers are Not the Same as Athletes!" *The Dancing Times*, March 1998, 557.

Rich, Frank. "The 'Falsetto' Musicals United at Hartford Stage," *New York Times*, October 15, 1991, C16.

_____. "Stage: 'First,' Baseball Musical: Back in Ebbets Field," *New York Times*, November 18, 1981, C25.

_____. "Theater: 'Diamonds,' A Revue about Baseball," *New York Times*, December 17, 1984: www.nytimes.com/1984/12/17/arts/theater-diamonds-a-revue-about-baseball.html (accessed October 19, 2012).

Ritzel, Rebecca. "'Carmen' Starts Up North, Then Heads to Charlotte," *Charlotte Observer*, August 19, 2013: www.charlotteobserver.com/2013/08/19/4248050/carmen-starts-up-north-then-heads.html#.Ux8u1M70g4A (accessed March 11, 2014).

Rizzo, Frank. "Legit Reviews: 'Johnny Baseball,'" *Variety*, June 3, 2010: www.variety.com/review/VE1117942916 (accessed November 12, 2012).

_____. "Trading Places: Athletes Turn to Dance at Jacob's Pillow for Artistic and Physical Edification," *Hartford Courant*, June 8, 1997: articles.courant.com/1997-06-08/entertainment/9706060045_1_dance-team-dance-workshop-choreographer-david-dorfman (accessed February 16, 2015).

Rosenberg, Howard W. "Recapping a Bit of Toledo's History," *Toledo Blade*, November 8, 2006.

Russell, Jenna. "Having a Ball on Stage: New Musical Traces the Bambino's Curse," *Boston Globe*, April 19, 2001, 6.

"Rube Marquard," National Baseball Hall of Fame, "Hall of Famers": baseballhall.org/hof/marquard-rube (accessed January 19, 2015).

Scheck, Frank. "Tapping into Baseball & Broadway Lore," *New York Post*, August 15, 2012: nypost.com/2012/08/16/tapping-into-baseball-bway-lore (accessed November 11, 2012).

Schonberg, Harold C. "Casey Bats Again with Same Result," *New York Times*, May 5, 1953, 34.

Schonberg, Harold C. "There is No Joy in 'Casey' Opera: TV Setting of Baseball Saga Strikes Out Esthetically—Poem Held More Musical," *New York Times*, March 7, 1955, 21.

Schwyzer, Elizabeth. "Cowboy Hats and Baseball Bats," *Santa Barbara Independent*, September 14, 2006 (updated September 28, 2006): www.independent.com/news/2006/sep/14/cowboy-hats-and-baseball-bats/ (accessed December 6, 2012).

"Season Tickets to Goodspeed at Last Year's Rates," *The Day* (New London, CT), March 14, 1985, 7.

Segal, Lewis. "Dance Review: Saxes, Music and Monologues at Santa Monica's Highways," *Los Angeles Times*, February 2, 1993: articles.latimes.com/1993-02-02/entertainment/ca-838_1_dan-froot (accessed February 16, 2015).

Seidel, Miriam. "Joining Messages with Movement," *Philadelphia Inquirer*, October 1, 1994: articles.philly.com/1994-10-01/entertainment/25870259_1_david-dorfman-dance-lisa-race-work-shapes (accessed February 16, 2015).

"Shadowball Jazz Opera Awarded Olympic Games 'Inspire Mark,'" *YES: Yamaha Education Supplement*, Spring 2010, 5.

Shepard, Richard F. "Going Out Guide: At Bat," *New York Times*, October 24, 1985, C22.

Siegel, Fern. "Stage Door: *National Pastime*," *Huffington Post*, August 16, 2012: huffingtonpost.com/fern-siegel/stage-door-pasti_b_1784343.html (accessed November 11, 2012).

Smith, Sid. "Jackie Robinson and the Great American Pastime: But Will His Life Make a Good Musical?" *Chicago Tribune*, April 11, 1993: articles.chicagotribune.com/1993-04-11/entertainment/9304110151_1_jackie-robinson-great-american-pastime-first-black-player (accessed January 30, 2015).

Spiselman, Ann. "Options: Summer Events Worth Staying in Town For," *Crain's Chicago Business*, August 5, 1995: www.chicagobusiness.com/article/19950805/ISSUE01/10009142/options-summer-events-worth-staying-in-town-for (accessed January 30, 2015).

"Stage Attracts Baseball Stars," *New York Times*, October 22, 1911, 33.

"Stars Play Baseball in Hollywood," British Pathé, issued November 8, 1938: www.britishpathe.com/video/stars-play-baseball-in-hollywood/query/US+BASEBALL (accessed February 23, 2015).

Stoop, Norma McLain. "Dancevision," *Dance Magazine*, November 1976, 98.

Stratyner, Barbara. "Ned Wayburn and the Dance Routine: From Vaudeville to the Ziegfeld Follies," Society of Dance History Scholars: https://sdhs.org/index.php?option=com_content&view=article&id=39&Itemid=1 (accessed September 27, 2012).

Sullivan, Dan. "Stage Review: Marcel Marceau: The World Behind the Mask," *Los Angeles Times*, March 29, 1984, M7.

_____. "Stage Review: 'Sporting Goods' Has Short Sizes," *Los Angeles Times*, July 2, 1984, H1, 4–5.

"Television Shows Include Comedians," *New York Sun*, May 27, 1939.

Thorn, John. "Baseball Film to 1920," MLBlogs Network, May 22, 2012: ourgame.mlblogs.com/2012/05/22/ (accessed February 22, 2015).

Trevino, Mariella. "Mary Ann Lee and Augusta Maywood," in *Celebrating Women in American History* (New York: Facts on File, 2011).

Ullrich, Lowell. "Forgotten Frasers Now Fiction," *The Province* (Vancouver, BC, Canada), June 5, 2011: www2.canada.com/theprovince/news/sports/story.html?id=242f5126–8aad-4acb-a1ce-4066199160ba&p=1 (accessed October 16, 2012).

Updike, John. "Sparky from St. Paul," *The New Yorker*, October 27, 2007: www.newyorker.com/magazine/2007/10/22/sparky-from-st-paul (accessed January 27, 2015).

Vecsey, George. "Dance: 'Baseball,' Unlike Anything the Babe Knew," *New York Times*, December 11, 1994: www.nytimes.com/1994/12/11/arts/dance-baseball-unlike-anything-the-babe-knew.html (accessed January 4, 2013).

Waleson, Heidi. "Street Scenes: Opera on a Brooklyn Sidewalk," *Wall Street Journal*, September 5, 2007: online.wsj.com/article_email/SB11889 4606447517416 (accessed November 23, 2012).

Wander, Robin. "Stanford Dance Reconstructs Anna Sokolow's Signature Work *Rooms*," *Stanford News*, February 9, 2012: news.stanford.edu/news/2012/February/dance-rooms-020912.html (accessed February 15, 2015).

Watrous, Mabel. "Dance Troupe Highly Praised: Mata and Hari Enliven Community Series," *The Spokesman-Review* (Spokane, WA), January 26, 1950, 9.

"Who Says Big Leaguers Don't Dance?" MLB.com/Entertainment, August 2, 2007: mlb.mlb.com/news/article_entertainment.jsp?ymd=20070802&content_id=2125248&vkey=entertainment&text=.jsp (accessed March 1, 2015).

Wilson, Tom. "Cap Makes Popular Showing in Galesburg," *The Galesburg Register-Mail* (Galesburg, IL), November 13, 2007.

Wu, Amber. "Nation's Trailblazing Giants of Dance Honored with Retrospective," *Taiwan Today*, December 12, 2008: taiwantoday.tw/ct.asp?xItem=46831&CtNode=450 (accessed December 6, 2012).

Zinser, Lynn. "Getting Out the Vote for Pablo," *New York Times*, July 10, 2009, 1. To view video: m.mlb.com/video/v5468463/the-giants-urge-fans-to-vote-for-pablo-sandoval (accessed March 15, 2015).

Index

Numbers in **_bold italics_** refer to pages with photographs.